COLONIAL POWERS AND ETHIOPIAN FRONTIERS 1880–1884

ACTA AETHIOPICA VOLUME IV

COLONIAL POWERS AND ETHIOPIAN FRONTIERS 1880–1884

EDITED BY SVEN RUBENSON

CO-EDITORS AMSALU AKLILU, SHIFERAW BEKELE AND SAMUEL RUBENSON

LUND UNIVERSITY PRESS

Lund University Press
The Joint Faculties of Humanities and Theology

P.O. Box 192
SE-221 00 LUND
Sweden
http://lunduniversitypress.lu.se

Lund University Press books are published in collaboration with Manchester University Press.

British Library Cataloguing-in-Publication Data
A catalogue record for this book is available from the British Library

Lund University Press gratefully acknowledges publication assistance from the Thora Ohlsson Foundation (*Thora Ohlssons stiftelse*)

ISBN 978-91-984699-6-7 hardback

First published 2021

Typeset in 10/12 Times New Roman and Warnock Pro by
Servis Filmsetting Ltd, Stockport, Cheshire

Contents

Preface

The background and aim of the series *Acta Aethiopica* was explained by Sven Rubenson, the editor of the series, in the preface and introduction to the first volume, *Correspondence and Treaties 1800–1854*, published by Addis Ababa University Press and Northwestern University Press in 1987. Co-editors of the first volume were Getatchew Haile, Collegeville, and John Hunwick, Evanston. The second volume, *Tewodros and His Contemporaries 1855–1868*, was published in 1994 by Addis Ababa University Press, with the Lund University Press of those days – a scheme of collaboration between various Lund University departments and the academic publisher Studentlitteratur – as co-publisher, and the third volume, *Internal Rivalries and Foreign Threats 1869–1879*, by Addis Ababa University Press and Transaction Publishers/ Rutgers University. These two volumes were co-edited by Amsalu Aklilu, Addis Abeba and Hamburg, Merid Wolde Aregay, Addis Abeba, and Samuel Rubenson, Lund. Sadly, the first two of them passed away in the subsequent years.

This volume, the fourth in the series, was prepared by Sven Rubenson with Amsalu Aklilu and myself as co-editors, but owing to health issues publication was delayed, and when Sven Rubenson passed away in 2013 the material was left in an unfinished state. It was only when Shiferaw Bekele offered to assist me as co-editor that I was finally able to finish the work. I am also deeply grateful to Wolbert Smidt and Marianne Thormählen who have both read the entire volume and contributed numerous corrections at the last stage.

As with previous volumes, many colleagues have shared their skills and knowledge with us as we have dealt with the archival research; with Arabic and Ethiopian philology; and with details of biography, history and geography. Hussein Ahmed, Ezra Gebremedhin, Fisseha Mekuria, Tekeste Negash, Kjell Norlin, Kevin O'Mahoney and Richard Pankhurst are but a few of the many who have assisted us in various ways and deserve to be mentioned with gratitude. Special thanks are due to Jocelyne Girgis who translated most of the Arabic documents. Where several translations are possible, or at least seem to be so, the final choice has been made largely on contextual grounds. It is thus only fair that I accept the ultimate responsibility for any shortcomings of the volume, linguistic as well as historical.

Also, as with previous volumes, special thanks are due to the Controller of Her Majesty's Stationery Office, London, to the *Conservateur en Chef* of the diplomatic archives of the French Ministry of Foreign Affairs, and to the authorities of the archives of the Italian Ministry of Foreign Affairs and the National Archives of Egypt, as well as to the librarians and keepers of all other archives concerned, for their kind permission to have documents in their possession published in *Acta Aethiopica*. Our gratitude goes to librarians and archivists who have generously assisted us in our search in Cairo and Jerusalem, in Athens and Rome, in Paris, London, Stockholm, Moscow and St. Petersburg. They are too many to be listed by name. The generous financial aid of the Department for Research Cooperation (SAREC) as well as of *Riksbankens Jubileumsfond* is acknowledged with deep gratitude.

Lund in October 2020
Samuel Rubenson

Introduction

The fourth volume of *Acta Aethiopica* only covers five years from the end of the previous volume, i.e. the start of 1880 to the end of 1884. The original plan was to include the entire decade up to the end of 1889, but the number of documents made this unrealistic, and with the passing away of the editor, Sven Rubenson, the material collected for the years 1885–1889 has been put aside waiting for a new editor to continue the work.

The title of this volume, *Colonial Powers and Ethiopian Frontiers*, refers to the fact that the documents included reflect the increasing colonial pressures on Ethiopia and the attempts of the Ethiopian rulers to define more clearly the frontiers of their country and their areas of influence. It is a period of tremendous importance as far as Ethiopia's position internationally is concerned. The internal rivalries of the 1870s are a matter of the past; the hegemony of Yohannis IV is no longer seriously questioned. Two major developments govern most of the writings included.

The first are the negotiations concerning the outcome of the Ethio-Egyptian wars of the 1870s. By 1880 that conflict had developed into a British-Ethiopian affair, which was finally ended with the Adwa treaty of June 1884. Although Ethiopia had clearly defended its frontiers and defeated the Egyptian offensive, European support for the Egyptians, as part of their colonial interests, made it extremely difficult for the Ethiopian emperor to make his voice heard and his conditions for a treaty accepted. The second major set of developments in the period are the increasing Italian and French colonial interests along the coast, in particular at Bab el-Mandeb and in today's Gulf of Djibouti, and the related commercial and political contacts with Shewa. Italy and France competed vigorously for support by local rulers and strongholds on the coast by inducing them to sell or donate territory and to enter into a series of treaties. This advance was to a great extent checked by the powerful ruler of Awsa, Maḥammad Hanfadhē (Amharic: Mehammed Hanferī; Arabic: Muḥammad Ḥanfarī), who on the one hand welcomed improved commercial links with Europe, but on the other defended his sovereignty and his close relations with the kingdom of Shewa.

* * * * *

The volume adheres to the principles and format of volumes I, II and III of the series. Thus, it contains all official letters and documents by Ethiopian rulers and notables we have been able to locate, with the exception of some minor notes that are of little significance and only preserved in translations. A special case is, however, created by the many letters written in Arabic by the rulers along the coast in response to the growing European activity in and around the Gulf of Djibouti. The large amount of often very brief and trivial letters about travel arrangements, and the difficulty in deciding which authors to include as "Ethiopians", have forced us to make a selection. Since they clearly relate to the issue of colonial interests in Ethiopia as well as the definition of the Ethiopian frontiers, we have included all letters of any importance by Maḥammad Ḥanfadhē of Awsa and most letters by Ḥamad La'īta, the Sultan of Gobad, Burhān Muḥammad, the Sultan of Raḥayta, and Ḥamad Muḥammad, the Sultan of Tajura.

Almost thirty percent of the letters were written by Yohannis IV, the undisputed emperor at the time. Most of the letters are, as in previous volumes, addressed to foreign heads of state or their representatives, and they almost exclusively deal with asserting Ethiopian sovereignty in the north against the attacks of the Egyptians and their allies. The two most significant documents signed by Yohannis in this connection are the two treatises negotiated with William Hewett in

June 1884 (docs 167, 168). In addition, a substantial proportion of Yohannis' letters is directed to religious officials or deals with issues of religion. A number of letters to the Ethiopian community in Jerusalem reflect the emperor's support for the Ethiopian monastery and the building of an Ethiopian church in the city (docs 43, 44, 57, 65, 76, 77, 127, 182, 192, 195). Three proclamations only preserved as reports in French are included under the emperor's name, although their authenticity may be disputed (docs 68–70). More important are the unfortunately few preserved letters of Yohannis to his subordinates, Minīlik and Tekle Haymanot. Furthermore, a few letters supply evidence of the emperor's relation with two independent European advisors, Gerhard Rohlfs and Demostenes Mitzakis.

The author represented by the second largest number of letters in this volume is, as expected, King Minīlik, who has contributed some twenty percent of the documents. Again, most of them are to European governments, but in contrast to those of Yohannis, Minīlik's letters are on the one hand all written to representatives of Italy and France, a vast majority to the Italians, and on the other they are – with a few exceptions – written to the consuls and agents of the states, not to the heads of state. The topics of the letters are, moreover, related primarily to commerce and the activities of explorers. This is also true of the two treatises signed by Minīlik in 1883 (docs 118, 122). The first is interesting in that it is signed by Minīlik even though it is between Italy and Maḥammad Ḥanfadhē, identified in the Italian version as the supreme head of the Danākil, and in the Amharic as the great Adal chief. Of special interest is the single letter by *Weyzero* Ṭaytu to the queen of Italy (doc. 166).

A special feature of this volume is the large number of letters, amounting to thirty percent, written by the rulers of Afar and the Red Sea littoral and their representatives. Taking into account that a large number of rather insignificant letters by them were excluded, this shows to what extent letter-writing was an established custom among the Muslim elite of the Afar. The letters reflect the Italian and French colonial interests in the area as a stronghold in relations to the interior. Of these letters more than half are by Maḥammad Ḥanfadhē, the ruler of Awsa. They clearly reveal his powerful influence on the local rulers on the coast, but also on all relations between the coast and Shewa, his willingness to support European commercial and exploratory interests, as well as his strong opposition to giving up any of his territory. In addition to him the most important figure was Ḥamad La'īta, the Sultan of Gobad and probably the most significant ruler at the time in the Gulf of Djibouti. The letters reveal his close cooperation with Maḥammad Ḥanfadhē and service to the Italians, as well as his hostility to Egyptian, British and French activities. Four agreements bear his signature, two with Italy and two with France (docs 157, 179, 194, 198). Except for the last, entitled "Donation", which is a rather strange document, they all focus on the protection of trade. The most important, the treaty with Italy, explicitly states that it should be ratified by Minīlik, a ratification of which we have found no trace (doc. 194). The third Afar author, Burhān Muḥammad, was the Sultan of Raḥayta under whose authority lay the coast and islands around and to the south of Aseb up to the territory of Obock. The letters reveal his animosity towards Egyptian claims as well as the tensions with the Italians about the borders of the territory sold to them. Sultan Ḥamad Muḥammad of Tajura is the signatory to three somewhat suspect documents, a so-called treaty and two so called donations, all evidently drawn up in French and poorly or never translated into Arabic (docs 184, 190 and 198).

Among Ethiopian notables included in the volume are *Nigus* Tekle Haymanot king of Gojjam, with four letters (7, 142, 143, 144), the first written before his appointment as king of Gojjam. All of them relate to his contact with the Italian explorers and the support gained from them for building the bridge across the Abbay river. *Ras* Alula is represented by 8 letters written to a number of European travellers and missionaries who were his friends or sought access to the emperor. A letter preserved in the archives of the Swedish mission (doc. 12) shows that Alula, in spite of good relations with the missionaries, totally opposed any teaching that might make Orthodox Christians convert to Protestantism. *Ras* Ar'aya is represented with three letters. Two of them, written to the Spanish envoy of King Alfonso XII (docs 72, 73), are of great interest as they deal with the secret collaboration of *Ras* Ar'aya with the Egyptians and the role of the *nā'ib* of Arkīko acting on behalf of Emperor Yohannis. The two letters by *Ras* Gobena to the king of Italy and the President of France are simply acknowledgments of gifts received.

A few letters were written by emissaries, secretaries and agents of Yohannis, Minīlik and Alula, either on their behalf or as more private communications, mainly in gratitude for gifts. They supply evidence of an evolving court bureaucracy slowly influenced by European standards. Most important are the five letters by *Azzazh* Welde Ṣadiq, minister at Minīlik's court, two of which are addressed to King Umberto of Italy. *Lij* Mirçha Werqē and Gebri'ēl Welde Gobena, represented by one letter each, had studied abroad and knew English. *Bejirond* Lewtē, represented by two letters and signing as the treasurer of Minīlik, was an active minister of the emperor. *Dej Agafarī* Tamrē *Abba* Sibsib, commander of Minīlik's rifle regiment, who signs his letter to King Umberto as *turk basha,* is otherwise unknown. Three letters were written by the brothers Yosēf and Gīyorgīs Nigusē, both agents of Minīlik in his relations with the Italians, and two letters by Gebru *Abba* Çhequn, Alula's lieutenant.

A few letters included here were written by Church officials, mainly to the Coptic patriarch. A few of them relate to the Ethiopian monastery in Jerusalem, others to relations with the patriarchate. An interesting letter by *Abune* Ṗētros (doc. 85) concerns an acquittal of seven local Ethiopians at Jenda, at least five of them belonging to the clergy. The reason is not stated, but may well have involved their collaboration with Catholic missionaries. Five letters from the archives of the Swedish mission give valuable insights into the views, experiences and activities of Ethiopian converts to Protestantism.

The documents are chiefly from the same sources as in previous volumes, that is the British, French and Italian official archives, with a clear dominance for the Italian archives because of the increased Italian colonial ambitions. Unfortunately, a number of important originals previously located in the Italian archives have since been misplaced or lost, and we have thus had to rely on contemporary translations. A small number of documents are from the official archives of Austria, Egypt and Germany. The archives of the Coptic patriarchate have still not been made accessible, but a few of its documents are produced from photographs made available to us from the collection of the late Mirrit Butrus Ghali. As in the previous volume, a number of documents come from the Ethiopian monastery in Jerusalem as well as from the Swedish Mission archives. Some documents are taken from publications by European travellers. A few very important letters are copied from Hiruy Welde Sillasē, *Tarīke Negest,* and others from the edition of a chronicle of Yohannis IV edited by Bairu Tafla.

* * * * *

Compared to previous volumes, linguistic diversity has increased. Gi'iz is surprisingly used in a number of letters by Yohannis and others, for example in the letter by *Abune* Ṗētros (doc. 85) and in one of Minīlik's letters (doc. 87). Although Amharic dominates, almost thirty percent of the letters are in Arabic, a fact that reflects the importance of the rulers in Afar and on the coast. The increased use of European languages is also significant. French is gradually becoming an important language of diplomacy in Ethiopia. By contrast, English is only used in one letter and Italian in none. In addition there are a few letters in Swedish written by Protestant converts.

A number of treatises and conventions are bilingual or even trilingual, although the Arabic of the bilingual agreements on the coast often seems secondary and of little importance.

A special problem has been the translation of the many Arabic documents. In addition to poor preservation, this is in many cases due to rather poor handwriting in combination with poor orthography, incorrect grammar, the absence of punctuation and non-standard use of the language. Thus, the meaning is quite often obscure or ambiguous. In some cases, we have thus had to resort to translations made at the time. Wherever we have been able to check, these have, however, appeared to be reliable. The many agreements entered into with the Afar rulers form an exception, though; it seems clear that they were generally drawn up in the European languages and either only drafted in Arabic or later translated into Arabic with little concern for a correct Arabic version.

In concordance with previous volumes, Ethiopian titles have not been translated but appear in italics in transliteration with the exception of *nigus*, which has consistently been translated as king, and *aṣē*, translated as emperor. When used for a non-Ethiopian *ato* has, however, been translated as Mr. Since *Acta Aethiopica* is a publication of historical documents, the designation "Galla" is preserved as used in the documents, in spite of its derogatory connotations.

Finally, a note about calendars and dates. Dates are retained in their original form, with Ethiopian, Coptic, or Arabic names of months and with the years as indicated in the different calendars. Dates in the list, at the top of documents, and in the notes are all according to the Gregorian calendar.

Seals

With a few exceptions, noted below, the original documents are generally sealed, and we may thus assume that the documents that have only been found in copies or translations were sealed as well. The exceptions are, on the one hand, the letters from ordinary people, such as the Protestant converts and royal servants of less distinction, and on the other a number of letters from Maḥammad Ḥanfadhē and local rulers on the coast, who normally sealed their letters. The seals used during the period covered by this volume of *Acta Aethiopica* represent an ongoing standardization already visible in the previous volume.[1]

Yohannis, the ruling emperor, used two seals, both introduced in 1879. Both of these are bilingual Gi'iz and Arabic and thus use two different references for his nation, *Ītyoṗya* (Ethiopia) and *Ḥabasha* (Abyssinia), here regarded as synonymous. The first seal was introduced to emphasize that Yohannis had defeated the invading Egyptian army. The traditional lion holds a cross in one of his paws, and the legend includes the statement: "the cross has defeated the tribe of Isma'ēl (*mesqel mo'a negede isma'ēl* and in Arabic *al-ṣalīb ghalaba 'umma ismā'īl*)". Below the lion the year 1864, the year of Yohannis' coronation according to the Ethiopian calendar, is written in Arabic numerals. Though the Ethiopians had literally defeated the "nation of [Khedive] Ismā'īl", Yohannis clearly wanted to convey this in religious terms: Christianity as opposed to Islam or – in Old Testament terms – Israel as opposed to Ishmael. Both the words and the cross in the paw of the lion bear witness to this. The seal is used in all letters to the European powers, but only occasionally in other letters. That circumstance underlines what we know from the content of his letters, namely that it was when addressing European rulers that Yohannis was eager to emphasize his role as the defender of Christianity. In his letters to Ethiopians as well as to the khedive (with one exception, doc. 173), we find the simple seal with the bilingual legend "Yohannis, King of Kings of Ethiopia (*niguse negest ze-ītyoṗya* and *mālik al-mulūk al-ḥabasha*)" and a cross between the Arabic and the Ethiopian text, as well as above the crown of the lion.

It is only in the first letter by Minīlik in this volume (doc. 10) that we find the seal he had acquired as early as 1870 and used throughout the 1870s (see *Acta* III). All subsequent letters are sealed with a seal of a more traditional Ethiopian style, although with the same motto: "The Lion of the tribe of Judah has prevailed (*mo'a anbessa zeimme negede yihuda*)". Although a quotation from the book of Revelation in the New Testament, the mention of "the tribe of Judah" called to mind the claims of the *Kibre Negest* according to which the Ethiopian kingship originated with Minīlik, the son of Solomon and the Queen of Sheba. The contemporary Shewan ruler was thus the second Minīlik, a designation he himself begins to use, although not consistently, from 1882 (see doc. 78 with note). Though Minīlik had been obliged to acknowledge Yohannis as his suzerain as early as 1878, he continued to use the seal and rule his kingdom autonomously, following his own foreign policy and concluding international treaties.

[1] For seals of Ethiopian dignitaries see Estelle Sohier & Serge Tornay, *Empreintes du temps*, Centre français des études éthiopiennes, Addis Abeba 2007.

1. King of Kings Yohannis, King of Zion in Ethiopia. The cross has defeated the tribe of Isma'ēl. Yūḥannā, King of Kings of Zion in Abyssinia. The cross has defeated the people of Ismā'īl. 1864

2. King of Kings Yohannis of Ethiopia; Yūḥannā, King of Kings of Abyssinia

3. Minyilik, King of Kings. The Lion of the tribe of Judah has prevailed

4. Minīlik, King of Shewa. The Lion of the tribe of Judah has prevailed

5. The seal of King Tekle Haymanot, appointed by Yohannis, King of Zion

6. The seal of *Weyzero* Ṭaytu

7. The seal of *Nebure id* Tekle Gīyorgīs

8. The seal of *Ras* Alula

9. The seal of *Ras* Alula who is the *turk basha*

10. The seal of *Bejirond* Lewṭē, *anbesa bē*?

11. *Azzazh* Welde Ṣadiq

12. The seal of *Turk Basha* Tamrē.

13. Sultan Muḥammad Ḥanfarī (Maḥammad Ḥanfadhē)

14. Abū Bakr

15. Burhan Muḥammad

16. Ḥamad La'ita

Note on orthography

There is no widely accepted simple system of transliteration from Ethiopic to Latin script, and many conventional spellings of the names of persons and places are by no means well-established. The system used for Ethiopic script in *Acta Aethiopica* is fairly simple, containing only three diacritical marks: a dash for two of the vowels, a dot for glottalized consonants, and an apostrophe to indicate a glottal stop where it is pronounced by at least some Amharic speakers; thus Ya'iqob and Gi'iz, but Alī (not 'Alī or 'Alī). The consonants or combinations of consonants have their normal English pronunciation, *g* (as in *g*et) standing for ገ, *j* (as in *j*am) for ጀ, *zh* (as *s* in plea*s*ure) for ዠ, and *q* (glottalized *k*) for ቀ. The seven vowels are transliterated *e*, *u*, *ī*, *a*, *ē*, *i* and *o*, and pronounced approximately as in b*e*t, r*u*le, mach*i*ne, f*a*ther, touch*é* (in French), f*i*t and l*o*rd. When the vowel is not pronounced in the sixth order, the *i* is omitted in the transliteration. In view of the ambivalent use of the labialized consonants, we have decided in favour of the simpler forms Gojjam and Gonder, as well as Goshu and Mekonnin. In cases where some authors have consistently used the labialized consonants, we have allowed both forms, e.g. Gwela and Gola. For a full presentation of the system, see Sven Rubenson, *Survival of Ethiopian Independence* (London: Heinemann 1976), pp. 413ff. In addition to this system and in order to achieve a better representation of names in Tigrinya, we have added a dot under the letter "h" where it represents a harsh "h", for example in Ḥalḥal, and an inverted apostrophe to represent a clearly pronounced glottal stop, as for example in 'Aylet.

The system is applied as consistently as possible for all names, as well as titles and other Ethiopian words written in Latin script, except for those geographical names where the English spelling is now practically uniform and has, in most cases, resulted in a distinctly different pronunciation (Abyssinia, Ethiopia, Eritrea, Massawa). In order to create consistency, place names are generally transliterated according to the Amharic spelling even in documents written in Arabic. Thus, Aseb and not 'Asab. Even where Ethiopian authors have transliterated their own names into Latin script differently, we have consistently used our own transliteration, thus for example Minīlik for Menilik (docs 88, 159, 175, 176) and Gebri'ēl Welde Gobena for Gabriel Welde Gobano.

As for names of persons and places in Arabic, the transliteration follows the established system of modern standard Arabic used, for example, in the *Cambridge History of Islam* in spite of the fact that the Arabic in the documents may often refer to Egyptian or Sudanese Arabic, for which a different transliteration would have been more appropriate in order to convey the local pronunciation. Since Arab names were also used by non-Arabic speakers, this unfortunately leads to what some may regard as annoying inconsistencies in the spelling of names of Arabic origin. We thus have both Aḥmad and Ahmed, 'Alī and Alī, Muḥammad, Maḥammad and Mehammed, and Ibrāhīm and Ībrahīm. For the ruler of Awsa, who in Amharic documents (and the previous volume of *Acta Aethiopica*) appears as Mehammed Hanferī and in Arabic documents, including his seal, as Muḥammad Ḥanferī, we have decided to write Maḥammad Ḥanfadhē, in order to respect his native Afar language. In fact, this concession to different orthographies in different languages is no different from the practice of writing Muhammad for an Arab but Mehmed for a Turk, or Butrus for an Egyptian but Petros (Ṗēṭros) for an Ethiopian, not to mention Peter for an Englishman. This principle does not solve all cases, but it does help establish some consistency.

Glossary

Abba	Father, monk (also used in *noms de guerre* or horse names)
Abbatē	Father, priest, monk
Abun, abune	Our father, bishop, metropolitan of the Ethiopian Orthodox Church
Aleqa	Chief, head, vicar of a church
Amba	Flat-topped mountain, mountain fortress
Anbā	Father, bishop
Aṣē, aṭē	Emperor
Ato	Master, Mr.
Azzazh	Chief, commander, supervisor
Balambaras	Officer, sergeant
Bejirond	Treasurer, chief of storehouse, "Finance Minister"
Bir Ṣāḥib	Lord, master
Blatta	Honorific title for achievement in learning and literature
Blattēngēta	More prominent honorific title for achievement in learning and literature
Debtera	Chorister, scribe (not ordained member of the clergy)
Degmaj	The second, added by King Minīlik to his name in 1882
Dej agafarī	Imperial guard
Dejjazmach, dejjach	"Commander of the entrance", general, governor
Ferenj	Foreigner(s), European(s) (by implication Roman Catholic)
Gezh	Ruler, Viceroy, Governor
Grazmach	Commander
Ḥajj	Honorific title for someone who has made the pilgrimage to Mecca
Ḥākim	Governor, ruler
Hijra	Year of the emigration from Mecca to Medina (632 C.E.)
Itegē	Queen, title of the consort of an Ethiopian monarch
Khawāja (Amharic *hawaja*)	Mr. (used in particular for Europeans)
Lij	Lit. "Child, son", honorific title, mostly used for young members of the higher aristocracy and royalty
Līqe papp̣asat	Archbishop, patriarch
Mekarī līq	scholarly advisor
Mel'ake Mihiret	Lit. "Lord of Mercy", honorary title of chief priest
Mel'ake Selam	Lit. "Lord of Peace", honorary title of chief priest
Memhir, memmirē	Master, teacher, abbot

Meridazmach	Provincial ruler (of Shewa), commander
Merīgēta	Scholarly chief priest, director of *debteras*, mentor
Muḥāfith	Governor
Musē	Term of address for Europeans, from "Monsieur"
Nā'ib	Deputy, agent; title given by the Turks to the Ethiopian chief on the mainland opposite Massawa
Negede	Tribe
Nibure'id, nebure id	Head of the church of St. Mary of Aksum and administrator of the territory belonging to the church
Nigus (Arab. *nikus*)	King
Niguse negest	King of Kings
Nigist	Queen
Nigiste negestat	Queen of Queens
P̣ap̣pas	Bishop
Pasha (Amharic *basha*)	Sir, honorific title for high civil or military official
Qēs	Priest
Qumuṣ	Chief priest
Ras	"Head", governor, commander, lord
Ṣāhib	Lord, master
Shaykh (Amharic *shēh*)	Chief of an Arab clan or village; religious official
Shifta	Rebel, outlaw
Shum	District or village chief, in Tigray provincial ruler
Ṣirag Maserē	Chamberlain
Tabot	Replica of Tablets of Law
Turk basha	Honorific title
Wakīl (Amharic *wekīl*)	Agent, representative
Wālī	Governor, ruler
Wazīr, wuzarā	High government official, minister of state in Muslim countries
Weyzero	Mrs., Madame, lady
Yumra	Tribe, clan

List of abbreviations

AAPA	Politisches Archiv des Auswärtigen Amts, Bonn
Acta	*Acta Aethiopica*
AEA	Archives of the Eparchy of Adigrat, Adigrat
AECP	Correspondance politique, Archives du Ministère des Affaires Étrangères, Paris
AECPC	Correspondance politique des consuls, Archives du Ministère des Affaires Étrangères, Paris
AED	Archives diplomatiques du Ministère des Affaires Étrangères, Paris
AEMD	Mémoires et Documents, Archives du Ministère des Affaires Étrangères, Paris
ANOM.OI	Archives Nationales d'Outre-Mer, Océan Indien
AP.DD	*Atti Parlamentari, Documenti Diplomatici*
ASMAE, AE	Archivio Storico dell Ministero degli Affari Esteri, Archivio Eritrea, Ministero degli Affari Esteri, Rome
ASMAI	Archivio Storico dell'ex Ministero dell'Africa Italiana, Ministero degli Affari Esteri, Rome
ASSGI	Archivio Storico, Società Geografica Italiana, Rome
BN	Bibliothèque Nationale, Paris
BSGI	*Bollettino della Società Geografica Italiana*
Chronicle	Bairu Tafla, *A Chronicle of Emperor Yohannis IV (1872–89)*, Äthiopistische Forschungen, Bd 1, Wiesbaden 1977
Dayr al-Sultan	Archives of the Dayr al-Sultan, Ethiopian monastery Jerusalem
Diplomatic History	Richard Caulk, *"Between the Jaws of Hyenas". A Diplomatic History of Ethiopia (1876–1896)*, Aethiopistische Forschungen 60, Wiesbaden 2002
EAE	*Encyclopaedia Aethiopica* Vols 1–5 (eds Siegbert Uhlig and Baye Yimam), Wiesbaden 2003–2014
EFS	Evangeliska Fosterlands-Stiftelsens arkiv, Uppsala
ENA	National Archives, Cairo
Ethiopia and Germany	Bairu Tafla, *Ethiopia and Germany: Cultural, Political and Economic Relations, 1871–1936*, Äthiopistische Forschungen, Bd 5, Wiesbaden 1981
Evangelical Pioneers	Gustav Arén, *Evangelical Pioneers in Ethiopia: Origins of the Evangelical Church Mekane Yesus*, Stockholm 1978
FO	Foreign Office Records, Public Record Office, London
Ghali Collection	Photographs of Ethiopian correspondence made by Mirrit Butrus Ghali and preserved in the library of the Societé d'archéologie Copte, Cairo

Hertslet	Edward Hertslet, *Map of Africa by Treaty*, London 1894
HHS	Haus-, Hof- und Staatsarchiv, Vienna
L'Italia in Africa	*L'Italia in Africa: Serie Storica, volume primo, Etiopia-Mar Rosso*, I–III (a cura di Carlo Giglio), Rome 1959–1960
Meine Mission	Gerhard Rohlfs, *Meine Mission nach Abessinien: Auf Befehl Sr. Maj. des Deutschen Kaisers im Winter 1880/81 unternommen*, Leipzig 1883
Survival	Sven Rubenson, *The Survival of Ethiopian Independence*, London 1976
Tarīke Negest	Hiruy Welde Sillasē, *Tarīke Negest* [Addis Abeba 1936]
Trattati	*Trattati, Convenzioni, Accordi, Protocolli Ed Altri Documenti Relativi All'Africa 1825–1906*, vol. I, Rome 1906
Wichale	Sven Rubenson, *Wichale XVIII: The Attempt to Establish a Protectorate over Ethiopia*, Addis Abeba 1964
Yohannis IV	Zewde Gabre-Sellassie, *Yohannis IV of Ethiopia: A Political Biography*, Oxford 1975

List of documents

1. Muḥammad ʻAbd al-Raḥīm to Jean-Baptiste Coulbeaux [Jan. 1880]
2. ʻAbd al-Karīm to Jean-Baptiste Coulbeaux 19 Jan. 1880
3. Mihiret Haylu to "friends in Sweden" 17 Feb. [1880]
4. Convention between Burhān Muḥammad and Rubattino Co. 15 March 1880
5. Yohannis IV to Victoria 29 April 1880
6. Yohannis IV to the British government 29 April 1880
7. Adal Tesemma to *Abba* Rago [April 1880]
8. Declaration by Afar chiefs *re* territory at Aseb 15 May 1880
9. Convention between Afar chiefs and the Rubattino Co. 15 May 1880
10. Minīlik II to Victoria 3 June 1880
11. Minīlik II to Giuglielmo Massaja 11 June 1880
12. Alula Ingida Qubī to Erik Emil Hedenström 18 June 1880
13. Convention between Burhān Muḥammad and Giuseppe Sapeto 20 Sept. 1880
14. Burhān Muḥammad to Giuseppe Sapeto [20] Sept. 1880
15. Minīlik II to Antonio Cecchi 6 Oct. 1880
16. Minīlik II to Onorato Caetani 16 Oct. (?) 1880
17. Minīlik II to Jules Grévy 1 Nov. 1880
18. Minīlik II to Albert Delagenière 1 Nov. 1880
19. Ratification by ʻAbdallah Shahīm of 15 May 1880 convention 5 Nov. 1880
20. Minīlik II to Benedetto Cairoli 9 Nov. 1880
21. Tekle Gīyorgīs to Kīrillus V 15 Nov. [1880?]
22. Alula Ingida Qubī to Gerhard Rohlfs 23 Nov. 1880
23. Alula Ingida Qubī to Gerhard Rohlfs [Nov. 1880]
24. Lewṭē Zewde to Gerhard Rohlfs [Nov. 1880]
25. Alula Ingida Qubī to Achille Raffray 10 Dec. 1880
26. Gebre Igzī' to Kīrillus V 15 Dec. [1880?]
27. Yohannis IV to Minīlik II 16 Dec. 1880
28. Gebru *Abba* Çhequn to Achille Raffray 16 Jan. [1881]
29. Yūsif al-Anṭūnī to Kīrillus V 22 Jan. 1881
30. Yohannis IV to Wilhelm I 17 Feb. 1881
31. Yohannis IV to Otto von Bismarck 17 Feb. 1881
32. Yohannis IV, power of attorney for Gerhard Rohlfs 17 Feb. 1881
33. Yohannis IV to Gerhard Rohlfs 23 Feb. 1881
34. Abū Bakr Ibrāhīm to Jules Grévy 6 March 1881
35. Alula Ingida Qubī to Kīrillus V 7 March [1881?]

36.	Minīlik II to Umberto I	30 March 1881
37.	Tekle Gīyorgīs to Kīrillus V	31 March [1881?]
38.	Gebre Gīyorgīs to Kīrillus V	[March 1881]
39.	Yohannis IV to Muḥammad Tawfīq	5 April 1881
40.	Yohannis IV to Muḥammad Tawfīq	5 April 1881
41.	Yohannis IV to Kīrillus V	5 April 1881
42.	Yohannis IV to Kīrillus V	5 April 1881
43.	Yohannis IV to Welde Sema'it Welde Yohannis	5 April 1881
44.	Yohannis IV to the Ethiopian community in Jerusalem	5 April 1881
45.	Burhān Muḥammad to the Italian representative in Aseb	[22 April] 1881
46.	Yohannis IV to Jean-Marcel Touvier, Jean-Baptiste Coulbeaux and Sixtus Barthèz	19 June 1881
47.	Maḥammad Ḥanfadhē to Louis Auguste Brémond	June 1881
48.	Minīlik II to Umberto I	11 July 1881
49.	Minīlik II to Umberto I	12 July 1881
50.	Minīlik II to Benedetto Cairoli	12 July 1881
51.	Yohannis IV to Achille Raffray	17 July 1881
52.	Yohannis IV to Gerhard Rohlfs	27 July 1881
53.	Yohannis IV, declaration on extent of Ethiopian territory	27 July 1881
54.	Burhān Muḥammad, declaration on relation with Egypt	19 Aug. 1881
55.	Nigusē Tasho and Amanu'ēl Hamed to Bengt Peter and Emelie Lundahl	[Aug.–Sept. 1881]
56.	Welde Ṣadiq to Umberto I	4 Sept. [?] 1881
57.	Yohannis IV to Welde Sema'it Welde Yohannis and the Ethiopian community in Jerusalem	5 Sept. 1881
58.	Isṭīfanos Fisseha to Mekonnin	15 Sept. [1881?]
59.	Onesimus Nesib to Johannes Neander	23 Sept. 1881
60.	Minīlik II to Onorato Caetani	9 Oct. 1881
61.	Minīlik II to Umberto I	14 Oct. 1881
62.	Yohannis IV to Victoria	4 Nov. 1881
63.	Yohannis IV to Jules Grévy	4 Nov. 1881
64.	Yohannis IV to Minīlik II	6 Dec. 1881
65.	Lewṭē Zewde to Kīrillus V	9 Jan. 1882
66.	Yohannis IV to Minīlik II	15 Jan. 1882
67.	Yohannis IV to Tekle Haymanot	30 Jan. 1882
68.	Yohannis IV, proclamation on the faith of *ferenj*	[Jan. 1882]
69.	Yohannis IV, proclamation on the practice of Islam	[Jan. 1882]
70.	Yohannis IV, proclamation on schismatics	[Jan. 1882]

71. Ar'aya Sillasē Dimṣu to Achille Raffray [Jan. 1882]
72. Ar'aya Sillasē Dimṣu to Juan Víctor Abargues de Sostén [Jan. 1882]
73. Ar'aya Sillasē Dimṣu to Juan Víctor Abargues de Sostén [Jan. 1882]
74. Yohannis IV to Muḥammad Tawfīq 14 Feb. 1882
75. Yohannis IV to Muḥammad Tawfīq 16 Feb. 1882
76. Yohannis IV to Welde Sema'it Welde Yohannis and the community of Dayr al-Sultan 20 Feb. 1882
77. Yohannis IV to Welde Sema'it Welde Yohannis and the community of Dayr al-Sultan 22 Feb. 1882
78. Minīlik II to Jules Grévy 7 March 1882
79. Minīlik II to François Soumagne 7 March 1882
80. Minīlik II to Pierre Arnoux 7 March 1882
81. Minīlik II to Pietro Antonelli 9 March 1882
82. Welde Ṣadiq to Pierre Arnoux 22 March 1882
83. Gebru *Abba* Çhequn to François Soumagne 24 March 1882
84. Maḥammad Ḥanfadhē to Pietro Antonelli 28 May 1882
85. P̣ēṭros to clerics and believers in Jenda 12 June 1882
86. Yohannis IV to Minīlik II 8 July 1882
87. Minīlik II to P̣ēṭros, Matēwos, Marqos and Luqas 11 July 1882
88. Minīlik II to Victoria 20 July 1882
89. Alula Ingida Qubī to Achille Raffray 20 July 1882
90. Yohannis IV to Achille Raffray 17 Aug. 1882
91. Yohannis IV to Gerhard Rohlfs 19 Aug. 1882
92. Ḥamad La'īta to Pietro Antonelli 28 Sept. 1882
93. Yohannis IV to Umberto I 30 Sept. 1882
94. Minīlik II to Paul Soleillet 9 Oct. [1882]
95. Maḥammad Ḥanfadhē to Sa'īd Awīḍan 16 Oct 1882
96. Minīlik to Giulio Pestalozza 18 Oct 1882
97. 'Abd al-Raḥmān Yūsif to Pietro Antonelli 20 Oct. 1882
98. Maḥammad Ḥanfadhē to Pietro Antonelli 24 Oct. 1882
99. Maḥammad Ḥanfadhē to Commissario Regio in Aseb 24 Oct. 1882
100. Maḥammad Ḥanfadhē to Giulio Pestalozza 25 Nov. 1882
101. Maḥammad Ḥanfadhē to Pietro Antonelli 25 Nov. 1882
102. Maḥammad Ḥanfadhē, power of attorney for 'Abd-al-Raḥmān 26 Nov. 1882
103. Maḥammad Ḥanfadhē to Pietro Antonelli 6 Dec. 1882
104. Burhān Muḥammad to Giulio Pestalozza 17 Dec. 1882
105. Ḥamad La'īta to Giulio Pestalozza 9 Jan. [1883]

106. Burhān Muḥammad to Giulio Pestalozza [Jan. 1883]
107. Burhān Muḥammad to Pasquale Stanislao Mancini 27 Jan. 1883
108. Maḥammad Ḥanfadhē to Pasquale Stanislao Mancini 14 March 1883
109. Maḥammad Ḥanfadhē and Burhān Muḥammad to Pasquale Stanislao Mancini 16 March 1883
110. Yohannis IV to Īyasu Dagmawī 19 March 1883
111. Ḥamad La'īta to Pasquale Stanislao Mancini 22 March 1883
112. Burhān Muḥammad to Pasquale Stanislao Mancini 25 March 1883
113. Yohannis IV to Victoria 9 April 1883
114. Yohannis IV to Wilhelm I 9 April 1883
115. Yohannis IV to Jules Grévy 9 April 1883
116. Yohannis IV to Kīrillus V 10 April 1883
117. Maḥammad Ḥanfadhē, Burhān Muḥammad and Ḥamad La'īta to Giovanni Branchi and Giulio Pestalozza 14 April 1883
118. Treaty between Maḥammad Ḥanfadhē and Italy 18 April 1883
119. Yohannis IV to Victoria 8 May 1883
120. Yohannis IV to Edward Malet 8 May 1883
121. Onesimus Nesib to Johannes Neander 14 May1883
122. Treaty between Shewa and Italy 21 May 1883
123. Minīlik to Giulio Pestalozza 21 May 1883
124. Minīlik II to Pasquale Stanislao Mancini 21 May 1883
125. Minīlik II to Giacomo Malvano 21 May 1883
126. Nigusē Tasho *et al.* to Bengt Peter and Emelie Lundahl 29 May 1883
127. Yohannis IV to Demosthenes Mitzakis 30 May 1883
128. Maḥammad Ḥanfadhē to Giulio Pestalozza 2 June 1883
129. Mirçha Werqē to Robert Fleming 12 June 1883
130. Minīlik II to the Ethiopian community in Jerusalem 25 June 1883
131. Minīlik II to Umberto I 30 June 1883
132. Tamrē *Abba* Sebsib to Umberto I 30 June 18[83]
133. Alula Ingida Qubī to Augustus Blandy Wylde [June (?) 1883]
134. Alula Ingida Qubī to Augustus Blandy Wylde [June (?) 1883]
135. Gobena Daçhī to Umberto I 3 July 1883
136. Welde Ṣadiq to Umberto I 10 July 1883
137. Maḥammad Ḥanfadhē to Pasquale Stanislao Mancini 30 July 1883
138. Maḥammad Ḥanfadhē to Pasquale Stanislao Mancini 21 Aug. 1883
139. Yohannis IV to Umberto I 1 Oct. 1883
140. Burhān Muḥammad to Giulio Pestalozza 9 Oct. 1883

141. Ḥamad La'īta to Giovanni Branchi 27 Oct. 1883
142. Tekle Haymanot to Umberto I 22 Nov. 1883
143. Tekle Haymanot to Pasquale Stanislao Mancini 22 Nov. 1883
144. Tekle Haymanot to Pasquale Stanislao Mancini 22 Nov. 1883
145. Minīlik II to Giulio Pestalozza 3 Dec. 1883
146. Maḥammad Ḥanfadhē to Giulio Pestalozza 16 Dec. 1883
147. Welde Ṣadiq to Giulio Pestalozza 18 Dec. 1883
148. Maḥammad Ḥanfadhē to Giulio Pestalozza 22 Dec. [1883]
149. Maḥammad Ḥanfadhē to Giovanni Branchi 24 Dec. 1883
150. Minīlik II to Pietro Antonelli 24 Dec. 1883
151. Maḥammad Ḥanfadhē to Giovanni Branchi 30 Dec. 1883
152. Maḥammad Ḥanfadhē to Giovanni Branchi 28 Jan. 1884
153. Maḥammad Ḥanfadhē to Giovanni Branchi 5 Feb. 1884
154. Maḥammad Ḥanfadhē to Giovanni Branchi [March 1884]
155. Yohannis IV to Muḥammad Tawfīq 14 March 1884
156. Yohannis IV to Muḥammad Tawfīq 17 March 1884
157. Convention between Ḥamad La'īta and Italy 17 March 1884
158. Maḥammad Ḥanfadhē to Giovanni Branchi 12 April 1884
159. Minīlik II to Pietro Antonelli 8 May 1884
160. Maḥammad Ḥanfadhē to Giovanni Branchi 8 May 1884
161. Welde Ṣadiq to Pietro Antonelli 22 May [1884]
162. Gobena Daçhī to Jules Grévy [May–June 1884]
163. Minīlik II to Pietro Antonelli 1 June 1884
164. Minīlik II to Giulio Pestalozza 1 June 1884
165. Minīlik II to Umberto I 1 June 1884
166. Ṭaytu to Margherita Maria Teresa Giovanna di Savoia 1 June 1884
167. Treaty between Ethiopia, Great Britain and Egypt 3 June 1884
168. Treaty between Ethiopia and Great Britain 3 June 1884
169. Maḥammad Ḥanfadhē to Giovanni Branchi 12 June 1884
170. Yosēf Nigusē to Pietro Antonelli 16 June 1884
171. Yohannis IV to Victoria 20 June 1884
172. Yohannis IV to Victoria 25 June 1884
173. Yohannis IV to Muḥammad Tawfīq 25 June 1884
174. Yohannis IV to Giovanni Branchi 25 June 1884
175. Minīlik II to Giacomo Malvano 9 Aug. 1884
176. Minīlik II to Giovanni Branchi 9 Aug. 1884
177. Gebri'ēl Welde Gobena to Giacomo Malvano 9 Aug. 1884

178.	Minīlik II to Pietro Antonelli	9 Aug. 1884
179.	Treaty between Ḥamad La'īta and France	9 Aug. 1884
180.	Gīyorgīs Gebre Sillasē Nigusē to Pietro Antonelli	11 Aug. 1884
181.	Yosēf Nigusē to Pietro Antonelli	[Aug. 1884]
182.	Yohannis IV to Gebre Igzī'	10 Sept. 1884
183.	Maḥammad Ḥanfadhē to Giulio Pestalozza	16 Sept. 1884
184.	Treaty between Ḥamad Muḥammad and Léonce Lagarde	21 Sept. 1884
185.	Maḥammad Ḥanfadhē to Pasquale Stanislao Mancini	5 Oct. 1884
186.	Maḥammad Ḥanfadhē to Pasquale Stanislao Mancini	5 Oct. 1884
187.	'Abd al-Raḥmān Yūsif to Pasquale Stanislao Mancini	5 Oct. 1884
188.	Ḥamad La'īta and 'Abd al-Qādir Ibrāhīm to Giulio Pestalozza	11 Oct. 1884
189.	Maḥammad Ḥanfadhē to Giulio Pestalozza	17 Oct. 1884
190.	Donation by Ḥamad Muḥammad et al. of territory to France	18 Oct. 1884
191.	Minīlik II to Giulio Pestalozza	4 Nov. 1884
192.	Yohannis IV to Welde Sema'it Welde Yohannis	5 Nov. 1884
193.	Maḥammad Ḥanfadhē to Giulio Pestalozza	11 Nov. 1884
194.	Treaty between Hamad La'īta and Italy	Nov. 1884
195.	Yohannis IV to Welde Sema'it Welde Yohannis	22 Nov. 1884
196.	Minīlik II to Umberto I	1 Dec. 1884
197.	Minīlik II to Pasquale Stanislao Mancini	2 Dec. 1884
198.	Donation by Ḥamad of Tajura and Ḥamad La'īta	14 Dec. 1884

THE TEXTS

Document no. 1

Muḥammad ‘Abd al-Raḥīm to Jean-Baptiste Coulbeaux, [Jan. 1880]

May [this message] from *Nā’ib* Muḥammad reach *Abba* Yohannis. May [God] give you health. Your letter reached me; I should have written to you. However, it was so unexpected. Since *Abune* Ya’iqob until *Abune* Yosēf yours has been mine and mine has been yours.

When we said goodbye to Gordon *Pasha* when he left Cairo for Alexandria, he praised you. He said to me, “Since they are my friends, protect them.” The consul that lives in Massawa (Raffray) said, “Do good things to them”. The consul is my friend. I have not changed at all (lit. in everything I am as before). But may [God] bring us together. Send this letter to *Abune* Yosēf on my behalf.

AEA, Amharic text copied into a diary kept at the eparchy of Adigrat. The letter is not dated, but copied into the diary together with the following letter and there assigned to January 1880. Muḥammad ‘Abd al-Raḥīm was *nā’ib* from 1856 to 1887 with some interruptions, and had been involved in the conflict between the Ottoman and Egyptian rulers and Tēwodros as well as Yohannis since the 1860s. See *EAE* 3, pp. 1046–1047. He travelled with Gordon to Cairo when Gordon left Massawa in Dec. 1879. *Abba* Yohannis refers to Fr. Coulbeaux and *Abune* Yosēf to Mgr. Touvier.

Document no. 2

‘Abd al-Karīm to Jean-Baptiste Coulbeaux, 19 Jan. 1880

May [this message] sent by *Nā’ib* ‘Abd al-Karīm reach *Abba* Yohannis. How have you been, really? I am well. The letter you sent to me has reached me. Fine, we will do everything that you have told [us to do]. As *Nā’ib* Muḥammad has been guarding, I will also do so. Even if it is your country, I will do even more than that. Otherwise I will guard like him. Again, I have sent to Asawirta and Tora that they should not come near you. May [God] let us meet. Amen.

Written at Massawa on the 9th of Ṭirr in the year 1872.

AEA, see above. ‘Abd al-Karīm was the cousin of Muḥammad and replaced him as *nā’ib* during his absence in 1880.

Document no. 3

Mihiret Haylu to “friends in Sweden”, 17 Feb. [1880]

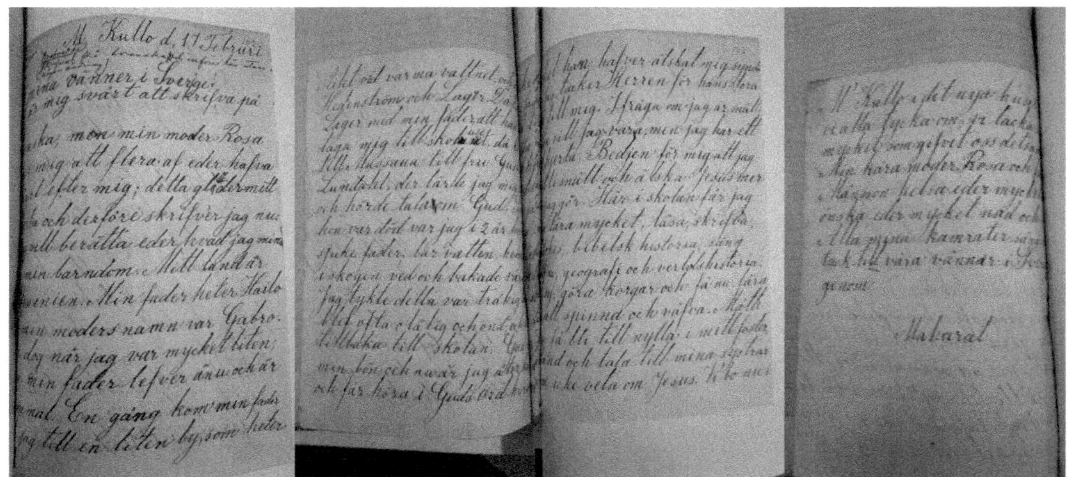

Imkullu (M’Kullu), 17 February

To my friends in Sweden.

It is hard for me to write in Swedish, but my mother Rosa says to me that many of you have asked about me; this gladdens my heart, and therefore I now write.

I want to tell you what I remember from my childhood. My country is Abyssinia. My father is called Haylu, and my mother’s name was Gabro. She died when I was very young, but my father is still alive, and he is old. My father and I once came to a small village called Aylet at the warm waters, and Hedenström and Lager were there.

Lager spoke with my father [and told him] that he should bring me to the schoolhouse. Then I came to Massawa to Mrs. Gustava Lundahl. There I learnt Swedish and heard about God. When she was dead, I lived for two years with my sick father, carried water, collected firewood in the forest and baked our bread. I found this tedious and often became impatient and angry and longed to go back to the school. God heard my prayer, and now I am back here and can hear from the word of God how much he has loved me, a sinner. I thank the Lord for his great mercy towards me. You ask if I am good; this I want to be, but I have a wicked heart. Pray for me that I may become good and love Jesus more than I do. Here in school I learn much: reading, writing, catechism, biblical history, singing, arithmetic, geography, and world history. We sew, make baskets and now learn how to spin and weave.

May I be of use in my country and speak to my sisters who do not know about Jesus. We now live in Imkullu (M'Kullu) in the new house, which we all like. We thank you very much, who have given this to us. My dear mother Rosa and father Månsson send many greetings and wish you much grace and peace.

Also all my friends say thanks to our friends in Sweden, through Mihiret.

EFS, E I 24 no. 133, Swedish original. The letter was forwarded to Sweden by Mrs. Rosa Månsson, the head-mistress of the school opened by the Swedish mission in Massawa in 1876 and moved to Imkullu in 1878, together with translations from Amharic of five more letters with a covering letter, also dated 17 February.

The writer was one of the girls taught in the school in Imkullu near Massawa at this time. Mihirit's father was *Aleqa* Haylu, a Gojjamē who had served as Tēwodros' secretary and later became a co-worker of the Swedish mission at Massawa (see *Acta* III, no. 80). Mihirit was entrusted by him to the Swedish missionary Gustava Lundahl (née von Platen) in early 1872 at the age of ten, after her father had become a friend of the Swedish missionaries Lager and Hedenström at Aylet in 1871. After Gustava Lundahl's death less than a year later, she had to go back to take care of her father, and it was only in 1880, most probably after her father's death, that she was able to return to the Swedish mission at Imkullu. Her command of Swedish and her handwriting are outstanding, especially as she had no formal education in the language. The school she joined had been opened in Massawa in 1876 and moved to Imkullu in 1878. In 1881, Mihirit married Onesimus Nesib and accompanied him on two missions to the Oromo area. She died at Imkullu in the epidemics of 1888. The letter is included as a specimen of letters by Ethiopian pupils in mission schools written for circulation among the supporters of the European missions in Europe. See *Evangelical Pioneers*, pp. 218, n. 36, 250–251.

Document no. 4

Convention between Burhān Muḥammad and the Rubattino Co., 15 March 1880

Shaykh Duran, 15 May 1880, Glory be to God.

Be it notified to those concerned, that this day, the 15th of the month of March 1880 and the 3rd day of the month of Rabī' al-ākhir of the year 1297 according to the Muslim era, I, Burhān Muḥammad, Sultan of Raḥayta, sovereign, absolute master and proprietor of the territory surrounding the village of Aseb, of Italian property, by virtue of a traditional and uncontested right declare that I stipulate, deliberately and with complete freedom (lit. spontaneity), on my own account and on that of my successors on one hand and on the other in favour of Professor Cav. Giuseppe Sapeto on behalf of the Rubattino Co. of Genoa, of which he is the legal representative, in the best of faith and under solemn oath the following contract, which is to be legally valid as if it had been drawn up by the public notary.

I, the above-mentioned Burhān Muḥammad, declare that I sell, am [now] selling, to the above-mentioned Cav. Giuseppe Sapeto in his capacity of procurator of the Rubattino Co. all the islands, none excluded, situated in the big bay of Aseb and between the parallels of *Ras* Sintyar and *Ras* Lumah, among which the principal ones are the islands of Fatmah, Darmabah, Makawah, Halem, Delkos, Arukia etc., and all the littoral extending between the above-mentioned *Ras* Lumah and *Ras* Sintyar together with a piece of the mainland that forms a territorial zone two nautical miles inland from the seashore along the whole coastline from the bay of Būya to Shaykh Duran and a territorial zone four nautical miles wide inland from the seashore along the whole coastline from Shaykh Duran to *Ras* Sintyar. And by this sale I renounce for me and my successors all rights of property and of sovereignty, investing the above-mentioned buyer with both these rights with the consequent right to raise the national Italian flag in the places sold and declaring that I am determined to respect and to make respected the sale itself at all times and places by all possible means. Professor Cav. Giuseppe Sapeto, as procurator of the Rubattino Co., undertakes, with reference to the sale that is the object of this document and in the name of the company itself, to pay the sum of 13,000 (thirteen thousand) thalers, of which I, Burhān Muḥammad, sultan as above, declare that I have received, on account and as an advance payment, the sum of 4,000 (four thousand) thalers, and it is agreed that the balance is to be paid as follows: 3,000 (three thousand) thalers after three months from today and the rest, 6,000 (six thousand) thalers, within a year from the date of this second payment. Finally, the contracting parties recognize that the present document must not in any way invalidate agreements that may prior to the present stipulations have been made by Messrs Rubattino & Co. and their representative, Professor Cav. Sapeto, with other holders of rights or interests, and they further declare that no contestation can or should be made as to the form in which the present document has been drawn up.

In faith whereof we, the contracting parties, sign with our own hands in the presence of the witnesses indicated below, and swear solemnly upon the Qurān and the Gospel respectively to keep the agreement stipulated above. So help us God.

Made and signed at Shaykh Duran (*sic*) the year, month and day as above.

Burhān Muḥammad, Sultan of Raḥayta; Giuseppe Sapeto, Procurator of the Rubattino Co. Witnesses: Giuseppe Bienenfeld Rolph; G. M. Giulietti; Sa'īd 'Awīḍān Sa'īd; Massaud Nahbur.

Trattati, no. 12, pp. 42–43, Italian text. No Arabic version is preserved, and it is unclear if there ever was one. Cf. doc. 45. Burhān Muḥammad signed as *wazīr* of Sultan Dīnī Muḥammad in 1862, but became the ruler of Raḥayta before 1870 (see *Acta* III, doc. 35). He died on 22 November 1883 (see *L'Italia in Africa*, I.3, p. 31)

Document no. 5

Yohannis IV to Victoria, 29 April 1880

Seal: King of Kings Yohannis, King of Zion in Ethiopia. The cross has defeated the tribe of Isma'ēl. Yūḥannā, King of Kings of Zion in Abyssinia. The cross has defeated the people of Ismā'īl. 1864.

May the message of the Elect of God Yohannis, King of Zion, King of Kings of Ethiopia, reach Queen Victoria, by the power of God [queen] of the United Kingdom [of] Great Britain [and] Ireland, defender of the faith, queen of India and all its dependencies.

I received your letter with its seal, which was written with good intent. I was extremely happy seeing this esteemed letter. The dignitaries and noblemen, after seeing this esteemed and honoured letter of yours, were also extremely happy. It is not only recently that you have done your best for my government. Did it not begin when Lord Napier came to fight Tēwodros 11 years ago today? Is it not because you gave me rifles, cannon and ammunition that I became a king under God? And now since I am your loyal son see to it that the issue is settled without delay.

As for Massawa and all the surrounding territories they are being occupied by force and deceit as they are not the countries and properties of the Turks. They are the property of the government of Ethiopia. And now see to it that they open an outlet for me so that the merchants can trade as in the past and not be hindered Still all the territories which are around Ethiopia that they have taken by force, I will never hand over identifying them with my seal. However, as for what they claim, that they are attacked and mistreated, send me good arbitrators from your government who will hear my and their complaints.

Earlier when you told me, "Live in peace and love with the governments that are your neighbours", I listened to your words and lived in peace and there is nothing that I have neglected. But the Turks claiming that they have progressed in knowledge felt stronger and came and fought me twice though I did not treat them badly. And Christian blood was shed without any offence [having been committed]. But since God is the God of the oppressed and not of the oppressor, he gave me power without any argument. Again, they misled a man called Welde Mīka'ēl, my servant from Ḥamasēn, for a lot of money and had him desert me. Twice they exterminated the surrounding people, not sparing even women and children. Let alone Ethiopians, finding a few Europeans they slew them all.

Believing that they would not let an Ethiopian get a passage, I sent an Englishman called "colonel" who lived with me, writing a letter to the English government indicating the occupation of my country and my being mistreated. They killed the messenger at Massawa and having torn up the letter they threw it into the sea. And now be informed that unless I found a town on the shore of the sea, so that Abyssinian and English traders [can] meet and trade with each other, it will be as before.

When the ruler (*gezh*) of Egypt, Tawfīq *Pasha*, sent a messenger, an Englishman called Gordon *Pasha*, I received him well with respect and honour. But he insulted and humiliated me saying "You are weak and have no power. I will bring an army along with me and fight you." After this, expecting that he would bring along an army with him and fight me, I armed myself, declared war and waited. However, I do not intend to start a war before I have received the reply to the letter I have written to you.

Written in the camp of Guba Lefto of the district of Yejju, 22 Mīyazya in the year of grace 1872.

FO 95/739, no. 215, Amharic original and English translation. The same day as the above, a letter was written to the British government (doc. 6 below). The letter mentioned in the text did reach the consul-general in Cairo (FO 78/2632). The Englishman "called colonel" whom Yohannis sent as his messenger to England but who died at Massawa was John Kirkham, a member of the British expedition to Meqdela 1867–68 who had remained behind and entered the service of the Ethiopian ruler. See *EAE* 3, p. 409. Welde Mīka'ēl Selomon had been appointed governor of Ḥamasēn by Yohannis but had revolted and joined the Egyptians who had made him *ras*. See *EAE* 5, pp. 1105–1107. On the role of *Dejjazmach* Welde Mīka'ēl see further *Survival*, pp. 326–327, 333–335, 337–341.

Document no. 6

Yohannis IV to the British government, 29 April 1880

መልእክተ፡ዘሥዩመ፡እግዚአብሔር፡ዮሐንስ፡ንጉሠ፡ጽዮን፡ንጉሠ፡ነገሥ
ት፡ዘኢትዮጵያ፡ይድረስ፡ኀበ፡ኩሎሙ፡መሳፍንት፡ወመኳንንት፡፡ዓታ
ብያን፡ቤት፡መንግሥት፡መማክርቲሃ፡ለንግሥት፡ቢክቶርያ፡፡ጸብጸቢ
ያቅ፡ሁሉም፡ደረሰኝ፡ስለኔ፡መንግሥት፡ስለ፡ሕዝቤ፡ባለጸግነት፡መጣ
ርእቻሁ፡የሀ፡እጅግ፡ደስ፡አለኝ፡የቱርኮች፡ነገር፡ግን፡ዜናቸ፡ጠላት፡
ልወጋ፡አገሬን፡ላሰቱ፡ብዙድ፡በኋላ፡ሠጥተው፡አገሬን፡ወሰዱት፡
ወደ፡ንግሥት፡እንዲህ፡አደረጉኝ፡ብዬ፡ደብዳቤ፡ጽፌ፡ብልክ፡ደብ
ዳቤውን፡ተደውክባሕር፡ጣሉት፡፡ከዚህ፡በኋላም፡መጥተው፡ስ
ቤቴ፡ድረስ፡የክርስቲያኑን፡ሁሉ፡ደም፡አፈሰሱት፡፡ደግመኛም፡
እማሴን፡ደጅች፡ወልደ፡ሚካኤል፡የሚባል፡ሎሌዬን፡ሹሚ፡
ብስደ፡በብዙ፡ገንዘብ፡እስተወ፡ብዙ፡ነፍሳት፡ስጥተው፡ሕዝቤ
ን፡ሁሉ፡ፈጁት፡፡ሁሉት፡ጊዜ፡፡ሲቶም፡እሽክርም፡ሳይቀር፡፡
እንኳን፡የኢትዮጵያ፡ሰውና፡የአውሮጳ፡ሰዎች፡ሞቱት፡ቢገኙ፡
ጩሞሮ፡እረዳቸው፡፡ዛሬም፡ከማህሉ፡አገሬ፡ምንስ፡ጦረቸ
ው፡ን፡እኔረውበሻል፡፡ክፉትር፡በቀር፡ክፉ፡እላደረገሁም፡ማለ
ቱ፡የምስር፡ገዥ፡ሐሰቱ፡ነው፡፡እሁንም፡አገሬን፡ሁሉ፡ኢትዮጵያ
ን፡ዙርያውን፡በእጁ፡እንዲያዘው፡አለ፡እስተፉልኝም፡በርም፡
ዘግቶብኛል፡፡መልሶ፡የእንግሊዝ፡ሰው፡የጎርደን፡ባሻ፡የሚባል፡
እንቷረት፡ብሎ፡ባክብኝ፡የምስር፡ገዥ፡እሺ፡ብሎ፡ወሰልኝም፡እድርጊ፡
እክብሬ፡ተቀበልሁት፡፡እሱ፡ግን፡ክፉ፡ቃል፡ተናገረኝ፡እንዲደው
ስ፡ም፡ን፡ጉ፡ልበት፡አለ፡ጠር፡አም፡ጥቂ፡እወጋ፡ሀለሁ፡ብሎ፡አደበኝ፡፡መል
እክቶኛው፡እንዲህ፡ሲለኝ፡ብዬ፡ሠራዊቴን፡ለብሰቤ፡ተቀመጥሁ፡ወዲያ
ውም፡እሰረኝ፡ብሎ፡ስለክ፡አስመታብኝ፡እክብሬ፡ስለተቀበልሁት፡፡እኔ
ማ፡ወዲ፡ንገሥታቱ፡ደብዳቤ፡ልኬ፡ምላሹ፡ሳይመጣልኝ፡እንደምን፡እ
ድርጊ፡እዋጋለሁ፡፡ሰ፡ወጀ፡የ፡መየሩ፡መት፡ምሕረት፡አመ፡ወየለሚያ
ዝያ፡ተጽሕፈ፡በጉጉ፡ጎፉች፡ሰፈር፡ብሒረ፡ዩጃ፡

Seal: King of Kings Yohannis, King of Zion in Ethiopia. The cross has defeated the tribe of Isma'ēl. Yūḥannā, King of Kings of Zion in Abyssinia. The cross has defeated the people of Ismā'īl. 1864.

May the message of the Elect of God Yohannis, King of Zion, King of Kings of Ethiopia, reach all the princes and notables, the ministers of the government and advisers to Queen Victoria.

I have received your letter. I am very pleased by your efforts for the prosperity of my kingdom and my people. But the question of the Turks! Earlier, when I went to fight [my] enemies and to expand my country, they came behind my back and took my country. When I wrote and sent a letter to the kings [of Europe] telling what they did to me, they tore up the letter and threw it into the sea. After this, they came up to my capital (lit. my house) and shed the blood of all the Christians.

Secondly, when I appointed and sent my servant *Dejjach* Welde Mīka'ēl to Ḥamasēn, they misled him with much money. By giving him many guns, they exterminated my people twice, not sparing women and children. Let alone Ethiopians, he slaughtered the few Europeans who were found amongst them. Even now, they have stationed their army in the centre of my country, in Bogos (Moges).

The ruler (*gezh*) of Egypt is lying when he says that he did not commit acts of aggression (lit. evil) but of friendship. At this time also, he is still in possession of all my country, of [all the lands] around Ethiopia. He has not restored them to me, and he has closed the ports to me. In addition to this the ruler of Egypt sent an Englishman called Gordon *Pasha* asking me to make peace with him. I agreed and welcomed him properly, honouring him. But he spoke evil words to me. He insulted me, saying, "In any case, what strength do you have? I shall bring an army and attack you." Since his messenger told me so, I gathered my army [and] waited. Right away he sent a telegram accusing me of imprisoning him, when I had received him with honour. As for me, how can I fight before I send letters to the kings and [have their] replies?

Written at the camp of Guba Lefto, in the land of Yejju on the 22nd of Mīyazya in the year of grace 1872.

FO 95/739, no. 217, Amharic/Gi'iz original and English translation. For the persons and circumstances see the footnote to the previous document. It may be noted that Emperor Yohannis is much more restricted in what he writes to the government than to the queen herself.

Document no. 7

Adal Tesemma to *Abba* Rago [April 1880]

Message from *Ras* Adal, chief of chiefs and prince of Gojjam, to the king of Gēra.

Abba Rago, how are you? I am well, by the grace of God, and my country, my cattle and my army are also well.

I have heard from some merchants that two *ferenj* had come to your kingdom. One of them is dead, the other one I know that you are keeping as a prisoner since a long time. I also know that you deprived them of all their merchandise and made them suffer much. I forgive you for everything and do not accuse you. As for the one who is dead – to the distress and vexation of you and of your relatives, the kings – God has willed it and there is nothing more to be said about it.

As for the one who is still alive, I desire and wish that you, as soon as you have received this letter of mine, concern yourself with this and make an agreement with the kings of Jimma, of Kefa, Goma, Limmu and Gumma, and send him to me with not even a thorn getting into his feet. Take away from him, if you like, what he has left, it matters little, but send this *ferenj* back to me, for I need him, and without excuses. If you send him to me, we shall be friends, and what grows in my country and not in yours I shall send to you, and what grows in your country but not in mine you shall send to me. If you refuse, I shall come and take him by force and close the roads and markets to your people, and we shall no longer be related.

Antonio Cecchi, *Da Zeila alle frontiere del Caffa*, vol. II, Rome, 1885, pp. 548–549, Italian text which is very clearly a translation from Amharic. No Amharic original has, however, been found. *Ras* Adal Tesemma was the ruler of Gojjam since 1874, and in January 1881 appointed *Nigus* with the name Tekle Haymanot. The addressee, here nicknamed *Abba* Rago, was in reality the queen of Gēra, Genne Gummiti. The two *ferenj* refer to Antonio Cecchi and Giovanni Chiarini who had been imprisoned by the queen in February 1879 on an expedition to the equatorial lakes. It is difficult to say when the news of Chiarini's death (5 October 1879) and Cecchi's captivity reached the outside world, but by April 1880 it was known *inter alia* through the above letter from *Ras* Adal. It was, however, only at the end of August 1881 that *Ras* Adal was able to have Cecchi liberated, and only in October that he could join Pietro Antonelli, Alfred Ilg and finally Gustavo Bianchi north of the Abbay.

Whether "without excuses", "senza scuse" in the Italian text, refers to the writer, "I feel no need to excuse myself", or the receiver, "don't bother about excusing yourself", is not clear.

Document no. 8

Declaration by Afar chiefs re. territory at Aseb, 15 May 1880

Glory be to God.

Today, the 15th of the month of May of the year 1880 according to the Christian era, and the 6th day of the month of Jumāda al-ākhira of the year 1297 according to the Muslim era, we Ḥasan Aḥmad, Ibrāhīm Aḥmad and Rāj Aḥmad, deliberately and of our own free will (lit. with complete spontaneity), in virtue of a traditional and uncontested right and with a view to an increase of the economical prosperity of our country and to future benefits for ourselves and the Danākil tribes inhabiting the same territory, benefits deriving from the creation of new working means, declare that we irrevocably cede, as if sold by us, the territory of Bar Assoli and that of the locality of Behtah, both situated north of Beylul, our exclusive and uncontested property, to Professor Cavalier Giuseppe Sapeto as representative of the Rubattino Co. of Genoa, for him to have at his disposal and use as he pleases as a true owner with no possibility for us to intervene in any way or to claim any sort of compensation. We, the undersigned Ḥasan Aḥmad, Ibrāhīm Aḥmad and Rāj Aḥmad, recognize that the present document of cession is legally valid as if drawn up by the public notary. In faith whereof we sign with our own hands and in the presence of the witnesses indicated below, solemnly swearing upon the Qurān, and undertake to keep valid the integrity of the present cession of the localities of Bar Assoli and Behtah at all times and places with all possible means.

So help us God.

Made and signed at Aseb, the year, month and day as above.

Ḥasan Aḥmad,
Ibrāhīm Aḥmad,
Rāj Aḥmad.

Sa'īd 'Awīḍān confirms the above
Ja'dar confirms the above
Giuseppe M. Giulietti.

I, the undersigned, declare that the cession of the localities of Bar Assoli and Behtah made to me by the brothers Ḥasan, Ibrāhīm and Rāj is subject to the conditions stipulated by me as representative of the Rubattino Co. of Genoa with the parties involved for all purchases made by me in the bay of Aseb. In faith whereof, etc.

Professor Giuseppe Sapeto,
representative [of] the Rubattino Co.

Aseb 15th May 1880.

Seen for legalization of the signatures on board SS. Avviso Italiano Esploratore, the Bay of Aseb 15th May 1880. The officer in charge of port consular authorities.
Seal: SS. picket Esploratore.

Seen for registration at the Royal Consulate of Italy in Aden. Aden, 28th May 1880. The Royal Consul Bienenfeld Rolph. Seal: Royal Consulate of Italy at Aden.

ASMAI, no file or identification number; Italian, signatures of Afar chiefs in Arabic inserted; printed in *Trattati*, pp. 47–48. As sultans of Aseb, Ḥasan and Ibrāhīm Aḥmad signed the contract with Sapeto on 15 November 1869 (*Acta* III, doc. 22) as well as the contract of 11 March 1870 (*ibid.*, doc. 43). Sa'īd 'Awīḍān, on whose boat the first contract was signed, later became the interpreter and agent of the Italians in Aseb. As with these earlier contracts, it is highly unlikely that an Arabic version ever existed. The third of the signatures is spelled 'Raghe' in the Italian text, which probably represents Egyptian pronunciation.

Document no. 9

Convention between Afar chiefs and the Rubattino Co., 15 May 1880

Aseb, 15th May 1880

Glory be to God.

Be those concerned notified that this day, the 15th of the month of May of the year 1880 according to the Christian era and the 6th day of the month of Jumādā-al-ākhira of the year 1297 according to the Muslim era, we, Ḥasan Aḥmad, by virtue of the traditional and uncontested right, declare that we stipulate, deliberately and with complete freedom (lit. spontaneity), on our own account and on that of our successors and the parties involved, and especially ʻAbdallāh Shaḥīm, of whom we are the legitimate representatives, on one hand, and in favour of Professor Cavalier Giuseppe Sapeto, on behalf of the Rubattino Co. of Genoa, of which he is the legal representative, on the other, in the best of faith and under solemn oath the following contract, which is to be legally valid as if it had been drawn up by the public notary.

We, Ḥasan Aḥmad, Ibrāhīm Aḥmad and Rāj Aḥmad, declare that we have sold, [and are] selling, to the aforementioned Cavalier Giuseppe Sapeto in his quality of procurator of the Rubattino Co. the island of Sennabor as well as all the region on the mainland between *Ras* Darmah and *Ras* Lumah; for an extension of six nautical miles inland from the seashore. And by this sale we renounce for us, for our successors, and for the parties involved, all right of property and sovereignty, investing the above-mentioned buyer with both these rights with the consequent right to raise the national Italian flag in the places sold, and declare that we are determined to respect and to make respected the sale itself at all times and places by every possible means.

Professor Cavalier Giuseppe Sapeto, as procurator of the Rubattino Co., undertakes, with reference to the sale that is the object of this document and in the name of the company itself, to pay the sum of 1,500 (one thousand five hundred) thalers, of which we, Ḥasan Aḥmad, Ibrāhīm Aḥmad and Rāj Aḥmad, declare that we have received two hundred (200) as an advance of payment on the day of 22 April 1880 of the Christian era and 12 Jumada-al-awal 1297 of the Muslim era, 300 (three hundred) thalers at the moment of the signing of the contract, and the remaining one thousand (1,000) thalers within a year from today.

And, in order to satisfy a wish expressed by the above-mentioned sellers, Professor Cavalier Giuseppe Sapeto, as procurator of the Rubattino Co., undertakes, as a gracious concession, for his own part as well as that of the Rubattino Co. and that of other holders of rights or interests, to leave full and complete freedom of action to the Danākil tribes living in the territory purchased according to the document with regard to habits, customs, practices and traditions, in so far as such freedom af action does not in any way interfere with the legitimate rights and interests of the above-mentioned Rubattino Co. or other holders of rights or interests.

Finally, the contracting parties recognize that the present document must not in any way invalidate agreements that prior to the present stipulations may have been made by Messrs Rubattino & Co.

and their representative Professor Cavalier Giuseppe Sapeto with other holders of rights or interests; and they further declare that no objection can or should be made as to the form in which the present document has been drawn up.

In faith whereof we, the contracting parties, sign with our own hands in the presence of the witnesses indicated below and swear solemnly upon the Qurān and the Gospel respectively to keep the agreement stipulated above.

So help us God.

Made and signed at Aseb the year, month and day as above.

Ḥasan Aḥmad	Giuseppe Sapeto
Ibrāhīm Aḥmad	Representative of the Rubattino Co.
Rāj Aḥmad	
Witnesses:	'Abdallāh Muḥammad, Sa'īd 'Awīḍān, Giuseppe Maria Giulietti, Ja'dar.

Trattati, pp. 44–46. The Italian original of this document is reported to have been located in ASMAI, but we have not been able to find it. This seems to be a revised and elaborated version of the previous document including a reference to 'Abdallāh Shaḥīm, who ratified the convention only in November 1880 (see doc. 19), a much more precise definition of the area sold, including the island Sennabor, the right to raise the Italian flag, and detailed accounts of payments and previous agreements. This long version was probably produced for the Italian legal system and was never sealed or signed by the sultans.

Document no. 10

Minīlik II to Victoria, 3 June 1880

የተላከ፡ከንጉሠ፡ምኒልክ፡በእግዚአብሔር፡ኃይል፡የሸዋ፡ንጉሠ፡የሆነ፡ይድረ
ስ፡ወደ፡ከበረች፡ወደ፡ታፈረች፡የዓለሙ፡ሁሉ፡እናት፡የነገሥታት፡ንግሥት፡፡የታላ
ቂቱ፡ብሪታንያ፡ንግሥት፡፡አንድ፡የሆኑ፡ነገሥታት፡ንግሥት፡የኢርላንድ፡ንግሠ
ት፡የክርስቲያን፡ሃይማኖት፡ጠባቂ፡፡የህንድ፡ነገሥታት፡ንግሥት፡የቅሪ፡የቅሪ፡የቀ
ረውንም፡በጅዋ፡የተያዘ፡በእግርዋ፡የተረገጠ፡መንግሥት፡ሁሉ፡ንግሥት፡ከሰላም
ታዎን፡እንደ፡ብዙ፡በረከት፡በታላቅ፡ፍቅር፡ይቀበሉልኝ፡፡ከንግሥት፡የመጣውን፡የጥቅ
ርና፡የምክር፡ደብዳቤ፡ከብዙ፡ማክበር፡ጋራ፡ተቀበልሁ፡፡በኔም፡ዘንድ፡እጅግ፡የከበረ፡
የተወደደ፡የሚያስደንቅ፡የሚያከመስግን፡ደብዳቤ፡ነበረ፡፡ይልቁንም፡የንግሥትቷ
ላ፡መንግሥቴን፡የሚያቀና፡በአገሬም፡ጥበብን፡የፍቅርንም፡መንገድ፡የሚያሳዩ፡፡
ከጐረቤቶቼም፡ጋራ፡የሚያፋቅር፡ምክር፡የሚነገር፡ደብዳቤ፡ነበረና፡፡ደግመኛም፡
ከባቴ፡ከወደጄ፡ከእኔ፡የውሐንስ፡ጋራ፡በመስማማቴ፡አንድ፡አካል፡በመሆኔ፡እጅግ፡ደ
ስ፡እንደ፡ለው፡በሰማ፡ደስታዩ፡ያለ፡መጠን፡ያለ፡ልክ፡የበዛ፡ሆነ፡፡ስለንግሥቲቱም፡ከእግዚ
አብሔር፡ኃይል፡ጋራ፡የሁለታችን፡ፍቅር፡እንዲጠነክር፡አልጠራጠርም፡፡ሥራዬም፡በን
ግሥት፡ፊት፡የክርስቲያን፡ነገሥታት፡ሥራ፡ሁሉ፡ከለተገኘልኝ፡እጅግ፡ደስ፡በሎኛል፡፡
የኔ፡ሥራ፡ንግሥት፡ለጠቁ፡ክርስቲያን፡በሚሠሩት፡መልክም፡ሥራ፡ፊት፡ከባሕር፡
ውስጥ፡እንዲገባ፡እማሌ፡ይጠለኝ፡ነበርና፡፡ደግመኛም፡ንግሥት፡ስለኤትዮጵያ፡ፍቅ
ር፡የመንግሥትዎን፡ምኒስቴር፡እኛን፡ለማፋቀር፡እንዲ[illegible]ጥር፡ስለአዘዙት፡እጅግ፡አመ
ሰግናለሁ፡፡እኔም፡የንግሥትን፡ምክር፡ይዤ፡ከጐረቤቶቼ፡ጋራ፡የሚያፋቅር፡ነገር፡ሁሉ፡አ
ደርጋለሁ፡፡ከንግሥትም፡ረዳትነት፡ጋራ፡የጋርመርሁትን፡የፈለጉትን፡ነገር፡ሁሉ፡ከባሕር፡
ዳር፡እንዲደክለክልብኝ፡ትስፋ፡አለኝ፡፡የጋርመርሁትንም፡የማይገባውን፡የባርያን፡ን
ግድ፡ማጥፋት፡በትቻለኝ፡ሁሉ፡እኔ፡በምገዛው፡አገር፡እንዲጠፋ፡አደርጋለሁ፡፡ንግ
ሥትም፡ክርስቲያን፡ወገኖቿ፡የምገዛን፡እኛን፡ከሰላም፡ባርነት፡እንዲገባ፡የጋርመ
ሩትን፡የክርስቲያን፡በዝነት፡እንዲጨርሱ፡ተስፋ፡አለን፡፡የማይጠገብ፡ፍቅርዎንም፡
ከኛ፡እንዳይርቅ፡ከብዙ፡ሰላምታ፡ጋራ፡ፈቃድዎን፡በ፡መፈጸም፡እጠብቃለሁ፡የን
ግሥትን፡ዕድሜ፡መንግሥትዎ፡ሰይናወጥ፡እግዚአብሔር፡እንዲያረዝመው፡ከብ
ዙ፡ማሰብ፡ጋራ፡እለምናለሁ፡፡ እግዚአብሔር፡ጤና፡ይስጥዎ፡፡
በግንቦት፡፳፯ በደብረ፡ብርሃን፡ከተማችን፡በ፲፰፻፸፪ ዓመት፡ምሕረት፡እምል
ደት፡ክርስቶስ፡መድኃኒን፡፡ ዳግማዊ፡ምኒልክ፡ንጉሠ፡ሸዋ፡በነገሠ፡በ፲፭ዓመ
ት፡ተጻፈ፡፡

May [this message] sent by King Minīlik, who has become king of Shewa by the power of God, reach the honoured and respected mother of all the world, the Queen of Queens, the queen of the United Kingdom of Great Britain and Ireland (lit. queen of Great Britain, the kingdoms that have become one, queen of Ireland), defender of the Christian faith, empress of India, the queen who has grasped in her hands and placed under her feet [all] the governments that remain (that remain, that remain), the queen of all kingdoms.

[Please] accept my greetings with great friendship as if they were many gifts. I received with great honour the letter of friendship and advice which came from you, the queen. It was for me a highly respected, appreciated, wonderful and praiseworthy letter. For it was above all a letter which [contained] the queen's words that would stabilize my government, show the path of wisdom and friendship in my country [and] give advice which would establish friendship with my neighbours.

Secondly, my happiness became great, beyond limit [and] beyond measure, when I heard that you were very pleased that I agreed with my father [and] friend *Aṣe* Yohannis becoming one body [with him]. I do not doubt that in the future also, with the power of God, the friendship between the two of us will grow stronger. I am very happy that in the eyes of the queen my deed was found to be a deed of Christian kings. For I used to think that compared with the deeds that the queen did in favour of oppressed Christians my deed was like a block of salt which was thrown into the sea.

Furthermore, I thank you, the queen, much because out of friendship for Ethiopia you have ordered the minister of your government to make an effort to create friendship between us. And I, following the queen's advice, shall do everything to establish friendship between me and my neighbours. I hope that what I have begun with the help of the queen [and] that everything I want on the seacoast will not be withheld from me.

[As for] the abolishing of the unlawful trade in slaves, which I have already begun, I shall to the best of my ability attempt to abolish [it] within the country that I rule. We have hopes that you, the queen, on your part, will complete the well-being of Christians, which you have already started by protecting us who are your Christian partisans from being enslaved by Islam.

I await, fulfilling your will with much care so that your friendship, of which one cannot have enough, will not be far from us. I pray to God, with much solicitude, that He may prolong the queen's life without your kingdom being shaken. May God give you health.

In our town of Debre Birhan, on the 27th of Ginbot in the year of grace 1872 after the birth of Christ our Saviour.

The second Minīlik, King of Shewa. Written in the 15th year of his reign.

Seal: Minīlik, King of Kings.
The Lion of the tribe of Judah has prevailed.

FO 95/739, no. 223, Amharic original; no. 224, French translation sealed with the same seal as the Amharic.

Document no. 11

Minīlik II to Giuglielmo Massaja, 11 June 1880

የተላከ፡ ከንጉሥ፡ ምኒልክ፡ ይድረስ፡ ወደ፡ ማሳያስ፡፡ እንዴት
ከረመው፡ እኔ፡ እግዚአብሔር፡ ይመስገን፡ ደኅና፡ ነኝ፡፡ ሠራዊቱም፡ ሁሉ፡
ደኅና፡ ነው፡፡ አባቴ፡ እኔ፡ ጃንሆይ፡ አሁስወን፡ ወደ፡ አገሮዎ፡ መ
ልሰው፡ ስለሰደድዎ፡ እጅግ፡ አዝኜአለሁ፡ እኔ፡ አታለለው፡ ነው
የሰደድዎ፡ ለኔ፡ የነገሩኝ፡ ነገር፡ ሌላ፡ ነበረ፡፡ አሁንም፡ በኔ፡ አይዘኑ
ልጆችዎንና፡ አባ፡ አትቴዎስን፡ (P. Ferdinand) በደኅና፡ አስቀምጫ
ለሁ፡ እንዳይራቡም፡ ምግባቸውን፡ አገራቸውንም፡ እስ
ጠብቄ፡ ሰውነታቸውንም፡ እንዳይጐሳቆሉ፡ አድርጌ፡ አስቀ
ምጫለሁ፡፡ ከቀረው፡ ነገር፡ የናናምባን፡ ለሰው፡ መስጠቴ፡
ከሰው፡ ሐሜት፡ ለመዳን፡ ነው፡ በዚያው፡ ፈንታ፡ ቀለባቸውን፡
እሰጣለሁ፡ የቀረውን፡ እንዳይነኩባቸው፡ አስጠብቄአለሁ፡
አባ፡ ያዕቆብና፡ አባ፡ ጎንዛግ፡ እንዴት፡ ናችሁ፡፡ ሰኔ፡ ፭፡
በሰኔ፡ ፲፰፻፸፪፡ በደብረ፡ ብርሃን፡ ተጻፈ፡፡

May [this message] sent by King Minīlik reach Massaja.

How have you been? Thank God, I am well. And all my army is well.

My father, I am extremely sad that His Majesty has sent you back home. He sent you deceiving me. What he had told me was something else. And now do not feel sorry because of me. I have given your children and *Abba* Atinatēwos (P. Ferdinand) a place to stay. I am giving them food so that they will not starve. I have kept them with me so that their land will be protected and have seen to it that their bodies do not suffer.

Moreover, I gave Yananamba (?) to other people in order to avoid people's malicious gossip. In exchange for this I am giving them their provisions. And so that what remains might not be taken away from them, I have supplied them with guards.

How are *Abba* Ya'iqob and *Abba* Gonzague?

Written at Debre Birhan, 5th Senē 1872.

BN, Orient. Abb. 254, no. 293, Amharic copy in Antoine d'Abbadie's handwriting. Apparently he has had some problems reading the original of the letter. The place name Yananamba could be a misreading of 'Ayn Amba. A possible alternative is "that *amba*".

In the above text d'Abbadie added "P. Ferdinand" after "*Abba* Atinatēwos", misspelt "Atitēwos", but failed to explain that the foreign missionary called *Abba* Ya'iqob was Mgr. Taurin. *Abba* Gonzague, also known as Louis Gonzague di Lasserre, was sometimes known as Iyyakem.

Below the Amharic text there is a note in Italian mentioning seals and warning that the letter should not be published because it might cause inconvenience or trouble.

Document no. 12

Alula Ingida Qubī to Erik Emil Hedenström, 18 June 1880

መልእክት፡ ዘራስ፡ አሉላ፡ ይድረስ፡ ከአስተሮም።
እንዴት፡ አለህ፡ እኔ፡ እግዚአብሔር፡ ይመስገን፡
ደህና፡ ነኝ። ስፍራማ፡ እሺ። ተቀመጥ። ነገር፡ ግን፡
ሃይማኖታችን፡ የብቻ፡ ነው። ሰው፡ አሳምናለሁ፡
አስተምራለሁ፡ አትበል። ሁላችን፡ ክርስቲያን፡ ብንሆን፡
በሃይማኖት፡ ማንም፡ የለንምና። አስተምራለሁ፡ ሰው፡
እሰበስባለሁ፡ ያልህ፡ እንደሆን። ካገሬ፡ አትቀመጥ።
ቀድሞም፡ ያጣላን፡ ይህ፡ ነው። ነው፡ እንጂ።
ሌላ፡ ምን፡ አድርገኸኝ። ከስፍራው፡ እሺ፡ ተቀመጥ።
በዓይን፡ ሥጋ፡ ለመተያየት፡ ያብቃን። የሰደድህልኝ፡ ጠበንጃ፡
እግዚአብሔር፡ ይስጥልኝ። ማፍሰሻ፡ ስደድልኝ።
ተጽሕፈ፡ አመ፡ ፲ወ፪፡ ለሰኔ። ።

May the message of *Ras* Alula reach Hedenström (Asterom). How are you? I am well, thank God.

As for the place (*sifirama*), yes, stay [there]. But since our faith is different, do not say, "I will convert people. I will teach." [Even] if we are all Christians we are not in harmony about [our] faith. If you say, "I will teach I will convene people", do not stay in my country. This is what made us quarrel before; it is only this. What else did you do to me? All right. Stay at the place

May He make it possible for us to meet (lit. see each other with our bodily eyes). Thank you for the rifles you sent me. Send me a *mafiseshe*.

Written on the 12th of Senē.

EFS, E I 24, 146d, Amharic text, almost certainly a copy produced by the Swedish missionary E. E. Hedenström, who was stationed at Geleb at this time. Below the text a date, "21 June", is added *in Swedish*! That Hedenström has been turned into 'Asterom' is not too far-fetched. What is referred to by "*mafiseshe*" is hard to say, probably some simple kind of machinery for road-work, perhaps a shovel.

Hedenström, moreover, mentions an exchange of letters with Alula in correspondence with the mission headquarters in Stockholm. "21 June" beneath the text probably refers to the day on which the letter was received.

Both calligraphy and orthography indicate that the text has been copied by a non-Ethiopian.

Document no. 13

Convention between Burhān Muḥammad and Giuseppe Sapeto, 20 Sept. 1880

Glory to God.

In the year 1880, on the 20th day of the month of September according to the Christian era, 2197 (*sic*), Hijra, the 15th of the month of Shawāl. Burhān Muḥammad, the Sultan of Raḥayta, and Giuseppe Sapeto, the legal agent of the Rubattino Co. at Aseb, having met at Dumeira, have reached agreement on the following convention:

The afore-mentioned Burhān Muḥammad, by the right of succession recognized by the Adal and Danākil [as] Sultan of Raḥayta and proprietor of all the country and the littoral from 'Assal in the Gulf of Tajura, to the present Italian possessions in the Danākil region, with the exception of the French possession of Obok, has, owing to his long acquaintance with the aforementioned Giuseppe Sapeto and his friendship with him, made good use of this friendship by freely (lit. spontaneously) and for the good of his own country, come to the following decisions:

1. to request protection from His Majesty Umberto I, King of Italy, while remaining invested with the full authority of sultan, and without paying any tribute;
2. to undertake not to permit nor tolerate slave trade in either sex (lit. all sexes), in all the territories of his own sultanate, unless he makes any further agreements with the Italian government in this matter;
3. to undertake to give to the said Rubattino Co. and to all Italian subjects of His Majesty the King of Italy ample possibilities to establish themselves and to freely transit in all parts of the sultanate for reasons commercial or whatever, and this without the obligation, for them, to have to pay to the same sultan or to his dependents any charges whatsoever for toll or residence;
4. to undertake to defend by all possible means in his power the Italian possessions in the bay of Aseb, the entire littoral acquired by the Rubattino Co. [and] the Italian agents or caravans staying in or crossing the territory of the sultanate;
5. to undertake to assist efficiently the Italian colony in the intent which the same has to open all the most convenient routes for putting Aseb in direct communication with Abyssinia, whether by Awsa or by Kwalima (?), or any other localities;
6. to undertake not to sell or transfer any part of his dominions and territories without the approval of the royal Italian government;
7. (and finally,) to undertake not to make war against foreign enemies and other Adal and Danākil tribes without the prior notice of the Italian authorities in Aseb, who will in all cases be called upon to examine the internal and external difficulties in order to make peace among the quarrelling tribes in a friendly way.

In exchange for such offers, submissions, obligations and privileges, the afore-mentioned Burhān Muḥammad, sultan as above, requests:

1. the authority to make known to all indigenous and foreign inhabitants, as soon as it is considered, in accord with the agent of the Italian government, that the opportune moment has arrived;

and in what manner and by what measures it seems most suitable, that he, Burhān Muḥammad, on behalf of himself and his successors, places himself under the protection of the Italian government;

2. (and finally,) to be considered while remaining under his own authority and his own rights of sultan, not discussed in the present document, a functionary of the royal Italian government is therefore compensated by an annual fixed stipend, to be decided by the government of His Majesty the King of Italy in conformity with the position of sultan and the services which he intends to grant to Italian subjects.

On his part, Giuseppe Sapeto, agent of the Rubattino Co. at Aseb and friend of the afore-mentioned Sultan Burhān, undertakes to convey the present agreement to the government of His Majesty the King of Italy for his acceptance.

Waiting for such adherence and as a token of the sincerity of his intentions Burhān Muḥammad, in accordance with the above declarations, swears on the Qurān to immediately execute, to the extent which concerns him, everything which is stipulated in the present agreement, while Giuseppe Sapeto, the representative of the Rubattino Co., swears on the Gospel to do everything which depends on him in order that this document shall be accepted by the royal government of Italy in its entirety.

In faith of which the contracting parties place their signatures on the present convention, signing in the presence of the witnesses mentioned below.

Confirming the above	Witnessing the above
Sign. I, Sultan Burhān bin Sultan Muḥammad	Sign. Ibrāhīm Ḥasan Sign. Sa'īd Awīḍan
Sign. Giuseppe Sapeto, legal procurator of the Rubattino Co.	Sign. Pietro Villani, witness Sign. Giuseppe Nozzoli, witness

Seen for the ratification of the signatures:

Sign. G. Galaezzo Frigerio, commander
Commander of the royal frigate "Ettore Fieramosca"

ASMAI 1/1–7, fol. 134, Italian text. Printed in *Trattati*, pp. 49–51 as well as in *L'Italia in Africa*, I.2 no. 158, allegato, pp. 152–153. No Arabic text is known to exist. There are several rather different Italian versions in the Italian archives as noted by Giglio in *L'Italia in Africa*, I.2, p. 152, note 1. The above translation is based on the version in *Trattati*. The text printed by Giglio deviates slightly from this version, including a misprint of the year 1297 into 2197, which is also found in the manuscript in ASMAI. According to Giglio the passages marked in italics above were substituted by the Italian ministry for earlier less definitive versions. There are no signatures except Frigerio's whose signature verifying that the text is a true copy is, strangely enough, found on several rather different versions. It is obvious that the Italian government and its representatives felt they could revise the text of the so-called convention as they wished without regard for the Ethiopian part. Thus, it is unlikely that any one of the Italian versions conforms to an Arabic version, if such a version ever existed.

Document no. 14

Burhān Muḥammad to Giuseppe Sapeto, [20] Sept. 1880

Praise be to God alone.
To Mr. Giuseppe Sapeto,

Your letter has reached me and I have been informed of its content. As far as the allowance which the *pasha* pretends that I have long since been receiving, that is a lie. As for me, I have never accepted the Egyptians, neither an allowance nor a flag. It is they who have wanted me to do so, but as for me I have always refused. I take an oath on the Qur'ān that my words are true.

In faith [of which] etc.
Signed: Burhān Muḥammad, sultan

Ibrāhīm Ḥasan
His authorized agent is witness to the signature.

September 1880.

AP.DD, XXIII, p. 330 annex to number 104, French translation. Behind the French text an Arabic original can be recognized.

Document no. 15

Minīlik II to Antonio Cecchi, 6 Oct. 1880

Letter of His Majesty Minīlik, King of Shewa, to Mr. A. Cecchi.

How are you? I, by the grace of God, am well, and [so is] also all my army. I am very happy and pleased that the Good Lord has saved you by delivering you from the hands of the king of Gēra. I was very grieved when I heard the news about the death of poor Mr. Chiarini and that of your captivity. I have done much for your release by writing to the son of *Abba* Jifar of Jimma telling him to ransom you, whatever the cost, and if necessary to cede half of his kingdom, and in case this is refused he should notify me; and that it will then be up to me to free Captain Cecchi, by making an expedition to Gēra.

Today I am aware that you are released but robbed of all your belongings. If these belongings are lost for the moment do not worry. I undertake to return them to you to the last needle. All my preoccupations until now have been to achieve your release. At present I have no other wish than to see you, and I send you Mr. Count Antonelli and Mr. Ilg in order that they may bring you to me. I hope that you all return in good health. The guides who accompany these gentlemen are charged with bringing you back.

By the means of these gentlemen I am sending you a mule.

ASSGI, busta 21, fasc. 6, fols 14–15, French and Italian translations from what was most probably an Amharic original. The translation has been made from the French. The Italian is published in BSGI, XVI, XVII (1881), p. 168, and the French in Antonio Cecchi, *Da Zeila alle Frontiere del Caffa*, Rome, 1885, vol. II, p. 570. The date assigned to the document appears only on the Italian version, albeit in a different handwriting from the letter itself. For the circumstances, see doc. 7 with note. The closing sentence about the mule appears only in the French translation.

Document no. 16

Minīlik II to Onorato Caetani, 16 Oct. (?) 1880

We, Minīlik II, by the grace of God King of Shewa, to His Excellency Mr. President of the Italian Geographical Society, Rome.

How are you? By the grace of the Almighty we are well and so are all our armies.

We have duly received your letters and the objects which you have addressed to us through Mr. S. Martini. Once more, we thank you very much for it. This we have already done by the hand of Count Antinori.

We take the opportunity of this letter to communicate our joy, which is also yours, relative to the rescue of Captain Cecchi, who is now in Gudru, the land of *Ras* Adal, a land the possession of which he owes to our generosity. We have sent Mr. Ilg, our engineer, and Mr. Count Antonelli to meet Captain Cecchi with the necessary personnel and mules. We hope that he will soon be with us and we shall neglect nothing to send him to the coast in a proper manner, if such is his will.

As for the objects of which Captain Cecchi has been robbed by the king of Gēra, we undertake to have them restored to the last needle (*Fr.* aiguille, *It.* spillo).

Written at Debre Birhan, 16th October 1873 (Abyssinian calendar).

ASSGI, busta 20, fasc. 5, fol. 1, French version; fols 2–3, Italian version. The opening line with its use of *pluralis majestatis* and the reference to the grace of God indicates that the letter was written in French or Italian. Printed in *BSGI*, XVII (1881), p. 168. It is impossible to know for sure if "Abyssinian calendar" refers only to the year or also to the date of the month. If the latter is the case the date should be 16 Ṭiqimt, i.e. 25 October. For the circumstances see also docs 7 and 15.

Alfred Ilg was a Swiss engineer who had arrived and settled in Shewa in 1879. He rapidly learned Amharic and played a crucial role in the development of Ethiopian manufacture, industry and building, including the city of Addis Abeba, and was highly trusted and decorated by Minīlik. Pietro Antonelli was a young Italian adventurer (born 1853) who had come to Ethiopia in late 1879 and settled at the Italian exploration centre at Liṭ Marefīya. He soon became one of the most important suppliers of weapons to Minīlik and the chief agent in the attempt to set up an Italian protectorate over Ethiopia finalized in the treaty of Wiçhalē in 1889. See *Diplomatic History*, pp. 25–34, and *Survival*, pp. 384–395.

Document no. 17

Minīlik II to Jules Grévy, 1 Nov. 1880

Sent by King Minīlik, who by the power of God has become king of Shewa, to Mr. Jules Grévy, president of the French republic.

How are you? We, by the grace of the Almighty, are very well as are also all our armies. After having offered our best wishes for good health and prosperity to our brother, we write as follows:

We have written several times to your government without ever receiving an answer. We assumed that the afflictions which France suffered for a time were the only reasons that prevented the French government from concerning itself with us and our kingdom. Today, however, when all news that reaches us is that France is more prosperous than ever, we thank God, and again address this great nation, the first to have brought to us the ideas of progress and civilization. Why do you not respond to our supplications? Why should it not be possible for them to come to us? The effects of the European civilization have made themselves felt in our kingdom.

The slave trade has disappeared. Day by day we are destroying the plague of robbers. Once they have been subdued by us, they do what the fear of God and the fear of our created nature orders us to observe.

Egypt, guided by a spirit envious and hostile to the Ethiopian people, a people essentially Christian, raises all sorts of obstacles to our relations with civilized Europe. The door of Ethiopia is in its hands, and everything that might be favourable to progress, to the civilization of our people, faces insurmountable obstacles.

The civilized and disinterested nations seem to ignore that Ethiopia exists, and that it is the desire of the Ethiopian people to adjust to the ideas of its European brothers. If we are to believe the disquieting rumours that have reached us, we are menaced by some nations that harbour a spirit of conquest against our country.

We would therefore like to see our European brothers respond favourably to our appeal. By occupying all ports of the Red Sea, Egypt allows us to have only what pleases it. France, a disinterested nation protective of the oppressed, could if it chose put an end to this abuse of power.

Why should not Obok, a French point, be the natural port of Shewa? This is what we ask our brother, beseeching him to study this question carefully.

All the powers seem to wish to concern themselves with us. Only France remains silent and yet it is to her we appeal in order that she may accord us paternal protection and thus make those powers reconsider who would like to profit from our inexperience and weakness. If the port of Obok were regarded as the natural port of Shewa, it would in our opinion serve to put an end to the rigorous demands of Egypt. French commerce would perhaps gain from it and our kingdom would find in it incontestable advantages for which we would be grateful to your government.

If the port of Obok becomes, as we hope, the centre of friendly and commercial relations between Shewa and Europe, we ask of your government the favour of having us represented there by authorizing the installation there of one of our sons, Muḥammad Abū Bakr, son of the *pasha* of Zeyla. He is our son, completely devoted to our interests, Abyssinian and not Egyptian. He alone has up to this day kept us, as far as is possible, in a relationship with Europe.

It was our intention to send an embassy to Europe, especially to France. However, the prominent men of the kingdom, the only persons we could turn to for such a mission, refuse to engage on a journey they regard as more perilous than it actually is. We have therefore resolved to rely for the time being entirely on M. Brémond, a French citizen, who has stayed with us for two years and whom we have come to know and appreciate just as Muḥammad Abū Bakr, our son in whom we have the greatest confidence.

Both of them will tell you how much we love the Europeans [and] about the reception they get here and the sympathy that we feel for them. Perhaps the peoples of Europe say that we have expelled the teachers of the Catholic mission. There is nothing in this; in this respect we do not have to justify ourselves, and if necessary we would undoubtedly be forced to do away with certain ideas and break with a too conciliatory policy.

What we, however, cannot write to our brother, our envoys can tell him, and what they say will be what we think, will be the truth. Our ignorance lets wealth remain buried in our kingdom. We have placed all the important matters in the hands of M. Brémond. We hope to conclude a convention with the agreeable French.

O my brother, may God inspire you and make you do something in favour of our people, whom we would like to see enlightened and civilized by that great light that the government you represent can spread with an impartiality of which this great nation alone is capable.

The Geographical Society of Rome had sent out, under the patronage of the king of Italy, our friend and brother, an expedition with the mission to cross Central Africa as far as Zanzibar.

We have, as far as our means allow, accorded efficient protection to it, and no reproach can be made about us.

If the success has not been complete, we have warned His Majesty the King of Italy about the difficulties that might occur beyond the borders of our territory, and we regret that our previsions have come true. We have managed by threats to liberate Captain Cecchi, who was held prisoner at Gēra near Kefa. Captain Cecchi is now in good health in our kingdom and we even hope that he will be able to return to his country by caravan.

We take advantage of the departure of the caravan of Mr. Brémond and Muḥammad Abū Bakr to bring to our brother in France in testimony of our high regard and great friendship:

1. A war coat;
2. A dignitary bracelet;
3. A shield and two lances;
4. A complete harness for a horse;
5. A complete harness for a mule;
6. Two drinking horns;
7. A sabre that has the merit of having belonged to *Meridazmach* Abbiyē, the founder of Shewa;
8. A zebra and two ostriches which our brother, if he so wishes, will offer in his name to the big garden of the government in Paris;
9. Our diploma and cross of the grand cordon of our order Honour and Friendship.

May God in His grace grant you long life (lit. age) and health.

Seal: Minīlik, King of Shewa. The Lion of the tribe of Judah has prevailed.

AEMD, Afrique 62, Abyssinie 3, fols 479–480, Amharic original; 482–484, French translation which is also sealed. The French translation is dated at the bottom: "Written in our royal city of Debre Birhan the first of the month of November 1880." Chris P. Rosenfeld has recorded a second letter written on the same date to the Chamber of Deputies; see *A Chronology of Menilek II of Ethiopia*, East Lansing 1976, p. 90. However, this letter has not been found.

Louis Brémond was a French arms dealer who had gained Minīlik's confidence and was sent to France with gifts and money to buy rifles. Muḥammad Abū Bakr was the son of the ruler of Zeyla, Abū Bakr Ibrāhīm.

Document no. 18

Minīlik II to Albert Delagenière, 1 Nov. 1880

Minīlik II, by the grace of God King of Shewa, to our good friend Mr. Delagenière, consul of France at Aden. How are you? We, by the grace of God, are well and so are all our armies.

We have received all your letters, and we thank you very much for all the information which you give us. We have also taken into consideration your recommendations with regard to your compatriot, Mr. A. Brémond, whom we have kept close to us for about two years during which time we have been able to convince ourselves that we could place full confidence in him.

We do so by acknowledging him as our general agent and charging him to give his attention to the conflict which exists between us and the firm of Turrer and Escher of Aden, a conflict, you will see, for which we have gathered the Europeans and on which they had not dared to pass judgement because of the insufficiency of the documents. In this business we have taken the liberty to appoint you, you and the consul of Italy, arbitrators, and we hope that you accept this task as a friend.

We would very much have wished that Mr. Turrer would have presented himself to us with acceptable accounts, but in spite of our ignorance of European matters simple common sense informs us that it was assumed that the largesse of a king could be counted on. We would have been able to be equal to such assumptions if some services had been rendered us, but on the contrary we have received from this unhappy affair nothing but disagreements, deceptions and a very distressing impression. You may judge about this yourself. We have given to Mr. Brémond our full authority to carry out some business in France. Our best wishes follow him, that he may achieve that your government will reckon us among the number of its friends and protégés.

Our greatest desire would be to see the port of Obok considered as the natural port of Shewa. This would then put an end to the Egyptian obstacles which cause Abyssinia to find itself in an iron ring, which the civilization which we call ours cannot break. The most disturbing rumours reach all the way to us. Egypt and perhaps other powers seem to have their eyes set on our kingdom in a spirit of conquest. We therefore seek the friendship of the disinterested powers and we would like to see France, which we love, accord us its high protection. We have not forgotten that the first ideas of civilization were brought to us by a French subject, and all the old people of our kingdom still mention the name of Rochet with veneration. This is well-nigh exactly the mission which we have confided to Mr. Brémond and we beg you to bring to it from your side all your good will with regard to us. This would give you [but] even greater right to our friendship, which as you know is already yours.

We are sending to the president of the French republic some small gifts, insignificant you may say, but which nevertheless give an idea of the industry of our country, even if it is still in its infancy. In line with this we ask you to grant Mr. Brémond the bracelet [implying] high rank, which has been deposited at your consulate since the unhappy Arnoux affair. If Mr. Brémond manages to make some installations at Obok in favour of our kingdom, we have designated Muḥammad Abū Bakr, the son of the *pasha* of Zeyla, to represent us there. Muḥammad is our son and we know him to be totally devoted to our interests. He is Abyssinian and not Egyptian. His influence along this still difficult route is uncontestable and we do not see among our subjects anyone we can entrust the [task to], the notables of our kingdom imagining such a journey too perilous, and this is the only reason that has prevented us from sending an embassy to Europe. It is therefore in Mr. Brémond and Muḥammad that we place confidence in all matters. May God grant you health and prosperity.

Made in our royal city of Debre Birhan on the 1st of the month of November 1880.

The seal of the king.

AEMD, Afrique 62, fols 510–512; also AED, Protocole C 41, French translation of a reportedly sealed Amharic original of which no trace has been found. C.-X. Rochet d'Héricourt was a French trader and explorer who played an important role in Ethiopian foreign relations in the 1840s; see *Survival*, pp. 147–164. Pierre Arnoux was a French artisan and adventurer who had won Minīlik's confidence and been entrusted in 1876 with a significant diplomatic and commercial mission to Egypt and France. The mission was, however, a failure, and Arnoux was killed in Afar in 1882. See *Survival*, pp. 372–375, and *Diplomatic History*, pp. 19–31.

Document no. 19

Ratification by ‘Abdallah Shahīm of 15 May 1880 convention, 5 Nov. 1880

Aseb 5th November 1880
Glory be to God.

I, ‘Abd Allāh Shaḥīm, sultan, declare in all conscience that I have given my consent to and accepted the contract stipulated in my name and in that of Ḥasan, Ibrāhīm and Rāj Aḥmad with Mr. Giuseppe Sapeto, procurator of the Rubattino Co., the 15th of the month of May of the year 1880, according to the European era, and the 6th of Jumād al-Ākhir of the year 1297 according to the Arabic era, for the sale in my name and in theirs to Mr. Giuseppe Sapeto of the island of Sennabor and the mainland from (*Ras*) Lumah to *Ras* Faranah.

Likewise, I approve the cession of the territories of Bar Assoli and Behtah made by the above-mentioned persons in my name and in theirs by another contract in favour of Mr. Giuseppe Sapeto. I also confirm that I have received from Mr. Giuseppe Sapeto one hundred thalers of the one thousand that remain of the total payment of the price for the purchased localities, which he has committed himself to paying within the terms established in the above-mentioned contract.

Aseb, on the 5th of the month of November of the year 1880 according to the Christian era and the 3rd of the month of Dhū al-Ḥijja of the year 1298 according to the Arabic calendar.

I, ‘Abd Allāh Shaḥīm, confirm as above.
Witnesses: Sa’īd ‘Awīḍān – Francesco Sa’īd Maryam.

Trattati, p. 52, no. 16, Italian text. There is no trace of any Arabic version and probably there has never been one. The document refers back to the convention with the Rubattino Co. of 15 May (doc. 9), here called a contract, as well as the declaration by the Afar chiefs of the same date (doc. 8). *Ras* Darmah in the convention has, however, been exchanged for *Ras* Faranah in this document. The name Francesco Sa’īd Maryam strikes us as rather strange. We have, however, not been able to identify the person.

Document no. 20

Minīlik II to Benedetto Cairoli, 9 Nov. 1880

የተላከ፡ ከንጉሥ፡ ምኒልክ፡ ይድረስ፡ ከኢጣሊያ፡ አ
ገር፡ ከታላቁ፡ ምኒስቴር፡ የባዕድ፡ አገር፡ ነገር፡ ሁሉ፡ የሚ
ያደርግ፡ እንደምን፡ ነህ፡ እኔ፡ እግዚአብሔር፡ ይመስ
ገን፡ ደኅና፡ ነኝ፡ ሠራዊቴም፡ ሁሉ፡ ደኅና፡ ነው።
ባለፈው፡ ዓመት፡ በግንቦት፡ በደብረ፡ ብርሃን፡ ከተማዬ፡
ተቀምጬ፡ ማርኪዝ፡ አንቲኖሬ፡ የጆግራፊያ፡ ማኅበ
ር፡ ጋራ፡ ተስማምታችሁ፡ የጻፋችሁትን፡ ደብዳቤ፡ አሳይቶ
ኝ፡ ነበር። አዋሽን፡ እንመርምረው፡ ከአሰብ፡ ሸዋ፡ ድረ
ስ፡ መንገድ፡ እንዲደርስ፡ ለደብዳቤ፡ ሁሉ፡ መመላለሻ፡ የ
ሚሆን፡ በአውሳ፡ ማኽል፡ የሚል፡ ደብዳቤ፡ አሳይቶኝ፡ ነበር።
አሁን፡ ደግሞ፡ ከዘመቻ፡ ስመለስ፡ ይህን፡ በር፡ ጨርሳች
ሁ፡ መያዛችሁን፡ የኢጣሊያ፡ መንግሥት፡ መያዙንና፡ ቤ
ትም፡ መሥራታችሁን፡ በዚህ፡ በር፡ ካጠገቡ፡ ከአለው፡ ሡ
ልጣን፡ ጋራ፡ የንግድ፡ ውል፡ መዋዋላችሁን፡ ነገረኝ።
እኔም፡ ከዚያ፡ የራቁ፡ ሌሎች፡ አሉኝ። የኔም፡ ሥራ፡ ከና
ንተ፡ ሥራ፡ ቢጋጠም፡ ደኅና፡ እወድ፡ ነበር። ይህን፡ መንገድ፡
ለማቅናት፡ የእነዚህን፡ ሁለት፡ አገሮች፡ ንግድና፡ የፍቅር፡ መ
ገናኘትም፡ ይቀና፡ ነበር፡ በሕዳር፡ ፩፡ ቀን፡ በ፲፰፻፸፫ በ
ደብረ፡ ብርሃን፡ ከተማ፡ ተጻፈ።

Seal: Minīlik, King of Shewa. The Lion of the tribe of Judah has prevailed.

May [this message] sent by King Minīlik reach the land of Italy, the great Italian minister of foreign affairs who handles all matters with foreign countries.

How are you? I am well, thank God, and all my army is well.

In Ginbot last year when I was staying in my city Debre Birhan, Marquis Antinori showed me the letter that you had written after agreeing with the Society of Geography. He showed me a letter which said: "Let us explore Awash so that a route which reaches from Aseb to Shewa can be built, suitable for the communication of letters by way of Awsa."

Now, when I returned from the war, he told me that you have occupied this port definitively, that the government of Italy has done so, and that you have even built houses. He has also told me that you have concluded a treaty of commerce with the sultan who lives near this port. I too have subjects who are [not] far from there. I too would have liked my endeavours to be joined to yours in improving this route. Thus the commerce, love and communication of these two countries would have been enhanced.

Written at the town of Debre Birhan on the 1st day of Hidar 1873.

ASMAI 36/1–4, doc. 155, Amharic original and French translation. The French "1er 9bre 1873 (cal. Abyss.)" is obviously a direct translation of the Amharic, not a conversion of the date. Benedetto Cairoli was both Italian prime minister and minister of foreign affairs 1879–1881. Orazio Antinori was an Italian botanist who travelled in Ethiopia in the early 1870s and returned in 1877, representing the Italian Geographical Society. He was instrumental in founding the scientific station at Liṭ Marefīya close to Ankober and died there in 1882.

Document no. 21

Tekle Gīyorgīs to Kīrillus V, 15 Nov. [1880?]

May [the message] sent by *Nibure'id* Tekle Gīyorgīs reach the honoured and exalted, the teacher of the world, the sun of righteousness, the light of those who are surrounded by darkness, the forgiver of sins, the apostle, *Abune* Kīrillus, *līqe pappasat* of Alexandria and Ethiopia.

May the Saviour of the world enable me to see you. I raise my hands saying, "May He give [you] health. Bless me. Absolve me, absolve me, absolve me from the sins I committed knowingly [and] unknowingly."

I am sending a monk who is on his way to Jerusalem, together with (lit. making him join) *Dejjazmach* Meshesha. So see him off, for my sake, as you see best, when he goes and when he returns, as he is my friend.

Written on the 7th of Hidar.

Seal: The seal of *Nibure id* Tekle Gīyorgīs.

Ghali Collection, no. 41, Amharic/Gi'iz original. The author is otherwise unknown, but in *Yohannis IV*, p. 108, he is identified with *Aleqa* Fenta referred to in docs 40 and 41. A note added in Arabic at the top of this letter defines it as "the fourth". Most probably Meshesha here stands for *Lij* Meshesha Werqē, a distinguished officer at Yohannis' court, who owing to his knowledge of European languages served in a number of diplomatic missions.

Document no. 22

Alula Ingida Qubī to Gerhard Rohlfs, 23 Nov. 1880

መልእክት፡ ዘራስ፡ አሉላ፡ ይድረስ፡ ከሮፍ
ልስ፡ የኒምሳ፡ ነገሥታት፡ መልክተኛ፡ እንዴት፡
አለህ፡ እኔ፡ እግዚአብሔር፡ ይመስገን፡ ደኅና
ነኝ፡ ከጃንሆይም፡ እኸ፡ ቶሎ፡ ብየ፡ አገሥግሼ፡ እ
ሊድልኝ ለሁ፡ ወረቀት፡ እንቶግም፡ ቶሎ፡ ብለህ፡
ና። ጃንሆይ፡ ከቀርብ፡ ሲሉ፡ እን፩ ድሲ ዪህ፡
በክብር፡ ቃልም፡ የሰደድልሕልኝ፡ ደብዳ
ቤ፡ ደረሰኝ። በ፲፭ ወበ፲፰፻፡ ፸ ወ፫ ዓመተ፡ ም
ሕረት፡ በፀአዘጋ፡ ከተማ፡ ተጽሕፈ አመ፡ ፲ወ፭ ለ
ኅዳር።

May the message of *Ras* Alula reach Rohlfs, the envoy of the kings of Austria. How are you? I am well, thank God.

Yes, I shall at once send an express messenger with a letter to His Majesty on your behalf, and you will hurry [to tell] that I am informing you, as soon as His Majesty orders that you be given an audience. The politely worded letter, which you sent me, has reached me.

Written in the camp of Ṣe azzega on 15th Hidar in the year of grace 1873.

Seal: The seal of *Ras* Alula.

HHS, RA 14.80 (3), Amharic original; *Meine Mission*, pp. 89–90, German translation. Gerhard Rohlfs was one of the great explorers of Africa and had taken part in Napier's expedition to Meqdela in 1867–1868 on behalf of the Prussian government. He was sent by Emperor Wilhelm I to Yohannis in late 1880 in reply to Yohannis' letter of 20 November 1879 (*Acta* III, doc. 231) offering assistance in finding a solution to the conflict with Egypt.

Document no. 23

Alula Ingida Qubī to Gerhard Rohlfs [Nov. 1880]

መልእክት፡ዘራስ፡አሉላ፡ይድረስ፡ለክቡር፡
ገርሃልት፡ሮልፍስ፡ወዩሴ፡ክጵሩስያ፡ንጉ
ሥ፡እንደት፡ሰነበትህ፡እኔ፡እግዚአብሔር፡
ይመስገን፡ደኅና፡ነኝ።ስትመጣ፡በዓይለት፡
አድርገህ፡እንድትመጣ፡በጊንዳ፡እስላሞች፡
ወንበዴዎች፡አሉ፡የሚቀሙ።በጊንዳ፡አት
ምጣ።ዓይለት፡ስትደርስ፡ላክብኝ።ከጥጉ፡ሰ
ው፡እሰድልሀለሁ፡የሚቀበሉ።

May the message of *Ras* Alula reach the honoured Gerhard Rohlfs, servant of the king of Prussia.

How have you been? I am well, thank God. When you come, arrange so that you come to Aylet. At Jenda (Ginda) there are Muslim robbers who plunder. Do not come to Jenda. When you arrive at Aylet write to me. I will at once send you people who will escort you.

Seal: The seal of *Ras* Alula.

HHS, RA 14.83 (7), Amharic original; *Meine Mission*, pp. 91–92, German translation. Rohlfs writes (p. 91) that he received a "rechtzeitig schnell" reply to the letter of 27 November – in all probability the above letter. The letter itself has no date, but on top of the document "1 Dez. 1880" is added, probably the date when the letter was received.

Document no. 24

Lewṭē Zewde to Gerhard Rohlfs [Nov. 1880]

የተላከ፡ከበጅሮንድ፡ለውጤ፡ይድረስ፡ከመካሪ፡ሊቅ፡ዶክ
ተር፡ጌርሀርድ፡ሮልፍ፡እንዴት፡ሰነበቱ፡እኔ፡እግዚአብሔር፡
ይመስገን፡ደኅና፡ነኝ፡ልጅዎ፡ነኝና፡አይርሱኝ፨ ፨ ፨

May [this letter] sent by *Bejirond* Lewṭē, reach the scholarly advisor (*mekarī līq*) Dr. Gerhard Rohlfs. How are you? I am well, thank God. Since I am your son, do not forget me.

Seal: The seal of *Bejirond* Lewṭē.

HHS, RA 14.78, Amharic original. Lewṭē Zewde was an important official in the service of Yohannes, responsible for the finances of the court. See *EAE* 3, pp. 525–526. According to doc. 43, he was sent to Jerusalem with provisions in 1881 and it was most probably in this connection that he wrote to the patriarch in January 1882 (doc. 65). We have not been able to establish what *anbesa bē* in the legend of the seal refers to.

Document no. 25

Alula Ingida Qubī to Achille Raffray, 10 Dec. 1880

May the letter of *Ras* Alula reach the consul of France, Raffray.

How are you? As for me, I am well, thank God. The letter in which you have sent me a good message (lit. bonne parole) has reached me. Let the person whom you have recommended so well to me come.

Written in the town of Ṣe'azzega on 2 December 1873 (10 Dec. 1880).

Signed: The seal of *Ras* Alula.

AECPC, Massaouah 4, fol. 194, French translation. Achille Raffray was a French naturalist and traveller who travelled in Ethiopia in the 1870s and was French vice-consul at Massawa 1880–1881. The person referred to was a French officer, Captain Lombard, who planned scientific research in Ethiopia.

Document no. 26

Gebre Igzī' to Kīrillus V, 15 Dec. [1880?]

May [this letter] reach my father and my master, the honoured and exalted *Abune* Kīrillus, *līqe pappasat* of Alexandria and Ethiopia, who sits on the chair of [St.] Mark the Evangelist, the servant and apostle of Christ.

I bow down at your feet and prostrate myself in the hall of your house. I have put my confidence in your holy prayer and your orthodox faith. Amen. I am well, by the mercy of God, and through your prayer, praise to the glory of the God of [St.] Mark.

Grieve for Ethiopia for she is dead and buried because she does not have a teacher in soul and in body, except for you. My thoughts (lit. eyes of my heart) are with you. The love of Christ and the love of you have overwhelmed me.

I have been kept busy by the work on the church commanded by *Aṭē* Yohannis, but when I have finished [the work] on the church I shall need the honoured letter from you.

Since the clothes you gave me are worn out, I am asking for clothes for myself, just as a son asks his father for his clothes and his food.

Written on 7th Ṭahsas.

Seal illegible.

So says your son *Abba* Gebre Igzī'.

Ghali Collection, no. 49. Amharic original. We have not been able to identify the author. Most probably he was a monk in the service of Yohannis. If it is the same person as mentioned in doc. 155 and the addressee of doc. 182, he served as an envoy to the patriarch in Cairo and to the community in Jerusalem. The dating does not include the year, and the contents do not reveal much. We have tentatively put in 1880, but it could well belong to 188[illegible] or even later.

Document no. 27

Yohannis IV to Minīlik II, 16 Dec. 1880

መልእክት ፡ ዘሥዩመ ፡ እግዚአብሔር ፡ ዮሐንስ ፡ ንጉሠ ፡ ጽዮን ፡ ንጉሠ ፡ ነገሥት ፡ ዘኢትዮጵያ ፤ ይድረስ ፡ ከንጉሥ ፡ ምኒልክ ፡ በአማን ፡ እስራኤላዊ ፡ ዘአልቦ ፡ ጽልሑት ። ሰላም ፡ ለከ ፡ ወሰላመ ፡ እግዚአብሔር ፡ የሃሉ ፡ ምስሌከ ። እኔ ፡ በእግዚአብሔር ፡ ቸርነት ፡ በእምነ ፡ ጽዮን ፡ አማላጅነት ፡ አምላከ ፡ ቅዱሳን ፡ ይክበር ፡ ይመስገን ፡ ደህና ፡ ነኝ ። ምሕረቱ ፡ ለዘለዓለም ፡ ነውና ።

ራስ ፡ አዳልን ፡ የጥምቀት ፡ ዕለት ፡ የምሾመው ፡ የማነግሠው ፡ ነኝ ። ሲሆን ፡ ቢሰላ ፡ አብረን ፡ ሁነን ፡ መሾም ፡ ይገባን ፡ ነበር ። ቀኑ ፡ የሚያጥር ፡ የማያዳርስ ፡ እንደ ፡ ሆነ ፡ አንድ ፡ ደህና ፡ ሰው ፡ ሁነታውን ፡ ሁሉ ፡ የሚያይ ፡ ገስግሶ ፡ ለጥምቀት ፡ እንዲገባ ፡ ይሁን ። እኔ ፡ ይህን ፡ ማለቴ ፡ ንጉሠ ፡ ነገሥት ፡ ተብዬ ፡ እኮራለሁ ፡ ብዬ ፡ አይደለም ። አንድ ፡ ጊዜ ፡ ስሙም ፡ ወጥቶልኛል ። የእግዚአብሔር ፡ ሃይማኖቱ ፡ እንዲጸና ፡ እንዲሠፋ ፡ አሕዛቦች ፡ እንዲጠፉ ፡ ብዬ ፡ ነው ። ለኢትዮጵያ ፡ ምቀኛዋ ፡ ብዙ ፡ ነውና ፡ ጸላቶቻችን ፡ እንዲደክሙና ፡ እንዲያፍሩ ፡ ብዬ ፡ ነው ።

ደግሞ ፡ ይህነን ፡ ጉዳይ ፡ ከደረግን ፡ በኋላ ፡ ወደ ፡ አምናችን ፡ የምመጣ ፡ ነኝና ፡ መምጣቱ ፡ የሚቸግር ፡ እንደ ፡ ሆን ፡ ከዚያው ፡ እንድንገናኝ ፡ ይሁን ።

የኢጣልያ ፡ ንጉሥ ፡ አምና ፡ በረከት ፡ ሰዶልኝ ፡ ነበር ። ዕቃውን ፡ አኑሮ ፡ ሰዎቹን ፡ መልሶ ፡ ወሰዳቸው ። ፍቅር ፡ ጀምሮ ፡ ሰዎቹን ፡ መልሶ ፡ መውሰዱ ፡ ብልሃቱ ፡ ጠፍቶኛል ። የዚህ ፡ ነገሩ ፡ ወደርሱ ፡ ይገኛል ፡ ይሆንን ።

ተጻሕፈ ፡ በአምባጫራ ፡ ከተማ ። አመ ፡ ሰሙኑ ፡ ለታኅሣሥ ፤ በ፲ወ፰፻፸፫ ፡ ወ፫ ፡ ዓ ፡ ም ።

May the message from the Elect of God Yohannis, King of Zion, King of Kings of Ethiopia, reach King Minīlik, an Israelite indeed, in whom is no guile. Peace be to you, and the peace of God be with you.

By the mercy of God and the intercession of Our Mother Zion, I am well. May the Lord of the saints be praised, for His mercy is forever.

I am going to appoint and crown *Ras* Adal king on the day of Ṭimqet. It would have been appropriate for us to appoint him together. If, however, there is not sufficient time, see to it that a competent man be sent without delay [in time] before Ṭimqet to come here and observe everything.

The reason I say this is not because I am a proud king who can say anything he wishes to say. No, I am not like that. I am already elected King of Kings; I do not need to do that. The reason why I do this is to make firm the religion of God and expand it, [and] at the same time eliminate the pagan, since those who are jealous of Ethiopia are so many. That is why I do this. By doing this we weaken and disgrace our enemy. When we have dealt with this matter I will return to last year's business.

If you have difficulties coming here, I will come to where we met last year; let us meet there. Last year the Italian king sent me a gift. He ordered the people who came with the gift to return to him when they had delivered it. I do not understand why he ordered them to return after entering into a friendly relationship, and I am confused about this. Is it possible to find an explanation of the enigma from him?

Written at the town of Amba, Chara on the 8th of Tahsas in the year of grace 1873.

Tarīke Negest, p. 71, printed Amharic text. *Blattēngēta* Hiruy's *Tarīke Negest* was at the stage of being printed in 1936 when the Italians entered Addis Abeba and prevented its publication. See Asfa-Wossen Asserate, *Die Geschichte von Šawā (Äthiopien) 1700–1865*, Wiesbaden, 1980, pp. 18–21. It has not been possible to trace the original or a copy of the letter in any collection in Ethiopia. Very few copies of the text were saved. In one, which was preserved by *Qēs* Badima Yalew, a few pages from the manuscript were added in handwriting. The biblical quotation "an Israelite indeed, in whom is no guile" (John, 1, 47) is also found in Yohannis' letters to Minīlik and to Tekle Haymanot. See docs 64, 66, 67 and 86.

Document no. 28

Gebru *Abba* Çhequn to Achille Raffray, 16 Jan. [1881]

May the letter from *Blatta* Gebru reach my friend Raffray, the consul of France.

How are you? As for me, by the grace of God, I am well. You will rejoice with me in learning that I have been appointed governor of Mereb Melash. You ask me to tell you the reason for Captain Lombard's return. He has come back because of his dragoman and because he did not feel well in the country. He did not want to stay with us, but has wanted to go to another place. The *ras* has not hurt him; he is the one who has become unfriendly.

As a token of our friendship, send me a watch and a gold-embroidered dress.

Written on 16th January.

AECPC, Massaouah 4, fol. 199, French translation. The preserved document states that it is a copy of a translation annexed to a letter from Massawa 29 Jan. 1881. No original has been found. Achille Raffray was the French vice consul at Massawa 1880–1881. Gebru *Abba* Çhequn of Tembēn had been appointed *blatta* by *Ras* Alula in 1877 and served as his lieutenant and deputy until he was killed at the battle of Kufit in Sept. 1885. See Haggai Erlich, *Ras Alula and the Scramble for Africa*, Lawrenceville, 1996, pp. 16, 33, 68–69.

Document no. 29

Yūsif al-Anṭūnī to Kīrillus V, 22 Jan. 1881

الي قدس الاب الاكرم والانا المفخم متى رقى منبر رياسة الكهنوت ذات الاصل الزاكي وتخلق لمرقسيه
المصطفى في الكرسي الاسكندري واذ نبوا الشده الابويه لبس من الوقار والبها الحله الكهنوتيه القابض
بيمينه عصا السياسه والباسط بشماله علا الرياسه اعني رييس الروسا وبعل الاغنا والناطقه
والهادي خرافه الي مناهج الحق بتعاليمه الصادقه انبا كيرلس البطريرك الكرسي المرقسي المعظم
ادام الله تعالي قدسه بالبقا المستطاب واعاد علينا من بركات دعاه المستجاب علي مدي الازمان والاحقاب
غب لثم مواطي الاقدام الطاهره والتماس درر ادعيتكم الفاخره مع رفع الدعا المستمد بطول بقا ايام رياستكم
الزاهره وخلود الانعام علي قداستكم الباهره ثم السوال عن شريف خاطركم الكريم وافتقاد مزاجكم الفاخر
السليم فنترجا من العزه الالاهيه ان يكون وجود غبطتكم باحسن صحه ورفاهيه فالمعروض لدي
سيادتكم المنيفه ومسامعكم الشريفه هو ان ملك الملوك يوحنس ارسل ابوه الروحاني الي الحبري
ابونا مرجس وقال لي اكتب لحضرة ابونا البطريرك بالوصيه علي المذكور وقول له وداعة
الله عليكم عطيتكم في الارض اقبلوا منكم في السما هنا ونرجو عدم ابراحنا من فيوضات غبطتكم
وادعياتكم في خطة دايرة احاطتكم وانتمالنا بالسير انتظار قداستكم وبكل احترام وتمام نكرر لثم
مواطي اقدامكم الاطهار ونرجوكم يا سيدي الحل والبركه وبالخضوع والاحنا نلتمس فاخر ادعيتكم
المستجابه للدوام ثانيا وثالثا ولد سيادتكم

تلميذكم القسيس يوسف
الانطوني تلميذ المطران
سلامة
١٥ شهر طوبا

وعبدكم الحاج منصور يقدم
مطانوات اقدامكم ودمتم

To His Holiness, the most noble father and most honoured *anbā* who has ascended the pulpit of the presidency of the priesthood, the incumbent of the pure foundation, appointed as the successor of St. Mark, elected for the chair of Alexandria. Since he holds the See of the Fathers, he is vested with the dignity and splendour of the priestly vestments. He holds in his left [hand] the sceptre of government and stretches out his right over the presidency. I mean the supreme head, the guardian of the rational herd, by his righteous teaching guide of the lamb on the road of truth, *Anbā* Kīrillus, Patriarch of the Chair of St. Mark the venerated May God Almighty perpetuate his sainthood in eternal bliss and return upon us the blessings of his indispensable intercession in the course of time and days.

After repeated kissing of the soles of the pure feet, the petition is that your lofty supplications together with the elevation of everlasting prayer may flow copiously throughout the remaining days of your brilliant leadership and [likewise] the perpetuity of favours upon Your Dazzling Holiness.

Then, as for the question of the nobleness of your honoured mind and the review of your excellent perfect condition, we expect from the divine might that Your Beatitude might be found to be in the best health and comfort.

What is well known to Your Excellency and to your noble ears is that the King of Kings Yohannis sent his spiritual father to me together with Father Girgis and said to me: "Write to His Honour, our Father the Patriarch for instruction about the above mentioned. Say to him: 'The comfort of God be with you! Your gift on earth will be accepted from you in heaven.'" This is what we ask for, that we may not be deprived of the abundance of Your Beatitude.

Our seclusion is within the realm of Your protection and our inclusion is in the course of the jurisdiction of Your Holiness. With all reverence and dignity we repeatedly kiss the imprints of your pure being. We ask you, our Master for absolution and blessing and in humility and respect we request the most splendid of your prayers for ever granted twice and thrice.

The son of Your Lord, the priest Yūsif al Anṭūnī, the disciple of Salāma.

15 in the month of Ṭūbā, the year 1298.

And your servant *al-Ḥajj* Manṣūr lies prostrate under your feet. May you live [for ever].

Ghali Collection, no. 147, Arabic text. Yūsif al-Anṭūnī is not known from any other letter, but was probably a Coptic monk from the monastery of St. Antony who had worked with *Abune* Selama and remained in Ethiopia after Selama's death at Meqdela in 1865. He was apparently used by the court as an Arabic secretary for relations with the Coptic patriarchate in Cairo.

Document no. 30

Yohannis IV to Wilhelm I, 17 Feb. 1881

In the name of the Father, and the Son, and the Holy Ghost, one God. Praise be to him.

May the message from the Elect of God Yohannis, King of Zion, King of Kings of Ethiopia, reach the revered [and] respected Wilhelm, by the grace of God, emperor of Germany [and] king of Prussia.

How are you? I, together with my army, am well, praise and thanks to the God of the righteous, since His mercy lasts forever. I received your respected letter with its seal, written in clear conscience and enlightened spirits, through the hands of the scholarly advisor (*mekarī līq*) Dr. Gerhard Rohlfs. I am very pleased to learn of the well-being of your people, the prosperity of your country, and your concern for peaceful reconciliation. On this matter I had written to Your Majesty last year, informing you about the injustices done to me by the Turks. Up to the present day they have not refrained. As recently as last November, they ambushed and killed my emissaries sent to the Barya country to collect taxes; and they also Islamize the Christian population. Yet, my restraint is not due to lack of power, thank God, but because of uncertainty as to the stand which the Powers may take on the issue. It is because I thought I should not take any measures before I get permission from you, the kings, that I have not made any move to recapture even the nearby lands, let alone those farther out.

I shall be satisfied if Your Majesty will mediate, as long as it is done on the basis of what my ancestors, the emperors of Ethiopia, held prior to the fall of the regime due to the advent of Grañ. After Grañ the empire was regained during Serṣe Dingil, Īyasu, and Fasīl, and later was lost by a certain Gugsa. There are not many things of which you, the European Powers, are aware with regard to Ethiopia. To the east and the south the boundary is the sea. To the west and the north, where there are no seas, it is bounded by Nubia (Nuba), Sewakin, Khartoum, Berber, Sinnar, Inariya, Sudan, Belew, Dingula, Hadendowa (Harendawa), Gashī, Massawa, Bedew, Shēho, and Ṭilṭal. Further, the regions inhabited by Galla, Shanqilla, and Adal are all mine, and yet recently, in the middle of Shewa, a place known by the name of Harer was taken [from us]. All the same I listed these places so that my country's boundaries be known. Previously, during the Era of Judges in the times of Alī and Wibē, and recently during the times of the King Tēwodros, and even in my times, the areas taken from us are: Borī, Asawirta, Zula, Asgedē Beqla, Ad Habte Maryam, Marya Qeyyaḥ (Barya Qeyyih), Marya Ṣellam (Barya Ṣellīm), Ad Welette Maryam, Ḥalḥal, Bogos (Moges) Te'ander, Ḥibub, Mensa', Bīdel Çhetel, Guḥmet, Dumē, Dahmīla, Shēho, Weyta, Taka (Takuy), Nara (Inariya), Habab, Kunama, Bazēn, Galla Bēt, Gedaref, and Harer. This is [the list]. Please do mediate in these affairs, for unless the worldly powers enable me to make peaceful reconciliation, how else can there be reconciliation; for the heavenly powers will not intervene. If I regain the areas I have enumerated, all right, I am willing to be reconciled. I request Your Majesty to permit your servant, the scholarly advisor (*mekarī līqi*) Dr. Gerhard Rohlfs, to be delegated by me to negotiate on my behalf.

Written at the camp of Samera, on the 11th day of Yekkatīt in the year of grace 1873.

Seal: King of Kings Yohannis, King of Zion in Ethiopia. The cross has defeated the tribe of Isma'ēl. Yūḥannā, King of Kings of Zion in Abyssinia. The cross has defeated the people of Ismā'īl. 1864.

AAPA, Abt. A, I.B.9, Africa, Abessinien, vol. 2, Amharic original. Printed in *Ethiopia and Germany*, p. 200. The letter was a response to a letter by Wilhelm I, dated 18 Sept. 1880, and brought to Yohannis by Rohlfs in Feb. 1881. A very similar list of places is found in doc. 53 in which Yohannis makes an attempt to define the borders of his country. Inariya in the text must have been confused with Nara, since Inariya is in a different area and the adjacent names are direct neighbors of Nara. For identifications see Wolbert Smidt: "History, Historical Arguments and the Ethio-Eritrean Conflict. Between Xenophobic Approaches and an Ideology of Unity", in: *Stichproben, Wiener Zeitschrift für kritische Afrikastudien, Vienna Journal of African Studies* 22 [Umstrittene Geschichte/n], 12. Jg., 2012, 103–120.

Document no. 31

Yohannis IV to Otto von Bismarck, 17 Feb. 1881

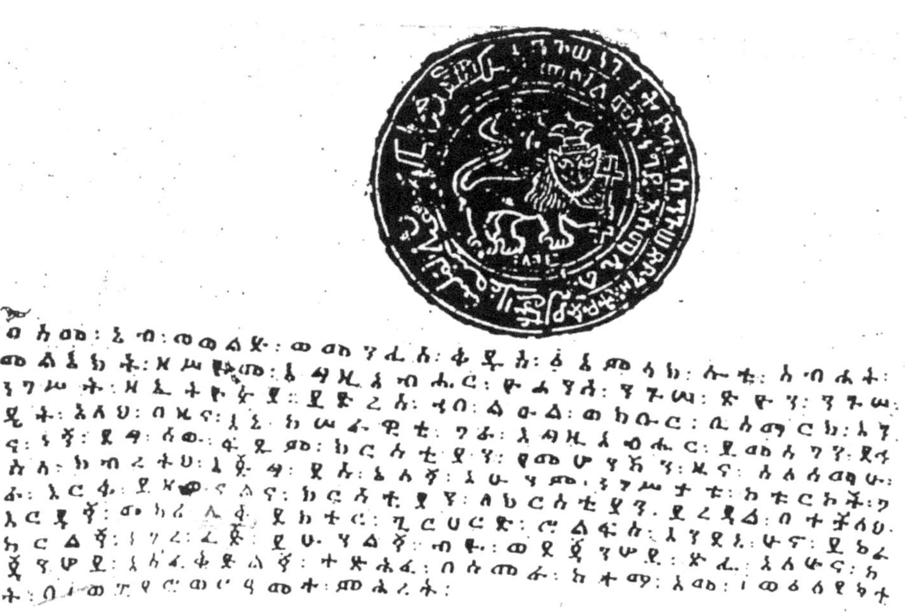

Seal: King of Kings Yohannis, King of Zion in Ethiopia. The cross has defeated the tribe of Isma'ēl. Yūḥannā, King of Kings of Zion in Abyssinia. The cross has defeated the people of Ismā'īl. 1864.

In the name of the Father, and the Son, and the Holy Ghost, one God. Praise be to Him.

May the message of the Elect of God Yohannis, King of Zion, King of Kings of Ethiopia, reach the exalted and honoured Bismarck.

How are you, [although known to me only] by hearsay? I and my army are well, thank God. I am very happy to hear that you are a kind man and a perfect Christian, and [to learn] about your good reputation.

And now, since the kings are trying to reconcile me with the Turks, and since a Christian ought to help another Christian, do your best to assist me. The scholarly advisor (*mekarī līq*) Dr. Gerhard Rohlfs is negotiating on my behalf. As I had written to His Majesty that he is my lawyer (lit. finisher of my case), [please] have His Majesty give him permission.

Written in the town of Semera, on 11th Yekatīt in the year of grace 1873.

AAPA, Abt. A, I.B.9, Africa, Abessinien, vol. 2, Amharic original. Printed in *Ethiopia and Germany*, p. 204.

Document no. 32

Yohannis IV, power of attorney for Gerhard Rohlfs, 17 Feb. 1881

መልእክት ፡ ዘሥዩመ ፡ እግዚአብሔር ፡ ዮሐንስ ፡ ንጉሠ
ነገሥት ፡ ንጉሠ ፡ ጽዮን ፡ ዘኢትዮጵያ ። መካሪ ፡
ሊቅ ፡ ዶክቶር ፡ ጌርሐርድ ፡ ሮልፍስ ። ነገሬን ፡
ከለኔ ፡ ሁነህ ፡ ከነገሥት ፡ ፊት ፡ ጨርስልኝ ፡
ብዬ ፡ ሰድጀዋለሁ ። በ፲፰ወ፻፸ወ፫
ዓመተ ፡ ምሕረት ፡ እመ ፡ ፲ወ፩ ለየካቲት ፡
በሠመራ ፡ ከተማ ፡ ተጻፈ ። ። ።

Seal: King of Kings Yohannis of Ethiopia; Yūḥannā, King of Kings of Abyssinia.

Message of the Elect of God Yohannis, King of Kings, King of Zion of Ethiopia.

I have sent the counsellor, the scholarly advisor (*mekarī līq*) Dr. Gerhard Rohlfs, with the instruction, "Carry out my business with the governments on my behalf."

Written at the camp of Semera in the year of grace 1873, on the 11th of Yekatīt.

HHS, RA 15.6, Amharic original. The document carries a note: "Vollmacht des Negus für mich" reportedly in Rohlfs's own handwriting. For Rohlfs mission see doc. 22. Rohlfs did not only gain Yohannis' trust but was, as the above shows, appointed to be his delegate and conclude peace on his behalf (see further *Survival*, p. 348). The title *mekarī līq* is only, but consistently, used for Gerhard Rohlfs. It denotes a counsellor as well as a scholar and manifests the high regard Yohannis had for him. See further docs 33, 52, 53 and 91.

Document no. 33

Yohannis IV to Gerhard Rohlfs, 23 Feb. 1881

መልእክት፡ዘሥዩመ፡እግዚአብሔር፡ዮሐንስ፡ንጉሠ፡ጽዮን፡ንጉሠ፡ነገሥ
ት፡ዘኢትዮጵያ፡ይድረስ፡ከመካሪ፡ሊቅ፡ዶክተር፡ጊርሀርድ፡ሮልፍ፡እንዴት፡
ሰነበትህ፡እኔም፡ሠራዊቴም፡ሁሉ፡እግዚአብሔር፡ይመስገን፡ደኅና፡ነኝ፡ከ
ጋላ፡ዘመቻ፡ቀርቻለሁ፡የነገሥታት፡መልክተኞች፡ብዙ፡ሁነው፡መጥተዋል፡
ሰምቼ፡የነዚያን፡ቃል፡ሳልሰማ፡አሕዛብን፡አጠፋለሁ፡አልሄድም፡ብዬ፡ቀርሁ፡ተጽሕፈ፡
በገላውዴዎስ፡ሰፈር፡አመ፡፲ወ፯ለየካቲት፡በ፲፻ወ፰፻ወ፸ወ፫ዓመተ፡ምሕረት፡

Seal: King of Kings Yohannis of Ethiopia; Yūḥannā, King of Kings of Abyssinia.

May this message of the Elect of God Yohannis, King of Zion, King of Kings of Ethiopia, reach the counsellor, the scholar (*mekarī līq*) Dr. Gerhard Rohlfs. How are you? I and all my army are well, thank God.

I have refrained from the Galla campaign. Having heard that many messengers from the authorities have arrived, I said: "I shall not go to eliminate the pagans without hearing the words of the messengers."

Gelawdēwos Sefer, on 17th Yekatīt in the year of grace 1873.

HHS, RA 13.99. Amharic original.

Document no. 34

Abū Bakr Ibrāhīm to Jules Grévy, 6 March 1881

To His Highness, the exalted president, the magnificent prince, president of the state council of [the] great [nation of] France. May its power increase.

After presenting respectful greetings befitting your rank, we honestly and gratefully inform Your Loving-kindness that Monsieur Brémond, who is travelling in the lands of Ethiopia, observing appropriate manners, has completed his mission in full friendship. This is how he became one of the most faithful people surrounding King Minīlik.

In fact, as King Minīlik wishes to be introduced and honoured to meet with the honourable and exalted president of the French government, he assigned Monsieur Brémond and our son Muḥammad Abū Bakr to go to the land of France and inform you of what they have seen on our side. This is what we would like to propose to Your Excellency and tell Your Highness. And since our above-mentioned son Muḥammad has neither been to Europe nor elsewhere, I beseech you to be concerned and generous and to take him under your wings; we will be grateful for [this] additional favour of yours. On the other hand, your demands will be fulfilled. All you have to do is to issue orders which we will fully execute and completely implement. In addition, we shall receive your honoured officers who come to us by land or by sea and offer them all good services. Our laudable son is subject to King Minīlik's orders and intentions. He is assigned solely for this mission. Concluding greetings.

I affix here my name, on 6th March 1881.
The governor (*muḥāfith*) of Zeyla.
Seal: Abū Bakr Ibrāhīm.

AEMD, Afrique 62, Abyssinie 3, fol. 507, Arabic original; fol. 506, French translation. The seal differs from the seals used earlier by Abū Bakr.

Document no. 35

Alula Ingida Qubī to Kīrillus V, 7 March [1881?]

ይድረስ፡ ከመምህረ፡ ዓለም፡ ብፁዕ፡ ወክቡር፡ አቡነ፡
ቄርሎስ፡ ሊቀ፡ ጳጳሳት፡ ዘእለእስክንድርያ፡ ዘይነብር፡ በመ
ንበረ፡ ማርቆስ፡ ገብሩ፡ ወሐዋርያሁ፡ ለክርስቶስ።
እስዕም፡ እደዊከ፡ ወእገሪከ፡ በአምኃ፡ መንፈሳዊ
ት፡ እንተ፡ አበዊነ፡ ሐዋርያት፡ ፍቱኒ፡ ወአንጽሐ
ኒ፡ አ አቡየ፡ ለወልድከ፡ ገብረ፡ ሚካኤል፡ ራስ፡ አሉላ፡
ዘውእቱ፡ ቱርክ፡ ባሻ፡ መድኃኔ፡ ዓለም፡ ጤና፡ ይስ
ጥልኝ፡ ብዬ፡ እጄን፡ እነሣለሁ፡ ለማርያም፡ መነዌ፡ ደ
ወል፡ ሊገዛበት፡ ብር፡ ፻ ብር፡ ሰድጃለሁ፡ አባቴ፡
ሆይ፡ አስገዝተው፡ መልካም፡ ደወል፡ ይስደዱልኝ፡
ተጽሕፈ፡ አመ፡ ፳ወ፱፡ ለየካቲት፡ በሐማሴን፡ ከተማ።

May [this letter] reach the teacher of the world, the blessed and honoured *Abune* Kīrillus, *līqe pappasat* of Alexandria who sits on the chair of Mark, the servant and apostle of Christ.

I kiss your hands and your feet with the spiritual kiss of our fathers, the apostles. Absolve me and cleanse me, O my father, me, your son Gebre Mika'ēl, *Ras* Alula, who is the *turk basha*. I raise my hands saying, "May the Saviour of the world give [you] health". I am sending 100 thalers to purchase a bell for Maryam Menewē. O my father, have a good bell bought and send it to me.

Written in the camp of Ḥamasēn, on the 29th of Yekkatīt.

Seal: This is the seal of *Ras* Alula who is the *turk basha*.

Ghali Collection, no. 43, Amharic/Gi'iz original which is followed by an Arabic translation. This is, however, not literal. The most important difference is that the Arabic includes the name of the emissary sent to buy the bell, *Abba* Mel'ake Birhan. Menewē was the place of origin of Alula.

We have tentatively dated this letter to 1881 assuming that it has a connection with the synod held on 8 July 1881 to solve the problem of a new leadership for the Ethiopian Church.

Document no. 36

Minīlik II to Umberto I, 30 March 1881

Message sent by King Minīlik, King of Shewa, to King Umberto I, King of Italy, Jerusalem and Cyprus.

How is Your Majesty? I, by the grace of God, am well, and all my army is well. May God glorify Your Majesty for having sent to me the decoration of the Cross of the Kingdom of Italy and for all the other very beautiful gifts, and the letter.

Now, by this letter, I let Your Majesty know that Captain Cecchi has been released and is [here] with me. I have done much work and made as many efforts as I could to save this man. In order to get him released, I sent three letters to the Queen of Gēra by [the hands of] *Abba* Jīffar, [promising] that if they released him in a friendly way I would give them great riches; but if they refused I would, once the winter had passed, have them destroyed.

Now, by this letter, I let Your Majesty know the honour I feel and the care I take of the Italians who come to my country and who stay here. I would have liked to do more, but I do not have any arms. Three years ago rifles should have arrived at Zeyla, where I sent 300 camels, but those who said they would bring them did not bring them.

Now, send me 2,000 Remingtons which I will purchase. These rifles can come from Your Majesty's country as far as to Aseb, and from there I will bring them here. If this is done, we will with the help of Your Majesty set the route in order and it will be possible to come and go regularly from my country to Your Majesty's and vice versa.

Written at Debre Birhan on the 22nd of Meggabīt 1873 (March).

ASMAI 36/1–6, Italian translation. No Amharic original in the archive. *L'Italia in Africa*, I.2 no. 176, p. 172 has dated this letter "27 Marzo". On the document itself someone has added the note "1880 del calendario gregoriano" which is obviously an error, Meggabīt 1873 corresponding to March *1881*. The release of Cecchi was already communicated to Italy in Nov. 1880 and is apparently an introduction geared to the actual message about the purchase of arms.

Document no. 37

Tekle Gīyorgīs to Kīrillus V, 31 March [1881?]

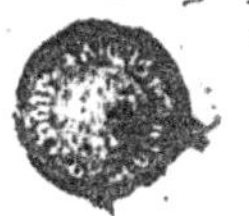

May [the message] reach the Father, the honoured and exalted *Abune* Kīrillus, *līqe pappasat* of Alexandria, the upright in faith, who sits on the chair of Mark the Evangelist, the servant and apostle of Christ.

Absolve me. Do not forget me. May God enable us to see each other in the life of this body. I, *Nibure'id* Tekle Gīyorgīs, raise my hands, saying, "May the Saviour of the world give [you] health."

Written on the 23rd of Meggabīt.

Seal: *Nibure id* Tekle Gīyorgīs.

Ghali Collection, no. 51, Amharic original; opening greetings in Gi'iz. The year 1881 is based on the assumption that this letter and the following one relate to the mission to Egypt in April 1881; see docs 41–44. For the author see doc. 21.

Document no. 38

Gebre Gīyorgīs to Kīrillus V [March 1881]

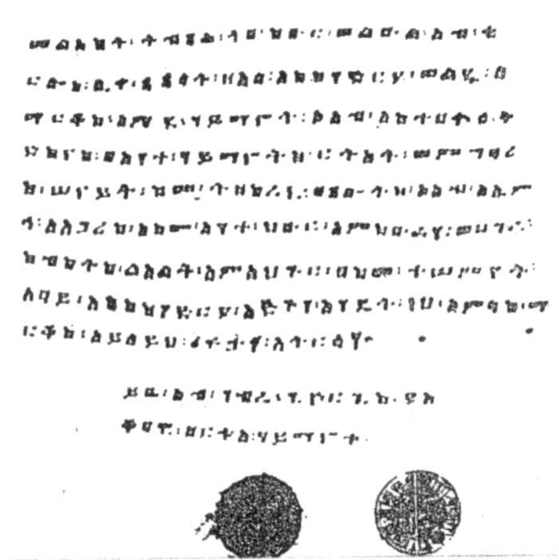

May the message reach the honoured and exalted *Ab[ba]* Kīrillus, *līqe pappasat* of Alexandria, son of Mark, the pillar of faith.

O father, I implore Your Holiness on account of your upright faith and good deeds that you may remember me in your prayers. O father, I kiss your feet, for you are more honoured than the honoured, and the land where you teach is the most exalted of countries as it is called Alexandria the Great.

How are you, really? May the God of Mark be always with you. Absolve me. Do not forget me.

[Thus] says *Ab[ba]* Gebre Gīyorgīs, the Jacobite of Orthodox faith.

Seals: illegible.

Ghali Collection, no. 50, Gi'iz/Amharic original. For date see document above.

Document no. 39

Yohannis IV to Muḥammad Tawfīq, 5 April 1881

Seal: King of Kings Yohannis of Ethiopia; Yūḥannā, King of Kings of Abyssinia.

In the name of God, the forgiving and compassionate, praise be to Him.

May the message of the Elect of God Yohannis, King of Zion, King of Kings of Ethiopia, reach the honoured and exalted Khedive Muḥammad Tawfīq *Pasha*, King of Misr and Gibṣ (Egypt) and those who follow his example.

Peace be to you, and the peace of God be with you. By the grace of God and the intercession of our Mother Zion, praise be to the God of our Fathers, I am well.

Owing to my strong friendship for you and your exalted position and your honoured and beloved government I have sent five engraved golden cuffs and one golden saddle.

Written in the land of Delanta, on 28th Meggabīt in the year of grace 1873.

ENA, Soudan 5/3/8, Gi'iz/Amharic original. The letter seems to be an opening letter presenting the gifts brought by Yohannis' delegation to Cairo in April 1881 to bring new bishops to Ethiopia. The real issues are presented in the next letter, of which there is also an Arabic account, doc. 41. A second Arabic account, doc. 42, about the transfer of money and trade through Massawa does not correspond to any preserved Amharic text. The letters were written within three days after Yohannis had received a conciliatory letter from Tawfīq opening up for negotiations. In his letter to Yohannis, 6 Dec. 1881, Muḥammad Tawfīq refers to the letters and the gifts received with the delegation sent to procure new bishops. The designation of a metropolitan and three bishops for Ethiopia is discussed in Antūn Sūryāl, 'Abd al-Sayyid, *Al-kanīsa al-Masriyya al-Qibtiyya wa-l-kanīsa Ithyūbiyā*, Cairo 1985, pp. 129–134, Yolande Mara, *The Church of Ethiopia*, Asmara, 1972, p. 25 and *Yohannis IV*, pp. 108–109. Both Misr and Gibṣ refer to Egypt, the first is Arabic the second Gi'iz.

Document no. 40

Yohannis IV to Muḥammad Tawfīq, 5 April 1881

በስመ፡ እግዚአብሔር፡ መሐሪ፡ ወመስተሣህል፡ ሉቱ፡ ስብሐት። ።
መልእክት፡ ዘሥዩመ፡ እግዚአብሔር፡ ዮሐንስ፡ ንጉሠ፡ ጽዮን፡ ን
ጉሠ፡ ነገሥት፡ ዘኢትዮጵያ፡ ትብጻሕ፡ ኀበ፡ ክቡር፡ ወልዑል፡ ኬዲ
ቪ፡ መሐመድ፡ ጠውፊቅ፡ ባሻ፡ ንጉሠ፡ ምስር፡ ወሻም፡ ወእለ፡ ይት
ለውዎሙ፡ በጸድሉ፡ ሰላም፡ ለከ፡ ወሰላመ፡ እግዚአብሔር፡ የሃሉ፡ ም
ስሌከ። እንሰ፡ ጀፋኝ፡ ወሰላም፡ በኀይሉ፡ እግዚአብሔር፡ ፀባዖት፡ ወ
በጸሎቱ፡ ለእግዚእትነ፡ ማርያም፡ ወሰጊዮር፡ እምላእክ፡ ጽዮን፡ ቅዱስ
ት፡ ስብሐት፡ ለእግዚአብሔር፡ ለዘእንበጽሐነ፡ እስከ፡ ዛቲ፡ ሰዓት። ።
ወክብር፡ ጠማሪ፡ መልእክትከ፡ ዘተጽሕፈ፡ በኔኝት፡ ፤ ገሪ፡ ጳጳሳ፡
ወኢጲስ፡ ቆጳጳሳት፡ ዘጸሐፍነ፡ ለከሙ፡ ከመ፡ ይትፈነዉ፡ እምኔከሙ፡
ወይምጽኡ፡ ተባዕ፡ ወበእንተ፡ ነገድ፡ ደዋይ፡ እለ፡ ሀለው፡ ይነብሩ፡ በገሐ
ር፡ ወበይብስ፡ ወበእንተ፡ ቱእሶዙ፡ ለእንቀጽ፡ ፍኖት፡ እለ፡ የሐው
ሩ፡ በቱ፡ ነገድ፡ ዘኢትዮጵያ፡ በጽሐ፡ ኀቤነ፡ እመ፡ ፳ወ፭ ለመጋቢት፡
በዕለት፡ ሩሉት፡ ቀዳሚት፡ ሰንበት። ወተወከፍናሁ፡ በክብር፡ ተወ
ክቡ፡ ወእምድኅረ፡ ከሠትናሁ፡ ወርኢናሁ፡ ለዝንቱ፡ መጣረ፡ መልእክ
ትከሙ፡ ክቡር፡ ወስቡሕ፡ ተፈሣሕነ፡ ወተሐሠይነ፡ እስመ፡ ዘተጽሕፈ፡ ነ
ገረ፡ ፍቅር፡ ከሙ፡ ጥዑም፡ ወጥቁ፡ እጅግ። ወንሕነሂ፡ እምድኅረ፡ ሰማዕነ፡
ወርእነ፡ ፍቅረ፡ መልእክትከሙ፡ ርቱዓ፡ ሐሳበ፡ ልበ፡ ከሙ፡ ፍጡነ፡ ነገረ፡ ም
ጽኢቶሙ፡ ለጳጳሳት፡ ወኤጲስ፡ ቆጶሳት፡ ወፈነውነ፡ ሰአምጽኦቶሙ፡ ወተ
ቀብሎቶሙ፡ በክብር፡ ወበፍቅር፡ ፍሡሐ፡ ሊቀ፡ ውንቶ፡ ወማእምራኒ፡ እ
ለ፡ ይስመዩ፡ እስማቲሆሙ፡ መልእክ፡ ምሕረት፡ ደስታ፡ ወጸሐፊ፡ ማኅደረ፡
ፊያቱ። ወመምሕር፡ ወልዩ፡ እረግጊ፡ ወእሳቄ፡ እሥራት፡ ወበጆሮጌዩ፡ እ
ቡስጣሊ፡ ባሒቱ፡ ይኩን፡ ፈቃድ፡ ክሙ፡ ፍጡን፡ ምጽአቶሙ፡ ጳጳሳ፡ ወኢጲስ፡ ቆ
ጳሳት፡ ወተመይጦቱ፡ እሑ፡ ልዑካን፡ እንበለ፡ ደባ፡ ወመፍዕ፡ ክሬምቱ፡ ኔ
ለመ፡ ወርኄ፡ ክረምት፡ ዘብሂሮ፡ ጽኑዕ፡ ውእቱ፡ በከመ፡ ሰምዕነ፡ እግ
ዚከሙ፡ እኑ፡ ሠናይ፡ ሐዊረ፡ ፍኖት፡ እምድኅረ፡ በዐት፡ ክረምት፡ ተጽሕፈ
በምድረ፡ ደባብቷ፡ እመ፡ ፳ወ፯ ለመጋቢት፡ በ፲ወ፰፻፸ወ፫ ዓመተ፡ ምሕረት፡

Seal: King of Kings Yohannis of Ethiopia; Yūḥannā, King of Kings of Abyssinia.

In the name of the God, the merciful and forgiving, praise be to Him.

May [this] message of the Elect of God Yohannis, King of Zion, King of Kings of Ethiopia, reach the honoured and exalted Khedive Muḥammad Tawfīq *Pasha*, King of Misr and Egypt and those who likewise are [his] subjects. Peace be to you and may the peace of God also be with you. As for me, I am well and live in peace by the power of God Sabaoth and by the prayers of our Lady Mary, the mother of the Lord [of] Holy Zion. Praise be to God who has helped us to reach this hour.

Your respected letter written on the subject of the bishops and archbishops about whom we had written to you, [requesting] that they be sent from you to us, and about the merchants who used to trade by land and sea, and the closure of the gate through which the Ethiopian merchants used to pass, has reached us on the 25th of Meggabīt, the chosen day of the first Sabbath.

We received it with honour. As we opened and saw your honoured and praiseworthy message we were extremely happy and joyous because the words that were written by you were pleasant and very beautiful. And after having heard and seen your straightforward message, we wrote to you at once concerning the bringing of the archbishop and the bishops and their reception with honour and great joy, and [for this reason] we sent the scholars and knowledgeable people by the name of *Mel'ake Mihiret* Desta and *Ṣirag Maserē* Fenta and *Memhir* Welde Aregawī and *Aleqa* Asrat and *Bejirond* Abustelī.

Only, let the bishops and archbishop come quickly and the messengers return before the rainy season starts, since the rainy season of our country is heavy. As you might know, it is not good to travel during the rainy season.

Written in the land of Delanta, 28th Meggabīt in the year of grace 1873.

ENA, Soudan 5/3/1, Gi'iz original. None of the envoys are known from other documents. The last name is most probably Amharic for Apostoli and refers to an envoy of Greek descent, perhaps related to *Merīgēta* Matēwos Apostoli, the Bible translator, and his brother Ingida Apostoli, who worked for the d'Abbadie brothers. For the Apostoli brothers see *Acta* I, docs 30, 101, 105. Two of the titles used in the letter are fairly unusual ecclesiastical titles. *Mel'ake mihiret* refers to the chief priest of a church or monastery called Mihiret, where *melake* is an alternative to *aleqa*. *Ṣirag maserē* means chamberlain, in Amharic *ye-nigus albesh*.

Document no. 41

Yohannis IV to Kīrillus V, 5 April 1881

رسالة من الملك يوحنا ملك ملوك الحبشه الى قداسة الاب الطوباني البطريرك ابنا كيرلوس
فى ١١ طوبه ٩٧ ارسلتم لنا خطابات وبوصولها حصل لنا الفرح والسرور وشكرنا فضل الله على صحة
سلامتكم والان مرسل لقدسكم المعلمين وهم ملاك السلام دستا وسراج اسارى فانتا والاب
ارجاوى والكه اسرات وبجروند ابوسطولى وصحبتهم تابعوهم لاجل تسليمهم المطران والاساقفة
اللازمين والمقصود الاسعاف بارسال المطران والاساقفة الثلاثة قبل الشتا وعن اذن
قدسكم ترسلوهم حالا وهانحن تحت امر سيادتكم بحيث يكونون من الانام الانقيا الممدوحين
العلمين حيث وانه ان الله شا بانتقال نفسه ابنا المطران ابنا اثناسيوس الذى كان حسن السيره
فنترجا دائما فرحين بوجود قدسكم بغاية الصحه طالبين منكم الدعاء الصالح على الدوام فى ٢٨ برمهات ٩٧

A letter from King Yohannis, King of Kings of Abyssinia (al-Ḥabasha) to His Holiness, the blessed father, the patriarch, *Anbā* Kīrillus, dated 11 Ṭuba [15]97. You have sent me letters. When we received them joy and pleasure befell us. We give thanks for God's favour towards the health of your well-being.

Now we send our teachers to Your Holiness. They are *Mel'ake Selam* Desta and *Sarāj Asārī* Fenta and *Abba* Aregawī and *Aleqa* Asrat and *Bejirond* Abusteli together with their followers so that you may hand over the metropolitan and the bishops asked for to them. The purpose is to facilitate the sending of the metropolitan and three bishops before the rainy season. With the permission of Your Holiness they should be sent immediately. Behold, we are under the command of Your Excellency, that they be [elected] from among the pious, praiseworthy, educated, since it was the will of God that the metropolitan *Anbā* Atinatēwos, who was of good character, passed away. We always hope that Your Holiness will remain in the utmost health and we ask from you devout prayers forever.

28th Baramhāt [15]97.

ENA, Soudan 5/3/8. Arabic account of a letter most probably kept in the archives of the Coptic Patriarchate. Letters from Yohannis to the Coptic Patriarchate were regularly registered and copied by the Egyptian authorities and preserved as part of the correspondence of the khedive. The letter of which this is an account must have had approximately the same content as the previous letter to the khedive. The titles of the members of the delegation are, however, rendered somewhat differently: *Mel'ake Mihiret* Desta is here *Mel'ake Selam, Ṣirag Maserē* Fenta is *Sarāj Asārī* Fenta, and *Memhir* Welde Aregawī is *Abba* Aregawī. The reference to *Anbā* Atinatēwos is missing in the previous letter. On the other hand, the Arabic account omits the reference to the trade issue.

Document no. 42

Yohannis IV to Kīrillus V, 5 April 1881

مرسول لابينا قدس البطريك مبلغ عشرة الاف ريال

خطاب رعي . بعد اداء السلام

وثلاثة الاف ريال برسم مصروف الثلاثة اساقفة

وبرسم مصروف المطران المرغوب برسم الفينه ريال

ثم ومن حيث انه قد سبق صدور امر

كذا خمساية ريال ثمنه الاجراس السابق ارسالها من طرف قدسكم

ودخول تجار مصوع لجهة الحبشة فالمأمول من فضلكم

الجناب العالى الخديوى بدخول تجار الحبشة لمصوع

ان تشاوروا جنابه السامى بشأن مشترى جانب بندق ويرسل لطرفنا ولذلك ارسلنا

جانب نقديه برسم مشترى البندق اللازم ٢٨ برمهات سنة ٩٧

After extended greetings. The amount of ten thousand riyāl has been sent to our father, His Holiness the patriarch. Two thousand riyāl are for the expenses of the requested metropolitan, and three thousand riyāl are for the expenses of the three bishops. Consequently, five hundred (*sic*) riyāl is the price of the bells sent previously by Your Holiness.

Then, as for the fact that orders were previously issued by His Highness the Khedive concerning the entrance of Abyssinian merchants to Massawa and merchants from Massawa into Abyssinia, what we hope from your goodness is that you will consult the highest authority in the matter of the purchase of some rifles, and let him send [them] to us. Likewise, we will send the necessary amount in cash for the purchase of the rifles.

28th Baramhāt [12]97.

ENA, Soudan 5/3/8. See previous note. No Amharic text with the equivalent content is preserved. The opening phrase of this text clearly indicates that we are dealing with a report about a letter, which does not exclude the possibility that what follows is a translation of the text of the letter itself.

Document no. 43

Yohannis IV to Welde Sema'it Welde Yohannis, 5 April 1881

Seal: King of Kings Yohannis of Ethiopia; Yūḥannā, King of Kings of Abyssinia.

May the message of the elect of God Yohannis, King of Zion, King of Kings of Ethiopia, reach *Abba* Welde Sema'it. How have you been? As for me and all my army, I am well, thank God.

I have sent 25,000 thaler so that you can build a church and 50,000 thaler for your allowances. The total is 70,000 thaler. I have sent 200 thaler for your provision, 100 thaler for *Abba* Hayle Īyyesus, 100 thaler for *Abba* Welde Maryam, and 100 thaler for the monk who is with you. I have given you this for provisions. As long as you love one another and do not quarrel, I will never fail you. Build the church very fast. See to it that much soil from Golgotha, the tomb of the Lord, and water of Jordan in many cans are sent to me. I have sent *Bejirond* Lewṭē to count and deliver the things. Send me oil, wood and tabots not yet carved and consecrated, in abundance, as much as can be found, in order that they may be prepared here. And let a doctor who knows the medicine for everything come to me, so that he may live with me, and let a man who knows about plants from that region, come to me with the seeds of all plants, so that he may live with me. I shall keep them salaried and make them all happy.

Written at the camp of Yibaba (Baba), on the 28th of Meggabīt in the year of grace 1873.

Dayr al-Sultan, no. 6, Gi'iz/Amharic original. Printed with English translation in *Chronicle*, no. 9, pp. 170–171, from a copy of a chronicle of *Aṣe* Yohannis. The addressee was the superior of the Ethiopian monastery in Jerusalem. The figures in the letter are confusing in so far as 25,000 + 50,000 make 75,000. In the letter as reported in the chronicle the amount designated for the building of the church is given as 17,000 and for the allowances 15,000. A sum of 20,000 thalers is, moreover, included to buy the land. The following letter of the same date has 15,000 + 7,000. Bairu Tafla in the *Chronicle* (p. 171) suggests that "forgery of some kind must have taken place". The translation erroneously writes Welde Īyyesus where the text, as in the letter above, has Hayle Īyyesus.

Document no. 44

Yohannis IV to the Ethiopian community in Jerusalem, 5 April 1881

Seal: King of Kings Yohannis of Ethiopia; Yūḥannā, King of Kings of Abyssinia.

May the message of the Elect of God Yohannis, King of Zion, King of Kings of Ethiopia, reach my saintly fathers, the monks of the Orthodox faith, the monks of the community of Jerusalem, who live in Dayr al-Sultan. Peace be to you and may the peace of God be with you.

By the mercy of God and the intercession of our mother Zion – may the God of the saints be praised – I am well. His mercy is everlasting. I have sent 35,000 thaler for the building of a church [and] 50,000 thaler for your allowances. The total is 85,000.

As long as God instils love amongst you, [and] I am informed about it, I do not have any problem and, as of now, I will not let you be worried regarding your food. Let alone you who do not have a share in taxes and appointments. I maintain the clergy of the churches of Ethiopia by giving them, in addition to appointments, taxes, salaries and provisions. Moreover, you consulted one another and testified that *Abba* Welde Sema'it is a good man like *Abbatē* Gebre Gīyorgīs, and appointed him. Now, if he wrongs you, since it is unbecoming to quarrel, you have the archbishop (*līqe pappasat*) there. Write to me and inform me, but do not quarrel over nothing. Do whatever he orders you, and do nothing against his will. Now then, if you disobey me, I will confuse and scatter you.

Moreover, you know the case of Egypt. Not only the clergy, even the soldiers, draw their rations together. In the same manner, buy [your] provisions together. But if you want to live like soldiers (lit. divisions), the divisions that are [here] with me are more numerous.

Written at the camp of Yebaba (Baba), 28th Meggabīt in the year of grace 1873.

Dayr al-Sultan, no. 7, Gi'iz/Amharic original. Printed with English translation in *Chronicle*, no. 10, pp. 170–173, no. 10. The amount for building the church differs from the amount in the previous letter of the same day, but here the total sum is correct. In the *Chronicle* the sums are 15,000 and 7,000 and the total 22,000.

Document no. 45

Burhān Muḥammad to the Italian representative in Aseb, [22 April] 1881

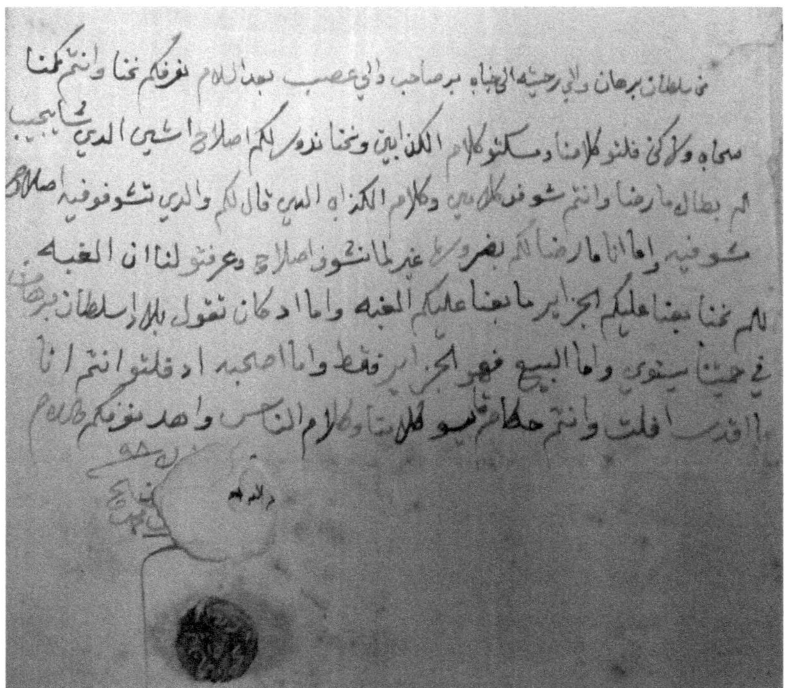

From Sultan Burhān, ruler of Raḥayta to His Honour, *Bir Ṣāḥib*, the ruler of Aseb.

After greetings we want you to know that we and you were friends, but you have disregarded our words and listened to the words of liars. We seek your welfare and wish you nothing evil (?). You should observe my words and the liar's words, which he told you, and follow the ones you think are good. You have told us that the gulf is yours. We sold you the islands. We did not sell the gulf. But if you say that all the land belongs to is under your protection, it is fine. But as for the purchase it was for the islands only. As for our friendship even if you untie it, we will not untie it.

22nd Jumād al-Awwal 1298 (21st April 1881).

ASMAE, AE 2. Arabic original and French translation. The Arabic original is damaged and difficult to decipher. The translation above is thus partly based on the French version where the addressee is designated as "gouverneur". The date is lost in the Arabic original and taken from the French version. The letter reveals that the Italian version of the so-called "convention" of 15 March 1880 (doc. 4) did most probably not agree with the Arabic version, if there ever was a written Arabic text. The French text summarizes the argument and specifies Markable as the issue at stake, where the Arabic speaks about the gulf. See further doc. 112 in which Burhān returns to the issue and explains his reason for demanding Markable to be returned to him, and doc. 140 in which he finally renounces his claim and asks for compensation for the injustice done to him.

Document no. 46

Yohannis IV to Jean-Marcel Touvier, Jean-Baptiste Coulbeaux and Sixtus Barthèz, 19 June 1881

May the letter from the Elect of God (lit. the Lord) Yohannis, King of Kings of Ethiopia reach *Abba* Yosēf (Mgr. Touvier), *Abba* Yohannis (Mgr. Coulbeaux) and *Abba* Ṗēṭros (Mgr. Barthèz). How are you?

I and my army are well, thank God. Since the Lord helps me, I am not afraid of anyone; why do you always trouble me? You have come to my country and devote yourself to teaching; however, does not that mean, "My teaching is better?" Seeing that you teach, do not many countries with pagans remain? But now leave my country. Go to your country! I have given orders to return your property to you. All persons who devote themselves to teaching do so only with the approval of the king; to teach without his approval is to take sides for the opposition. What you love, you other [people], is to make Christian blood flow in vain. Earlier you wrote to king Tekle Gīyorgīs and caused him to come and fight me. Now in contempt of my edicts you arrange to sell and trade in tobacco. You banquet with *shifta* (rebels) and offer them refuge. All of this does nothing but create hostility and destroy all friendship. If I speak like this it does not mean that I have given orders to plunder you. That was done without my approval. For the time being, this is the answer I send you.

Written at the camp of Zobil, 14th June (19th June) in the year of grace 1873 (1881).

AECPC, Massaouah 4, fol. 226, French translation of what must have been an Amharic original now lost. Not only are the three Catholic priests called by their names as missionaries in Ethiopia, i.e. *Abba* Yosēf, *Abba* Yohannis and *Abba* Ṗēṭros, but the Amharic word *shifta* appears with a translation into French. The Catholic mission had been robbed and the three missionaries taken captive by *Dejjach* Tedla, a cousin of Yohannis, and *Dejjach* Meshesha, Yohannis' nephew, on 1 June. For a detailed account see Kevin O'Mahoney, *The Ebullient Phoenix: A History of the Vicariate of Abyssinia 1860–1881*, book II, Asmara, 1987, pp. 242–249. Although Yohannis, in order not to create diplomatic problems, ordered them to be released as soon he was informed (see doc. 51), it is evident that he had no sympathy for them. In fact, the letter reiterates what Yohannis had already written in 1872 about the Catholics meddling in Ethiopian politics and supporting his rivals. See *Acta* III, docs 88 and 100.

Document no. 47

Maḥammad Ḥanfadhē to Louis Auguste Brémond, June 1881

In the name of God, the compassionate and merciful.

Praise be to God alone and blessings and peace be upon him after whom there is no prophet, and upon his companions who sacrificed themselves for God.

Now, if you inquire about us, we are well and healthy. May God make you likewise. We pray God [to grant] us and yourself health.

From His Excellency, the most noble and most honoured, the pious and pure, Sultan bin Sultan Maḥammad Ḥanfadhē (Muḥammad bin Ḥanfadhē) to His Excellency the deputy of King Minīlik, by this I refer to Brémond, the Frenchman, general agent of Minīlik. We beseech God for health for us and for you. What we want to tell you is, that the letters you sent with ʻAbd al-Raḥmān, bin Shaykh Yūsif, the deceased, reached us. We read it, your message, and understood its content, and we accept what you and Sultan Minīlik have said. But please, if you address us, do not address us except through ʻAbd al-Raḥmān Yūsif. We heard you wish to embark at Obok. For the sake of King Minīlik we approve of your coming to Obok. If you come, support and sustenance will be [supplied] from Obok. You will stay with me. But for now, no one should set out with you except yourself. And do not set out except with ʻAbd al-Raḥmān Yūsif. As for the brotherhood, we accept it and will benefit from each other, God willing, in this world. When you come to me, do not fear or feel saddened about what is happening, it is of the creatures and not of the Creator. If you come to me, the grace you knew in me is still there. Do not worry about provisions, not even a needle, except for what your heart says. As for the news, you will find them with ʻAbd al-Raḥmān Yūsif, who is our and your confidant. Do help him in all ways. I am likewise his friend and trustee. Concluding greetings.

From Maḥammad Ḥanfadhē.

Seal: Muḥammad Ḥanfadhē.

AEMD, Afrique 62, Abyssinie 3, fol. 519, Arabic original; fol. 520, French translation. The letter is undated, but annotated "reçue le 27 Juin". The author, Maḥammad Ḥanfadhē, was the Sultan of Awsa from 1862 to 1902. Fighting against the Egyptians and their ally, Abū Bakr Ibrāhīm, he was responsible for the attacks on the caravans of Arnoux and of Munzinger in 1875 (see *Acta* III, no. 125 and 179). For details on him see *EAE* 3, pp. 647–648. Since Brémond stayed at Obok it was most probably written a week or two earlier. ʻAbd al-Raḥmān Yūsif was the trusted agent of Maḥammad Ḥanfadhē.

Document no. 48

Minīlik II to Umberto I, 11 July 1881

Message sent by King Minīlik to His Majesty Umberto I, King of Italy, our friend.

How are you? I, by the grace of God, am well and all my court is well.

Your Majesty! In the past I had already written a letter to Your Majesty in order to let you know that Captain Cecchi had been released and what I had done to get him free.

This very day Captain Cecchi unexpectedly comes to me to tell me that because of illness he wishes to go back to his country. On his departure from here I supplied him with all he needs for the journey so that no accident will occur to him and I have sent him away. God will bring him, as I hope, in good health to Your Majesty. He will not fail to tell you everything we have done for the Geographical Society.

I pray to God that he will grant Your Majesty a long life and guard our friendship.

Written at Werre'īlu, our city, the 5th of July, 1873.

ASMAI 36/1–6, fols 101–102, Italian text. Printed in *AP.DD*, XV, p. 71 as dated 11 July 1880 (*sic*), which is an obvious mistake since Cecchi was released in August 1880 (see docs 15–17). The cover (101) gives the correct date '11 Luglio 1881', which corresponds to Hamlē 5 in the Ethiopian calendar. It thus seems obvious that 'luglio" in the text above is simply a translation of Hamlē, leaving the date of the month unchanged just like the year. No Amharic version of this letter or the two following ones is recorded in ASMAI.

Document no. 49

Minīlik II to Umberto I, 12 July 1881

Message sent by King Minīlik to Umberto I, King of Italy.

How is your health? I, by the grace of God, am well. Today I add to the letter of the 5th of July the current month as follows: Earlier I had written to Your Majesty through Captain Martini about the rifles, but Captain Martini has not concluded this matter. If I had had a quantity of rifles and war-materials, Captain Cecchi would not have returned like that from halfway (uncompleted journey). What I lack today are rifles. Your Majesty on the other hand, since your heart is benevolent, will not be embarrassed. As for us we do lack weapons against our enemies, but we lack nothing else. Among us a chief with a hundred men flees and abandons his land in front of ten riflemen. The Egyptians, our neighbours all around us, close our way and prevent us from purchasing any with our own money. As for getting rifles our only hope lies with Your Majesty's calculations and goodness and we have no other hope. Only Your Majesty's heart with regard to such injustice, and that alone, can put an end to this situation of ours.

Written at Werre'īlu (from) our city, the 6th of July 1873 of our salvation (according to the Julian calendar).

ASMAI 36/1–6, fols 105–106. Italian text. Printed in *AP.DD*, XV, p. 72, dated 11 July 1880 (*sic*). See doc. 48 above for our dating.

Document no. 50

Minīlik II to Benedetto Cairoli, 12 July 1881

Message sent by King Minīlik so that it will reach the Ministry of Foreign Affairs under the direction of the minister of the king of Italy, Mr Cairoli.

How are you? I, by the grace of God, am well. I have already written to you about the release of Captain Cecchi, telling you about all my efforts in that matter. Today Captain Cecchi suddenly wants to leave because of illness, and so I send him away hoping that it will please you. He will tell you everything that was said and done here.

As for the past, the reason why Captain Cecchi came back in the middle of his journey was shortage of weapons. If I had had many rifles, I would have had him accompanied by many people and everything would have turned out well. Today I am short of rifles, but as for all the rest I do not lack anything.

From all sides the Turks, having closed the door, intercept our passage. I have always been at peace with the realm of Egypt and to this day I do not know of having given them any reason for offence; in spite of this they always shut their doors to us. For this reason, I appeal to your heart so that you do everything possible to make rifles arrive to me. Of course, I intend to buy them.

Written at Werre'īlu, our city, the 6th of July 1873 of the Christian era (according to the Julian calendar).

ASMAI 36/1–6, fols 103–104, Italian text. Printed in *AP.DD*, XV, p. 71 as dated on 12 July 1880 (*sic*). See doc. 48 above for dating. Cairoli had actually resigned as early as 29 May 1881.

Document no. 51

Yohannis IV to Achille Raffray, 17 July 1881

Message from the Elect of God Yohannis, King of Zion, King of Kings of Ethiopia, to Consul Raffray of France.

How are you? I and my army are well, thank God. I have subdued the Wello and the Adal, and made them Christians; I tell you this, I have left. After my [departure] (lit. behind me) *Dejjach* Tedla wrote to me, "I have found *Abba* Yosēf, Yohannis and Ṗēṭros with the *shifta*. I have laid hold of them." It is with my permission that they have baptized and taught the ignorant. I have told him, "Who has given you the right to their goods? Restore everything, release them. I am very angry. Look what I wrote to him. Now, have them come. I will make him come who has done evil to them, and I shall render justice."

Written in the camp at Zobil, 17th July (Greek calendar).

AECPC, Massaouah 4, fol. 240, French translation, copied in a sixteen-page report by the French vice-consul of Massawa Achille Raffray, dated 22 November. The original was reportedly kept in the archives of the vice-consulate at Massawa and may very well have been lost. When claiming to have subdued Adal, Yohannis IV refers to his Afar campaigns, during which he gained control of the Afar area nearby Meqelē, where he constructed the Mika'ēl church. Further Afar areas such as Awsa entertained a political relation with Shewa, as further letters show, but no campaign to subdue them took place. The three priests mentioned are the Catholic missionaries J-M. Touvier, J-B. Coulbeaux and S. Barthèz, who had been captured by *Dejjach* Tedla, a cousin of Yohannis, and *Dejjach* Meshesha, Yohannis' nephew. See doc. 46.

Document no. 52

Yohannis IV to Gerhard Rohlfs, 27 July 1881

መልእክት፡ ዘሥዩመ፡ እግዚአብሔር፡ ዮሐንስ፡ ንጉሠ፡ ጽዮ
ን፡ ንጉሠ፡ ነገሥት፡ ዘኢትዮጵያ፡ ይድረስ፡ ከመካሪ፡ ሊቅ፡
ዶክቶር፡ ጌርሃርድ፡ ሮልፍስ፡ እንዴት፡ ሰንበትህ፡ እኔ፡ ከሠ
ራዊቴ፡ ጋራ፡ እግዚአብሔር፡ ይመስገን፡ ደኅና፡ ነኝ፡ ደብዳቤ
ህም፡ ደረሰኝ፡ እኔም፡ በዚያው፡ በጻፍክልኝ፡ ምላሺ፡ እንደሌ
ክኝ፡ አድርጌ፡ መልእክቱንም፡ አትሜ፡ እንግዳሸትንም፡ አድ
ርጌ፡ ሰድጀለሁ፡፡ ነገር፡ ግን፡ እቶበዝን፡ የሆነውን፡ ሁሉ፡ የጧ
ቱ፡ የማታውን፡ ንገር፡ ጻፍልኝ፡ በኛ፡ ጉዳይ፡ እንዳትበለጥ፡
ሁኝ፡፡ ተጽሐፈ፡ በዞቢል፡ ከተማ፡ እመ፡ ፳ወ፩ ለሐምሌ፡ በ፲
ወ፰፻፸ወ፫ ዓመተ፡ ምሕረት፡፡

Seal: King of Kings Yohannis of Ethiopia; Yūḥannā, King of Kings of Abyssinia.

May the message of the Elect of God Yohannis, King of Zion, King of Kings of Ethiopia, reach the counsellor, the scholarly adviser (*mekarī līq*) Dr. Gerhard Rohlfs. How have you been? I, together with my army, thank God, am well. I have also received your letter. And I have done according to what you wrote to me in the response to your letter. I have sealed the letter and also sent Ingidashēt. However, don't stop writing to me what is happening day and night. Don't be fooled (lit. outsmarted) on our case.

Written in the town of Zobil, on the 21st of Hamlē in the year of grace 1873.

HHS, RA 15, Amharic original. The sealed letter Yohannis refers to is most probably the following declaration in which Yohannis sets out his territorial claims in view of the negotiations that Gerhard Rohlfs, on behalf of the German government, had promised to arrange. See doc. 31. Ingidashēt refers to *Lij* Ingidashēt Schimper, the son of the German botanist Georg Wilhelm Schimper, who had settled in Adwa in 1837, and his wife Mirṣit. Cf. doc. 91. He studied in Germany 1868–1878 and was later in the service of Yohannis and instrumental in making Meqelē the new capital.

Document no. 53

Yohannis IV, declaration on extent of Ethiopian territory, 27 July 1881

Seal: King of Kings Yohannis of Ethiopia; Yuḥannā, King of Kings of Abyssinia.

Elect of God, Yohannis, King of Siyon, King of Kings of Ethiopia. The numbering of the lands Ethiopia. On the east and south side, the boundary is the sea. But on the west and on the north, where there is no sea, [lie] Nubia (Nuba), Sewakin, Khartoum, Berber, Sinnar, Inariya, Sudan. Belew, Dingula, Hadendowa (Harendawa), Gashī, Massawa, Bedew, Shēhu, Ṭilṭal, and, as to the rest, all the regions occupied by Galla, Shanqilla and Adal. In the middle of Shewa, a place known as Harer has been occupied. Already during my reign, Borī, Asawirta (Amawirta), Zula, Asgēdē, Beqla, 'Ad Habte Maryam, Marya Qeyyaḥ (Barya Qeyyih), Marya Ṣellam (Barya Ṣellim), 'Ad Welette Maryam, Ḥalḥal, Bogos (Moges), Te'ander, Ḥibub, Mensa', Bīdel Çhetel, Guḥmet, Dumē, Dahmīla, Shēho, Weyta, Taka (Takuy), Habab, Kunama, Bazēn, Galla Bēt, Gedaref, Harer, have been captured. Let the scholarly adviser (*mekarī līq*), Gerhard Rohlfs, thresh out the territories enumerated above on my behalf, in consultation with the ruler (*gezh*) of Egypt, Khedive Tawfīq *Pasha*.

Written in the town of Zebil, on 21st Hamlē 1873.

HHS, RA 16.38, Amharic original. This document carries the same date as the letter above which mentions the visit of Rohlfs to Yohannis. The calligraphy is also the same. In all probability it was drawn up by someone at the court of Yohannis. For the list of places, compare with doc. 30.

Document no. 54

Burhān Muḥammad, declaration on relation with Egypt, 19 Aug. 1881

I, the undersigned Sultan Burhān bin Muḥammad, declare that as far as I know no act of submission to Egypt has ever been made until this day, neither during the time of my father, nor that of my forefathers, the sultans of Raḥayta, neither by myself, nor by my above-mentioned predecessors, nor has the Egyptian flag ever been raised at Raḥayta, nor has the Egyptian government ever exercised any jurisdiction whatsoever at Raḥayta, as they do not have any rights whatsoever to the country of my father and my forefathers.

In faith of which I have signed, 1298, 23rd Ramadān (August 1881).

(Seal)

Signed: Burhān.

AP.DD, XXIII, no. 150, Italian text. The date in the Muslim calendar and the style of the text indicate that this is a translation from Arabic, but it is unclear if there ever was an Arabic document.

Document no. 55

Nigusē Tasho and Amanu'ēl Hamed to Bengt Peter and Emelie Lundahl [Aug.–Sept. 1881]

To our father Lundahl and our mother Emelie. We wonder very much how you are; we are well. Yohannis, however, has long been ill. When we went to Shewa, we stayed a week at the Abbay without being able to cross, but then we gave one thaler and crossed. When we had crossed, our belongings were examined, and they took our saw from us. We were allowed to keep the other things.

The reason why we left Agewmidir is this: When we were sitting and teaching children, *Abba* Welde Gīyorgīs, a priest, came in order to Christianize the Mohammedans by forcing them to [accept] baptism. Then the priests accused us and he said: "Bring them", and then we were brought to him. "Why do you say that Mary and the saints do not intercede for us; why do you eat during the fast?" he said and fettered us in iron for five days. "Whether Abyssinians or Galla, we teach them. You are not allowed to do so." And then they took our books.

Then we went to Shewa, as we had heard that the missionary Mayer had received a district in Galla and freedom to work [there]. So, we decided to go to them, and went.

From Agewmidir to the Abbay is four days' journey. Very lovely country! From the Abbay to Ballī, Mayer's station, seventeen days' journey. Christ got us through safely. From Ankober to Ballī, four days. It is situated at the border of Minīlik's kingdom. He often comes into Galla and kills.

O our father, do not forget us in [your] prayers! Tell your children and brothers to pray for us. The German brothers received us with joy. They still had no houses, but they gave us a tent, where we still live. We have been here two months. In Agewmidir, I took myself a wife, after having conferred with the brothers. Her name is Mihiret and she can read the Bible. A respected person named Meharī accompanied us with his wife – persecuted as we are.

Yohannis has much pain in his body. He suffers so that he cries day and night. He has been ill four months. Pray for him. Mayer and Greiner said that Lundahl has written to us and asked if he could send missionaries here. Therefore, we stay until you write further to us. We are building ourselves a house here, and Greiner has helped us cut [trees] for timber.

Greet all the brothers, big and small, each one by his [own] name. O my brothers, when we stood fettered in front of the high priest, we recalled the word of Christ, which he told his disciples, Matthew 10, 16–18.

The grace of Our Lord Jesus Christ be with you.
Nigusē, Amanu'ēl, Yohannis, Ēlsabēṭ.

EFS, E I 24, 173a–d, Swedish translation incorporated in a letter dated 2 Oct. 1881, from B. P. Lundahl to J. Neander at mission headquarters in Stockholm. Since Nigusē's and Amanu'ēl's letter has first travelled from Ballī, a Protestant mission station in Oromo to Imkullu, our dating is obviously very tentative. The writers of the letter are Nigusē Tasho and Amanu'ēl Hamed, both mentioned by Lundahl as the authors. The blessing, however, comes from all four. Amanu'ēl was an Oromo Muslim who had been baptized by the Swedish missionaries in 1872 and Nigusē was an Oromo merchant who entered the Swedish mission service in 1877. They had been ordained as evangelists and sent to the Oromo people in November the same year. Yohannis was their assistant and Ēlsabēṭ Amanu'ēl's wife. For details about the authors and their activities see *Evangelical Pioneers*, pp. 234–238 and 243–248.

Document no. 56

Welde Ṣadiq to Umberto I, 4 Sept. [?] 1881

I raise my hands, wishing you good health in the name of the Saviour of the world. I pray to God that he will save your kingdom that is so honoured and has done so much good for the realm of Shewa.

I have received the most beautiful and precious revolver, sent to me by the Italian Geographical Society through the travelling geographer, the illustrious Captain Martini, as a sign of his highly desired friendship. And when I, Your Majesty's slave, unworthy of polishing your shoes, thought of the great gift you sent me, I took immense pleasure in it. As I lack something worthy of Your Majesty to let you know my love and gratitude, I [nevertheless] send you something from my country, i.e. a ceremonial garment (*lemd*), which a warrior of great merit usually dresses in, and a buffalo horn, which our *dejjazmach*, or army general, usually drinks from, in the hope that you will receive it as if it were a great gift, since it is a sign of my most sincere friendship and veneration. So I hope that your affection for me, your slave, and for my master, a great friend of Your Majesty, will always keep increasing and that the agreement that has been made about the rifles with Count Antonelli will be accomplished. Then my king will be satisfied in all his plans, helped by Your Majesty, and God will bless you.

I beg Your Majesty to receive the gift I send you through Captain Cecchi, sent out by this Geographical Society. I for my part will not fail to show every consideration I can for the representatives of the Society that remain here and for those that will come later on.

Written at Ankober the 30th of August 1873 (according to the Julian calendar).

Azzazh Welde Ṣadiq.

ASMAI 36/1–6, fols 107–108, Italian translation of a supposedly Amharic original. The date is confusing in the sense that we cannot know with certainty whether "30 agosto" refers to the Gregorian or the Julian calendar. Concluding from the reference to the Julian calendar and the year 1873 we have read "30 agosto" as 30 Nehasē and converted the whole date to 4 September 1881. The indication that this letter was sealed, "loro sigilli" (their seals), is confusing. If a sealed original of this letter has existed, it is hard to understand why it should have had more than one seal. In a document of Jan. 1875 (*Acta* II, doc. 125), *Azzazh* Welde Ṣadiq is referred to as the "minister of the king's palace". He was apparently closely involved in the work of the Italian explorers. See also docs 82, 136, 147 and 161.

Document no. 57

Yohannis IV to Welde Sema'it Welde Yohannis and the Ethiopian community in Jerusalem, 5 Sept. 1881

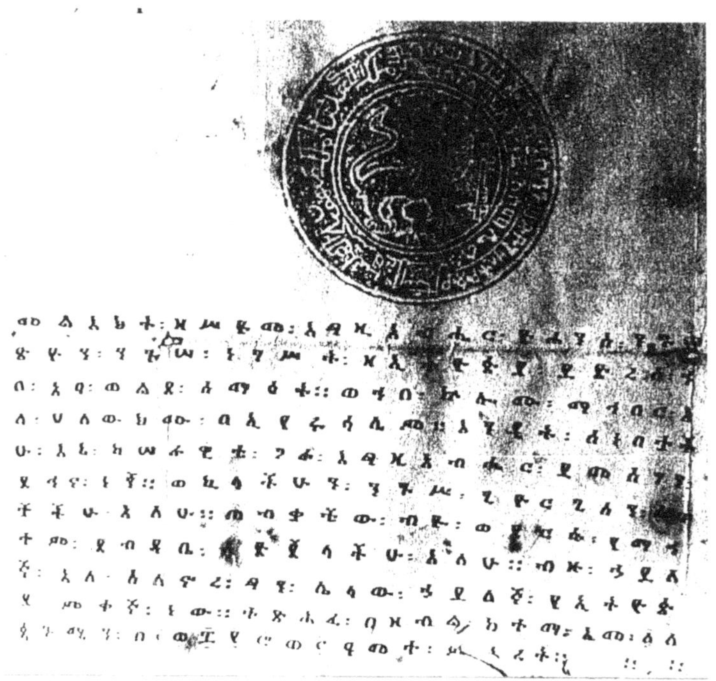

Seal: King of Kings Yohannis, King of Zion in Ethiopia. The cross has defeated the tribe of Isma'ēl. Yūḥannā, King of Kings of Zion in Abyssinia. The cross has defeated the people of Ismā'īl. 1864.

May the message of the Elect of God Yohannis, King of Zion, King of Kings of Ethiopia, reach *Abba* Welde Sema'it and all you [members of] the community, who live in Jerusalem.

How have you been? I, together with my army, am well, thank God. I have given you King George (*Nigus* Giyorgīs) as your representative (*wekīl*). As there are many trouble-makers, I have sent him a sealed letter, saying "protect them for me". One of the powerful persons, however, is an enemy of Ethiopia.

Written at the town of Zobil on the 1st of Ṗagumē in the year of grace 1873.

Dayr al-Sultan, no. 8, Amharic/Gi'iz original. Printed with English translation in *Chronicle*, no. 8, pp. 168–171, where the king is called "Welde Gīyorgīs". Probably Yohannis is referring to King George of Greece who, being so much closer to Jerusalem, had better opportunities to protect the Ethiopians there than Yohannis. But we have not been able to find any letter that fits the letter mentioned here.

Document no. 58

Isṭīfanos Fisseha to Mekonnin, 15 Sept. [1881?]

May [this letter] reach *Ato* Mekonnin. How have you passed the rainy season? I am well, thank God. I have sold six *tabots*. I still am left with one *tabot*. At the end of Meskerem I shall arrive in Egypt. I have sold all my goods.

May [God] enable *Abba* Kīrillus to live for a thousand years. That woman, the sister of Mary, is coming with (lit. having) a certificate.

I present many greetings in a (one word incomprehensible) written letter.

Written at the town of Asmera, on 6th Meskerem.

As there are those who want seven marble *tabots*, you and I ought to act as partners. There is much profit in it. We [sell] the small cheap, the big ones dear.

So says Isṭīfanos Fisseha [from] Gura‘.

Stephanos Fessaha.

Ghali Collection, no. 54, Amharic text. We have not been able to identify the author nor the addressee. Apparently he was well connected with the church in Egypt and trading in *tabots*. The handwriting is almost illegible in some places; thus, the translation must be regarded as tentative. Though writing to a countryman, Isṭīfanos apparently wanted to show that he could use the Latin alphabet.

Document no. 59

Onesimus Nesib to Johannes Neander, 23 Sept. 1881

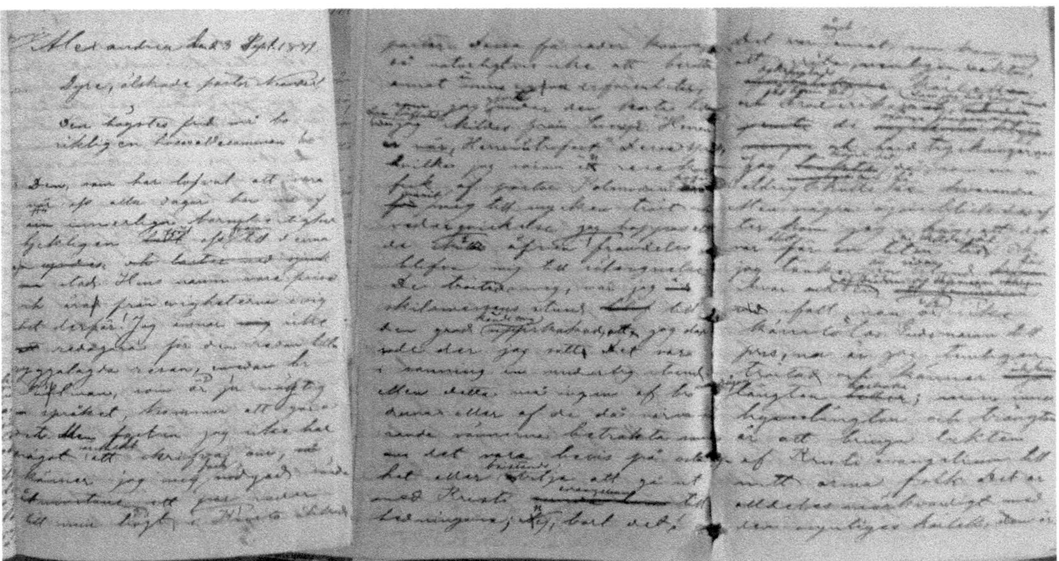

Alexandria 23rd Sept. 1881

Dear, beloved Pastor Neander,

May the peace of the Highest be abundantly with us all.

He who has promised to be near us every day has now in his compassion brought us safely to this town. His name be praised and honoured from ages of eternity for this. I do not intend to give an account of the journey already covered, as brother Påhlman who is capable of the language will do that. But although I do not have anything in particular to write about, I do, however, feel compelled to send at least a couple of lines to my pastor highly beloved in Christ. These few lines will not of course tell other than my own experiences which I have met with during the short time which has passed since I was separated from Sweden. "The lord is near, the lord is faithful". These sayings which I received as provisions for the journey from Pastor Kolmodin have been much comfort and refreshment. I hope that they will be a blessing to me in the future as well. They consoled me when I in the moment of separation felt so upset that I was shaking where I sat. It was in truth a remarkable moment. But may none of the brothers or the friends present regard this as if it was a sign of uncertainty or failing desire to proceed with the gospel of Christ to the heathen.

No, God forbid! It was something else which made me weep, namely all the pure ingenuous love, and the evidence of brotherhood, which I was given the opportunity to experience, and the many hugs and shaking of hands. I felt then as if we never more would see each other. But some moments later I remembered that it was only for a short period we were separated here. And I believe that each and every one of the brothers will experience such a moment at separation, unless they are without feelings.

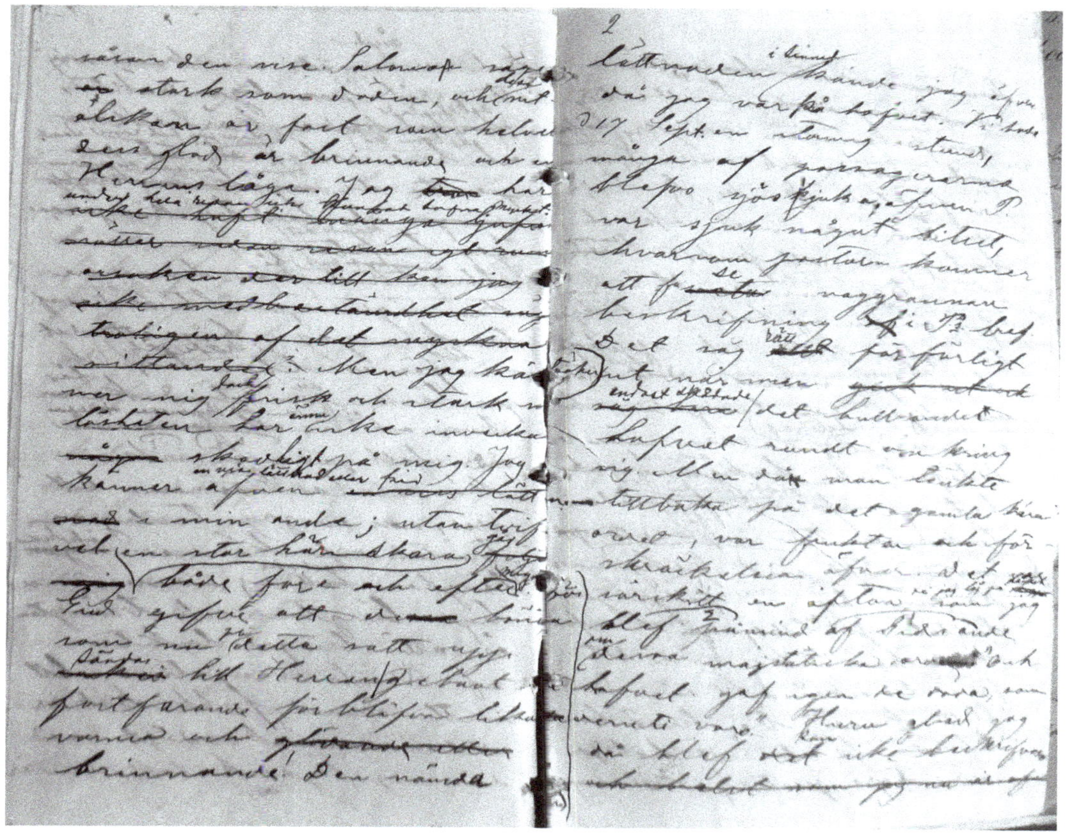

The name of God be praised, I am now quite comforted and do not feel any longing to go; my yearning and wish is to bring the savour of the gospel of Christ to my poor people. It is very strange with the love of the Unseen; it is as the wise Solomon says: “strong as death, and its jealousy as solid as hell, its ardour is burning and a flame of the Lord.”

I have not been able to sleep much during the whole journey. I do, however, feel healthy and strong, and the sleeplessness has not yet affected me. I also feel a certain relief and peace in my spirit; an army of hosts is no doubt both before and after me. God grant that the prayers that are now in this way sent to the Lord Sabaoth will remain strong and burning! I felt the mentioned relief in my mind also while being at sea. 17 September, we had a stormy moment. Many of the passengers were seasick, and P. was also a little ill, about which the Pastor will hear a more detailed description in P.’s letter. Only seeing the rumbling ocean on all sides, it looked quite frightful. But thinking back on the dear words, the fear and the fright was over. Particularly one evening, when I was lying on deck, I was reminded by the Spirit of God of these majestic words: “And the sea gave up the dead which were in it.” The joy I then felt, cannot be described. However, the waters, as the psalmist says, roared and were troubled, but we did not fear since God, our God, was with us and chased away all fear through his blessed presence – and consequently we now want to praise and exalt His Holy Name with all our heart.

Nevertheless, the longest and most difficult part of the journey still remains, but we do not need to be worried with restless thoughts about the future; instead we may throw all our worries on the Lord.

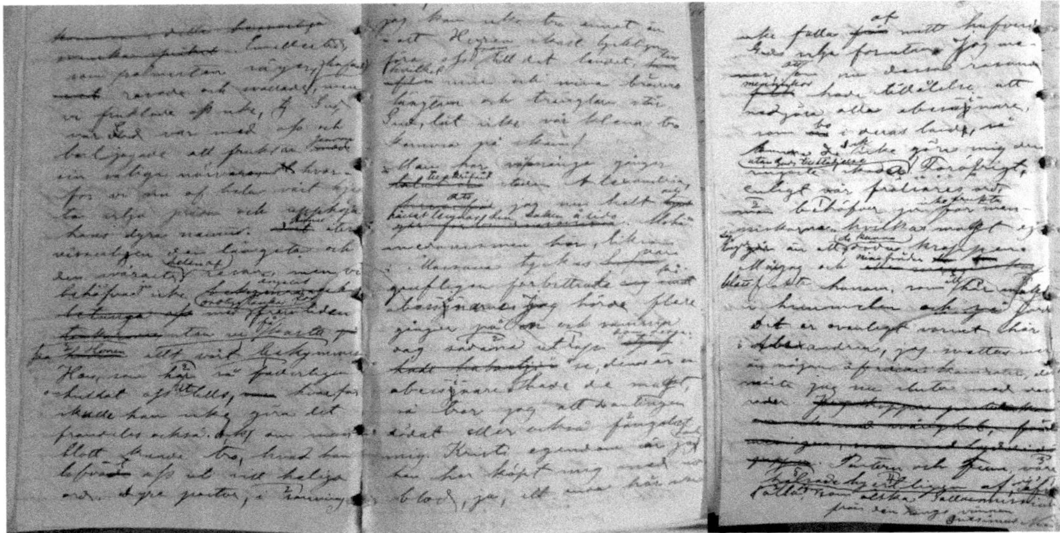

He who has in such a fatherly manner cared for us until now, why should he not do that in the future as well. Oh! if one could only believe what he has promised us in His Holy Word. Dear Pastor, I can honestly not believe other than that the Lord shall bring us happily all the way to the land to which my and my brothers' longing and desire stands. God, do not let our weak faith come to nought.

The city Alexandria has been described so many times that I now leave that matter entirely aside. The Mohammedans here, just the same as in Massawa, seem to be terribly angry with the Abyssinians. I heard several times on the same day exclamations like the following: "Look! This man is an Abyssinian." If they had power, I believe that they would either have killed or imprisoned me. However, I am the property of Christ, He has bought me with His blood, yes not a single hair shall fall from my head without God's will. I mean that if these furious people had permission to cut down all Abyssinians who live in their land, would they nevertheless be able to do me the least harm without the permission of God? Besides, according to the words of Our Saviour, one does not need to fear men whose power does not extend further than that they can kill the body. Be it so that I and my brother fear him alone who has all power in heaven and on earth.

It is unusually warm here in Alexandria. I sweat more than any of the others, so I must now finish with these lines.

The Pastor and [his] wife, as well as all others who love the mission to the Galla, be cordially greeted from the humble friend,

Onesimus Nesib.

EFS, E I 24, Swedish original. Onesimus Nesib was an Oromo who had been sold as a slave, liberated by Werner Munzinger and entrusted to the Swedish mission at the age of fourteen in 1870. He was baptized two years later. In 1876 he was sent to Sweden where he studied at a theological training institute until September 1881. This letter reports on his journey back, but also on his thoughts about the forthcoming mission to his own Oromo people. See further *Evangelical Pioneers*, pp. 164–167 and 249–251. Pastor Kolmodin refers to the Swedish theologian, Adolf Kolmodin, who taught at Johannelunds Theological seminary when Onesimus studied there. He was the father of the Ethiopianist scholar and later adviser of *Ras* Teferi, Johannes Kolmodin.

As a rule we have turned to the King James' version for quotations from the Bible. The Swedish text of the above letter, however, differs so much from the King James' version that a literal translation seems preferable in this particular case.

Document no. 60

Minīlik II to Onorato Caetani, 9 Oct. 1881

May [the] message, sent by King Minīlik, by the grace of God King of Shewa, reach the President of the Italian Geographical Society.

How are you? By the grace of God I am well and all my army is well.

I intend to send an order to Count Antinori to leave with all his people. As the letter arrived the very day of the departure of Captain Cecchi, and I had much business waiting with Count Antinori, for this reason, I have forbidden Count Antinori to leave until we have finished our business. Thus, since I have forbidden him to leave, I hope that you are not feeling anxious about him (alt. do not think evil of him.) Otherwise, being a respected elderly gentleman, who has the witness of everyone about what he has done (lit. pro e contro), this seems a very just case; and therefore, do not reprimand me for making him wait.

Written at Ankober, the 9th of October 1874 (Julian calendar).

Place of the seal.

ASSGI, busta 20, fasc. 5, fol. 5, Italian translation of a supposedly Amharic original. It cannot be taken for granted that the day and the name of the month should be understood according to the Ethiopian calendar even if it is indicated that the year, in this case 1874, is according to the Julian calendar. We have come to the conclusion that the day and month here may just as well be Gregorian and have only converted "1874" to 1881. This is supported by the fact that "9 ottobre" is clearly written in the handwriting of the letter itself while the year 1874 seems to have been added in a different hand. Moreover 1881 has been added at the bottom of the document without bothering about "9 ottobre". For Antinori, see doc. 20.

Document no. 61

Minīlik II to Umberto I, 14 Oct. 1881

Letter written by Minīlik, King of Shewa, to His Majesty Umberto I, by the power of God King of Italy.

[Your] Majesty,

Because of the friendship which I had with your venerated and amiable father [and because of] my friendship with Your Majesty and your [agent] who has come to me as a consequence, I give to the learned men of Italy a place in which to rest and live called Liṭ Marefīya, where the invited persons from the Italian Geographical Society can stay in peace; and because of this I ordered all my subjects and officials to receive them and to respect them as they are entitled to be. If the two invited persons from the Italian Geographical Society who have departed for the South are not successful with regard to the outcome of their travels, the fault is not mine. Your Majesty should know, and that is what I have written to your father, the king, namely that I will not be able to protect them outside my kingdom, whatever evil might happen to them. Now I have heard to my great dismay the news that fourteen Italians have been betrayed in the dependency of the kingdom of Awsa; and that your government is sending a warship with soldiers to punish the assassins. I for my part intended to descend and help to destroy the guilty. Because of what the government of Italy has already begun by this expedition, I am prepared for everything. I shall descend or send soldiers to Aseb to receive the rifles which Count Antonelli should bring to me, and on this trip I expect that they shall be able to speak about the exchange of merchandise between the land of Shewa and that of Italy. This could be an affair of great advantage to both countries.

Your Majesty should know that on my side I shall do everything to instruct my people well. I have already communicated another matter, which is to abolish the trade in slaves who come from Kefa and to prevent the slave-traders from passing through any longer.

Your Majesty, I love Italy and respect its king, however in order that our relations shall become strong it is necessary that the government of Italy makes a treaty of friendship and commerce with us. Five years have already passed, during which Count Antinori has stayed in my country, where he is much loved. If Your Majesty consents, I wish that Count Antinori might continue to remain there as before as the head of the geographical expedition, with the addition of a [consular] representative, who can finish all issues and conclude the treaties and conventions which might be required with the government of Italy. For this purpose it is not necessary to send another person. Your Majesty should be able to do me this favour for the good of the two countries in agreement with the president of the Geographical Society.

With regard to the blood shed on the borders of the kingdom of Awsa, I have sent a messenger to investigate if this king really has the intention to come to an agreement about restitution for the Italian blood, as he has informed me. This done, which I am waiting for with impatience, I shall come down with my soldiers resolved to give Italy proof of the very particular friendship which I have always harboured until this day, and a token of my recognition and love.

May God meanwhile preserve you for a long time for the welfare of your country.

Written at Debre Birhan, 5th October 1874 (Julian calendar).

ASMAI 36/1–6, fols 109–111, Italian translation. For the date, see note at doc. 48. We once located the Amharic original in ASMAI 1/3–17, but the document seems later to have been misplaced. At any rate we have not been able to acquire a copy for publication in this volume. For Minīlik s earlier contacts with Umberto and his father Victor Emmanuel II, see *Acta* III, docs 165, 187, 208 and 211.

Document no. 62

Yohannis IV to Victoria, 4 Nov. 1881

Seal: King of Kings Yohannis, King of Zion in Ethiopia. The cross has defeated the tribe of Isma'ēl. Yūḥannā, King of Kings of Zion in Abyssinia. The cross has defeated the people of Ismā'īl. 1864.

May the message of the Elect of God Yohannis, King of Zion, King of Kings of Ethiopia, reach Queen Victoria, by the grace of God queen of the United Kingdom of [Great Britain and] Ireland, defender of the faith, the queen of India and all its dependencies. How have you been, really, since I [last] wrote to you? I, together with my army, am well. May God, the God of the righteous, be honoured and praised. Your honoured letter, with its seal, has reached me. The peace agreement with the Turks has not been settled for me.

An envoy called Gordon Pasha came. He started saying he would have me reconciled. Because his words were not acceptable to me, we parted disagreeing; I have not demarcated the borders of my country; I have not obtained a port on the sea coast.

Until I get your permission, I remain without doing anything still suffering from the injustice. Now, however, I have obtained a bishop by sending gold, according to the ancient custom. As for the gifts, let alone when there is a reason, even in the midst of war, gifts can be exchanged. Now too, since you are someone who has, since long ago, been concerned about my kingdom, settle my affairs by enabling me to get a port on the sea coast, by enabling me to demarcate the domain of my fathers, the boundaries of Ethiopia. If this cannot take place, I do not mind, as long as I have your permission. So send me a reply.

Written in the town of Meqelē on 26th Ṭiqimt in the year of grace 1874 (?).

FO 95/740, nos. 82–83, Amharic original and English translation. The letter is a reply to a letter from Victoria dated March 8, 1881, in response to Yohannis' letter dated 29 April 1880 (doc. 5). For the circumstances of this letter and the following, see *Survival*, pp. 347–351.

Document no. 63

Yohannis IV to Jules Grévy, 4 Nov. 1881

Seal: King of Kings Yohannis, King of Zion in Ethiopia. The cross has defeated the tribe of Isma'ēl. Yūḥannā, King of Kings of Zion in Abyssinia. The cross has defeated the people of Ismā'īl. 1864.

May this message from the Elect of God, Yohannis, King of Zion, King of Kings of Ethiopia, reach the appointee over the French government, the exalted and honoured Jules Grévy. How are you really since I wrote to you last? I, with my army, by the graciousness of God – may the Lord of the saints be praised and honoured – am well, since His mercy is forever. I received your respected letter with its seal, written on Yekkatīt 10. I also received from the hands of the French consul Raffray 12 rifles, 2 pistols and 4 swords which you have sent as a sign of friendship. Thank you. Regarding my reconciliation with the Turks, a man called Gordon *Pasha*, who claims to be sent to make the reconciliation, came earlier, and as he disagreed with me, we parted after quarrelling. However, there is nothing I agreed to (lit. made reconciliation) with the Turks. And now, as customary, I have sent gold and had a bishop brought. Concerning the gift, apart from there being a good reason, it is normal to have an exchange of goods even between parties at war. But if I get reconciled it will be through you, the king, or after they have evacuated my land, [which] they have occupied demarcating their and my borders. Otherwise, am I so easy to become reconciled with? And now, please finalize as soon as possible the case of the reconciliation. However, if this becomes impossible, I would like to get the permission of you, the kings.

Please send me the response through the French consul Raffray. Regarding the messenger, since he is an envoy of the palace, I have received him humbly and with respect. I gave him an engraved golden metal cuff, a golden scabbard, a golden sword, golden lion fur, a horse-cloth, a shemma with fringes, [a medal of] the seal of Solomon.

Written in the town of Meqelē, on 26th Ṭiqimt in the year of grace 1874 (4th November 1881).

AEMD, Afrique 62, Abyssinie 3, fol. 538, Amharic original. Like others, this document was sent to Antoine d'Abbadie for translation (BN, Abb. 254, no. 281). When returned to the Ministère des Affaires Étrangères, it was placed upside down in the bound volume.

Document no. 64

Yohannis IV to Minīlik II, 6 Dec. 1881

መልእክት ፡ ዘሥዩመ ፡ እግዚአብሔር ፡ ዮሐንስ ፡ ንጉሠ ፡ ጽዮን ፡ ንጉሠ ፡ ነገሥት ፡ ዘኢትዮጵያ ። ይድረስ ፡ ከንጉሥ ፡ ምኒልክ ፡ በአማን ፡ እስራኤላዊ ፡ ዘአልቦ ፡ ጽልሑት ። ሰላም ፡ ለከ ፡ ወሰላመ ፡ እግዚአብሔር ፡ የሃሉ ፡ ምስሌከ ፤ እኔ ፡ በእግዚአብሔር ፡ ቸርነት ፤ በእምነ ፡ ጽዮን ፡ አማላጅነት ፡ አምላከ ፡ ቅዱሳን ፡ ይክበር ፡ ይመስገን ፡ ደኅና ፡ ነኝ ። ምሕረቱ ፡ ለዘለዓለም ፡ ነውና ። ደብዳቤውም ፡ ደረሰኝ ። ለንጉሥ ፡ ተክለ ፡ ሃይማኖት ፡ ከዚህ ፡ በፊትም ፡ ልኬአለሁ ፡ እንግዴህም ፡ እሺ ፡ እልክለሁ ። ደግሞ ፡ ለየራሳችሁ ፡ አንዳንድ ፡ ሰው ፡ አለመስደዴም ፡ ወደ ፡ ሸዋ ፡ የሔደው ፡ ለሸዋ ። ወደ ፡ ጐጃም ፡ የሔደውም ፡ ለጐጃም ፡ ያደላልና ፡ ነገሩ ፡ አያምርም ፡ ብዬ ፡ ነው ። ነገር ፡ ግን ፡ አንድ ፡ ጳጳስ ፡ ሶስት ፡ ኤጲስ ፡ ቆጶሳት ፡ አራት ፡ ሁነው ፡ ሲወጡ ፡ በኢትዮጵያ ፡ ተደርጎ ፡ የማያውቅ ፡ ሐዲስ ፡ ነገር ፡ ሲደረግ ፡ የረከሰ ፡ በሚቀደስበት ፡ የተጣላ ፡ በሚታረቅበት ፡ ጊዜ ፡ እላንተ ፡ ትጣላላችሁን ። እኔም ፡ ለሠራዊቴ ፡ ስንቅ ፡ አሲይዝ ፡ ብዬ ፡ ነው ፡ እንጂ ፡ ምን ፡ አደርጋለሁ ፤ ይኸው ፡ መጣሁ ፡ ተነሥቼአለሁ ። ሲሆን ፡ ወይ ፡ ከዋድላ ፡ ወይ ፡ ከቤጌምድር ፡ ላይ ፡ ከእኔ ፡ ስንገናኝ ፡ አለያያችኋለሁ ፤ አትቸኩሉ ፡ እስክመጣ ፡ ድረስ ፡ ቆዩ ። የቸኮላችሁ ፡ እንደ ፡ ሆነ ፡ ግን ፡ ካለሁበት ፡ ድረስ ፡ እየራሳችሁ ፡ የሚለያይ ፡ አንድ ፡ አንድ ፡ ሰው ፡ ስደዱ ። የሚመጣው ፡ ሰው ፡ ግን ፡ በጥንቱ ፡ ውሉ ፡ ተጋጥሞ ፡ የሚለያይ ፡ ነው ። ተጽሕፈ ፡ በመቀሌ ፡ ከተማ ፡ አመ ፡ ፳ ወ፰ ፡ ለኅዳር ፡ በ፲ ወ፰፻፸ ወ፬ ዓመተ ፡ ምሕረት ።

A message of the Elect of God Yohannis, King of Zion, King of Kings of Ethiopia.

May it reach King Minīlik, an Israelite indeed, in whom there is no guile. Peace be to you and the peace of God be with you.

By the grace of God and the intercession of our mother Ṣiyon, may the God of the saints be honoured and praised, I am well. For His mercy is forever.

The letter has reached me. I have written to King Tekle Haymanot earlier and, yes, I will write also in the future. Furthermore, the reason why I did not send one person for each of you is because I thought that the one who goes to Shewa would be partial to Shewa and the one who goes to Gojjam to Gojjam, and that the matter would not look good. However, when an archbishop and three bishops, four [in all], come, and when something new that has never been done in Ethiopia is done, and when the defiled should be blessed and the quarrelling reconciled, how come that you quarrel?

As for me I now want to get hold of provisions for my army; what else have I to do? I shall come; I have started. I will have you reconciled when we meet either in Wadla or in Begēmdir. Don't hurry; wait until I come. If, however, [both of] you are in a hurry send a man each at the place where I am, who should reconcile you. However, the man that should come [to me] should be a man who remains firm on former terms to make peace.

Written in the town of Meqelē on 28th Hidar in the year of grace 1874.

Tarīke Negest, p. 56, Addis Abeba [1936], printed Amharic text. For the reference to "an Israelite indeed, in whom there is no guile", see doc. 27.

Document no. 65

Lewṭē Zewde to Kīrillus V, 9 Jan. 1882

The holy God, the sacred Father, the all-benevolent, he who is full of virtue, of the seat of the Coptic church of Alexandria, the slave of the Lord, son of St. Mark, the apostle in the land of Alexandria which is called the land of all the apostles and which lives under the umbrella of the Jacobites and the firm foundation of Abyssinia, the fourth of the evangelists and the second most beloved of the apostles, the father and benevolent *Abba* Kīrillus, patriarch of the see of St. Mark. May He prolong his life.

After greetings and prostration (lit. under your feet), and reception of your blessing from your respected hands, we pray always that you may live in peace for a long time. Indeed, that this has taken such a long time is because we wished to have it in the mind of Your Holiness, since we are your sons and you will forgive us. If there is a wrong or sin that we have committed, the Deity, the Son of the living God, who is wanted by all, has given you the key to redeem the wanted ones from among the unwanted and to turn as your sons the kings that have committed sins.

And we implore you that you visit your son with your fatherly zeal, with your peaceful power, and bless and absolve the sins of our wives and sons. May the Lord prolong your potential with long life with all justice. Amen. And now we have sent to your holiness by the hands of my father *Qumuṣ* Mīka'ēl, and for the sake of your beloved son Tamru, presents of two bells for the church. May the Lord prolong your life for our sake.

Your son the *bejirond*, the treasurer of the king (one word illegible)
The year 1598, 2 Ṭuba. (one word illegible) 58
Bejirond Lewṭē.

Seal: The seal of *Bejirond* Lewṭē.

Ghali Collection, no. 156. Arabic original. This Arabic text has been extremely difficult to decipher and understand, thus the above translation must be regarded as a paraphrase. For the author, see doc. 24.

Document no. 66

Yohannis IV to Minīlik II, 15 Jan. 1882

መልእክት ፡ ዘሥዩመ ፡ እግዚአብሔር ፡ ዮሐንስ ፡ ንጉሠ ፡ ጽዮን ፡ ንጉሠ ፡ ነገሥት ፡ ዘኢትዮጵያ ። ይድረስ ፡ ከንጉሥ ፡ ምኒልክ ። በአማን ፡ እስራኤላዊ ፡ ዘአልቦ ፡ ጽልሁት ። ሰላም ፡ ለከ ፡ ወሰላመ ፡ እግዚአብሔር ፡ የሃሉ ፡ ምስሌከ ፡ እኔ ፡ በእግዚአብሔር ፡ ቸርነት ፡ በእናችን ፡ ጽዮን ፡ አማላጅነት ፡ አምላከ ፡ ቅዱሳን ፡ ይክበር ፡ ይመስገን ፡ ደህና ፡ ነኝ ። ምሕረቱ ፡ ለዘለዓለም ፡ ነውና ።

ደብዳቤውም ፡ ደረሰኝ ። ከዚህ ፡ በፊትም ፡ የሁለታችሁን ፡ መልእክት ፡ በደብዳቤ ፡ አመላልሳለሁ ። አትጣሉብኝ ፡ ተፋቀሩልኝ ። እንደ ፡ ሽማግሌ ፡ እንደ ፡ እናት ፡ እንደ ፡ አባት ፡ እመክራለሁ ፡ አገለግላለሁ ፡ እንጂ ፤ እንደ ፡ ንጉሥ ፡ ይህ ፡ ይሁን ፡ ብዬ ፡ ያዘዝሁት ፡ ነገር ፡ የለኝም ። አሁንም ፡ የአሕዛብና ፡ የሰይጣን ፡ መሳለቂያ ፡ እንዳንሆን ፡ ከባሕር ፡ ወዲህ ፤ ከባሕር ፡ ወዲያ ፡ ብዙ ፡ ጠላት ፡ ሳለን ፡ እርስ ፡ በርሳችን ፡ ብንዋጋ ፤ የክርስቲያን ፡ ደም ፡ በከንቱ ፡ ቢፈስ ፡ ለክርስቶስ ፡ ደስ ፡ አይለውም ። አሁንም ፡ የሁለታችሁ ፡ ጦር ፡ አይገናኝ ፤ ከተገናኘ ፡ ዘንድ ፡ ከመዋጋት ፡ ይደርሳል ። እኔ ፡ እስክመጣ ፡ ድረስ ፡ ታገሡልኝ ፤ ጦራችሁ ፡ በያለበት ፡ ይቆይ ። ደግሞ ፡ እኔ ፡ ፊቴን ፡ ወደ ፡ ትግሬ ፡ ብመልስ ፡ በወረ ፡ ባቦ ፤ ባርጎብ ፡ በወሎ ፤ ብዙ ፡ ነገር ፡ ይደረጋል ፤ ማተቡን ፡ ይቆርጣል ፡ ሲሉ ፡ እሰማለሁ ፡ ከቀድሞውም ፡ ያጠፉ ፡ ያባ ፡ ዋጠው ፡ ምክር ፡ ይሆንን ፡ ብዬ ፡ ነበር ። አሁንም ፡ ቢመከርበት ፡ ይሻላል ። ነገር ፡ ግን ፡ እኔ ፡ ባጠፋው ፡ ቸግሮኝ ፡ አይደለም ፡ ከወንድሜ ፡ ጋራ ፡ እንዳልከፋፋ ፡ ብዬ ፡ ነው ፡ እንጂ ። ተጽሕፈ ፡ በጭኒ ፡ ሰፈር ፡ አመ ፡ ፰ለጥር ፡ በ፲ወ፰፻፸ወ፬ ፡ ዓመተ ፡ ምሕረት ።

May the message of the Elect of God Yohannis, King of Zion, King of Kings of Ethiopia, reach King Minīlik, an Israelite indeed, in whom there is no guile. Peace be to you and the peace of God be with you.

By the grace of God and the intercession of Our Mother Zion – may the God of the saints be honoured and praised – I am well, since his mercy is forever.

The letter has reached me. Earlier I have answered both of your messages by letters: "Please, do not quarrel, love one another." I advise and serve as an elder, as a mother, as a father but it is not something that I ordered you, like a king saying "Have this done". And now let us not be the target (?) of the mockery of gentiles and of Satan. As we have many enemies on this side of the sea and from the other side, if we fight against one another and if Christian blood is shed in vain Christ will not be happy.

And now let not the armies of you two meet. If they meet it will come to fighting. Please, have patience until I come. Let your armies stay where they are. Besides, if I turn my face towards Tigrē many things will happen in Werre Babo, in Argobba and in Wello. I hear [people] saying that the neckband (*mateb*) will be cut; they will become Muslims. I was saying, "Can it be the lost advice of *Abba* Waṭew?" And now it is better if it is discussed. However, it is not that it would have been difficult for me to destroy him but [I have no desire] to be on bad terms with my brother.

Written in the camp of Çhinī on 8th Ṭirr in the year of grace 1874.

Tarīke Negest, p. 56, Addis Abeba [1936], printed Amharic text.

Document no. 67

Yohannis IV to Tekle Haymanot, 30 Jan. 1882

መልእክት ፡ ዘሥዩመ ፡ እግዚአብሔር ፡ ዮሐንስ ፡ ንጉሠ
ጽዮን ፤ ንጉሠ ፡ ነገሥት ፡ ዘኢትዮጵያ ። ይድረስ ፡ ከንጉሥ ፡
ተክለ ፡ ሃይማኖት ፡ በአማን ፡ እስራኤላዊ ፡ ዘአልቦ ፡ ጽል
ሁት ፤ ሰላም ፡ ለከ ፡ ወሰላመ ፡ እግዚአብሔር ፡ የሃሉ ፡ ምስ
ሌከ ። እኔ ፡ በእግዚአብሔር ፡ ቸርነት ፤ በእምነ ፡ ጽዮን ፡
አማላጅነት ፡ አምላከ ፡ ቅዱሳን ፡ ይክበር ፡ ይመስገን ፡ ደ
ህና ፡ ነኝ ፤ ምሕረቱ ፡ ለዘለዓለም ፡ ነውና ።

ደብዳቤውም ፡ ደረሰኝ ፡ እኔም ፡ የሁለታችሁን ፡ ነገር ፡
እየሰማሁ ፡ መከራ ፡ እየተቀበልሁ ፡ ተቀምጫለሁ ። ነገር ፡
ግን ፡ ኢትማእ ፡ ለእኩይ ፡ በእኩይ ፤ አላ ፡ በገቢረ ፡ ሠናይ ፡
ነው ። እንኳን ፡ በቅርብ ፡ ያለውን ፡ ጠላቴን ፡ በሩቅ ፡ እ
ንኳን ፡ ያለውን ፡ ጠላቴን ፡ እግዚአብሔር ፡ በቸርነቱ ፡ ይ
ጎዳልኛል ፡ እንጂ ፡ እኔ ፡ አልጎዳውም ። አሁንም ፡ መ
ግፋት ፡ ክፉ ፡ ነው ፡ እንጂ ፤ የተገፋ ፡ ሰው ፡ ምን ፡ ተጐድ
ቶ ፡ ያውቃል ። ለሁሉም ፡ እኔ ፡ ወደዚያው ፡ መጣሁ ፡ ሁ
ሉም ፡ ስንገናኝ ፡ ይሆናል ። ተጽሕፈ ፡ በአድዋ ፡ ከተማ ፡
አመ ፡ ፳ወ፫ ለጥር ፡ በ፲ወ፰፻፸ወ፬ ዓመተ ፡ ምሕረት ።

May the message of the Elect of God Yohannis, King of Zion, King of Kings of Ethiopia, reach King Tekle Haymanot, an Israelite indeed, in whom there is no guile.

Peace be to you and the peace of God be with you.

By the grace of God and the intercession of Our Mother Ṣiyon, may the God of the saints be honoured and praised, I am well, since his mercy lasts forever. I have received the letter. Having heard the case of both of you I remain anticipating trouble. But since it is said "Do not overcome evil with evil, but by doing good", let alone [against] my enemy who is near by; but even he who is far away, not I but God, by His grace, takes steps on my behalf. And now it is bad to do wrong; I do not act wrongly. For a wronged person has never been disadvantaged. Anyway I am coming there. Everything will be done when we meet.

Written in the town of Adwa on 23rd Ṭirr in the year of grace 1874.

Tarīke Negest, pp. 56–57, Addis Abeba [1936], printed Amharic text. The messenger carrying this letter is also said to have been entrusted with an oral message from Minīlik intended for Tekle Haymanot. It has been preserved in Hiruy's book as follows: "Why do you always humiliate me? Some time ago you came in force and had my country Gojjam destroyed, and [then] left. And now again you have appointed people over the country of the Galla which I have brought under my control. Now after this I am coming; don't go away. Choose a place which you prepare in Haro, Jimma [or] Chelliya and wait for me in an open field. I am not sending this message in a letter believing that you would read it alone by yourself, tear it into pieces and throw it away, pretending not to have heard about it and run away. But if it is delivered orally and if you have heard and flee, your servants would make critical observations against you. It is for that reason that I have sent it orally."

Document no. 68

Yohannis IV, proclamation on the faith of *ferenj* [Jan. 1882]

Look here, I have brought you an *abun*. Approach him and receive his benediction. You have entered [into] a foreign creed, i.e. one different from mine, return; you have accepted the creed of the *ferenj*, return to the creed of your fathers, return to the *abun* and swear the oath to him, in order to make yourself liked and blessed by him . . .

If you say, "I will do nothing of [the kind]", know that your hand is at stake! [You will give] your hand to me and your property to your accuser.

AECPC, Massaouah 4, fol. 267, French translation. The person who has recorded this and the following two proclamations dated them "Vers le 10 Janvier", "Vers la fin du même mois" and "Le même jour" respectively. Whether he ever saw them in writing is impossible to know; indeed they may have been proclaimed orally, which may explain the lack of proper, solemn introductions and dates. In any case the proclamation is clearly addressed to Catholics. The last phrase indicates the punishment of having one hand cut off and the property handed back to the missionaries.

Document no. 69

Yohannis IV, proclamation on the practice of Islam [Jan. 1882]

You who were a Muslim I made a Christian three years ago; if you do not remember it, calculate yourself. But [in reality] you are a Christian only by day and exercise Muslim practices by night. You do not eat meat together with Christians, you do not partake of the Communion. Be a real Christian, come to the *abun* to be blessed, take a confessor, eat Christian meat . . . If you marry, marry a Christian girl, and do not give your daughter to anyone but a Christian. Whoever does not do [anything of] this, may he be killed like a Ṭilṭal or a Galla, and the killer may receive the insignia of an elephant killer.

AECPC, Massaouah 4, fol. 267, French translation. For the date, see doc. 68. The insignia of an elephant killer was reportedly a small silver chain rolled round the *mateb*, the blue ribbon of a Christian.

Document no. 70

Yohannis IV, proclamation on schismatics [Jan. 1882]

While I am bringing back the Muslims to Christianity, braggarts (*foucarotes*) and *ferenj* have come who say, "We are the ones who have the true creed, we are the ones who have the *abun*." Regard them and those who have the same creed as Muslims. If you find any of them, tell them: "Return to the creed of your fathers." If he refuses, do not bring him to me, I do not want to see him, shoot him like a Ṭilṭal and receive the insignia of the elephant killer.

Whoever uses tobacco, kill him likewise. . . .

AECPC, Massaouah 4, fol. 267, French translation, ending with four dots. For the date, see previous document. We have concluded that "*foucarotes*" is a form of the Amharic *fokkara*, "to brag, to boast". It is quite obvious from this text, if authentic, that Yohannis had as little sympathy for, or patience with, the European missionaries coming to Ethiopia as with propagators of Islam.

Document no. 71

Ar'aya Sillasē Dimṣu to Achille Raffray [Jan. 1882]

May the letter of *Ras* Ar'aya, a notable of the nation, reach the vice-consul of France

How are you? You are my representative (*wekil*); find what has been taken from me, and try to have it returned to me. Bichou has carried out your commission for me; you have acted well in this matter. O my son and my friend, you have begun; now finish it. Tell me what you want from my country. You have been of service to me, I shall not forget it. Continue to look for what belongs to me so that it will not be lost.

(His seal at the bottom.)

AECPC, Massaouah 4, fol. 270, French translation. No date, but assigned to January 1882 since it is preserved in the archive together with the two following documents. *Ras* Ar'aya served Yohannis successively as governor of Inderta, Akkele Guzay and Dembiya and was killed at the battle of Metemma in March 1889. We have not been able to find out who the person named Bichou was, nor what was the concern of the commission.

Document no. 72

Ar'aya Sillasē Dimṣu to Juan Víctor Abargues de Sostén [Jan. 1882]

Ras Ar'aya to his friend the consul of Spain.

How are you? I know the interest which you take in me. Thank you for the good message which you have sent me. It is full of hope for me. I do not ask for anything else but that the measures you take for the fulfilment of this promise will lead to the solution I desire. If His Highness the viceroy accepts my services, nothing but my name will be useful for him. If His Highness 'Alā' ad-Dīn *Pasha* tells me, in accordance with his orders, "We will gladly receive you in our ranks", let him just say how, and I will accept any condition. If he tells me, "Come to us", I will descend with the number of faithful soldiers he decides for me, be it few or many; all I have, or very few or even no one, whatever he wishes. If, on the contrary, he tells me, "Stay in the high country, until we tell you", I have an *amba*, Debre Mēla, near the Sahos where I can seek refuge and wait for his message, and pass the evil days before undertaking anything in union and agreement with you. But on this *amba* and during this time of waiting I cannot expect from anyone but you the supplies necessary for me and the men you tell me to keep. If our offers are not accepted, I ask of you, my lord, the consul, that the greatest secrecy as to the subject of my request be maintained. My head is at stake, and my defeat will be certain. I beg you to take the greatest possible precautions in communicating this to His Excellency 'Alā ad-Dīn *Pasha*, because in his entourage there are spies and informers who denounce me in front of Emperor Yohannis. If my plan is successful, I am assured of the consent of King Minīlik (Shewa) and King Tekle Haymanot (Gojjam) as soon as I have notified them. Above all I ask of you the greatest secrecy and the greatest precautions, especially if you doubt success. You understand why I do not write in Amharic, nor place my seal [here]. The roads are not safe.

AECPC, Massaouah 4, fol. 268, French translation. No date. In the archival copies the letter follows upon the proclamations above (docs 68–70) dated January 1882 and is thus assigned to January 1882. As stated, the letter was not written in Amharic, but it is impossible to know if the original was in Arabic or in a European language. Juan Víctor Abargues de Sostén had been sent by the Madrid Geographic Society to Ethiopia in 1881 with a letter from King Alfonso XII. A note on the document states that the letter was attached to a letter no. 1 to Abargues de Sostén, 1st April. This letter has not been found and it is impossible to know if the date refers to 1881 or 1882. It is obvious from the last words of this letter that Ar'aya was very anxious that his treason against his nephew, Yohannis IV, should not be discovered.

Document no. 73

Ar'aya Sillasē Dimṣu to Juan Víctor Abargues de Sostén [Jan. 1882]

Letter from *Ras* Ar'aya to his friend Abargues de Sostén, consul of Spain. How are you?

I have received the messenger whom you sent to me. Thank you for what you for friendship's sake have done for me with His Excellency 'Alā' ad-Dīn *Pasha.* The signed and sealed letter which you demand from me I am entirely disposed to send you, having absolute confidence in your friendship. But now the king's great spy, the most dangerous enemy of Egypt in Abyssinia, *Nā'ib* Muḥammad, has been sent and will arrive at Massawa to inform the king about everything that is happening, is being decided, plotted, or prepared at Massawa and overseas against Abyssinia. This man, who has been educated by Egypt and has not served anybody but Yohannis until this day, has associations that are kept most secret from the government, and by him I am sure to be denounced at once as soon as he is there so all planning is useless since he has in his hands all the secrets and will turn them all to the advantage of the king while at the same time appearing to serve his masters. The military and diplomatic failures of Egypt have no other cause. I am therefore obliged not to undertake anything compromising. And if the governor believed me, he would remove him or keep this spy of the king whom the Egyptian chiefs have been unlucky enough never to distrust under good guard (they have failed to follow this advice!).

Only 'Alā' ad-Dīn *Pasha*, this I know, will have understood, and it is no doubt because of this that the *Nā'ib* has worked so much against him with the king. I therefore and above all fear this man and it is this that forces me to be prudent. However, I understand that engagements are necessary where mutual oaths are given, but at the decisive moment when all is agreed upon it will be necessary to go into action. After this preliminary agreement, I am prepared to swear loyalty in the terms which you have sent me, but in a way less (word illegible) than [on] paper. So, by an intermediary in whom you have confidence I myself even said to your messenger, "Accept yourself my oath and convey it". If Egypt then wants to take up arms again, I am its man, and in that case I am prepared to sign an agreement and to place myself at the disposal of His Excellency. If it should begin with reprisals, I am prepared, at the first notice of the arrival of troops, to go where I am told. If there should be a delay, I can wait on my *amba*, near the frontier as I have already told you.

But if it should be more or less lengthy, it would be better that I remain pretending to be in the service of the king until the time (word illegible) provided that the secret is protected between us. Otherwise it will be my defeat, that of my children and of those faithful to me. For the moment I rely on you and completely trust you, a European and a Christian, and by (word illegible) 'Ala' ad-Dīn *Pasha*, but not on the *divan* where all the secrets are always sold, which I know with certainty. I also ask you for secrecy between (word illegible) and 'Ala' ad-Dīn *Pasha* alone, and all necessary precautions so that nothing is allowed to transpire until our desires are fulfilled. But even if these desires would not have any result at this moment, from the day the Egyptian government begins the fight, it will be able to judge the sincerity of my present plans.

Please destroy this letter and my preceding one.

AECPC, Massaouah 4, fol. 269, French translation. No date, but a note in the margin of the French translation says 24 January, and the archival copy follows upon the preceding document. See the note on the previous document for context. The four places indicated as illegible are because the binding of the volume covers the text.

Document no. 74

Yohannis IV to Muḥammad Tawfiq, 14 Feb. 1882

بسم سيدنا يسوع المسيح كلمة الله الازليه الذي به كان كل شي له السبح دايماً

رسالت المويد من الله يوحنا ملك صهيون ملك ملوك الحبشة

الى المعظم المحتشم العالي القدر حامي الخيريه وثابت النيه المكرم المحترم الخديوي محمد توفيق باشا الزايد الفهم وحب المحبة داعيه
السلام لكم وسلام الله يحل عليكم انا وكل الجيوش طيبين بقوة الله الصباوت المجد لله الذي ارصلنا الى هذه الساعه
وها قد كتبنا لكم لننبا لاجل عظم شرفكم وسبب تايدكم المعظم ولاجل ثبات ضميركم الطاهر رسالة هديه صالحه من زيادت
الفرح والابتهاج بما فعلتموه معنا من مراسلة المطران والاساقفه بكما طلبتنا ان يكونوا حاضرين بداخل مملكتنا ايتوبيا
وثانياً لاجل مراسلتكم لنا الهديه الكريمه التي عددها ٨٠٠ جماية بندقيه لاثبات المحبه ولذلك ابتهج قلبنا ومجدنا الله الملوك
والروسا وارباب الدوله جميعاً وفرحوا وابتهجوا لاجل هذا الصنيع قايلين بالهذا التواضع والحب العظيم وايضاً فلنسبح
الله لاجل نيالكم كل النعمه والخيرات ويتبارك اسم مجده القدوس الذي انعم عليكم بنعمته واجلسكم بكرسي
والدكم سماعل باشا وسابق تاريخه لاسماعل باشا لاجل المحبة كنا قد ارسلنا لجنابه هديه [illegible] فلاجل ان ابتهج بها ابتهاج
كامل جداً قايلاً ان من قبل هذا كان ملكاً يدعا اسمه المدعو تاودروش حين اخي سعيد باشا ارسل له هديه من
جنابه فبذل التشكرات بالمائه والثنيه وعوض الجزيل والان يوحنا ملك صهيون ملك ملوك الحبشه بمقدار
هذا طالب المحبة الرجل [illegible] قايل بالابتهاج ومن زود ابتهاج المحبه ارسل الينا اثناسيوس المطران وقال هذا
مبارك هو الله الذي اقام لنا الرجل المومن يوحنا المويد من الله ملك صهيون ملك ملوك الحبشه
وبعد ذلك بسبب الناس الاشرار تدتعدينا عداوه عظيمه والان انا اطلب المحبه منك فقط وتكون [illegible]
محلات مملكتنا الاصليه بكما كانت منذ القديم لكيلا يكون عداوه ما بين بعضنا بعض وتنعزل الحدود
التي لمملكة ايتوبيا التي كانت منذ الاصول باياديب ملوك الحبشه ويكون ما يخص الحبشه للحبشه وما لمصر لمصر
وقد شرحنا سابق هذا للمرسل اوربا قايلاً لهم اعزلوا وافرقوا لنا الحدود الحبشيه والمصريه لكيلا يكون لنا عداوه معكم ودام حكم

١٨٧٤
٨ امشير

Seal: King of Kings Yohannis of Ethiopia, Yuḥannā King of Kings of Abyssinia.

In the name of our Lord Jesus Christ, the everlasting wisdom of God, to whom the time and the days belong, a message of the beloved of God, Yohannis, King of Zion, King of Kings of Abyssinia. To the august, respected and potent, without self-aggrandizement and firm in his will, the honoured and revered Khedive Muḥammad Tawfīq *Pasha*, endowed with understanding and one who likes friendship. Peace be to you and may the peace of God be with you. I, and all my army, by the power of God the Sabaoth, are well. Praise be to God who has brought us to this hour.

We have written you a letter in respect for your exalted honour and splendid strong support and in respect for the constancy of your pure consciousness, a message righteously guided by the abundance of happiness and joy.

What you have done to us by sending an archbishop and bishops, based on our request, to become apostles inside our kingdom Ethiopia, and secondly by sending us respectful presents whose number is 800 guns in order to prolong our friendship, for all this our heart became happy and as a result we praised God, the possessor of all; and the dignitaries of our nation were very happy regarding the present, saying, "What humility and great love!".

Therefore may God bestow on you all blessings and benevolence and may His glorious name be sanctified who has given you all his blessings, who made you sit on the throne of your father Ismā'īl Pasha: And Ismā'īl Pasha owing to our friendship towards him, we sent him presents and he was fully satisfied with it saying, "The one who was before, whose name was Tēwodros, when Said Pasha sent him presents instead of thanking him responded by calling him bad names, therefore, returning evil for good. However, now Yohannis, King of Zion, King of Kings of Ethiopia, to the extent of his love he accepted our presents with happiness and joy". And as a result of his happiness and friendship, Atinatēwos, one of the bishops, said, "Blessed be God who raised to us a believer called Yohannis, King of Zion and King of Kings of Ethiopia."

And after this owing to wicked people we became fatal enemies. But now I don't ask only friendship but also [that we] stay in our respective original kingdoms, as it used to be in former times so that no enmity arises between us, and demarcate the borders of the Ethiopian kingdom which used to exist for ages in the hands of Abyssinian monarchs. Therefore, what may belong to Abyssinia be awarded to Abyssinia (al-Ḥabasha) and that of Egypt to Egypt.

1874, on the 8th of Amshīr.

ENA, Soudan 5/3/4, Arabic original. A copy of the letter from Muḥammad Tawfīq to Yohannis dated 6 Dec. 1881. A list of the gifts for Yohannis is found in ENA 5/3/2 and 5/3/5 respectively.

Document no. 75

Yohannis IV to Muḥammad Tawfiq, 16 Feb. 1882

በስመ፡ እግዚእነ፡ ኢየሱስ፡ ክርስቶስ፡ ሎቱ፡ ስብሐት። ። ። ።
መልእክት፡ ዘሥዩመ፡ እግዚአብሔር፡ ዮሐንስ፡ ንጉሠ፡ ነገሥት፡ ንጉሠ፡
ጽዮን፡ ዘኢትዮጵያ ።።። ይድረስ፡ ኀበ፡ ክቡር፡ ወፍቁር፡ ዋሊዩ፡ ወልሁል፡ ግ
ሁመ፡ ዜና፡ ወርቱዓ፡ ሐሊና። ኪዲቪ፡ መሐመድ፡ ተውፊቅ፡ ባሻ፡ ማዕም
ር። ወመፍቀሬ፡ ፍቅር። ሰላም፡ ለከ፡ ወሰላመ፡ እግዚአብሔር፡ የሃሉ፡ ምስ
ሌከ። አነ፡ ወሠራዊትየ፡ ዳኅና፡ ብኃይሉ፡ እግዚአብሔር፡ ሀባዎት፡ ስ
ብሐት፡ ለእግዚአብሔር፡ ለዘአብጽሐነ፡ እስከ፡ ዛቲ፡ ሰዓት። ወናሁ፡ ጸሐ
ፍኩ፡ ለከሙ፡ በእንተ፡ ዕበይከሙ፡ ወልዕልና፡ ሢመትክሙ። ክብርት
ወበእንተ፡ ርትዕት፡ ሕሊናከሙ። ንጽሕት። ቃሉ፡ እምኀ፡ ሠናይ፡ እምብዝ
ኃ፡ ፍሥሐ፡ ወሐሤት፡ ዘገበርክሙ፡ ሊተ፡ በእንተ፡ ምጽአተ፡ [illegible]፡ ወ[illegible]
[illegible]ት። ዘኃሠሥኩ፡ እነ፡ ይኩኑ፡ ሐዋርያተ። በውስቴቱ፡ መንግሥትየ፡
ዘኢትዮጵያ። ወበእንተ፡ ዘፈነውክሙ፡ ሊተ፡ ግጽ፡ በረከት፡ ዘኑኃቲሁ፡ ፲
፱ መበዓጅ። ለእጽንፆ፡ ፍትር፡ በእንተዝ፡ ተፈሥሐ፡ ልብየ፡ ወእእኩት፡ ክም
ለእግዚአብሔር፡ ነገሥትነ። ወመጸንዕት፡ ተፈሥሐ፡ ወተፈሥሐ፡ በእን
ተ፡ ዝንቱ፡ ነገር፡ እንዘ፡ ይብሉ፡ ዘመጠነዝ፡ ትሕትና፡ ወፍቅር። ወዓዲ፡ እ
ሴብሖ፡ ለእግዚአብሔር፡ በእንተ፡ ዘሰ፡ ጸጋ፡ ዘነሣእክሙ። ወይትባረ
ክ፡ ስመ፡ ስብሐቲሁ፡ ቅዱስ። እስመ፡ ወሀበ፡ ለክሙ፡ ሢመተ፡ ወመንበረ
ዘአቡክሙ። እስመ፡ ኢሌ፡ ባሻ። ወእምቅድመዝ፡ ለእስማዒል፡ ባሻ፡ በእን
ተ፡ ፍቅር፡ ንስቲት፡ ግጽ፡ በረከት፡ ለእመ፡ ፈነውኩ፡ ሎቱ፡ ፍጹመ፡ ተፈሥሐ
ወይቤ፡ ወእምቅድመ፡ ዝሰ፡ ዘነበረ፡ ዘስሙ፡ ካሣ፡ አኮኑ፡ ሰደዶ፡ ባሻ፡ ለእ
ሰመ፡ ይሬኢ፡ ሎቱ፡ ግጽ፡ በረከት፡ ሚጠ፡ ሎቱ፡ ህየንተ፡ ውዱሴ፡ ጸርፈ፡ ወ
ህየንተ፡ ሠናይት፡ እኪተ። ዘዮምሰ፡ ንጉሠ፡ ነገሥት፡ ዮሐንስ፡ ንጉሠ፡ ጽ
ዮን፡ ዘኢትዮጵያ። ዘመጠነዝ፡ ኃያል፡ ፍቅር፡ ብእሲ፡ ምእመን፡ እንዘ፡
ይብል፡ ተፈሥሐ። ወእምብዝኃ፡ ፍሥሐሁ፡ ፈነወ፡ ሊተ፡ [illegible]
ሃ፡ [illegible]። ወይቤ፡ ይትባረክ፡ እግዚአብሔር፡ ዘአንገሠ፡ ለነ፡ ብእሲ፡ ም
ዕመነ፡ ዮሐንስሃ፡ ሥዩመ፡ እግዚአብሔር፡ ንጉሠ፡ ጽዮን፡ ንጉሠ፡ ነገ
ሥት፡ ዘኢትዮጵያ። ወእም ድኅረዝ፡ በምክንያተ፡ ሰብእ፡ እኩያን፡ ተ
በአስስነ፡ ዲቢየ፡ ባዕሰ። ወይእዜኒ፡ እንሰ፡ እኅሥሥ፡ ምስሌከ፡ ፍቅረ፡
ባሕቲ፡ ንቲም፡ በበመካን፡ ሢመትነ፡ ዘቅንት፡ ከመ፡ ኢይኩን፡ ባዕስ
ማ እከሊን። ወይትሌለይ፡ ወሰን፡ ዘመንግሥተ፡ ኢትዮጵያ፡ ዘዮ፡ እም
ቅንት፡ በእዴሆሙ፡ ለነገሥተ፡ ኢትዮጵያ፡ ከመ፡ ይኩን፡ ዘኢትዮጵያ፡
ለኢትዮጵያ። ወግብፅ፡ ለግብፅ፡ ትኩመኒ፡ ጸሐፍኩ፡ ለነገሥተ፡ ሮም፡
እንዘ፡ አብሎ፡ ፍጹመ፡ ሊተ፡ ሀገርየ፡ ከመ፡ ኢይትበዓስ፡ ምስሌክሙ። ተ
ጸሐፈ፡ በአድዋ፡ ከተማ፡ በ፲፱ ወበ፲፰፻ ወ፸፬ ዓመተ፡ ምሕረ
ት፡ አመ፡ ፲ ለየካቲት።

Seal: King of Kings Yohannis of Ethiopia; Yūḥannā, King of Kings of Abyssinia.

In the name of our Lord Jesus Christ, praise be to Him.

May the message of the Elect of God Yohannis, King of Kings of Ethiopia, reach the honoured and respected, the great and exalted, [he who enjoys] pleasant reputation and an upright mind, Khedive Muḥammad Tawfīq *Pasha*, the scholar (lit. knowledgeable) and lover of friendship. Peace be to you and the peace of God be with you. By the might of God Sabaoth, I and my army are well. Praise be to God who has kept us until this moment.

And now, I had written to you about your greatness and the greatness of your honoured appointment [which is] due to your upright and pure mind. A word of gratitude for the great happiness and pleasure for what you have done for me regarding the coming of the archbishop and the bishops whom I wanted to be teachers in my kingdom of Ethiopia, and regarding the gifts you sent me for the strengthening of friendship, numbering eight hundred rifles. For this reason my heart was joyful and happy about this matter saying, "What modesty and friendship!"

Again I praise God for all the grace that you have received. And may His Holy Name be praised because He has granted you the appointment to the throne of your father, Ismā'īl *Pasha*. And earlier when I had sent a small present of friendship to Ismā'īl *Pasha* he was very happy and said, "He who was before by the name of Kasa, when my brother Sa'īd Pasha sent him presents instead of praise he paid him back by calling him bad names. But the King of Kings of today Yohannis, King of Zion of Ethiopia, is earnestly (lit. very much) looking for friendship". [Ismā'īl] said, "Be happy", and to the extent of his happiness he sent me *Ṗappas* Atirnatēwos. And he said, "praise be to God who has elected for us a faithful man, Yohannis, elect of God, King of Zion, King of Kings of Ethiopia."

And after this we quarrelled very badly because of wicked people. And now I am seeking friendship with you; let us abide by the early positions of our agreement in order that quarrels may not arise between us, and may the borderlands of Ethiopia which were in the hands of the Ethiopian kings be demarcated, so that what was Ethiopia's [may be awarded] to Ethiopia and [what was] Egypt's [may be awarded] to Egypt. Earlier I had written to the kings of Europe saying, "Demarcate my land so that I will not quarrel with you."

Written in the town of Adwa in the year of grace 1874, on the 10th of Yekkatīt.

ENA, Soudan 5/3/[illegible], Gi'iz original. The letter seems to be a Gi'iz version of the previous letter, but dated two days later. The only significant difference is that the Arabic text does not mention the letters sent to the rulers of Egypt asking them to assist in demarcating the borders.

Document no. 76

Yohannis IV to Welde Sema'it Welde Yohannis and the community of Dayr al-Sultan, 20 Feb. 1882

May the letter of the Elect of God Yohannis, King of Zion, King of Kings of Ethiopia, reach *Abba* Welde Sema'it and the whole Ethiopian community of Dayr al-Sultan in Jerusalem.

How are you? I, thanks to God, am well with my army. I have received your letter and I have written concerning you and the piece of land to the patriarch, and to Sultan 'Abd al-Hamīd, King of Ottoman Istanbul. I have written to all these; but it is because of you that I am blamed so much; not because I am guilty.

If the problem is solved as a result of the dispatched letters, you may stay where you are. If it does not come through, you may reside at the place I have bought. If that is found impossible, you should give it up and come and stay in Aksum as I have already instructed you earlier. All is the land of God. Man is saved by his good deeds, and God relieves him with His mercy. I have sent you seven thousand thalers for your maintenance. But a country does not make one righteous.

Written on the 14th day of Yekkatīt in the year of mercy 1874, in the town of Adwa.

Chronicle, no. 11, pp. 172–175, Gi'iz/Amharic text and English translation. The original could not be located at the monastery in Jerusalem.

Document no. 77

Yohannis IV to Welde Sema'it Welde Yohannis and the community of Dayr al-Sultan, 22 Feb. 1882

Seal: King of Kings Yohannis of Ethiopia; Yūḥannā, King of Kings of Abyssinia.

In the name of Our Lord Jesus Christ. Praise be to Him.

May the message of the Elect of God Yohannis, King of Zion, King of Kings of Ethiopia, reach *Abba* Welde Sema'it and the whole community of Jerusalem, which is the Dayr al-Sultan of Ethiopia, the upright in faith, who endure oppression like Naboth who died by the hands of Jezebel, the queen, because of his vineyard

Peace be to you all. I am well and in peace through your strong prayers. Praise be to God who has brought us up to this hour. And now, I have sent you some money, amounting to 6,000 [thalers], by the hands of *Abba* Hayle Īyyesus and another person.

However, do not be discontented with me because it is [so] little. The reason why the money is [so] little and why I send [it] to you in small amounts is because the strangers who speak ill of me and who want money have become numerous. Do not give up praying because of the oppression that you are suffering. The God of the oppressed will hear your prayers and He will give you the reward for your oppression. For He judges justly.

Written in the town of Adwa, on 16th Yekkatīt in the year of grace 1874.

Dayr al-Sultan, no. 9, Amharic/Gi'iz original. Printed with English translation in *Chronicle*, no. 12, pp. 174–175. Here the second person is identified as *Abba* Welde Tensa'ē. The translation erroneously writes Welde Īyyesus for Hayle Īyyesus in the text.

Document no. 78

Minīlik II to Jules Grévy, 7 March 1882

ዳግማዊ፡ ምኒልክ፡ በእግዚአብሔር፡ ኃይል፡ የሸዋ፡ ንጉ
ሠ፡ የሆነ፡ ይድረስ፡ ወደ፡ ክቡር፡ ወደ፡ ታፈረ፡ የፈረንሲስ፡ ፕረዚዳን፡ ጁል፡
ግረቢ፡፡ እንዴት፡ ነው፡ እኔ፡ እግዚአብሔር፡ ይመስገን፡ ደኅና፡ ነኝ፡ ሠራዊቴም፡
ሁሉ፡ ደኅና፡ ነው፡፡

ያለፈው፡ ዓመት፡ ካፒ፡ ብረሞ፡ ጋራ፡ ሰዎቼንና፡ የፍቅር፡ ደብ
ዳቤ፡ በረከት፡ አከዪጎ፡ ሰድጄ፡ ነበር፡፡ መድረሱን፡ ሰማሁ፡ ምላሹን፡ ግን፡ አላገኘሁም፡
የላክሁት፡ የበዱ፡ አህያ፡ ቃረስ፡ በገባ፡ በአክሬሊ፡ ምክት፡ ቀኑ፡ ሞተ፡ ብሎ፡ አከከሬ፡ ነገረ፡
ሠላሴ፡ ንጉዜ፡ ጻፈልኝ፡ እርሰዎም፡ አዘኑ፡ ሊሉ፡ ሰማሁ፡ ምንም፡ የሚቸግር፡ ነገር፡
የለም፡ ባገሬ፡ ያለ፡ ነገር፡ ለኔ፡ አይቸግረኝም፡ የሚቸግረኝ፡ ነገር፡ በየውሮፓ፡
ያለ፡ ነገር፡ ነው፡፡ አሁን፡ በኔ፡ ሰዎች፡ በተጋጀሬ፡ የሚኖሩ፡ ብርቱ፡ ታላቅ፡ ግፍ፡ ተሠራ፡

ከቅድመ፡ አያቶቼ፡ ጋር፡ ምሮ፡ ሹመታቸውን፡ ያልተናወጠ፡ ባመት
ባመት፡ ሁለት፡ ሁለት፡ ፻፻ እንካቦ፡ ጨው፡ የሚገብሩልኝ፡ ጨውም፡ የኔ፡ ያባ
ቶቼ፡ ያያቶቼ፡ የሆነ፡ ከተጋጀራ፡ ጋር ምሮ፡ ሸዋ፡ ድረስ፡ ያለት፡ አይለጡትም፡ የኔ፡ ዜጋ
ች፡ እንደሆኑ፡ ዓለም፡ ሁሉ፡ የሚያውቀው፡ ካንዱ፡ ወገኖች፡ በፊር፡ ሽፍተው፡ የሚ
ኖሩ፡፡ ወደ፡ ምክር፡ የላክሁት፡ መልእክተኛዬ፡ ሰይመለስ፡ ቶርኮች፡ ሹሞቼን፡ አስጠ
ርተው፡ ወደ፡ መርከብ፡ አግብተው፡ አዋረዱዋቸው፡ ከመርከብም፡ ወደ፡ ጋርል
ባ፡ ጣሉዋቸው፡ ጨውን፡ በግድ፡ ሸጡ፡ አያሉ፡ ማንም፡ ማን፡ ሊሸጠው፡ የማይቻ
ለውን፡ በግድ፡ ሸጡ፡ ብለው፡ አዋረዱዋቸው፡ እኒህም፡ ሰዎች፡ ወደኔ፡ ሮጠው፡ ጉል
በት፡ የላትውምና፡ እኔም፡ የየውሮፓ፡ ነገሥታት፡ ከጕረቤትህ፡ ጋራ፡ ተስማሙ፡ ብሎኛል፡ እሺ፡ በ
ዬ፡ ነበር፡፡ ነገር፡ ግን፡ ፍቅርና፡ ነብር፡ ካንድ፡ በረት፡ ማሰደር፡ አይቻልምና፡ የማልዘልቀው፡
ሆነ፡፡ እንግሊዞች፡ ወደ፡ ሐበሻ፡ የመጡ፡ ጊዜ፡ በየውሮፓ፡ ነገሥታት፡ ሠራት፡ ተመልሰ
ው፡ ሄዱ፡ ይህም፡ ምስጋና፡ ለፈረንሲስ፡ መንግሥት፡ ከኃ ስጣዋለን፡፡ ዛሬ፡ ቶርኮች፡ አፋችኒ
ን፡ ሊዘጉ፡ ይፈልጋሉ፡ በራችንን፡ እንዲዘጉ፡ እኛም፡ ጨርሰው፡ ከከቴ ዘጉብን፡ እንጠ
ብቅም፡ ቢሆን፡ በሠራት፡ አገራችንን፡ ይለቃሉ፡ ከለዚያ፡ በግድ፡ የበረታ፡ ይወስደዋል፡
ከእኛ ገሩና፡ ከለሕዝቡ፡ መሞት፡ ነውር፡ አይደለም፡፡ በቃየክ፡ የፈረንሲስ፡ መንግሥት
ስም፡ ሊሾሙ በት፡ ነው፡ ብለው፡ ግዴን፡ ያሉት፡ ሰዎቼ፡ ቢጽፉልኝ፡ ከዚያ፡ ደስ፡ አለኝ፡፡ እንግዲ
ህ፡ ያድርጉ፡ ሁነት፡ አይሆኑ፡ መንገድ፡ ይቀና፡ ነበር፡፡ እርሰዎ፡ ቢበረቱ፡ በዚህ፡ ነገር፡ የፈረንሲ
ስ፡ ሕዝብ፡ በኛ፡ ዘንድ፡ እጅግ፡ የከበረ፡ ይሆን፡ ነበር፡ የጋጀሏ ግረቢ፡ ከምም፡ በኛ፡ ዘንድ
በገዳፀሕይ፡ ያበራ፡ ነበር፡፡ እኔ፡ ሜና፡ ጤናውን፡ ይስጠዎ፡፡
በየካቲት፡ ፳፰ በ፲፰፻፸፬ በአንኮበር፡ ከተማ፡ ተጻፈ፡፡

[May the letter of] the second Minīlik, who by the power of God has become king of Shewa, reach the honoured and respected president of the French, Jules Grévy.

How are you? I am well, thank God. All my army is also well. Last year I sent my people with Mr. Brémond with a letter and gifts of friendship. I have heard that they have arrived, but I have not yet received a reply. My servant Gebre Sillasē Nigusē has written to me saying that the zebra I sent died 15 days after arriving in Paris. I have also heard that you were sorry [for this]. This is no problem. I have no difficulty about anything that is found in my country. What is difficult for me are things [found] in Europe.

Now a serious injustice has been done against my people who live in Tajura. The whole world knows that, except for some clans who live as bandits, the Adal who live from Tajura up to Shewa are my subjects; that the salt belongs to me [as] to my fathers and to my grandfathers; and that from [the days of] my grandfathers, with no one challenging their right (lit. governorship), they pay to us every year a tribute of 2,000 bags (*ankabo*) of salt. Before my messenger whom I sent to Egypt returned, the Turks summoned my officials, made them board a ship and humiliated them. Then forcing them out of the ship, they threw them into a boat, compelling them to sell the salt. They humiliated them by compelling them to sell the salt, which no one, whoever he may be, had the right to sell. These people have appealed to me because they have no power [themselves]. And I have agreed to live in peace with my neighbours, as the kings of Europe told me. But as it is impossible to make a goat and a leopard live in the same pen, it has become something I cannot endure. When the English came to Abyssinia they returned according to the law of the Europeans. We are indebted for this to the French government also.

Today, the Turks want to shut our mouths just as they have closed our ports. And we shall not wait until they shut us in completely. In fact, they ought to leave our lands lawfully. If not, [the ports] will be taken by force, by whoever is stronger. It is not a shame to die for one's country and one's people. I was very pleased when my people who are in Aden wrote to me saying that the French government is going to appoint an official over Obok. May God make it a reality. If it turns out [to be] true, the route would be opened up. If you acted vigorously on this matter, the French people would be much respected amongst us and the name of Jules Grévy would shine like the sun amongst us.

May [God] give you long life and health.

Written at the camp of Inṭoṭṭo, on the 29th of Yekkatīt 1874.

Seal: Minīlik, King of Shewa. The Lion of the tribe of Judah has prevailed.

AECPC, Angleterre, Aden, 1858–1884, 57, fol. 251, Amharic original fols 254–255, French translation. This seems to be the first letter preserved in Amharic where Minīlik styles himself as *degmaj*, "the second". Earlier letters in French and Italian add "II" after his name, but we cannot know how this was represented in the Amharic texts. *Degmaj* is, however, not used consistently until 1884 at a time when his letters were often written in French.

The letter was reportedly translated by *Azzazh* Gebre Sillasē Nigusē, who was recommended for the task by Minīlik. He is to reappear in many of the following letters as a trader and messenger of Minīlik in relation to Maḥammad Ḥanfadhē and the rulers along the coast as well as the Italians. He is sometimes referred to as Gīyorgīs Gebre Sillasē or Gīyorgīs Nigusē.

Document no. 79

Minīlik II to François Soumagne, 7 March 1882

Please forward my letter to Grévy. You already know, perhaps, what has happened to my subjects and tributary chiefs at the hands of the Egyptians.

I have been the friend of the Egyptians until now. I have never sought conflict with them. I have even sent emissaries with gifts, and now look how the Egyptians have seized the salt which nourishes all Ethiopia. My chiefs who have been maltreated are Sultan Ḥamad from Tajura, *Wazīr* Ibrāhīm and Aḥmad La'īta.

The salt plains belong to me since the days of my forefathers. Moreover, I know, and many know, that Tajura is the port of Shewa.

No one should give up what is his unless he is forced to do so. You have with you my trusted man Gebre Sillasē Nigusē. You also have 'Abd al-Raḥmān. You can ask them.

I protect the French and ask for your assistance to my people. I want all French to have passports when they come. If they do anything wrong, I will send them back to you. If they have no passports, I will punish them according to our laws. Those who come without papers or recommendations will be treated as Abyssinians. I have sent letters through Awsa, and I have been told that these letters were given to Arnoux and that he has kept them. If this is true, ask him to send them.

Seal: Minīlik, King of Shewa. The Lion of the tribe of Judah has prevailed.

29th Yekkatīt 1874.

AECPC, Angleterre, Aden, 1858–1884, 57, fols 252–253, French text. Whatever the reason it is quite obvious from this letter that the task of forwarding Minīlik's letter to the French government was entrusted to Soumagne rather than to Arnoux. Soumagne replaced Raffray as French vice-consul of Massawa at the end of 1882. Aḥmad La'īta is probably Sultan Ḥamad La'īta. Gebre Sillasē refers to Minīlik's chief agent on the coast, Gebre Sillasē Nigusē. Ḥamad Muḥammad was the Sultan of Tajura from 1880 to 1912. 'Abd al-Raḥmān Yūsif was the trusted agent of Maḥammad Ḥanfadhē.

Document no. 80

Minīlik II to Pierre Arnoux, 7 March 1882

May [this letter], sent by King Minīlik, reach Mr. Arnoux.

How are you? I am well, thank God. All my army is well.

The letter you sent to me has reached me. I have received all the earlier letters. They came on 16 Nehasē 1881 [and] 1 Ṭirr 1882.

I have heard about the trouble which you experienced in Egypt. The picture of you and your son has reached me. And now I am sending you 100 camels in care of Maḥammad Ḥanfadhē for the sniders and the ammunition. Write to me. If the doctor and the workers are available, send them to me. We shall speak of everything else later. I will give you the money for the sniders, I am sending it with Maḥammad Ḥanfadhē.

Written at the camp of Inṭoṭṭo on the 29th day of Yekkatīt in the year of grace 1874.

Seal: Minīlik, King of Shewa. The Lion of the tribe of Judah has prevailed.

BN, Ethiop. Abb. 254, no. 295, Amharic original; 293, French translation, and 294, address reading "Vice-consulat de France à Aden, *yidres kato arnus*, Monsieur Arnoux (Obok)". As with so many other letters from Ethiopian rulers to the French, this letter was translated by Antoine d'Abbadie. The "snider", more properly the Snider-Enfield, referred to was a breech-loading rifle widely used by the British army in the late nineteenth century.

Document no. 81

Minīlik II to Pietro Antonelli, 9 March 1882

I have heard how Mr. Martini has written things against me, but I do not believe they have done any damage. I would have been able to write to the Geographical Society of Italy and to the king himself about what has happened here in this country. But it would be a dishonour for me to occupy myself with such a small matter. He opens his mouth to disseminate false information against me, but you, Count Antonelli, and Captain Cecchi, and all the Europeans who are living in Shewa, know his conduct and how he has squandered my goods. All the same, what should I say? May God repay him. I would not have spoken if he had not been impossible to reach. Be aware of this!

ASSGI, busta 20, fasc. 5, no. 16, Italian translation. The document is prefaced by the following paragraph: "A letter from King Minīlik to Count Pietro Antonelli dated 9 March 1882, in which he expresses himself according to the translation [made by] Father Massaia on behalf of S. Martini." In all probability the text is a genuine translation of an Amharic original, in which case the opening paragraph was part of the letter itself. We have omitted it above because of the information about the translation and the fact that the text, beginning "Ho sentito come . . .", is within quotation marks in the document. We have translated SGI into "the Geographical Society of Italy" because of the unusual form "d'Italia" used instead of "italiana".

Document no. 82

Welde Ṣadiq to Pierre Arnoux, 22 March 1882

May [this letter] from *Azzazh* Welde Ṣadiq reach the greatly respected, honoured, beloved, and trusted Mr. Arnoux (Arnos).

How are you really, really? Thank God, I am well, including my servants. Since the camels and the packers have arrived, see to it that [the goods] are quickly packed, and keep them at hand, so that they do not [have to] wait and remain there. If the goods are kept in boxes it will wear out the camels. If they are in bundles, it will be easy (lit. turn out well) for them; there is time [to make them] into bundles.

Written on the 14th day of Meggabīt in the year 1874.

Seal: *Azzazh* Welde Ṣadiq.

BN, Orient. Abb., 254, no. 297, Amharic original.

Document no. 83

Gebru *Abba* Çhequn to François Soumagne, 24 March 1882

Letter of *Blatta* Gebru to the honourable who is above the honourable, who is our friend, who is the consul of France. [May] the Saviour of the world keep you in good health.

As for my soldiers, they are prepared; they did not recognize them and did not know that these men are your friends and mine. They have done badly and I became angry when I heard about their conduct. I have treated the Europeans well, I have sent them back with excuses and compliments, so now rejoice. The king has entrusted the government of these provinces to me, and when he arrives write to me and count on me. Please send me a nice watch.

16th Meggabīt 1874.

AECPC, Massaouah 4, fol. 256, French translation. For the author, see doc. 28.

Document no. 84

Maḥammad Ḥanfadhē to Pietro Antonelli, 28 May 1882

To His Excellency, the respected friend of His Majesty King Minīlik, Count Pietro Antonelli. I wish you good health, and as for us, we are, thank God, very well.

We have received your letter of the month of March, and we have acquainted ourselves with it. As for the merchandise for King Minīlik, have no fear; when it comes to Aseb, you will consign it to Gebre Sillasē and 'Abd al-Raḥmān, who will inform me as soon as they have received it, and from that moment on it will be my responsibility and it will be my task to protect it till it is consigned to King Minīlik.

It is not true that I oppose the passage of Europeans in my territory, but since (text missing) without distinction of nationality (text missing) all Europeans, I have dissuaded [Europeans] from passage in my territory. But I am not opposed [to them]. And when the Italian government con[sults] me and King Minīlik, I shall come to an agreement with the Bedouins in order to open a safe route for both men and merchandise, and for this purpose we shall make a treaty between us to be valid for the future.

In the meantime, I shall provide a safe way for you and the merchandise for King Minīlik. As soon as you reach Aseb, you will inform 'Abd al-Raḥmān, who will undertake to inform me. I ask you to present the translation of this letter to your government to let them know that the route is clear.

Sultan Maḥammad Ḥanfadhē.

10th Rajab 1299.

N.B. Ḥanfadhē writes to Gīyorgīs that the letters he has sent to King Minīlik are on their way to their destination. This is for your information.

ASMAE, AE 2, Italian translation. No Arabic document has been found. There is a hole through the paper of this letter, indicated above by "(text missing)". Described as a "traduzione approsimativa", the translation is clearly made by someone ignorant of Ethiopian and Arabic names; Gebre Sillasē, for instance, appears as "Gabriel Sallasi" and "Abd al-Raḥmān" as "Habdu Rheman". Gebre Sillasē refers to Minīlik's chief agent on the coast, Gebre Sillasē Nigusē. 'Abd al-Raḥmān Yūsif was the trusted agent of Maḥammad Ḥanfadhē. At the end of the translation there is a note in Italian stating: "Hanferī writes to Gīyorgīs that the letters he has sent to King Minīlik are on their way to their destination. This is for your information." Whether Gīyorgīs in the note refers to Gebre Sillasē, who was also known as Gīyorgīs Gebre Sillasē, it is impossible to know.

Document no. 85

Pēṭros to clerics and believers in Jenda, 12 June 1882

መልእክት፡ የተላከ፡ እምኀበ፡ ጴጥሮስ፡
ሊቀ፡ ጳጳሳት፡ ዘመንግሥተ፡ ኢትዮጵያ፡
ገብሩ፡ ወሐዋርያሁ፡ ለእግዚእነ፡ ኢየሱስ፡
ክርስቶስ፡ ወልዱ፡ ለቅዱስ፡ ማርቆስ፡
ወንጌላዊ፡ ዘሀገረ፡ ዓባይ፡ እስክንድርያ፡
ትብጻሕ፡ ኀበ፡ ውሉድየ፡ ወፍቁራንየ፡ ቀሳው
ስት፡ ወዲያቆናት፡ ወመሃይምናን፡ ወኵሎ
ሹሙ፡ [illegible] ቅዱስ፡ ጊዮርጊስ፡
ሰላመ፡ እግዚአብሔር፡ የሃሉ፡ ምስሌክሙ፡
አሜን፡ ደብተራ፡ ብሩ፡ ደብተራ፡ አረጋዊ፡ ቄስ፡
ኤልያስ፡ ቄስ፡ ትእዛዙ፡ ጎሹ፡ መርሻ፡ ደብተራ፡
ፈንታ፡ ወልደ፡ እስጢፋኖስ፡ ወንድሜ፡ አቡነ፡
አትናቴዎስ፡ ነጻ፡ እንዳወጣቸው፡ እኔም፡ አውጥ
ቻቸዋለሁ፡ አዲስ፡ እንግዳ፡ አይድረስባቸው፡ ወንድ
ሞቻቸውን፡ ይሳቡ፡ ሕገ፡ ወንጌልን፡ ያስተምሩ፡
እንዳሳዝናችሁ፡ ከፍቃዴ፡ አትውጡ፡ ከአባቱ
ፈቃድ፡ የወጣ፡ ልጅ፡ ርጉም፡ ነው፡ እግዚአብ
ሔር፡ ይፍታችሁ፡ እግዚአብሔር፡ ይባርካችሁ፡
በ፲፰፻፸፬፡ ዓመ፡ በ፮፡ ለወርኃ፡ ሰኔ፡ ተጽሕፈ፡

Seal: illegible.

A message sent from Pēṭros, *līqe pappasat* of the state of Ethiopia, the servant and apostle of our Lord Jesus Christ, the son of St. Mark, the evangelist of the great city of Alexandria, may it reach my sons and beloved, priests, deacons, believers and all appointees of the land of Jenda St. George. The peace of God be with you. Amen.

As my brother *Abune* Atinatēwos acquitted *Debtera* Birru, *Debtera* Aregawī, *Qēs* Ēlyas, *Qēs* Ti'izazu, Goshu Mersha, *Debtera* Fenta [and] Welde Isṭīfanos, I have also acquitted them. I do not want them to encounter any unexpected trouble. Let them win over their brothers and teach the laws of the Gospel. In order that I do not get angry with you, do not disobey me (lit. go out of my will). A son who disobeys his father is a cursed one. May God absolve you and bless you.

Written on the 6th of the month of Senē 1874.

Private archives of the Flad family, St-Légier, Switzerland, Gi'iz/Amharic original. Pēṭros was one of the four bishops sent to Ethiopia in 1881. The clerics acquitted are otherwise unknown. The seal is clearly in Arabic, but unfortunately illegible, except for the two numbers "59". This might indicate that the seal carries a year in the 1590s Coptic calendar, corresponding to 1874–1883 in the Gregorian calendar.

Document no. 86

Yohannis IV to Minīlik II, 8 July 1882

መልእክት ፡ ዘሥዩመ ፡ እግዚአብሔር ፡ ዮሐንስ ፡ ንጉሠ ፡ ጽዮን ፡ ንጉሠ ፡ ነገሥት ፡ ዘኢትዮጵያ ፡ ይድረስ ፡ ከንጉሥ ፡ ምኒልክ ፤ በአማን ፡ እስራኤላዊ ፤ ዘአልቦ ፡ ጽልሑት ፤ ሰላም ፡ ለከ ፡ ወሰላመ ፡ እግዚአብሔር ፡ የሃሉ ፡ ምስሌከ ። እኔ ፡ በእግዚአብሔር ፡ ቸርነት ፤ በእምነ ፡ ጽዮን ፡ አማላጅነት ፤ አምላከ ፡ ቅዱሳን ፡ ይክበር ፡ ይመስገን ፡ ደህና ፡ ነኝ ፡ ምሕረቱ ፡ ለዘለዓለም ፡ ነውና ።

በጌምድር ፡ ሳለሁ ፡ ሁለቱ ፡ ነገሥታት ፡ ተዋግተው ፡ ድሉ ፡ ለንጉሥ ፡ ምኒልክ ፡ ሆነ ፤ ንጉሥ ፡ ተክለ ፡ ሃይማኖትንም ፡ ይዘው ፡ ወደ ፡ ሸዋ ፡ ተጓዙ ፡ ሲሉ ፡ ብሰማ ፡ እግዚአብሔር ፡ የፈቀደውን ፡ ሠርቷል ፡ ብዬ ፡ የክርስቲያን ፡ ደም ፡ በማይረባ ፡ ነገር ፡ በመፍሰሱ ፡ የእናንተን ፡ ደብዳቤ ፡ ስጠብቅ ፡ ደብረ ፡ ታቦር ፡ ላይ ፡ ወር ፡ ሙሉ ፡ ተቀመጥሁ ፤ ኋላ ፡ ግን ፡ ወሬያችሁ ፡ ቢጠፋብኝ ፡ ይህስ ፡ ነገር ፡ አለበት ፡ ብዬ ፡ ስመጣ ፡ ሳይንትን ፡ ሳልፈው ፡ የንጉሥ ፡ ወረቀት ፡ ደረሰልኝ ። ደብዳቤውንም ፡ አይቼ ፡ መዘግየቱ ፡ በመንገዱ ፡ ርዝመት ፡ እንጂ ፡ ሌላ ፡ ተንኮል ፡ አለመኖሩን ፡ ባውቅ ፡ ወደ ፡ በጌምድር ፡ ለመመለስ ፡ አሰብሁ ። ነገር ፡ ግን ፡ ክረምቱ ፡ ተጭኗልና ፡ ሠራዊቱ ፡ የሚጎዳብኝ ፡ ሆነ ። ስለዚህ ፡ በወሎ ፡ እንድከርም ፡ ፈቃድ ፡ ይደረግልኝ ። እኔም ፡ አገር ፡ አልበድልም ። በጥቢ ፡ ተገናኝተን ፡ ሁሉንም ፡ ነገር ፡ ተማክረን ፡ ወደ ፡ በጌምድር ፤ መመለስ ፡ ይሻላል ፡ ብዬ ፡ ነው ፡ እንጂ ፡ ሌላ ፡ ጉዳይ ፡ ኖሮኝ ፡ አይደለም ።

ደግሞ ፡ ይህ ፡ የሚያሳዝን ፡ ነገር ፡ ሲሆን ፡ ተመልሼ ፡ ሠራዊቱ ፡ በውሀ ፡ ሙላት ፡ በጭቃ ፡ ያለቀው ፡ አልፎ ፡ የተረፈውን ፡ ይዤ ፡ መመለስ ፡ ይሻለኛል ። ሐምሌ ፡ ፪ ቀን ፡ ፲፰፻፸፬ ፡ ዓ ፡ ም ።

May the message of the Elect of God Yohannis, King of Zion, King of Kings of Ethiopia, reach King Minīlik, an Israelite indeed, in whom there is no guile. Peace be to you, and the peace of God be with you.

By the grace of God and the intercession of Our Mother Zion – may the God of the saints be praised – I am well, since his mercy is forever.

When I was in Begēmdir, I heard that the two kings had fought; that the victory was King Minīlik's, and that [you] captured King Tekle Haymanot and proceeded to Shewa. I said, what has happened was God's will, and since Christian blood was spilled for nothing I waited a whole month at Debre Tabor expecting your letters. Then not hearing from [any of] you I thought that there must be something strange going on, and as I passed Sayint I received the king's letter. After seeing the letter, I understood that the letter was delayed due to the distance and not to any other foul play.

I wanted to return to Begēmdir. However, since the rainy season has become so heavy, and in order that my soldiers should not suffer, may I have your permission to spend the rainy season in Wello?

As for me, I am not going to pillage the country. I am only considering that we should meet each other after the rainy season and discuss matters before I go back to Begēmdir. Otherwise I have no reason [to stay]. Moreover, this is a sad story. I thought it appropriate to return with the remainder of my army leaving behind those who have perished due to floods and mud.

The 2nd day of Hamlē in the year of grace 1874.

Tarīke Negest, p. 60, printed Amharic text.

Document no. 87

Minīlik II to Pēṭros, Matēwos, Marqos and Luqas, 11 July 1882

ትብጻሕ፡ ኀበ፡ ልዑላን፡ ወኅሩያን፡ በኀበ፡ እግዚአብሔር፡ አቡነ፡ ጴጥሮስ፡ ወአቡነ፡ ማቴዎስ፤ አቡነ፡ ማርቆስ፡ ወአቡነ፡ ሉቃስ፡ ጳጳሳት፡ ዘኢትዮጵያ። ብርሃናተ፡ ዓለም፤ ወሐዋርያቲሁ፡ ለእግዚእነ፡ ኢየሱስ፡ ክርስቶስ፡ ወውሉዱ፡ ለማርቆስ፡ ወንጌላዊ።

የተላከ፡ ከንጉሥ፡ ምኒልክ። እዴምኀክሙ፡ በአምኃ፡ መንፈሳዊት፤ ወአኃሥሥ፡ በረከተክሙ፡ ዘትረድእ፡ ለኵሉ፡ ፍጥረት። አነ፡ ዳህን፡ ወሰላም፡ በጸጋሁ፡ ለእግዚእነ፡ ፀባዖት፡ ወበስእለታ፡ ለእግዝእትነ፡ ወላዲተ፡ ሕይወት። በሰኔ፡ ፪ ቀን፡ የተጻፈ፡ የውግዘት፡ ደብዳቤያችሁ፡ በተዋጋን፡ በ፳ ቀን፡ ደረሰልኝ፤ እኔም፡ ንጉሥ፡ ተክለ፡ ሃይማኖትን፡ ለመውጋት፡ አልፈለግሁም፡ ነበር፤ እርሱ፡ ፎክሮ፤ ከወደ፡ ኋላዬ፡ ገሥግሶ፡ ቢመጣብኝ፡ አልሞት፡ ባይ፡ ተጋዳይ፡ እንደሚባለው፡ ዙሬ፡ ተዋጋን።

እኔ፡ ግን፡ ለመውጋት፡ ፈልጌው፡ እንደ፡ ሆነ፡ ያወገዛችሁትም፤ የረገማችሁትም፡ ይድረስብኝ። ደግሞ፡ ክርስቲያን፡ ለክርስቲያን፡ በመዋጋታችን፡ ጃንሆይን፡ አስቀየመን፡ ይሆናል። የጃንሆይም፡ ልቡና፡ እንዳይለወጥብኝ፡ ስለ፡ ሥላሴ፡ ብላችሁ፡ አስምሩኝ፡ እንጂ፡ በደለኛውንስ፡ እኔ፡ በጥቢ፡ ስመጣ፡ እዚያው፡ በጃንሆይ፡ ፊት፡ ታገኙታላችሁ። ሐምሌ፡ ፭ ቀን፡ ፲፰፻፸፬፡ ተጻፈ።

May [this message] reach the exalted and elected of God, *Abune* Pēṭros and *Abune* Matēwos, *Abune* Marqos and *Abune* Luqas, bishops of Ethiopia, lights of the world and apostles of Jesus Christ and sons of Mark the Evangelist.

[Message] sent by King Minīlik. I greet you with spiritual greetings and look forward to your blessing, which helps all creatures. I am well and live in peace by the grace of the Lord Sabaoth and the intercession of Our Lady, the mother of life.

Your letter of excommunication written on Senē 2 reached me twenty days after we waged war. On my part I did not want to fight King Tekle Haymanot. But since he bragged and attacked me from behind I fought with him in self-defence. However, if I fought with him deliberately, may your excommunication and curse fall upon me.

Moreover, when we Christians fought against Christians it might have hurt the feelings of His Majesty. In order that the attitude of His Majesty towards me does not change, for the sake of the Holy Trinity have him forgive me. As for [who is] the wrongdoer you will find out for yourselves, in front of His Majesty, when I come after the rainy season.

Written on 5th Hamlē 1874.

Tarīke Negest, p. 59, printed Gi'iz/Amharic text.

Document no. 88

Minīlik II to Victoria, 20 July 1882

Nous, Menilik II, par la grâce de Dieu. Roi de Choa, à Sa Majesté la Reine Victoria, Souveraine du Royaume Uni et des Indes.

Comment se porte Votre Majesté? Nous par la grâce du Tout-Puissant, sommes en bonne santé ainsi que Nos armées.

Nous sommes heureux de pouvoir annoncer à Votre Majesté qu'une longue et laborieuse campagne de sept mois contre les royaumes esclavagistes, musulmans pour la plupart, situés au Sud et à l'Ouest de Nos domaines et maîtres de la route du Choa à Kaffa, vient de Nous mettre à même de soumettre et de rendre tributaires les Rois de Limou, Gomma, Gouma, Ghera et le Roi chrétien de Kaffa. Nous avons détruit entièrement ces centres de l'esclavage, et avons rendu à la liberté des milliers de malheureuses Créatures humaines.

Unique descendant direct et légitime de la dynastie de Salomon, héritier et gardien jaloux du nom glorieux de Notre aïeul Sala Sallassie, Nous, Menilik II, avons voulu par cette guerre opiniâtre contre les États esclavagistes, prouver à toute l'Europe civilisée Notre sincère attachement à la cause de l'humanité inaugurée par le Christ.

Nos armées victorieuses commencaient à se retirer et regagnaient paisiblement leurs foyers, lorsqu'elles furent provoquées par des paroles injurieuses : par trois fois le Roi Tekla Haïmanot, Souverain du Godjam, Nous défia au combat dans les plaines mêmes du Godru, possession qu'il devait à Notre générosité. Blessé dans notre honneur, nous nous vîmes forcés d'accepter le combat.

La journée du 5 Juin restera mémorable dans les annales du Choa.

Une lutte acharnée dura jusqu'au soir, et la victoire Nous fut enfin assurée par l'impétuosité et la bravoure de Notre cavalerie Galla, qui armée de lances seulement et bravant les fusils et les canons, divisa en deux l'armée ennemie et parvint ainsi à la mettre en pleine déroute.

Tekla Haïmanot et ses deux fils, son général en chef Ras Derrasso ainsi que ses autres généraux et Choums en grand nombre, tous ses soldats, armes et bagages sont tombés entre Nos mains. Tekla Haïmanot, grièvement blessé, et les autres principaux chefs, conduits à Notre résidence royale, y sont chrétiennement traités. Les soldats et les femmes ont été renvoyés dans leur pays. Les Choums remis également en liberté ont préféré, pour la plupart, rester au Choa.

Nous aurions pu Nous emparer du Godjam et étouffer ainsi ce foyer du commerce des esclaves ; mais Nous devons penser à défendre Notre propre patrie. Nous savons, en effet, que Nos victoires Nous ont suscité de puissantes inimitiés, et ce n'est que confiants dans la Sainteté de la cause que Nous avons entrepris de défendre, confiant dans la protection de Dieu et la sympathie de la libre Europe que Nous attendons les évènements quels qu'ils soient.

Nous n'en poursuivrons pas moins Notre œuvre d'ouvrir et d'assurer à la Science, au Commerce et à l'industrie les routes qui conduisent aux riches pays du Sud, d'éloigner et de punir avec une sévère justice les avides et cruels marchands de chair humaines.

Nous Nous réservons de faire connaître à Votre Majesté les dispositions intérieures que Nous jugerons convenable de prendre pour que Notre oeuvre demeure efficace, et que les fruits du sang si généreusement versé ne soient point perdus.

Fait en Notre ville Royale d'Antoto, le 20 Juillet 1882.

We, Minīlik II, by the grace of God King of Shewa, to Her Majesty Queen Victoria, the sovereign of the United Kingdom and India. How is Your Majesty? We are in good health, and so are our armies by the grace of the Almighty. We are happy to be able to announce to Your Majesty that a long and laborious campaign of seven months against the slave kingdoms, for the most part Muslim, situated to the south and west of our domains, and masters of the route from Shewa to Kefa, has recently made us able to subjugate the kings of Limmu, Goma, Gumma, Gēra, and the Christian king of Kefa and make them tributaries. We have completely destroyed these centres of slavery and set free thousands of poor human beings. The unique direct and legitimate descendant of the dynasty of Selomon, heir and jealous guardian of the glorious name of our forefather Sahle Sillasē, we, Minīlik II, have desired to prove, by this unyielding war against the slave states, to all civilized Europe our sincere attachment to the cause of humanity initiated by Christ.

Our victorious armies began to retire and peacefully regain their bases when they were provoked by insulting words. Three times King Tekle Haymanot, the sovereign of Gojjam, challenged us to fight on the very plains of Gudru, a possession which he owed to our generosity. Our honour offended, we saw ourselves forced into combat. The day of 5 June shall remain memorable in the annals of Shewa. A furious battle lasted until evening and our victory was finally assured by the impetuosity and valour of our Galla cavalry which, armed with lances alone, and defying rifles and cannon, divided the enemy army into two and thus succeeded in routing it completely.

Tekle Haymanot and his two sons, his commander in chief *Ras* Dereso, as well as his other generals and numerous chiefs, all his soldiers, weapons and baggage fell into our hands. Tekle Haymanot, who was seriously wounded, and the other principal chiefs were conducted to our royal residence and are being treated there in a Christian manner. The soldiers and women have been sent back to their country. The chiefs, who were also set free, have for the most part preferred to stay in Shewa.

We would have been able to capture Gojjam and thus stamp out this centre of trade in slaves. But we have to think about defending our own homeland. We know in fact that our victories have aroused powerful animosity against us, and it is only through confidence in the sacredness of the cause which we have undertaken to defend and in the protection of God and the sympathy of free Europe that we await whatever events may come.

Nevertheless, we will pursue our work to open up and secure to science and commerce and to industry the routes which lead to the rich countries of the South, to expel and punish by severe justice the greedy and cruel traders in human flesh.

We reserve to ourselves [the privilege of making] known to Your Majesty the interior dispositions which we judge it convenient to make, in order that our effort remains effective and that the fruits of the blood so generously shed shall not be lost.

Made in our royal city of Inṭoṭṭo, 20th July 1882.

Seal: Minīlik, King of Shewa. The Lion of the tribe of Judah has prevailed.

FO 95/742, no. 128, French original. Identical letters were sent to several European heads of state. They were either written by a French-speaking secretary – but the handwriting is neither that of Yosēf Nigusē (see doc. 170) nor that of Gebri'ēl Welde Gobena (see doc. 177) – or possibly on his instructions by the French merchant L. A. Brémond, who was engaged in establishing Obok as a French trading base in 1882.

In addition to the above to Queen Victoria, the copies for King Leopold of Belgium and President Jules Grévy of France have been located, Archives des Palais Royaux, Brussels, and AEMD, Afrique 62, fols 567–568, respectively. The differences in the wording of, for instance, the letter to Leopold and the one to Victoria are insignificant, e.g. "defiant" instead of "bravant", "soignés" instead of "traités", and the explanation "pour rentrer dans leur patrie" added in the letter to Leopold. The original of the letter to Umberto seems to have disappeared, as affirmed by Carlo Giglio who published Umberto's reply in *L'Italia in Africa*, I.2, p. 251. A translation into Amharic in very poor handwriting, certainly made by a European, is found in ASSGI, 19, 5, fol. 35.

Document no. 89

Alula Ingida Qubī to Achille Raffray, 20 July 1882

May the letter of *Ras* Alula, who is *turk basha*, reach the consul of France, Raffray. How are you? As for me, thank God, I am well.

Your letter has reached me. As for the matter of the money, I have communicated the words of your letter to His Majesty. And he answered me, "Until today, no one has come to me; [it is] not that I have refused [to receive] him. So now, from Mesqel (26 September) onwards, as soon as an accredited person shall come to me, I shall willingly hand it over."

Besides, His Majesty has, at the news of a battle between King Minīlik and *Nigus* Tekle Haymanot, gone to Wello in order to find out the cause of their quarrel. And now, King Minīlik has sent this message to Yohannis: "It is he (Tekle Haymanot) who wanted to oppress me and who offended me; as for me, I have used no violence, sought no quarrel in order to join battle with him. It is not I who am responsible or at fault. So now, may His Majesty accord me the proper, and in his opinion just, judgement, and condemn me if I ought to be [condemned]. I am prepared to come bringing with me *Nigus* Tekle Haymanot and appear before you, and confront each other in every respect and on all points in dispute."

Now, His Majesty has established his camp at Werre'īlu, in order to keep an eye on them and wait for them until their arrival. Moreover, the Italians have written to him: "It is because Minīlik is our friend, that we are sending him cannon and arms and everything we have", and His Majesty has replied to them: "The French government is my friend. I have not written to it; otherwise it would not send me one or two, but a great number.["] If I write this to you, it is to let you know that His Majesty loves you and [will tell you] all that happens.

Written in the camp of Werre'īlu, 14 Hamlē in the year of grace 1874 (20 July 1882).

AECPC, Massaouah 4, fol. 287, French translation. The issue – the matter of the money – is somewhat obscure. Most probably it is the question of a purchase of arms for Yohannis, with Raffray as agent. The French text uses "roi" for Minīlik and "neguss" for Tekle Haymanot. While the Amharic original in all likelihood had *nigus* for both Minīlik and Tekle Haymanot, the French missionary M. Coulbeaux, who translated the letter, was obviously influenced by the fact that Minīlik was known also in Europe as the "King of Ethiopia". Thus, the translation of this and the following letter refers to Minīlik as king while using *nigus* for Tekle Haymanot.

Document no. 90

Yohannis IV to Achille Raffray, 17 Aug. 1882

May the letter of the Elect of God Yohannis, King of Kings of Zion and Ethiopia, reach the consul of France, Raffray.

How are you? As for me, by the grace of God and the intercession of Our Lady of Zion, I am well, blessed be her mercy forever. The two kings, King Minīlik and *Nigus* Tekle Haymanot, had by the instigation of Satan a distressing encounter on the borders of the Galla territories. To put an end to these hostilities and better see who is to blame in this case and reestablish accord, I had come to Wello. But now the two kings have submitted themselves. I have had returned the possessions that had been taken away, reconciled the hostile parties and reestablished accord through a solid convention. I have set up camp for the time being on a height in a territory called Werre'īlu.

I write these details to you as a friend in order to let you know what has happened. Since a long time back the kings of France have been the friends of my ancestors, the kings of Ethiopia, and up till now, up till my reign, it is from the French government that presents have come to us.

Moreover, and lastly, when its missionaries wrote about the burning of their church and the injury they had suffered, they nevertheless wrote good words to me and said nothing that hurt my heart. We are thus your friends of long standing, so let me therefore become friends with the French government. Please write to it on my behalf a letter of friendship. Please obtain for me from it the opportunity to have sent to me at my expense cannons, guns, gunpowder and all other munitions and arms that become a king. It is not difficult for it to provide this franchise for me by its will. If you are authorized to come and see me, I would be pleased to see you, since you are my friend. So if there is nothing to prevent you, please come and see me.

Previously, the English, in response to a letter from me, wrote to me, "You and the Egyptians are both our sons, we will reconcile you . . ." But I, fearing that this might seem like pride on my part, answered them: "Well, may some man suitable for this, among you or the French government, become aware of the injustice I suffer, and we shall each stay where we are until your arbitration."

After having started, they abandoned this matter of mine.

It is because you are my friend that I write this to you to let you know about the injustice and violence I am subjected to. It is not that my strength fails me or that I need someone to complain to. Do your best then to provide me with a solid and perfect friendship.

Written at the camp of Werre'īlu on the 13th of Nehasē (17 August 1882) in the year of grace 1874.

AECPC, Massaouah 4, fols 287–288, French translation.

Document no. 91

Yohannis IV to Gerhard Rohlfs, 19 Aug. 1882

May the message from the Elect of God Yohannis, King of Zion, King of Kings of Ethiopia, reach Gerhard Dr. Rohlfs.

How have you been? I, with my army, am well, by the grace of God, through the intercession of our Mother Zion, with the God of the saints, to whom be glory and praise, for His mercy lasts forever.

Your letter has reached us by the hand of *Lij* Ingidashēt. To the English, since they let my country Bogos (Moges) be taken away by the late Munzinger (Misinjir), I addressed a letter complaining about the taking away of my land. They said to me: "He has no right to this, instead your land should be vacated." With this they betrayed me, they did not see to the leaving of the land. With the words, "Go, fight him" they urged on the Turks and let me be attacked. After that they wrote to me again, "Do not quarrel with your neighbour. Christian blood should not be shed for nothing; we want to bring you peace; stay in your countries."

Since I deemed it good, I wrote to those who claim to want to bring me peace in a good way, inasmuch as I added the humiliation and the act of violence committed against me by the Turks the following answer, "Good! You may bring me peace, if you arrange so that I can stay in the land, possessed by the ancient kings; according to this you may determine my borders." However, they did not determine my borders and did not bring me peace. After examining my claim they said, "But you have peace." With this statement they gave up the matter which they had taken up.

Now this is nothing I care about any longer. It is God who made me king. My land is in his hands. Nevertheless, it is my wish that you should be informed about it; but as I have no one [here] to whom I want to express any complaint about [the matter], you should rather come here so that we can have a meeting. The two kings, King Minīlik and King Tekle Haymanot, had become enemies over the boundary and fought each other. Nowadays, both my sons and I have, after having restituted to both the property lost to them and thus reconciled them, taken residence in Wello and stay there. The wording of both, the Gi'iz and the Arabic, is the same.

Written in the camp of Werre'īlu, on 14 Nehasē in the year of grace 1874.

HHS, RA 14, Amharic original; AAPA, Abt. A, I.B.9, 1/1–3, German translation dated 20 August. The German text, a translation by Rohlfs (?), is poor. It attempts to translate the Amharic literally, and in some cases it is impossible to say with certainty what the text means. *Lij* Ingidashēt is the son of the German migrant Wilhelm Schimper; see doc. 52.

Document no. 92

Ḥamad La'īta to Pietro Antonelli, 28 Sept. 1882

Praise be to God!

To the respected and beloved Count Antonelli, may God protect him.

I give you my compliments and inform you that I have learnt about all your concerns from 'Abd al-Raḥmān. When he came, I had war in my country. The cause of it is Abū Bakr *Pasha*, the one who made himself great owing to our work. He sent the Egyptian soldiers to occupy my territory.

As for your imminent departure, it was 'Abd al-Raḥmān who told me about it. I shall be the one who lets you pass on my route and wherever you want. Maḥammad Ḥanfadhē and I are but one person, and with regard to the caravans I was appointed responsible by Sultan Ḥanfadhē. King Minīlik and all the Abyssinians know about this. As soon as I had received your letter, I sent 'Abd al-Raḥmān back to you in Aden, and my brother with 'Abd al-Qadir to Awsa, so that they bring you the protection of the sultan.

Since we know who you are, everything will be done, and you will have camels and your feet will not touch the earth; I myself will carry you on my head. From the letter that Maḥammad Ḥanfadhē will send, you will learn about my work and you will see that he tells you the same as I say. Before now, I already knew you by name, because Gīyorgīs and 'Abd al-Raḥmān had talked to me about you. Be assured that you, apart from possible misadventures sent by God, shall pass through our territories respected and untroubled.

In order that I may be able to send the caravan of the king (Minīlik) faster, I am sending 'Abd al-Raḥmān and Gebre Sillasē to Aden.

Health and prosperity [to you].

The 15th day of the month of Dhū al-Qa'da 1299.

(Seal of Ḥamad La'īta).

AP.DD, XV, p. 85, Italian translation. Gīyorgīs must here refer to Gebre Sillasē Nigusē who was also known as Gīyorīs Gebre Sillasē.

Document no. 93

Yohannis IV to Umberto I, 30 Sept. 1882

In the name of Our Lord Jesus Christ, praise be to Him.

May the message from the Elect of God Yohannis, King of Zion, King of Kings of Ethiopia, reach the honoured and respected Umberto I, King of Italy.

How are you, really? By the loving-kindness of God, by the intercession of Our Mother Zion, I am well. May the God of the saints be glorified and praised, for His mercy lasts for ever.

I have received your respected letter with its seal by the hand of your consul, Giovanni Branchi. The medal of honour you have sent me on red velvet with fringes, a silk cloak, eight rifles, two pistols, a gold embroidered cloth, a silk cloth, a golden umbrella, a golden girdle, and a pair of binoculars, together with all the other not enumerated things, have reached me. Thank you.

Written in the town of Semera on 21st Meskerem in the year of grace 1875.

Seal: King of Kings Yohannis, King of Zion in Ethiopia. The cross has defeated the tribe of Isma'ēl. Yūḥannā, King of Kings of Zion in Abyssinia. The cross has defeated the people of Ismā'īl. 1864.

ASMAI 36/2–13, Amharic original. Italian translation. Giovanni Branchi was, strictly speaking, not a "consul" of Italy. He had worked in the Far East as an Italian diplomat in the 1870s and been appointed civil commissioner (Regio Commissario Civile) of Aseb in 1880, taking up his post in 1881. He resigned in 1884 and subsequently became Italian consul-general in New York.

Document no. 94

Minīlik II to Paul Soleillet, 9 Oct. [1882]

May [this letter] sent by King Minīlik reach Mr. Soleillet (*musē* Soliyū). How are you, really? I am well, thank God.

And your letter has reached me. When I saw it I was very happy. But if you come to me today, I am busy, and it does not suit me. It is better if you wait there. I will not be staying many days.

When I have finished my business I will come quickly. As for what you told me, to release Gebre Maryam for you, I have sent orders to release him. May God make it possible [for us] to meet (lit. see each other with our bodily eyes).

Written on the 30th day of Meskerem.

Seal: Minīlik, King of Shewa. The Lion of the tribe of Judah has prevailed.

BN, Ethiop. Abb. 303, Amharic original. Soleillet arrived on the Red Sea coast in January 1882 as the agent of the French Company of Obok. Gebre Maryam is otherwise unknown and should not be confused with the Catholic convert *Abba* Gebre Maryam who was taken captive and later interrogated and tortured at the court of Yohannis in 1881. For the context of this letter, see Harold Marcus, *The Life and Times of Menelik II: Ethiopia 1844–1913*, Oxford, 1975, p. 60.

Document no. 95

Maḥammad Ḥanfadhē to Sa'īd 'Awīḍān, 16 Oct. 1882

God be praised and to Him prayer and salutation.

To our distinguished and generous friend Sa'īd 'Awīḍān. May God keep him healthy. If you ask about our condition, we are in good health and prosperity, and may God accord the same grace to you.

I let you know that I have received the letter and understood what you say to me. I have already defined the question a first time with Minīlik and with them (i.e. the Italians): if they wish to send goods to Minīlik, they should send them to me and I will see to it that they reach Minīlik. To them I have written these words and also to Minīlik. If they wish to accompany the goods, they should address themselves to 'Abd al-Raḥmān bin Yūsif, since we have accorded them passage on his behalf. I have only one word, and God is one. So if they wish to send the goods on my route, they can just send it, but if they wish to accompany the goods, may they go to 'Abd al-Raḥmān, to whom we have indicated a route in this vicinity. That is what I let you know.

From Sultan Maḥammad, bin Sultan Ḥanfadhē, the deceased. May God be gracious to him. May it be so.

ASMAE, AE 2, Italian translation. Printed in *L'Italia in Africa*, I.2 no. 275, allegato 1, p. 247. The Arabic original has not been located. A note above the letter states that it was received in Aseb on 15 November 1882 and written on 16 October. Another note in the margin states that the letter was accompanied by a letter from Sa'īd 'Awīḍān to Maḥammad Ḥanfadhē dated 4 October 1882 concerning Antonelli's travel to Shewa and request for a safe trading route, to which this is most probably the reply. The letter by Sa'īd 'Awīḍān has not been found.

Document no. 96

Minīlik II to Giulio Pestalozza, 18 Oct. 1882

Seal
Werre'īlu, 9th Ṭiqimt 1875

I have received the letter that you have sent me about which I am happy. I am satisfied with the news you give me of the arrival of Antonelli. Since I had earlier understood that Antonelli would come to Obok I have sent 60 camels. Since he has not disembarked there my camels have loaded merchandise to be sent with my people.

I now correspond with Maḥammad Ḥanfadhē to open the route, and I conduct negotiations for that purpose. Even earlier I have written to Maḥammad Ḥanfadhē in that sense. I have now asked Maḥammad Ḥanfadhē to provide the necessary camels for the escort. I added that Antonelli should come by way of Zeyla this time, but his luggage by way of Awsa. Ḥanfadhē had written to me that he would not receive a European on his territory and therefore the route of Zeyla is preferable for the moment, but when the new route finally will be open the Italians can pass by it. For the moment it is better to abstain since white people cannot travel there. If signor Antonelli would like to take this way I am not of his opinion and would take the other way. It would be better though that his luggage went by way of Awsa. I am conducting negotiations and will make it possible to open this way since this is to the advantage of my country and to the country of the king of Italy, and to make something that is approved by the king of Italy I will make every effort.

Mr Pierre (Labatut) has bought 40 rifles for me and since I hear that they are already in Aseb, I ask you to send these arms to me.

ASMAI 1/5–31, Amharic original, either misplaced or lost. Printed Italian translation in *L'Italia in Africa*, I.3 no. 296, allegato, p. 23. Giulio Pestalozza was appointed "segretario" with the title "Reggente il commissariato civile i Assab" from June 1882 to November 1883 after the transfer of the rights of the Rubattino Co. to the Italian government in June 1882 during the absence of the appointed "Regio Commissario Civile", Giovanni Branchi. He was reinstated as "Reggente" in August 1884. See *L'Italia in Africa*, I.2 p. 247. Pierre Labatut is known as a French arms dealer.

Document no. 97

'Abd al-Raḥmān Yūsif to Pietro Antonelli, 20 Oct. 1882

God be praised.

Salutation to the respectable Count Antonelli.

On my arrival at Obok, I did not find Gebre Sillasē Beddo to send camels to you, so I left my uncle *Shaykh* Osman so that he is the one who will bring you the camels and the men I will leave Sagallo on the 7th of Dhū al-Ḥijja and you will see how our business will succeed by the grace of God. *Shaykh* Osman is a man who will remain in our service in Aseb, so that he becomes our agent: try to make the consul accord him an employment, for without paying you cannot avail yourself of people. When he arrives with the camels, we ask you from our part to give him money to send to his family. Do this, I tell you. Do this.

As for myself, Maḥammad Ḥanfadhē has sent me two couriers and told me, "Come, come", and this is in order to make the necessary agreements for your journey in Abyssinia. Fear nothing, be calm. I beg you to give my compliments to the consul and tell him that I will not forget his words and that, with God's help, I shall arrive with all our affairs in order.

In the month of Dhū al-Ḥijja on Friday, the 7th day, 1299 (Gregorian calendar: 20 October 1882).

'Abd al-Raḥmān bin *Shaykh* Yūsif.

ASMAI 7/1–1, Italian translation. Printed in *AP.DD*, XV, p. 83. No Arabic version has been located. We have not been able to identify Gebre Sillasē Beddo, but it is quite probable that he is the same as *Azzazh* Gebre Sillasē Nigusē who appears in numerous documents in this volume as Minīlik's agent on the coast. The Italian administrators at Aseb were most often designated as "consuls" by the Afar. The administrator in Aseb at this time was Giulio Pestalozza. See further doc. 100.

Document no. 98

Maḥammad Ḥanfadhē to Pietro Antonelli, 24 Oct. 1882

Praise be to God. Prayer and salutation to the One Almighty.

To our distinguished and generous respectable friend Antonelli. May God always and everywhere be propitious to him.

We have received your good letter and have understood what you say to us. You intimate your wish to go from Aseb to Shewa. May it be so and fear nothing. God willing, I shall protect you and protect others. As for the camels, we have none at our disposal for the time being. They are all engaged for Shewa. One of my men will come to you with 'Abd al-Qādir bin Ibrāhīm and 'Abd al-Raḥmān bin *Shaykh* Yūsif, and he will accompany you. For my part, I send greetings and wishes of prosperity to you.

In the month of Dhū al-Ḥijja, on Tuesday the 11th day, in the year 1299 of Hijra (this date corresponds to 24 October 1882, in the Gregorian calendar).

Sultan Maḥammad bin Sultan Ḥanfadhē.

ASMAI 7/1–1, Italian translation. Printed in *AP.DD*, XV, p. 84.

Document no. 99

Maḥammad Ḥanfadhē to Commissario Regio in Aseb, 24 Oct. 1882

Praise be to God and prayer and salutation to Him, the one Almighty.

To my illustrious, generous and dear friend the Italian consul. May God always and everywhere be favourable to him.

If you ask about us, we are, thanks to God, well and content. I let you know that I have received the letter that you sent me earlier and have studied it. As to the person that you tell me that he intends to go to Shewa, there is neither any difficulty nor anything to fear, and God willing, I shall protect him and protect others. This I have written to him as well as to you in answer to your letter brought to me by messenger. I have agreed to all this merely in order to please Minīlik and ʿAbd al-Raḥmān Yūsif and because ʿAbd al-Raḥmān wanted that route. ʿAbd al-Raḥmān is my agent and Minīlik's and I have granted him a (illegible word), and if you help me on your part I will help you. Greetings.

From Sultan Maḥammad bin Sultan Ḥanfadhē, on the 11th day, Tuesday, of the month of Dhū al-Ḥijja in 1299.

ASMAE, AE 2, Italian translation. Printed in *L'Italia in Africa*, I.2 no. 275, allegato 2, pp. 247–248. The Arabic original of ASMAI 1/4–28 has been misplaced or lost. The Italian translation carries a note stating that the letter arrived in Aseb on 17 November 1882 with ʿAbd al-Qādir, a Danākil messenger sent by Antonelli from Aden together with a letter to Maḥammad Ḥanfadhē in which he advised him to answer the letter from the Commissario in Aseb.

Document no. 100

Maḥammad Ḥanfadhē to Giulio Pestalozza, 25 Nov. 1882

تاريخ في شهر محرم الحرام خلي منه رابع عشر يوم الاحد سنة ١٣٠٠ من الهجرة

الدعاء الوافر والثناء المتكاثر يهديان جناب عالي والياه والجباه سلالة الاجلاء
الاكابر الاجل الافخم الاكمل الاشيم محمود السجايا والشيم الصاحب الحليم
قنصر عصب حرس الباري من الاكدار ذاته وحماه من الاضرار صفاته ولا زال
في بارخ المجد والاجلال وشامخ العز والاقبال امين ثم امابعد فالباعث التحرير
ذريعة الاخلاص هو السوال عن صحة ذاتكم السنية واعتدال اوقاتكم الزكية
الهنان هي الامل من حضرة عالم الازال لا زال الجناب في اكمل الخير والسرور ربيع
الحقيقي من كرم الله تعالى في اتم الخير والسرور يسال عن حال الجناب بالغدوات
والبكور ثم لا يخفى محترم الجناب ان الشيخ عبد الرحمن بن الشيخ يوسف بلغني سلامتك
واما من جهة الجوابات امر سفركم الى سفركم شوى نصبنا لكم شيخ عبد الرحمن بن شيخ يوسف
اعتمد واعليه بكل ما بدا لكم بطريق او غيره للحبيث انه كفاية ونهاية وهو جعلناه محل النفع
بكل امر كان ما كان وارسلنا بيده علامة من عندنا تصديقا لكم واعتمد واعليه بدوام الدوام
وارسلت لك هدية منا لاجل ارتباط المحبة وعقد اساس المودة ثوب حبشي منقشات ومعلمات
حربة وترس وجنبيه وخلخال بيد شيخ عبد الرحمن بن شيخ يوسف فتفضل منه بالقبول
كان ما يليق بنا لكم هذه الهدية حتى القليل من الخليل جليل للحبيث عبد الرحمن المذكور ونستعجل بالرجوع
الكم لا تلومنا ما دمنا في الحيوة وان شاء الله تتمم المراد دايم والدوام

واما الجوابات الذي يجي من عندكم بما اردتم
خلي تجينا بطريق عبد الرحمن يوسف

مستمد الدعاء من
عند سلطان محمد
سلطان حنفري دوم

وان تفضلتم من احسانكم
السابق ولاحق من الهدية
فتقبضون بيد عبد الرحمن
بن شيخ يوسف المرحوم
يا لديكم معلوم

Dated in the month of Muḥarram, the sacred, fourteen days having elapsed, on Sunday, the year 1300 Hijra.

Abundant prayers and generous eulogy presented to His Honour, the high-standing and honoured, offspring of the illustrious and the majestic, the most illustrious and magnificent, the most perfect and most virtuous, the laudable of nature and conduct, the clement friend, the consul of Aseb. May the Creator protect his person from all distress and preserve his felicity from all harm. May he live in glory and fame, and remain in might and prosperity. Amen.

And now, the reason for writing [and] the affirmation of our loyalty, is the inquiry about your noble health and about the harmony of your pleasant times, which are what we hope for from the Knowledgeable of eternity. May Your Honour remain in complete health and happiness. Thanks to God's kindness, your true beloved is well and pleased and prays for your well-being morning and forenoon. As is not hidden from Your Honourable Highness, *Shaykh* 'Abd al-Raḥmān, bin *Shaykh* Yūsif, the deceased, has reassured me of your health. As for the letters, your trip to Shewa has been authorized [and] we have assigned *Shaykh* 'Abd al-Raḥmān bin *Shaykh* Yūsif to you; count on him whatever faces you on the way since he is sufficiently aware and fully authorized. We have given him authorization to settle and resolve any issue. In fact, we have also given him a power of attorney so that you could trust him. Rely on him at all times. Finally, I have sent you a present to tie us together in love and establish friendship; actually, I have sent you an Ethiopian dress, engraved pieces, milestones, a lance, a shield, a pound and an anklet with *Shaykh* 'Abd al-Raḥmān bin *Shaykh* Yūsif. Please accept it, even though you deserve better than this present, since from a friend the insignificant is significant [and] since the named 'Abd al-Raḥmān was hurrying back to you. Do not reproach us as long as we live. If it is the will of God Almighty, your wishes will be fulfilled for ever and ever. As for any other correspondence, please do send it only with *Shaykh* 'Abd al-Raḥmān Yūsif.

And if you wish in accordance with your former and further benevolence to offer me a gift, please send it to me through 'Abd al-Raḥmān, bin *Shaykh* Yūsif, the deceased. Of this you have been informed.

The sender of the message is Sultan Maḥammad, bin Sultan Ḥanfadhē, the deceased

Seals: Sultan Maḥammad Ḥanfadhē.
Sultan Maḥammad Ḥanfadhē.

ASMAE, AE 2, Arabic original; ASMAI 7/1–1, Italian translation. The letter is written to "the consul of Aseb", a designation often used by the local rulers referring to the Italian administrator in Aseb. Giovanni Branchi had taken up his post as *Regio Commissario Civile* in Aseb in 1881, but in his absence from early 1882 it was Giulio Pestalozza in the capacity of "Segretario" with the title *Reggente* who was responsible until Branchi returned to his post as from November 1883 until August 1884, when Pestalozza was again reinstated as *Reggente*. The mentioning of "your trip to Shewa" must be understood as a reference to the Italian expedition of Pietro Antonelli, interpreted by Maḥammad Ḥanfadhē as an official Italian expedition.

Document no. 101

Maḥammad Ḥanfadhē to Pietro Antonelli, 25 Nov. 1882

Praise be to God.

To my highly respected and very wise friend Count Antonelli, may God always and everywhere keep him safe; may it be so.

What urges us to address this friendly letter to you is our wish to be informed about your health, which we hope that God will always grant to be perfect. As regards your true friend he is, due to God's generosity, well and keeps asking with great interest for news about you. We wish to let you know that the one who brought your letters was *Shaykh* 'Abd al-Raḥmān bin *Shaykh* Yūsif, your friend, who arrived here in good health. We know your feelings and from 'Abd al-Raḥmān we have learnt the truth of your word. We put our hope in God and in the growth and continuation of our friendship. We send you a gift with 'Abd al-Raḥmān to confirm our friendship, an Abyssinian mantle, a shield, a lance, a knife and two bracelets; receive them and enjoy them. The value is in the friendship with which the gift is given, for these things are certainly not worthy of being given by a man like me to a man like you, but 'Abd al-Raḥmān did not want to stay to give me time to prepare my gifts. For this reason, excuse me for sending you a small thing this time; under other circumstances we will complete what we want.

As of your departure to Shewa we have given the assignment to *Shaykh* 'Abd al-Raḥmān bin *Shaykh* Yūsif. Count on his word about the route and other matters, for he is a competent man and I have nominated him my agent and representative and we have given him our seal (?) to make this clear.

Both with regard to letters and other things that you may wish to send me, always use 'Abd al-Raḥmān.

May God help you.

Dated in the month of Muḥarram, the 14th day, Sunday, in the year of Hijra.

Sultan Maḥammad, bin Sultan Ḥanfadhē, the deceased.

(Seal of Maḥammad Ḥanfadhē.)

Translator: C. Hag.

ASMAI 7/1–1, Italian translation. Another copy with minor differences is found in ASMAE, AE 2. The translation is introduced as: "Translation from Arabic of a letter from Maḥammad Ḥanfadhē, Sultan of Aussa to Count Antonelli received in Aseb on 17 December 1882" (our translation of the Italian text). It is somewhat unclear what the Italian translation refers to in the phrase: "dato un nostro signo /si allude al bastone/ affinche ciò sia palese". We have interpreted it as referring to the sealed power of attorney dated the next day; see the following document.

Document no. 102

Maḥammad Ḥanfadhē, power of attorney for ‘Abd al-Raḥmān, 26 Nov. 1882

Seal.

I, Sultan Maḥammad bin [son of] Sultan Ḥanfadhē the deceased, herewith declare that I have written ‘Abd al-Raḥmān bin *Shaykh* Yūsif a power of attorney. He is appointed as my attorney in fact and therefore controls our interests and judges what is for our benefit and what is against it. I have delegated him my power; hence, his orders are valid and effective. Whoever contradicts and opposes his orders is considered to be one of the *ferenj* and their followers among the Shewa residents. Whoever disobeys him and does not abide by his word has betrayed me and will be severely punished whereas whoever follows him shall gain victory and triumph.

Dated in the month of Muḥarram the sacred after fifteen days had elapsed, Monday after the afternoon prayer, the year 1300 after the Hijra of the chosen; God bless him and grant him salvation. The writer of this letter is ‘Abd al-Raḥmān, bin Muḥammad Turāb.

Seal of Sultan Ḥanfadhē

ASMAE, AE 2, copy of Arabic original, Italian translation; ASMAI 7/1–1 has two different Italian translations, one of which is very close to the ASMAE, AE 2 version.

Document no. 103

Maḥammad Ḥanfadhē to Pietro Antonelli, 6 Dec. 1882

Praise be to God.

To the highly respectable and very wise friend Count Antonelli, may God keep him safe, may this be so.

We inform you that your letter as well as your gifts have arrived with ʻAbd al-Qādir on the 11th of Muḥarram. We have already sent you many letters announcing that we have sent gifts to you as well as to the consul. We now send you *Shaykh* ʻAbd al-Raḥmān bin *Shaykh* Yūsif and Bassitri, who will serve to protect you and let the Bedouins know that your blood is my blood; therefore fear nothing. You will hear all that we wish from you from ʻAbd al-Raḥmān's mouth. If you continue to let us know the truth and if you keep your word, you shall always have our ever-growing friendship. See to it that your word is not like that of the French. Help yourself and the consul, ʻAbd al-Raḥmān, and do not listen to the words of the house of Abū Bakr, who has betrayed the Danākil. He who uses him can never be our friend. As for the camels we have spoken to ʻAbd al-Raḥmān and Bassitri and we have informed Sultan Burhān.

In the month of Muḥarram, the 25th day of the year 1300.

From Sultan Maḥammad, bin [son of] Sultan Ḥanfadhē, the deceased.

(Seal)

ASMAI 7/1–1, Italian translation. Printed in *AP.DD*, XV, p. 89. The Italian text states that the letter arrived in Aseb on 17 December 1882 through ʻAbd al-Raḥmān.

Document no. 104

Burhān Muḥammad to Giulio Pestalozza, 17 Dec. 1882

Praise be to God alone, He who has no partner. To His Honourable Excellency, the most noble and most honoured, the respected and beloved, I refer to the true friend Giulio Pestalozza. Peace be upon you and the mercy of Allah, peace be upon you.

We inform you [that] Sa'īd 'Awīḍān reached us and spoke about the camels. We did not obtain camels for rent only for sale; we hope that you desire to buy some. We inform you we did not obtain any for rent. As for the letter that was sent to me from Sultan Maḥammad Ḥanfadhē, in it he mentioned the desire of the *ferenj* to send goods to Minīlik on my route. This is fine, they are authorized. They want to go with the caravan and take the route of Siar and below Sinkara. I gave orders [to take] that route. O true friend, I am willing, if Count Antonelli desires to travel, to send with him people from my route to Abyssinia (al-Ḥabasha) to King Minīlik.

As for the camels, we did not obtain camels for rent; I sent but obtained except (unintelligible word) only for sale, and you think that I did not look for camels thoroughly. Mr. Count Antonelli and I have become bound in friendship and affection. It is my desire that he reaches King Minīlik, and [my desire] to be generous to him, to the king and to you. As for the camels, we have none. Greetings. Dated the month of Safar, the sixth.

Signature half erased:
The greetings and the paper come from
Sultan [Burhān] bin Sultan Muḥammad, the deceased.

And don't forget the coffee O my friend.
Seal: Burhān Muḥammad

ASMAE, AE 2, Arabic original; ASMAI 7/1–1, Italian translation. In the Italian translation the date was misunderstood. Arabic *sanaa* (year) was read *sitta* (the sixth), thus *sesto* instead of *anno.* The sixth of Ṣafar corresponds to 17 December.

Document no. 105

Ḥamad La'īta to Giulio Pestalozza, 9 Jan. [1883]

And now, the message comes from Ḥamad La'īta to Mr. Pestalozza, the Governor (*ḥākim*) of Aseb, if you inquire about us, we are well. We would like to inform you that we are sending you this letter to announce that the delegation to Sultan Maḥammad Ḥanfadhē has left. Until I came to you a monthly payment has to be made for the months I have been away from you, counted according to the rules kept by you. And my arrival shall be soon, after our work is finished, and our money is collected from [the people] where I have been. I will come to you for the sake of friendship, and because you long to meet me.

As for the French, our relation has been different; we held opposing views, which lead to mutual aversion resulting in estrangement and separation. In addition, the French do not follow agreed conditions and do not respect fixed dates and deadlines. They show arms and power, and they withhold generosity and kindness. Their companionship is violent, and their conditions are haughty. It is necessary to inform you that this was the case with them; we disagreed and are not on good terms. And this is what we tell you. Furthermore, we are entitled to thirty riyal as monthly payment. God, God, and God, God.

Ḥamad La'īta.

Seal illegible.

Dated the last day of the month of Safar, Tuesday.

Seal illegible.

ASMAI 7/1–1, Arabic original. The addressee of the letter, "Busṭalūl", is obviously Giulio Pestalozza, the representative of Italy residing in Aseb at the time, in Arabic referred to as the *ḥākim* of Aseb. See doc. 100. The last sentence of the letter is unclear and the translation must therefore be regarded as tentative.

Document no. 106

Burhān Muḥammad to Giulio Pestalozza [Jan. 1883]

Praise be to God alone.

To His Honour, the dear and beloved, His Excellency, the pure friend, governor (*bir ṣāḥib*) of Aseb, Giulio Pestalozza. May God Almighty lead him. Amen.

The peace of God Almighty and His mercy and His blessing is what we bestow upon Your Excellency. What we tell you is that Count Antonelli is travelling to Abyssinia (al-Ḥabasha) by the route of Awsa with the authorization and protection of Sultan Maḥammad Ḥanfadhē. We agreed that he joins us to Sultan Maḥammad Ḥanfadhē, so that we can personally introduce them to one another. Thus, we are travelling with him to assure Your Excellency as representative of the Italian government, that we have done and will do our best and utmost in whatever benefits the above mentioned government whose protection we have not left.

We assert Your Excellency that we shall do our best, in agreement and alliance with Sultan Maḥammad Ḥanfadhē, to serve your interests and to exchange your merchandise in the land of Danākil depending upon his administration. Let it be known to Your Excellency that our travel is dedicated to this purpose which is of advantage. Therefore I ask Your Excellency to inform your sublime ministry of this. I present my greetings to Your Excellency.

The sender of the message is Sultan Burhān bin Sultan Muḥammad, the deceased.

Certified. (lit. It is true.)

ASMAE, AE, Arabic copy; ASMAI 7/1–1, Italian translation. The letter is not dated and has no seal. It is dated in the Italian archives 27–I 1883, but was probably written earlier, as suggested by a comparison with the following letter.

Document no. 107

Burhān Muḥammad to Pasquale Stanislao Mancini, 27 Jan. 1883

الحمد لله وحده كافي المهمات ودافع البليات الي العزيز سعادة المنستر هلنه الله
امين فان سالتم عنا فنحن في خير وعافيه نسلم عليك الف الف سلام ونعرفك الفرح
الشديد والاعتبار والفروح حق الصغير حق كنت انت نولي والاواخ حق
ملك منلك لمان عرفنا ان هو يودي حق ملك الطليان الي ملك منلك الذي
هو صاحبنا ومتوافقنا لاجل هذا ساعدناه بقلب فرح وقدمناله نفسنا و
أعطيناله الجمال ومحتاج الصغير الذي نقدر عليه سهلناله وخرجناه بالامان
وانا لمان عرفت ان هو رسول من طرفكم وكيل ويودي الهديات حق
ملك الطليان شاورت نفسي وقلت في نفسي هذي الالواصل نجعله إنكم انتم
دولة الطليان الذي وصلت عندي وقمت معه ومشيت بنفسي معه إلي
السلطان محمد حنفلي حتى نتمم إصلاح الطريق التجاريه ما بين عصب
وبشوي مع مساعدت ملك منلك وخصوصا الذي فرحني وقوّمني الحكم
والشرط الأمان والمحبة الذي انكتبت من سعادة المنستر في الكتاب الكريم
لمان فتر لي كنت انت نولي وانا نشكرجا عليك يا سعادة المنستر إنكتير
في لا فنصر عصب وللكمندار بانور حربي للعيال حقي وللمال
حقي حتى يصير نسولي مدة ما انا غايب مع كنت انت نولي وان شا الله انا
بروحي منا اوسه نخبر لك اخبار السفر حقه بالطيب والاشغال
الذي بانصلحها لا خصوصا ومنفعة عصب وان شا الله نحن
نفرح ونفرحكم بالامان والسلام

تاريخ شهر ربيع اول نهار الاثنين ثمنت عشر ١٣٠٠
١٨

من السلطان برهان رحيفه
ابن السلطان محمد

Praise be to God alone, He who dispels anxieties and makes afflictions disappear.

To His Eminence, the dear minister. May God Almighty lead him. Amen.

If you inquire about us, we are well and healthy, and we send you our very best regards. We are pleased to inform you that Count Antonelli has the full right to travel, the same right as the loyal people who obey King Minīlik. When we were informed that he is the messenger of the Italian king to our friend and provider King Minīlik, we were delighted to help him. So, we introduced ourselves and offered him, as much as we could, camels and provisions to travel. Then we did our best to facilitate his travel, and finally we sent him off in safety.

But, as soon as I realized that he was your representative and that he was bringing presents to King Minīlik, I thought and said to myself: We will treat this visitor as if it were you, [representing] the government of Italy, who had reached us. Thus, I accompanied him personally to Sultan Maḥammad Hanfadhē so that the commercial route between Aseb and Shewa would be improved with the help of King Minīlik.

What in particular made me delighted and happy were the provisions and terms for safety and friendship that were expressed by Your Eminence, the minister, in the legal letter which Count Antonelli explained to me. I beseech you eminent Minister to inform the Consul of Aseb and the commander of the warship that these are my people and this is my money, so that they guard them while I am away with Count Antonelli.

If it is the will of God Almighty, after I come back from Awsa I will report to you the news I gather during my travel about the improvements and works that we are doing, especially for the benefit of Aseb. And if it is the will of God Almighty, we will both rejoice in safety. Greetings.

Dated in the month of Rabī' al-Awwal, on Monday the 18th, the year 1300.

From Sultan Burhān [of] Raḥayta, bin [son of] Sultan Muḥammad, the deceased. May God bless him.

ASMAI 36/2–12, Arabic original and Italian translation. Pasquale Stanislao Mancini was the Italian minister of foreign affairs 1881–1885.

Document no. 108

Maḥammad Ḥanfadhē to Pasquale Stanislao Mancini, 14 March 1883

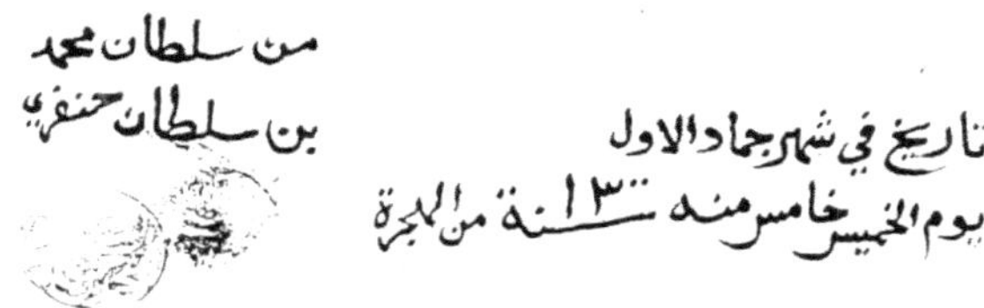
من سلطان محمد
بن سلطان حنفري

تاريخ في شهر جماد الاول
يوم الخميس خامس منه ١٣٠٠ سنة من الهجرة

الدعاء الوافر والثناء المتكاثر يهديان جناب عالي الجاه والجناب
سلالة الاجلا الاكابر الاجل الافخم الاكمل الاشيم محمود السجايا
والشيم الصاحب الحليم منستراي سد الاعظم حرس الباري من
الاكدار ذاته وحما من الاضرار صفاته ولازال في بارج المجد و
والاجلال وشامخ العز والاقبال امين اما بعد فالباعث التحرير ذريعة
الاخلاص هو السوال عن صحة ذاتكم السنية واعتدال اوقاتكم
الزكية اللتان هما الامل من حضرة عالم الازل لازال الجناب
في اكمل الخير والسرور ومحبكم الحقيقي من كرم الله تعالى في اتم الخير
والسرور يسال عن حال الجناب بالغدوات والبكور اما بعد الذي
اعرفكم وصل الينا من جنابكم المرسول منكم ووكيلكم كنت انتوانللي
فاويناه واكرمناه والزمناه واحشمناه على حسب طاقتنا واستخبرناه عن
حالكم واحوالكم وفهمنا من كل طرف من الصداقة والمحبة والكلامات الذي
انتم اصلحتم ورتبتم من طريق التجارية من عصب الى شوي بطريقنا قبلنا
وحبينا واعطينا الامر للرعيتنا حتى ينزلوا الى عصب القوافل للتجارة واما الشرط
والقنطرار خلينا على سلطان منلك حتى يقطع ويتوافق مع كنت انتوانللي و
وارسلنا معه جواباتنا ومرادنا ووكيلنا الى سلطان منلك ونحن فهمنا الحسد
والفساد الذي كان يباعد بيننا وبينكم حتى ما يكون العدو بيننا قبلنا صحبتكم
ومحبتكم بقلب طيب وفرح واما من جناب كنت انتوانللي شيعناه وجهزناه
الى شوى مع قافلتنا وهو اعطانا باسمكم هدية لنا فقبلنا منه بالعز والناموس
ونحن نعرفكم مرادنا من اباءنا واجدادنا ماسكين ملتنا ولا نتعدي على ملة
غيرنا ونطلب من دولتكم الحراسة من البحر بالبابورتكم من كل عدو وخاصة

من الحصابون الذي يتعدون بغير الحق ونحن نحرس في ارضنا تجارتكم ورعيتكم ونعطيهم كل الراحة
ونفاتح لهم طرقان في ارض حقنا بمنفعة التجارية

Abundant prayers and generous eulogy presented to His Honour, the high-standing and honoured, offspring of the illustrious and the majestic, the most illustrious and most magnificent, the most perfect and most virtuous, the estimable and laudable of nature, the clement friend, the minister of the Supreme Sovereign. May the Creator protect his person from all distress and preserve his felicity from all harm. May he live in glory and fame, and remain in might and prosperity. Amen.

And now, the reason for writing, the affirmation of our loyalty, is the inquiry about your noble health and about the harmony of your pleasant times, which are what we hope for from the Knowledgeable of eternity. May Your Honour remain in complete health and happiness. Thanks to God's kindness, your true beloved is well and pleased and prays for your well-being morning and forenoon.

And now, we inform you that your messenger and representative, Count Antonelli, has reached us. We welcomed him, sheltered him, served him and honoured him as much as we could. We asked him about your condition and your well-being, and we understood that there is friendship and kinship on all sides.

We accepted and appreciated the statement that you approved of and settled for the commercial route from Aseb to Shewa passing through our land. Thus we ordered our people to bring down their commercial caravans to Aseb. As for the conditions and the terms (*al-qanṭara*), we leave it for Sultan Minīlik so that he will conclude [the issue] and agree with Count Antonelli. Actually, we sent our letters, our wishes and our representative with him to Sultan Minīlik. We realized the envy and corruption that had estranged us from you. In order that there be no enmity between us, we have accepted your friendship and your kinship with joy and pleasure. As for Count Antonelli, we have equipped him and escorted him to Shewa with our caravan. He gave us a gift in your name, and we have accepted it according to law and honour. We would like to inform you of our objectives: since the days of our ancestors, we stick to our religion and do not offend any other religion. We ask your government to guard our coast with your steamer against any enemy especially the Egyptians who invade [our land] without any right. As for us, we will guard your people and your commerce on our land; we shall ensure their comfort and fix them routes on our legal lands for commercial benefits.

Dated in the month of Jumād al-Awwal, Thursday, the 5th, the year 1300 of *Hijra*.

From Sultan Maḥammad bin Sultan Ḥanfadhē.

Seals illegible.

ASMAI 7/1–1, Arabic original and Italian translation. The same day Maḥammad Ḥanfadhē sent a very similar accompanying letter to the consul in Aseb. See *AP.DD*, XV, pp. 112–113.

Document no. 109

Maḥammad Ḥanfadhē and Burhān Muḥammad to Pasquale Stanislao Mancini, 16 March 1883

الى جناب عالي الجاه والجناب سلالة الاجلاء الاكابر الاجل الافخم المفخم الاكمل الاشيم محمود السجايا وا
والشيم المراد به الصاحب الحليم منستراي سدر الاعظم سلطان تليان بلدة رومة حرس الباري من
الاكدار ذاته وحماه من الاضرار صفاته ولا زال في بارخ المجد والاجلال وشامخ العز والاقبال امين
اما بعد ناءكد ونظهر اليوم سبع في تاريخ جماد الاول ١٣٠٠ سنة الف وثلثمائة وفي الشهر اربا وي
في مرسواا ١٦ ١٨٨٢ سنة نفتح الطريق التجارية واصلاح التجارية مابين عصب واوسه ثم الى شوي
بحر استنا في ارض الدنا كل قبلنا نفتح الطريق لرعيت التليان بغير عشو لا الحشمة والناموس بحضو
حقكم كنت انت نلي وحملنا اخر كلامنا والشرط وقطعنا الكلام وينختم مع السلطان منلك ونطلب من جناب
المكرم سعادة منستر انك تحطي اخر تمام الامر للحيث كنت انت نلي نحنا مستمنين عليه ونطلبك تعرف
للرعيتكم حتى يوقفوا من الخروج الى البر حتى يرجع من شوى تمام الشرط والاتفاق مع كنت انت نلي وهو
المذكو كنت انت نلي يعرفكم مرادنا وعرفناه انه يذكر لكم في خطه ما في قلبنا من المحبة والصداقة لمجاورتكم هذا عرفنا لكم
ايضا نعرفكم الحراسة من البحر من كل عدو وخاصة من المصريون المتعدين بغير طريق ولا حق هذا عرفنا لكم

من سلطان محمد
بن سلطان حنفدي

Firma e Bolli del Sultano Mohamed Aufun

من سلطان برهان
بن سلطان محمد

صحيح

Firma del Sultano Berhan

Visto per l'autenticità dell'atto delle firme e dei Bolli
Pietro Antonelli

The high-standing and prestigious, offspring of the illustrious and the grandees, the most illustrious and magnificent, the most perfect and most virtuous, the estimable and laudable of nature, the clement friend, the minister of His Supreme Sovereign, the Italian ruler (sultan) of the city of Rome. May the Creator protect his person from all distress and preserve his felicity from all harm. May he live in glory and fame, and remain in might and prosperity. Amen.

We confirm and proclaim today, the 7th of Jumād al-Awwal, the year 1300, in the fourth month, 16 March, the year 1883, we open the commercial route and restore the commerce between Aseb and Awsa, and then to Shewa, under our protection in the land of Danākil. In the presence of your representative Count Antonelli, we have accepted opening the route for the Italian people without collecting any taxes whether dictated by law or by fair-mindedness. This is our final word and decision and King Minīlik will be the one to give the final word on this matter. We ask Your honourable Eminence, the Minister, to give Count Antonelli the final word since we trust Count Antonelli. We would like you to tell your people not to take these routes until Count Antonelli brings back the agreement and the terms from Shewa. In fact, Count Antonelli will inform you of our desire, and we asked him to mention to you in writing the friendship and kinship in our hearts for your neighbourliness. This is what we tell you. We would also like to ask you to guard the coast from all enemies and especially from the Egyptians who invade the lands for no reason and without any right. And this is what we tell you.

From Sultan Maḥammad bin Sultan Ḥanfadhē.
Two seals, both illegible.

From Sultan Burhān bin Sultan Muḥammad.
Certified. (lit. It is verily he.)

ASMAI 7/1–1, Arabic original and Italian translation.

Document no. 110

Yohannis IV to Īyasu Dagmawī, 19 March 1883

A letter of the Elect of God Yohannis King of Zion, King of Kings of Ethiopia.

May it reach ....

I am totally confused. I cannot go to Tigre hurriedly for I do not have time: Kremt is coming in. I have not given my soldiers food, clothes and salary. It will take me much time. The people will be disquieted and ask, "What has happened to him?" *Ras* Ar'aya Sillasē is in Wello. For this reason, I want some advice. The prophet and saintly David sought advice from the saintly and sinners alike. Why should I not do the same? I am troubled from two sides. The hour of the coming of God is not known. I am afraid for Tigre when I cross to the land of the Amhara. I do not feel fear for myself. On the other hand, I am afraid that these devils, the whites, will enter my land from behind. As for God, he has given me everything. I am not in want of anything. I seek your advice because I do not know what to do and I know that the fate of an undecided person is uncertain.

Semera, 11th Megabīt 1875.

Maryam Ṣiyon Church, Aksum. The above is the English translation by Gebre Medhin Kīdane, Addis Abeba, who copied and translated the document and to whom we are greatly indebted. Unfortunately, the phrase presenting the addressee was not translated. The most likely addressee is the *nibure'id* of the Maryam Ṣiyon Church, Īyasu Dagmawī. The "whites" mentioned most probably refers to the European colonial powers who tried to establish control of what was to become Eritrea in the aftermath of the Ethio-Egyptian war.

Document no. 111

Ḥamad La'īta to Pasquale Stanislao Mancini, 22 March 1883

الدعاء الوافر والثناء المتكاثر يهدي بان الى سعادة المنستر سلطان
طليان بلد رومه اما بعد نعرفكم لمان وصل كنت انت نوله انا
كنت غائب باشغال البدوان ومن بعد انا وصلت فى الاخر وتوا
جهنا مع كنت انت نوله والكلامات الذي كتبوا لكم سلطان محمد حنفلي
وسلطان برهان منهم ومن طرفي انا عندي مقبول الذي كتبوا لكم انا كذالك
من طرفي نحرس ونقبل تجار رعية الطليان انا نحرس فى ارض عده يمره
ومحمد حنفلي نحرس في ارض عسه يمره وكلنا نساعد للحرس احقكم وا
انتم احرسوا نحنا من البحر من طرفنا اعرفوا ان نحنا والسلطان منلك شورنا
وحالنا واحد ماهو اثنين هصدقوا هذا والسلام

تاريخ شهر جماد اول نهار جمعه ١٣ سنة ١٣٠٠

من السلطان حمد ابن السلطان لعيته المرحوم

Abundant prayers and generous eulogy presented to His Eminence the Minister of the Italians, ruler (sultan) of the city of Rome. And now, I would like to inform you that when Count Antonelli arrived, I was away because of the affairs of the Bedouins. Then, finally I came back and met Count Antonelli, and agreed to the letters written to you by Sultan Maḥammad Ḥanfadhē and Sultan Burhān. I agree with what they wrote to you and I am also willing to guard and accept the commerce of the Italians. I shall guard the land of the 'Idda (*yumra*) while Maḥammad Ḥanfadhē guards the land of the 'Isa (*yumra*). We shall all work on guarding your rights. On the other hand, you are to guard us from the sea. In addition, know that Sultan Minīlik and we have consulted and we are one and not two. Believe so and peace be to you.

Dated in the month of Jumād al-Awwal, Friday the 13th, the year 1300.

From Sultan Ḥamad bin [son of] Sultan La'īta, the deceased.

ASMAI 7/1–1, Arabic original.

Document no. 112

Burhān Muḥammad to Pasquale Stanislao Mancini, 25 March 1883

الى سعادة الاكرم المكرم الامجد الانجد الكامل الاكمل الاجل الجليل الاحشم المحشم العزيز المحترم
الصاحب الحليم سعادة منستراي سدر الاعظم السلطان تليان حرس الباري من الاكدار ذاته وحماه
من الاضرار صفاته ولازال في بارح المجد والاجلال وشامخ العز والاقبال اما بعد فالباعث التحرير
ذريعة الاخلاص هو السوال عن صحة ذاتكم السنية واعتدال اوقاتكم الزكية اللتان هما الامل من حضرة
عالم الازل لازال الجناب في اكمل الخير والسرور ومحبكم الحقيقي من كرم الله تعالى في اتم الخير والسرور يسال
عن حال الجناب بالغدوات والبكور ثم لا يخفى محترم الجناب بالاعتبار والمشي حقنا مع وكيلكم كنت انت نلي
الى اوسه ومع وكالة السلطان منلك وعساكره الى عند السلطان محمد بن السلطان حنفري ومشاقي الطريق بايسر طريق
بلا تعب ولا نصب ومع طيب القلب وقبلوه بالعز والناموس والاكرام غايت الاكرام ونعرفكم في جوابات الذي
كتبنالكم اثنين حقنا انه مسئلة الطريق صلحنا بحضور كنت انت نلي بالمحبة حقنا واقفة بالقلب الطريق مفتوح
بالطيب واشغالنا اشتوا بالكبير والحين حتى يصلح ويتم المحبة حقنا حتى لا يخرب انا وسلطان محمد نطلبكم تحكموا الذي
كانت تفارق بيننا وبينكم وهذا الكلام سلطنة حقي في مركبله والان الشرط الذي كتبنا انا والعالم سبينة ماكنت
نعرف ان بلاد مركبله في داخل الميلين ولا ذكرنا اسم المركبله وانا احلف بالله اني ماكنت اعرف كم قدر الميل
وعلى هذا تخالفنا والان نقل لكم انكم تخرجولي الحق وتردولي مركبله حتى تدوم المحبة وبالقلب الطيب ونعرف
ان حكومة التليان ماير ضا علينا ضروره هذا عرفناكم

تاريخ جماد اول ٦ ١٣٠٠ سنه
شهر مرسوا ١٦ ١٨٨٣ سنه

سلطان برهان
بن سلطان محمد
صحيح

To His Eminence, the most noble and most honoured, the bravest and most victorious, the most perfect and most virtuous, the most illustrious and most venerable, the most decent and most humble, the beloved and respected, the clement friend, the Minister of His Supreme Sovereign the Italian Sultan. May the Creator protect his person from all distress and preserve his felicity from all harm. May he live in glory and fame and remain in might and prosperity. Amen

The reason for writing, the affirmation of our loyalty, is the inquiry about your noble health and about the harmony of your pleasant times which are what we hope for from the Knowledgeable of eternity. May Your Honour remain in complete health and happiness. Thanks to God's kindness, your true beloved is well and healthy and prays for your Honour's well-being morning and forenoon. As is not hidden from Your Respected Honour, your representative Count Antonelli left for Awsa in full honour, truly, and with the authorization of Sultan Minīlik and his soldiers, he continued to Sultan Maḥammad bin Sultan Ḥanfadhē. He took the easiest way and met no fatigue nor hardship, but happiness. They received him in honour, glory, and dignity, full dignity.

In the two letters we wrote to you, we informed you, truly, that with love truly filling the heart we settled the issue of the route in the presence of Count Antonelli. We are pleased that the route has been opened; our work has been immense. In order that our friendship is truly restored and complete and so that Sultan Maḥammad and I are not ruined, we ask you to reconsider what had estranged us, that is my right to rule Markable.

And now the agreement which I and the learned Sapeto signed, we were not aware that the land of Markable was located within the two miles, nor did we mention the name of Markable, and I swear to God that I did not know how far a mile extended. On this we disagreed, but now I ask you to give me back my right and restore Markable to me so that friendship and good-heartedness prevail, knowing that the Italian government is not pleased if we are harmed. That is what we tell you.

Dated on the 16th of Jumād al Awwal 1300.
The 16th of the month of March 1883.

Sultan Burhān bin Sultan Muḥammad
Certified Burhān [himself].

ASMAI 7/1–1, Arabic original and Italian summary. The Italian summary is printed in *L'Italia in Africa*, I.3 no. 285, p. 7. The European date is obviously wrong, the secretary apparently equating Jumād al Awwal with March. Markable refers to the commercially important salt pans off the coast at Aseb, which Sultan Burhān apparently believed not to have been included in the agreements with Sapeto and the Rubattino Co. in 1880 (docs 4, 8, 9, 13 and 19). With the Italian government replacing the Rubattino Co., the issue of the sovereignty of the area came to a head, and Sultan Burhān felt he had been deceived. Some six months later he finally renounced his claim to Markable, declaring himself satisfied with economic compensation by the Italian government (see doc. 140).

Document no. 113

Yohannis IV to Victoria, 9 April 1883

May the message of the Elect of God Yohannis, King of Zion, King of Kings of Ethiopia, reach the honoured and exalted above all, Queen Victoria, by the grace of God [appointed] defender of the faith, queen of Great Britain and Ireland, Queen of Queens of India (Hindikē).

How are you, really? I am well, by the loving kindness of God. Previously I used to write to you frequently about all the injustices done to me by Ismā'īl *Pasha*, the territories that he took from me by trespassing, telling how he had my territories taken, by sending his servant Munzinger. It is Munzinger who brought us into all this conflict. And now, since the rule of the Muslims is destroyed and the country is in the hands of Christians, see to it that my country is restored to me. Last year you sent a letter telling me, "I will have your territories restored to you".

Even in former times, you were my helper. When all the kings rule their respective countries, their respective patrimonies, what have I done that my country should be taken away from me? Until now, I have not stopped writing and sending letters. However, the Turks tear them up and throw them into the sea. The reason why this happens is that the ports on the sea are closed to me. They have closed them in such a way that messengers cannot go back and forth, merchants cannot trade, goods that I want cannot be brought to me. [Please,] look at this letter and find the appropriate solution for all these matters. When we brought bishops according to ancient tradition, we brought them by giving money [and other] gifts. Accordingly, when I brought bishops by sending my men, Mr. Malet, your consul-general in Egypt, wrote to you saying, "He has made a peace agreement with Tawfīq *Pasha*." On the contrary, I have not made a peace agreement. I am writing all this because I am your son and friend, and you would not like me being wronged. And now, it is because I want the Kingdom of Christ to expand and the religion of the unbelievers to be destroyed. Except for this I have no quarrel with Christians. If the Kingdom of Christ does not expand now in your time and with your might, when will it expand?

The reason for my writing like this is that I want to get a port on the Red Sea so that I may have weapons and [other] goods that I want brought to me. I would not have appealed [to you] and complained about the Turks in order to restore my own territory, which is within my reach, had it not been for my desire to satisfy my claims with your permission.

Written in the town of Semera on 2nd Mīyazya in the year of grace 1875.

Seal: King of Kings Yohannis, King of Zion in Ethiopia. The cross has defeated the tribe of Isma'ēl. Yūḥannā, King of Kings of Zion in Abyssinia. The cross has defeated the people of Ismā'īl. 1864.

FO 95/743, no. 221, Amharic original and English translation. In the translation, the letter is dated "7 Mīyazya at the town of Samra", which is in parenthesis converted to 15 November 1883! The translation by Charles Speedy is rather free and occasionally totally misleading. A note in the printed records states that the letter was received 10 December. A draft copy of a reply from Victoria is dated 2 January 1884 (FO 95/744). For the circumstances of the letter see *Yohannes IV*, pp. 128–129, and *Survival*, p. 352. Two almost identical letters to Emperor Wilhelm of Germany and President Grévy of France were written the same day and all entrusted to the Austrian explorer Anton Stecker, who was returning to Europe after several years in Ethiopia (see docs 114 and 115).

Document no. 114

Yohannis IV to Wilhelm I, 9 April 1883

May the message from the Elect of God Yohannis, King of Zion, King of Kings of Ethiopia, reach the right honourable, the exalted, Wilhelm King of Kings of Germany, King of Prussia.

How are you, really? I, by the mercy of God, am well. Earlier I sent you a letter through Dr. Rohlfs and told you about all the injustice which Ismā'īl *Pasha* has done to me and how he advanced by force. He has taken away my country and taken possession of my territories through his servant named Munzinger. The dispute lasting ever since is the fault of Munzinger. The answer to this [letter] has not come to me. Now that the Muslim rule has been destroyed and the lands are in the hands of Christians, help me so that my land is given back to me. When all kings have possession of their lands, why should I let my land be stolen?

By old custom we obtain our bishop by giving money and gifts of honour. Accordingly, when I sent my people and had bishops come, Mr. Malet, the British consul-general in Egypt, wrote to my detriment to the British government saying that I have made peace with Tawfīq Pasha. I have not made peace at all. And now I insist that my country is given back to me that I may have a coast to the Red Sea and that the merchants can trade freely for the purpose of import and export of goods and different necessities. Furthermore, however, when in these days, the kingdom of Christ is not growing and the faith of the peoples is not complete, when will it then be? With the Christians I have no dispute.

Written on 2nd Mīyazya in the residence of Semera in the year of grace 1875.

Seal: King of Kings Yohannis, King of Zion in Ethiopia. The cross has defeated the tribe of Isma'ēl. Yūḥannā, King of Kings of Zion in Abyssinia. The cross has defeated the people of Ismā'īl. 1864.

AAPA, I.B.9, Afrika, Abessinien, vol. 1, Amharic original FO 1/30, pp. 64–68, German translation by Professor D. Dillmann with mistaken conversion of the date to 10 April. Printed with a slightly different English translation in *Ethiopia and Germany*, pp. 206–207. See the previous letter for the context.

Document no. 115

Yohannis IV to Jules Grévy, 9 April 1883

[illegible]

May the message of the Elect of God Yohannis, King of Zion, King of Kings of Ethiopia, reach the respected and eminent Jules Grévy, elected to the government of France. My brother, my friend, how are you, really? I, by the mercy of God, am well.

Earlier I informed you about all the injustice which Ismā'īl *Pasha* has done to me and how he advanced by force. He has taken away my country and taken possession of my territories through his servant named Munzinger. I sent a letter to the French government about this and that the dispute lasting ever since is the fault of Munzinger. No reply to this has reached me. Now, since the Muslim rule has been destroyed and the lands are in the hands of Christians, see to it that my country is restored to me. When all kings have possession of their lands, why should I let my land be stolen?

By old custom we obtain our bishop by giving money and gifts of honour. Accordingly, when I sent my people and had bishops come, Mr. Malet, the British consul-general in Egypt, wrote to my detriment to the British government saying that I have made peace with Tawfīq Pasha. I have not made peace at all. And now [I wish] that my country shall be returned to me, that the merchants shall be able to undertake their commerce and bring me from the littoral or the Red Sea arms and products which I seek [to buy for myself]. I have written so considering that since your times the Kingdom of Christ has not been extended and that the faith of the nations has not faded and shall never fade. I harbour no hostility against the Christians.

Written 2nd Mīyazya in the camp of Semera in the year of grace 1875 (9 April 1883).

BN, Ethiop. Abb. 254, no. 279, copy of Amharic text and French translation in Antoine d'Abbadie's handwriting. A copy of the translation without the Amharic text is filed as no. 283. The original of the letter has not been found and it is thus unclear if it ever reached its addressee.

Document no. 116

Yohannis IV to Kīrillus V, 10 April 1883

ترجمه

رسالة الملك يوحنا ملك ملوك الحبشه الوارده لغبطة السيد الاب البطريرك

تاريخها ٢ برموده سنة ١٥٩٩ وكان ورودها في ١٠ شهر توت سنة ١٦٠٠ قبطيه وهذه صورتها

شكر الله ونحمده الذي خلق السما والارض الي قدس الاب البطريرك الفايق القدامه

خامس الانجليين ثالث عشر الحواريين ذو المملكه والكهنوت خليفة الرسل الاطهار

حارس غنمه من الذياب الاريوسيه والنسطوريه عمود واساس الديانه المسيحيه

ساقي شعبه بالتعاليم الروحانيه المملوه من الاسرار الالهيه كما له الثمانيه وسبعه

عشرين عمود الديانه المسيحيه الحقيقيه العابد الساهر الطالب عن جميع شعبه البكر

الطاهر والراعي العالي الذي اضا علينا بضيا شمسه ابينا وريسنا ابنا كيرلس رييس

اساقفة اسكندريه والحبشه والنوبه وافريقيه وخمس مدن الغربيه اطلب من الله

ان اطمن قدسكم في خير واقبل الاقدام والايدي واغنا ان انظركم بعينايي امين

ايها الاب الاقدس انا ابنكم الساجد وجميع ملوكي يسجدون لقدسكم وجميع الوزرا

والباشاوات والقمامصه والقسوس والشمامسه وجميع الشعب الكبار والصغار يطلبوا

ويتضرعوا لقدسكم بان تدعوا بالصلوه عنا وعن جميع الشعب نعلمكم ان الاسقف

ابنا مرقس لما حضر مصوع كان حاصل له عيا ولما تقابلنا معه كان عيان واخيرا

ارسلته الي بلد تسمي (اوفو) وقد تنيح ابنا مرقس اسقف الحبشه في ١٦ كيهك ١٥٩٩

وجميع متروكاته ارسلناها صحبة الخواجه كزالي واما الصليب الذي له وضعناه في الدفن

معه كذا الخواجه نقولا المصوراتي لم تقابل معنا الا بعد خمس شهور بالنسبه لعياه

في مدينة عدوه وعرفنا بان يعلم المصوراتيه الموجودين بطرفنا وانما بعد

تعليم المذكورين الموجودين عندنا يحضر بالسلام لقدسكم وربنا يحفظكم علي الدوام امين

[illegible]

Translation:

A letter from King Yoḥannis, King of Kings of Abyssinia (al-Ḥabasha) written to His Beatitude the Father the Patriarch, dated on the 3rd of Baramūda 1599, received the 10th of Tūt of the year 1600 Coptic. This is its copy.

We thank God, and we praise Him who has created heaven and earth. To His Holiness the Father the Patriarch, the exceedingly holy, the fifth apostle, the thirteenth disciple, holder of the kingdom and the priesthood, successor of the virtuous apostles, protecting his herd from the Arian and Nestorian wolves, the pillar and foundation of the Christian religion, pouring spiritual teaching filled with divine mysteries on his people, he who makes the three hundred and nineteen complete, the pillar of the Christian religion, the truth of the vigilant worshipper, the pleader for all his people, the pure and unprecedented, the good shepherd who enlightens us with the brightness of his sun, our father and our master *Anbā* Kīrillus, the Archbishop of Alexandria, Abyssinia, Nubia, Africa, and the five cities of the West. I ask God that I may witness Your Holiness flourish, I kiss your feet and hands and I hope to see you with my own eyes. Amen.

O Holy Father! I am your son prostrating, and all my kings prostrate before Your Holiness, all the ministers (*wuzarā*), the *pashas*, the archpriests, the priests, the deacons, and all the people, elderly and youngsters beseech and implore Your Holiness to present your prayers for us and for all the people.

We inform you that when the bishop *Anbā* Marqos came to Massawa, he had already caught the plague and when we met him, he was very ill. Then, I sent him to a village called Arqūb, and *Anbā* Marqos, the bishop of Abyssinia, passed away on the 16th of Kiyhak 1599. We sent all his belongings with Mr. (*al-khawāja*) Manālī. As for his cross, we deposited it with him in the coffin. Mr. (*al-khawāja*) Nicola, the painter (?) (*masūrātī*) did not meet us until five months later because of the plague in the city of Adwa, and then we told him to inform the painters (*maṣūrātīya*) present on our side. If it is God's will after informing the above-mentioned who is with us, he will present himself to Your Holiness in safety.

May God guard you at all times. Amen.

His Excellency, the dear son, Mr. (*Khawāja*) 'Awaḍ Sa'dallāh, the revered, may God bless him abundantly, presents his greetings to you through this copy of the translation of the letter that reached us in the mail. May Your Excellency review it adequately. If the above-mentioned *khawāja* comes carrying the items that we sent, do take them from him and notify us officially.

Our greetings and blessings to their Excellences our children in the eminent council.

May God's peace engulf you all. To him all our thanks always.

11th Tūt 1600.

Ghali Collection, no. 3, Arabic text. As stated at the top this is a translation, probably of an Amharic original, although the letters by the Ethiopian rulers to the Coptic patriarch were generally written in Arabic. It is unclear if the reference to "this copy of the translation of the letter" is a note by the copyist and refers to the letter itself, or part of the original referring to another letter. *Anbā* Marqos was one of the four bishops who arrived in Ethiopia in October 1883. He died on 25 December 1883.

Document no. 117

Maḥammad Ḥanfadhē, Burhān Muḥammad and Ḥamad La'īta to Giovanni Branchi and Giulio Pestalozza, 14 April 1883

الى حضرة الجنابات العاليات الاكرامات الكرمات
العزيزات الاجلات الحليمات المحب برنكي
وصاحب عصب بستلوسي هداهما الله تعالى
في كل زمان واوان وان سالتم وعمن يلوذ بنا
فانا بخير وعافيه ولا نسال الا عنكم وعن
احوالكم التي هي القصد والمراد من رب العباد
وصل الينا جوابكم وفهمنا ما ذكرتم وصار لدينا
معلوم والجوابات الذي ارسلتموه لانت نلي
ارسلناه حالا وصل الينا وانشا الله يبلغه وبلغنا
من جهة بحرة ان المصريون يعمرون ساكلوا
للميت ابو بكر باشة وصل بنفسه مع عساكر المصريون
وكان بيننا وبينكم عهدا وميثاقا الحماية من
البحر منا وحماية البر منكم الان فكيف يعمرون
بلدانا وانتم في حيات لان الفرنساوي كتب لنا
كتاب لا تحاربون المصريون لان المصريون
نزوله في ساكلو بلادنا لا نعرفوا الان فنصل

To Their Excellences, the high-ranking, the most noble and the most honoured, the beloved and most illustrious, the clement friends, the beloved Branchi and the ruler (*ṣāḥib*) of Aseb, Pestalozza. May God Almighty guide them at all times.

If you ask about us and those who take refuge with us, we are well and healthy, and we are not concerned about anything except you and your well-being which is the ultimate aim and desire of the Lord of the faithful. Your letter reached us and we understood and took account of what you mention. As soon as we received the letters you sent to Count Antonelli we forwarded them to him, God willing he will receive them. We were informed from Tajura that the Egyptians had invaded Sagallo since Abū Bakr *Pasha* has arrived there himself with the Egyptian soldiers.

We had made an agreement and an accord between us and you that you guard the coast and we guard the land. So, how come they invaded our lands while you are still alive? In fact, the French sent us a letter asking us not to attack the Egyptians since the Egyptians landed at Sagallo with the permission of the English.

Now, the French Consul has written to the French authorities [that] we were in agreement with the English government. Then, after settling things with the English on behalf of the Egyptians, he ordered them: "By God by God, do not fight them". And now, what is your opinion and what is your suggestion on how to protect us and yourself on our land? Now, do inform us of your situation since you have to inform Sultan Burhān of everything. Sultan Burhān and we are one; there is no difference between us. Since he is closer to you, he shall be our authorized representative. Let it be known to you.

The sender of the message is Ṣulṭān Maḥammad Ḥanfadhē and Sulṭan Burhān Muḥammad and Ḥamad La'īta, dated Saturday afternoon, 6 Jumād al-Ākhir, the year 1300.

Sultan Maḥammad Ḥanfadhē and Ḥamad La'īta send their very best regards to Sa'īd 'Awīḍān.

Seal: illegible.

ASMAI 7/1–1. Arabic original with Italian translation. The letter clearly demonstrates the cooperation between the Danākil sultans in their opposition to the Egyptian attempts to capture their lands with the tacit support of the British and French and their anger at the failure of the Italians to prevent this in spite of their previous promises.

Document no. 118

Treaty between Maḥammad Ḥanfadhē and Italy, 18 April 1883

118a Arabic text

بيان الشروط

مع الطات نجيه بن [illegible] حومد هنفري مملكة إيطاليا كل الذي باقو من [illegible] اسب [illegible]

مدينة شو [illegible] محد حسن بي غافية وخراش

الاول

انوحبا دائما السلام [illegible] مع والي اسب المحمد هنفري وكل جمعتهم اهل [illegible]

بدبو دايمن

والثاني

من الثنين الاطراف يوالو كل واحد واحد والي الذي يخلص الشروط

والثالث

محمد هنفري ذامن وغافر لكل المسافرين في البر وفي الباحر ذامن وغافر مملكة الحا[illegible]

والرابع

محمد هنفري يتشاور مع المنابخ الدناكل ويقطع الجمرك ويسافروا اهل

الحاليا بلا جمرك ويطيعم الذفنيه والخمس

والخامس

محمد هنفري يطعي الحيه واحد محل للمسافرين يتزايه فيه الجمال الذي جا من

بلاد مملكت الحاليا والسادس

والبيات كل واحد في الدينا يجلس ويتكلم واحد على اليمان والدين

والسابع

كل اهل إيطاليا انوحابيت والسواحيين بسافروا على ماحلتهم و [illegible] اجنبهم

ويتو ينتصر محمد هنفري و مملكة الحاليا [illegible] وس اهل كل الدناكل

وجموعة محمد هنفري في الباحر والثامن

البابور الحاليا كل وقت في طرف الباحر [illegible] جمعت محمد هنفري و [illegible]

فيه حق الى محل الدناكل والتاسع

وهذا الشروط في ارت ملك منليك [illegible] في بلد كونت انتونيلي

والاشرا

هذا الشروط مكتوب في اللغا

الثلاثين لغا في عربي وفي الحبشي

و في الحاليان والسنام ختام

في شهر جوماد الثاني ١١

في السنة ١٣٠٠

List of clauses

between Sultan Maḥammad bin Ḥanfadhē, the deceased, [and] the Kingdom of Italy. Whoever travels from the village (*qarāya*) of Aseb to the city (*madīna*) of Shewa shall be protected and guarded by Maḥammad Ḥanfadhē.

First

There shall be perpetual peace and friendship for ever between the governor (*wālī*) of Aseb and Maḥammad Ḥanfadhē and all the people of Danākil.

Second

Each of the two parties shall appoint a representative to implement the clauses.

Third

Maḥammad Ḥanfadhē will be the guarantor and protector of all the travellers by land. On the sea, the Kingdom of Italy is the guarantor and protector.

Fourth

Maḥammad Ḥanfadhē will consult with the *shaykhs* of the Danākil and . . . the customs so that the Italian people shall travel without paying taxes and be exempted from transit duty.

Fifth

Maḥammad Ḥanfadhē will provide . . . a place for the travellers in which the camels and people who come from Italy can rest.

Sixth

As for the faith, each one shall remain (*yijlis*) in the religion and no one shall discuss faith and religion.

Seventh

All Italians, be they merchants or visitors, may come and go as they wish and are pleased. They are protected and guarded by Maḥammad Ḥanfadhē; and the kingdom of Italy will guard and protect the people of all the Danākil and the dependents of Maḥammad Ḥanfadhē from the side of the sea.

Eighth

The Italian steamship shall always protect and guard the dependents of Maḥammad Ḥanfadhē from the sea, and no one shall invade the land of the Danākil.

Ninth

These articles are in accordance with the will of King Minīlik and are concluded through Count Antonelli.

Tenth

This treaty is written in three languages, in Arabic, in Amharic, and in Italian.

Concluding Greetings
Dated on the 10th of Jumād al-Thānī, 1300 of *Hijra*.

Seal: Sultan Maḥammad Ḥanfadhē.
Seal: King Minīlik of Shewa.
Seal: Italian Antonelli.

118b Italian text

Progetto di una Convenzione fra il Governo di S.M. il re d'Italia ed il Capo supremo di tutti i Danakili, il sultano Mohamed Anfari.

Art. 1°

La pace e l'amicizia saranno costanti e perpetue fra le autorità italiane di Assab ed il sultano Mohamed Anfari e fra tutti i loro dipendenti.

Art. 2°

Ciascuna delle due parti nominerà un suo rappresentante pel disbrigo degli affari.

Art. 3°

Il sultano Mohamed Anfari garantisce al governo italiano ed a S.M. il re Menelik la sicurezza della via fra Assab, Aussa ed il regno di Scioa a tutte le carovane italiane da e per il mare.

Art. 4°

Il sultano Mohamed Anfari di comune accordo cogli altri sultani dichiara esenti da dazio [illegible] le carovane italiane provenienti o dirette per Assab.

Art. 5°

Il sultano Mohamed Anfari concede al governo di S.M. il Re d'Italia l'uso della terra di Ablis [illegible] parte del territorio di Aussa atto alla coltivazione [illegible] stabilirvi una stazione commerciale italiana.

Art. 6°

Saranno rispettate tutte le religioni.

Art. 7°

I sudditi di S.M. il re d'Italia viaggeranno liberamente [illegible] tutti i paesi dipendenti dal sultano Mohamed Anfari

Plan of a convention between the government of H.M. the King of Italy and the supreme head of all the Danākil, the Sultan Maḥammad Ḥanfadhē

Article 1.
Peace and friendship shall be constant and perpetual between the Italian authority of Aseb and Sultan Maḥammad Ḥanfadhē and between all their dependents.

Article 2.
Each of the two parties shall nominate a representative of his for the dispatch of business.

Article 3.
Sultan Maḥammad Ḥanfadhē guarantees to the Italian government and His Majesty King Minīlik the security of the route from Aseb and Awsa to the kingdom of Shewa, to all the Italian caravans.

Article 4.
Sultan Maḥammad Ḥanfadhē, in common accord with the other sultans, declares all Italian caravans proceeding from or directed to Aseb exempt from duty or tribute.

Article 5.
Sultan Maḥammad Ḥanfadhē concedes to the government of His Majesty the King of Italy the use of the land of Ablis/Awsa, on the part of the territory of Awsa which is suitable for cultivation in order to establish an Italian commercial station.

Article 6.
All religions shall be respected.

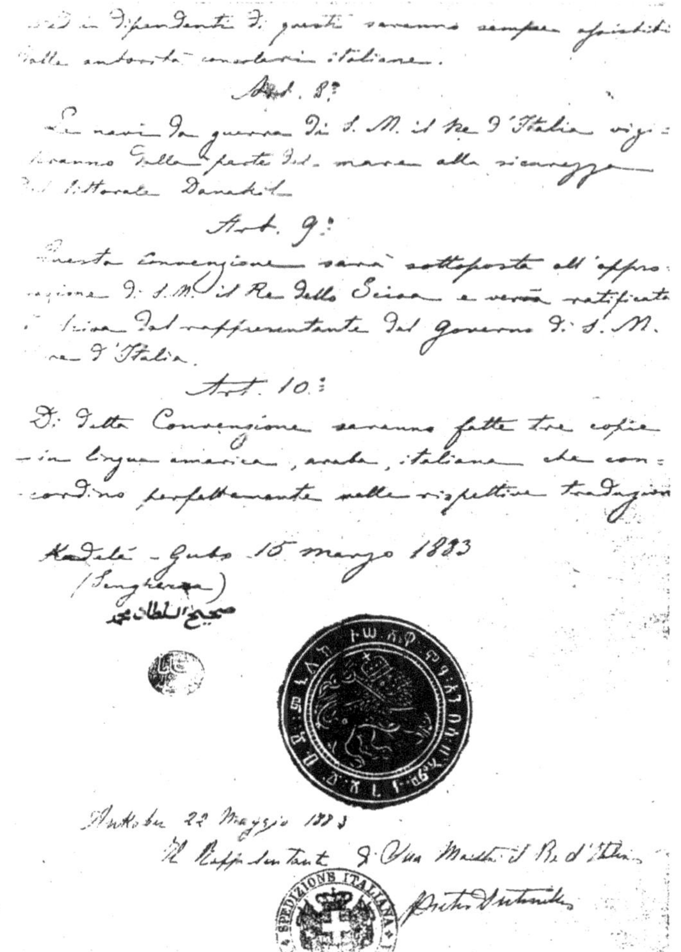

...ed i dipendenti di questi saranno sempre sottoposti alle autorità consolari italiane.

Art. 8°

Le navi da guerra di S. M. il Re d'Italia vigileranno dalla parte del mare alla sicurezza del littorale Danakil.

Art. 9°

Questa convenzione sarà sottoposta all'approvazione di S. M. il Re dello Scioa e verrà ratificata in Scioa dal rappresentante del governo di S. M. il Re d'Italia.

Art. 10°

Di detta Convenzione saranno fatte tre copie in lingua amarica, araba, italiana che concordino perfettamente nelle rispettive traduzioni.

Hadelé - Gubo 15 maggio 1883
(Sengherra)
صحيح السلطان

Ankober 22 Maggio 1883
Il Rappresentante di Sua Maestà il Re d'Italia
Pietro Antonelli

Article 7.
The subjects of His Majesty the King of Italy shall travel freely in all the land depending on Sultan Maḥammad Ḥanfadhē and his dependents shall always be under the Italian consular authority.

Article 8.
The warships of His Majesty the King of Italy shall supervise the security of the Danākil coast from the side of the sea.

Article 9.
This convention shall be submitted for the approval of His Majesty the King of Shewa and shall be ratified in Shewa by the representative of the government of His Majesty the King of Italy.

Article 10.
Of this convention, three copies have been made in the Amharic, Arabic and Italian languages, which agree perfectly in the respective translation.

Ḥadele Gubo, 15th March 1883 (Sengherra).
Certified: Sultan Maḥammad

Seal illegible
Seal: Minīlik King of Shewa. The Lion of the tribe of Judah has prevailed.

Ankober, 22nd May 1883.
The representative of His Majesty the King of Italy, Pietro Antonelli.

Seal: The Royal Italian expedition.

ከኍሳቁ፡ ከሽዷሬፉኙ፡ ሹም፡ ከመሐመድ፡ ሐንፈሬ፡
ጋር፡ የኢጣልያ፡ መንግሥት፡ የተዡሚመረው፡ [illegible]ል፡፡
መዠመሪያ፡
ፍቅርና፡ ሰላም፡ ከአሰብ፡ ሹምችና፡ ከመሐመድ፡ ሐ
ንፈሬ፡ ጋር፡ ዘመትር፡ ይኖራል፡ ከዚኅቻቾሙም፡ ጋር፡
ሁለተኛ፡
ከሁሉትም፡ ወገን፡ ፩፩ሰው፡ ሠሉን፡ የሚዟሬርስ፡ ይኖ[illegible]ል፡፡
ሦ[illegible]ተኛ፡
መሐመድ፡ ሐንፈሬ፡ በንጉሥ፡ ምኒልክ፡ ፊት፡ በኢጣልያ፡ መ
ንግሥት፡ ፊት፡ የመንገዱ፡ ተያዥ፡ ይሆናል፡ ለሚሄዱትም፡
ለሚመጡትም፡ ሰው፡ ሁሉ፡
አራተኛ፡
መሐመድ፡ ሐንፈሬ፡ ከአገዱሎቹ፡ ጋር፡ ተማክሮ፡ የኢጣልያ፡
ነጋዴች፡ ሲመላለሱ፡ ቀረጥ፡ እንዳይቀረጡ፡ ያደርጋል፡
አምስተኛ፡፡
መሐመድ፡ ሐንፈሬ፡ ለኢጣልያ፡ መንግሥት፡ [illegible]፡ አሰው፡
ላኧቃ፡ ለማመል፡ ይሰጣል፡፡ ስ[illegible]ስተኛ፡፡ ሁሉ፡ በእየ፡ ሣይ[illegible]
ቱ፡ ሊኖር፡ [illegible] ሰበተኛ፡ በመሐመድ፡ ሐንፈሬ፡ አገር፡
[illegible]፡ የኢጣልያ፡ ሰዎች፡ በነፃነት፡ ሲመላለሱ፡ እንደ፡ ወደዱ፡፡
ለመሐመድ፡ ሐንፈሬም፡ በ[illegible]ች፡ ኢጣልያኖች፡ ጭፍ፡ ኢ[illegible]ን
ትወ፡ ነው፡፡ ስምንተኛ፡፡ የኢጣልያ፡ መርከቦች፡ በባ[illegible]
ነገሩ፡ ሁሉ፡ እንዲረጋጭ፡ የእዳሎች፡ ቦታ፡ እንደ ይነ[illegible]
ጠቃሉ፡፡ ዘጠነኛ፡ ይህ፡ የተወጠነው፡ ውል፡ እንደ፡ ንጉሥ[illegible]
ኒልክ፡ ሐሳብ፡ ይሆናል፡ በኢጣ[illegible]ያ፡
ንጉሥ፡ እንዲደረሴ፡ በኮንት፡ ኤንቶኔሊ፡
ይጨረስል፡፡ ፲ኛ፡ ይህ፡ ውል፡ በ፫ ቋንቋ፡
በአ[illegible]ርኛ፡ በአረብኛ፡ በኢጣልያ፡ ተ
ጽፍዋል፡ በማኅበት፡ ፲፫ ሰ፤ ፲፰፻[illegible]

[illegible] 22 Maggio 1883

Pietro Antonelli

A treaty reached between the great Adal chief and the Italian government.

The first

Friendship and peace will always prevail between the chiefs of Aseb and Maḥammad Ḥanfadhē and their subjects.

The second

One person from each side will be appointed to implement the treaty.

The third

Maḥammad Ḥanfadhē will in front of King Minīlik and to the Italian government be the guarantor for the travellers, for all the people who come and go.

The fourth

Maḥammad Ḥanfadhē in consultation with the *shaykhs* (*abadulloch*) will see to it that the Italian traders shall not pay customs duties.

The fifth

Maḥammad Ḥanfadhē will give the Italian government one place as a residence for people, goods and camels. *The sixth*: We have accepted that every one lives according to his religion. *The seventh*: In the land of Maḥammad Ḥanfadhē Italian people may move around in liberty as they wish. The Italians will be the protectors of Maḥammad Ḥanfadhē's people. *The eighth*: Italian steamships shall supervise all areas in order to protect the land of the Adals so that they shall not be touched. *The ninth*: This agreed-upon treaty which accords with the will of King Minīlik, the King of Ethiopia, is concluded by the representative of the King of Italy, Count Antonelli. *The tenth*: This treaty is written in three languages, in Amharic, in Arabic and in Italian.

Ginbot 13, 1875

Ankober 22 May 1883, Pietro Antonelli

Seal: Spedizione Italiana. Regio di Scioa

Seal: Minīlik, King of Shewa. The Lion of the tribe of Judah has prevailed.

ASMAI 7/1–1, no. 17, Italian, Arabic and Amharic originals. Italian text printed in *Trattati*, pp. 60–61, with the date 15 March. The circumstances under which the signing of this agreement took place resulted in three versions of the treaty. The first to be written was the Italian plan dated "Kadelé-Gubo 15 marzo 1883" (Kadelé-Gubo, or rather Ḥadele Gubo, identified as Sengherra, that is Sinkara, the capital of Maḥammad Ḥanfadhē). We have decided to ignore this date since that version is called a "progetto", thus it may be seen as Antonelli's draft. Nevertheless, it must later have been regarded as a valid version of the treaty because of the seals below the text, added on 18 April and 22 May. We have put 18 April which is the date when Maḥammad Ḥanfadhē sealed it and the date on the Arabic version. But since Maḥammad Ḥanfadhē recognized the authority and the interest Minīlik had regarding the routes to the coast, Antonelli proceeded to Ankober, and an Amharic version dated 13 Ginbot 1875 (= 20 May 1883) was produced and sealed by Minīlik. Antonelli must have decided to postpone his signing until Minīlik had so to speak, ratified the treaty by applying his seal to all three versions; Antonelli signed and sealed all three versions two days later, on 22 May. The Amharic version was, however, never sealed by Maḥammad Ḥanfadhē.

Except for two important clauses the three versions are basically in agreement. In the fifth article the Italian version is more specific concerning Italian settlements. Where the Arabic and Amharic versions simply refer to a "place to rest", the Italian texts states that Maḥammad Ḥanfadhē concedes to the Italians the land of Ablis, part of Awsa, for cultivation and for establishing an Italian commercial station. In the seventh article, the Italian version refers to the assistance given by the Italian consular authority where the other versions speak about Maḥammad Ḥanfadhē's protection of the Italian travellers.

Document no. 119

Yohannis IV to Victoria, 8 May 1883

መልእክት፡ ዘሥዩመ፡ እግዚአብሔር፡ ዮሐንስ፡ ን
ጉሠ፡ ጽዮን፡ ንጉሠ፡ ነገሥት፡ ዘኢትዮጵያ፡ ይድ
ረስ፡ ኀበ፡ ክብርት፡ ወልዕልት፡ ቢክቶርያ፡ ዘበጸ
ጋ፡ እግዚአብሔር፡ ንግሥት፡ ንግሥታት፡ ውሁዳን፡
ዘውእቶሙ፡ ቢርታንያ፡ ወአይርላንድ፡ መሥተጋድ
ሊት፡ በእንተ፡ ሃይማኖት፡ ወአህጉረ፡ ልጅት፡ ዘህን
ዱ፡ እጅጉን፡ እንዴት፡ አሉ፡ እኔ ግን፡ በእግዚአብሔር፡
ቸርነት፡ አምላከ፡ ቅዱሳን፡ ይክበር፡ ይመስገን፡
ደኅና፡ ነኝ፡ ምሕረቱ፡ ለዘለዓለም፡ ነውና፡ ደብዳቤ
ውም፡ ደረሰኝ፡ ቃሉም፡ እጅግ፡ መልካም፡ ነው፡ ነገ
ር፡ ግን፡ እግዚአብሔር፡ መጨረሻውን፡ ይግበረው፡
ተጽሕፈ፡ በሠመራ፡ ከተማ፡ አመ፡ ፩ ለግንቦት፡ በ፲ወ
፰፻፸ወ፭ ዓመተ፡ ምሕረት፨

May the letter from the elect of God Yohannis, King of Zion, King of Kings of Ethiopia, reach the respected and exalted Victoria, who, by the grace of God, is the Queen of Queens, of the United Kingdom of Great Britain and Ireland, protector of the faith and of the country (*ahigure lidjīt*) of India. How are you, really?

As for me, I am well, by the grace of God, may the Lord of the saints be honoured and praised. His mercy is everlasting.

The letter has reached me. The message is very good. May God, however, bring it to completion.

Written at the city of Semera, on 1st Ginbot in the year of grace 1875.

Seal: King of Kings Yohannis, King of Zion in Ethiopia. The cross has defeated the tribe of Isma'ēl. Yūḥannā, King of Kings of Zion in Abyssinia. The cross has defeated the people of Ismā'īl. 1864.

FO 95/743, no. 216, Amharic original and English translation. The letter from Victoria, the reception of which Yohannis acknowledges here, was a letter of 9 November 1882 (FO 95/742, no. 130). See *Survival*, pp. 351–352.

Document no. 120

Yohannis IV to Edward Malet, 8 May 1883

May the letter from the Elect of God Yohannis, King of Zion, King of Kings of Ethiopia, reach Sir Edward Malet, minister plenipotentiary, commander and knight, consul of the kingdom of England in the country of Egypt, etc.

How are you? I also, by the bounty of God, am well, the holy God be exalted and praised for His mercy endureth forever. The letter which came by the hand of the *nā'ib*, has reached me, and its word is very good, but God grant its fulfilment.

Written in the royal residence of Semera, the first Ginbot in the year of Grace 1875.

FO 1/30, p. 72, English translation. No Amharic original has been found. Except for standardization of the spelling of names and some phrases, and the elimination of explanatory parentheses, the text is reproduced here as preserved in the translation. A letter by a Norwegian scholar attempting to explain one of the titles apparently used for Malet shows the Foreign Office had difficulties in translating the Amharic correspondence. See FO 1/30, pp. 145–146.

Document no. 121

Onesimus Nesib to Johannes Neander, 14 May 1883

Imkullo (Minkullo) 14 May 1883

Dear Pastor Neander,

Grace and Peace.

Our money is now nearly finished; we do not have more than 28 thalers left. Therefore we beg for help as soon as possible. The other day Hedenström's things were sold. There were many things among them which we would have needed for our coming expedition but because of lack of money, I bought nothing more than a little gunpowder and percussion caps. I was even allowed to keep my rifle hoping that you, as I asked you before, would pay him for it at home. There is common sadness as Hedenström was dismissed, not only in our congregation, but also by all those who knew him. People thought and hoped that he would come out even before the fall, but completely unexpected the sad mail was received from him, "Sell my things. I am not coming out."

Ras Adal is now free from his captivity and has been appointed [to rule] over some parts of his earlier territory. He is very eager to receive teachers whom he could send to Gudru. He would bring them there at his own cost. Two of the Felasha missionaries have gone there. That is at least what their servants who had come to bring money to them told [us]. And this is quite possible, since he has never been an enemy of the Gospel.

Our brothers were expelled from Gojjam without his knowledge. The *aleqa* who caused the expulsion of our brothers in secret agreement with other adherents [of the Orthodox faith] is said to have ended his days. It seems as if the slave trade will be started as usual; here and there one meets slaves who have recently been brought down and sold. One day I saw two middle-sized boys who were going to be sold then. I heard them speak genuine Galla (Oromo) with each other. Oh, how the zeal for my poor people gnawed at me; if I had the power, I would have done to the slave trader as Samuel did to Agag, 1 Sam 15.33.

The route to Harer is now safer than it was when Svensson was there. The governor there has been deposed; may God permit that the one who comes after him will be a man who will promote the spread of the Gospel. We sincerely long to reach our goal. Please do not forget us, nor the Galla (Oromo). Now, everything is well. Glory and praise be to God, we are in good health. Books in Galla (Oromo) [language] which we left in Khartoum are now on their way here to Massawa. In addition, some boxes will soon come from London, perhaps in the month of April. The only thing that is missing is to start, but nothing else. May the God above all gods kindle the hearts of all his faithful with the fire of his holy spirit so that they, as long as they remain in this foreign land, will be able to work faithfully in the vineyard of their Lord.

Greet all the friends of the Kingdom of God, especially the friends at Johannelund.

Onesimus.

EFS, E I 24, 230. Swedish original. Onesimus had studied in Sweden from 1876 to 1881 and his Swedish is quite good. Onesimus, himself an Oromo, used the word "Galla" without any negative connotations as simply referring to the Oromo and/or their language.

Document no. 122

Treaty between Shewa and Italy, 21 May 1883

በኢጣልያ፡መንግሥትና፡በሸዋ፡
መንግሥት፡መካከል፡የተደረገ፡የፍቅር
ና፡የንግድ፡ውል፡ይህ፡ነው።

መ፩መርያ፡ክፍል

በኢጣልያ ንጉሥና በሸዋ ንጉሥ መካከል
በልጆቻቸውና በዘመዶቻቸውም መካከል
ልጅ፡ልጅ፡የሚኖር ፍቅር ይደረጋል
ሁለቱም ወገኖች ለዘለዓለም በፍቅር በ
ሰላም ይኖራሉ

ሁለተኛ ክፍል።

እነዚህ ሁለቱ ንጉሥታት ከየመንግሥታ
ቸው ሲኖሩ እንደ ክንድ ንጉሥ ምስ
ለኔ ወን እያኖረ በየምስለኔያቸው ጉዳ
ያቸውን ይጨርሳሉ። ምስለኔዎቻቸው
ም ነጋዴዎቻቸው፡ በመሻታቸው፡ የመሰከሩ
ላቸውና ነው። እንደ ባንድ አገር ነጋዴ
ዎቻቸው እንዲልባቸው እንዲነግዱ። ቆ
ንሱልም፡ቢሆን፡የቆንስል ወኪል፡ቢሆ
ን፡መሾም፡ይቻላቸዋል። እነዚህም፡ቆንስል፡
የመንግሥትን ሥራ፡የሚጠብቁ፡ናቸውና፡መከበ
ር፡ይገባቸዋል፡ሥልጣንም አላቸው። እንዲሁ አገ
ሩ፡ልማድ፡እንዲወደዱ እንዲከበሩ
ቸው፡ይደረጋላቸዋል

ሦስተኛ፡ክፍል

የነዚህ፡የሁለቱ ወገኖችና ዘጐቹ፡የንግድ
ና፡እቃቸውና፡ሌላም ገንዘባቸውን፡እየያዙ፡
በነዚህ፡ሁለት ንጉሥታት አገር እንደ፡ልባቸው፡
መሄድና፡መምጣት ይቻላቸዋል። በባሕርም
ቢሆን በየብስም ቢሆን መሄድ ይቻላቸዋል
በየመንግሥታቸው ጥብቅነት በየዘጐቻቸው፡
ጥብቅነት፡ደስ ብሎአቸው፡ይኖራሉ።

አራተኛ ክፍል።

የኢጣልያ፡ሰዎች፡በሸዋ መሬት፡የሸዋም፡
ሰው፡በኢጣልያ፡አገር፡እንደ፡አገሩ፡ልማድ፡
ይኖራሉ፡በንግዱም ቢሆን፡በማኅበርናም፡ቢ
ሆን፡እንደ፡አገሩ ልማድ፡ያገሩ ሕግጋት
ይልክለከውን፡ሥራ፡ሁሉ፡እየደረጉ፡ይኖራ
ሉ። በቀረው ነገር ተስማምተው ይኖራሉ።

This is the treaty of friendship and commerce made between the government of Italy and the government of Shewa.

Article 1. There shall be a perpetual peace and constant friendship between the king of Italy and the king of Shewa as well as between their children and their subjects from generation to generation.

Article 2. These two kings, as long as they live in their respective realms, shall place representatives and accomplish their affairs through their envoys. Each king can appoint a consul or a representative of a consul in the respective countries to make it possible for their merchants to trade as they wish. Since these consuls protect the activities of governments, they should be honoured. They also have authority. Steps shall be taken so that they will be loved and honoured according to the custom of the country.

Article 3. Those who belong to these two and their citizens are allowed to take their goods and other properties and come and go as they wish within the countries of these two kings. They are allowed to travel both by sea and by land. They shall live happily under the protection of the respective governments and their subjects.

አምስተኛ፡ ክፍል፡

የኢጣልያ፡ ሰዎችና፡ የሸዋ ሰዎች፡ በየሃይ
መኖታቸው፡ ይኖራሉ፡ አለመቀስቀስ፡ የኢጣ
ልያ፡ ሰዎች፡ ግን፡ ሃይማኖታቸውን፡ በሸዋ፡ መ
ሬት፡ ማስተማር፡ አይችሉም፡ የሸዋም፡ በኢጣ
ልያ፡ እንደዚሁ፡ አይቻላቸውም፡፡

ስድስተኛ፡ ክፍል፡፡

በሸዋ መሬት፡ የኢጣልያ፡ ሰው፡ የሞተ፡ እንደ
ሆነ፡ የሸዋ፡ መኳንንት፡ ገንዘቡን፡ ሁሉ፡ ይ
ጠብቃሉ፡ የኢጣልያን፡ ሹሞች፡ ፈቃድ፡ እስ
ኪያገኙ፡ ድረስ፡ ወይም፡ ያጣም፡ የኢጣልያ፡ መ
ንግሥት፡ ያዘዛቸው፡ ሰው፡ ፈቃድ፡ እስኪመጣላ
ቸው፡ ድረስ፡ አስቀምጠው፡ ይጠብቃሉ፡፡ በኢ
ጣልያም፡ አገር፡ የሸዋ፡ ሰው፡ የሞተ፡ እንደሆ
ነ፡ የኢጣልያ፡ ሹሞች፡ አሁን፡ እንደ፡ ተናገርነ
ው፡ ያደርጋሉ፡፡

ሰባተኛ፡ ክፍል፡

የሸዋ፡ መንገድ፡ ለወሰንተኛ፡ አይመችምና፡
የመንገዱ፡ ክፋት፡ ከዚህ፡ ቀደም፡ ስላየነው፡፡
ንጉሥ፡ ምኒልክ፡ በርሰዎ፡ በኩል፡ ያለውን፡ የ
ኢጣልያ፡ ነጋዴች፡ ሲመጡ፡ በቻሉዎ፡ መን
ገዱን፡ እንዲያቀኑላቸው፡፡ የሚሰጡትን፡ ኪ
ራይ፡ በጥቂት፡ ገንዘብ፡ እንዲያደርጉላቸ
ው፡ ለኢጣልያ፡ ሰው፡ በዚህን፡ ያህል፡ ይሁ
ን፡ ብለው፡ ክርክሩን፡ እንዲቈርጡላቸው፡
ይሆናል፡፡

ስምንተኛ፡ ክፍል፡፡

የኢጣልያ፡ ሰዎች፡ የንግድ፡ እቃ፡ በሸዋ፡ መሬ
ት፡ ሲገቡና፡ ሲወጡ፡ ቀረጡን፡ ይህን፡ ያህል፡
ከ፻፡፭፡
ይሁን፡ ብለው፡ ይቈርጣሉ፡ ንጉሥ፡ ወደ
ሌላ፡ አገር፡ አልፎ፡ የሚሄድ፡ እቃ፡ የሆነ፡ እን
ደሆን፡ ግን፡ ቀረጥ፡ የለባቸውም፡ አልፎ፡ ሂ
ያጅ፡ ነውና፡፡ እቃው፡ ሲሄድ፡ ግን፡ ንጉሥ፡ ነፍ
ጥ፡ እንደሆነ፡ አይተው፡ ያሳልፉ፡፡ ነፍጥ፡ ያለ
ንጉሥ፡ ፈቃድ፡ አይሸጥም፡፡ በዚህም ለውጥ፡
የሸዋ፡ ነጋዴች፡ የንጉሥ፡ ዚጎች፡ የሚያመጡ
ት፡ የንግድ፡ እቃ፡ በዚህኑ፡ ውል፡ የተጻፈው፡ ቀ
ን፡ እስኪደርስ፡ ሲገቡም፡ ሲወጡም፡ ምንም

Article 4. Italian people in Shewa and Shewan people in the country of Italy can live according to the custom of the country. As far as trade and agriculture are concerned, they shall live according to the custom of the country doing all the things which the laws of the country do not forbid. As to the rest they shall live in concord.

Article 5. The people of Italy and the people of Shewa shall live according to their own religions without provocations However, the people of Italy cannot teach their religion on Shewan soil, neither can the people of Shewa do so in Italy.

Article 6. If an Italian dies on Shewan soil the noblemen of Shewa will guard all his property. Until Italian authorities get permission, or until persons authorized by the Italian government receive their permit, they shall store and guard it. If a person from Shewa dies in Italy, the Italian authorities shall do according to what we have said.

Article 7. As we have seen before, the routes of Shewa are not comfortable for strangers. King Minīlik, from your side see to it as much as possible that the routes are made accessible to them when Italian merchants come. Make the rent that they pay low. Determine the costs of pack animals for the Italians, saying: "Let it be so much."

Article 8. When mercantile goods belonging to Italians enter and leave Shewa, the king shall determine the duty ("5 %" is added between the lines). But if it is a matter of goods which pass to go to another country, they are not obliged to pay duties because the goods are in transit. But when the goods move on, the king shall check if there are rifles and then permit transit. Rifles cannot be sold without the permission of the king. In exchange, the goods which are brought in by merchants of Shewa and by subjects of the king are not liable to duties during the period of the validity of this agreement. According to this agreement, beginning from January 1883, they do not have to pay at the Italian gate at Aseb.

፫

ቀረጥ፡ ሳይከፍሉም፡፡ ይህም ውል፡ ከጥር፡
፲፰፻፸፰ ዓምሮ፡ በአሰብ፡ በኢጣልያ፡ በር
መክፈል፡ የለባቸውም፡፡

ዘጠነኛ፡ ክፍል፡፡

እነዚህ፡ ሁለቱ፡ ነገሥታት፡ የንግድ፡ መንገድ፡
ከሸዋ፡ መንግሥት፡ እንግሥቱ፡ እስተ፡ ኢጣልያ፡
በር፡ አሰብ፡ ድረስ፡ የቀና፡ የረታ፡ የተከፈተ፡
መንገድ፡ እንዲሆን፡ ያደርጋሉ፡፡ ኢጣልያም
በባሕር፡ በኩል፡ አይለይለው፡ ይጠብቃሉ፡፡
የሸዋም፡ መንግሥት፡ በበኩሉ፡ የሃገሩን፡
መንገድ፡ መቅናቱን፡ በጣም፡ ያያሉ፡ ይጠብ
ቃሉ፡፡ ንጉሥ፡ ምኒልክ፡ ወደ፡ አሰብ፡ ነጋዴ፡ እ
ንዲሄዱ፡ ያደርጋሉ፡፡

አሥረኛ፡ ክፍል፡፡

ንጉሥ፡ ምኒልክ፡ የሚገዙዋቸውን፡ ሹሞች፡
ሁሉ፡ የኢጣልያ፡ ነጋዴዎች፡ እንደልባቸው፡ እንዲ
ነግዱ፡ እንዳይከለክሏቸው፡ እንዲፈቅዱላ
ቸው፡ ለሹማምንቶቻቸው፡ ያሳውቋቸዋል፡፡ የተበደሉ
ም፡ እንደሆነ፡ የተገባ፡ ዳኝነት፡ ያወጡላቸዋል፡
ደግመኛም፡ ንጉሥ፡ ምኒልክ፡ ከአውሳ፡ ሹም፡ጋራ፡

፬

ከአሰብና፡ ከሸዋ፡ መካከል፡ ያለውን፡ መንገድ፡
መቅናቱን፡ እያዩ፡ የተቻላቸውን፡ ሁሉ፡
እያደረጉ፡ ከአዳልና፡ ከሱማሌ፡ ይጠብቁዋ
ቸዋል፡ ያድኗቸዋል፡ ይከላከሉላቸዋል፡
ይህም፡ መንገድ፡ እንዲቀና፡ የኢጣልያ፡ መን
ግሥት፡ ለአውሳው፡ ሹም፡ የሚከፈለውን
ገንዘብ፡ ንጉሥ፡ ምኒልክ፡ ይቈርጣሉ፡ ይ
ህም፡ ሰፈር፡ በወጣ፡ ቁጥር፡ ለአውሳው፡ ሹም፡
ይህን፡ ያህል፡ ተቀበል፡ ወይም፡ በዓመት፡ ይህን፡
ያህል፡ ተቀበል፡ ብለው፡ ይቈርጣሉ፡፡

፲፩ኛ፡ ክፍል

የኢጣልያ፡ ንጉሥ፡ ወደ፡ አሰብ፡ የሚመጡትን፡
የሸዋ፡ ሰዎች፡ ምድር፡ ያለገንዘብ፡ ይሰጡዋ
ቸዋል፡፡ ቤት፡ ሠርተን፡ እንኖራለን፡ ያሉ፡ እንደሆ
ን፡፡ በሰጧቸው፡ ምድር፡ ሥልጣን፡ ይሰጧቸዋል፡፡

፲፪ኛ፡ ክፍል፡፡

የሸዋ፡ ሹሞች፡ ከኢጣልያ፡ ዜጎች፡ ጋራ፡ ጠብና፡

Article 9. These two kings shall see to it that the commercial route from the government of Shewa to the Italian gate at Aseb is fully accessible. Italy shall keep guard thoroughly on the side of the sea. On its part the government of Shewa shall diligently see to it that the internal routes are accessible and guard them. King Minīlik shall see to it that merchants go to Aseb.

Article 10. King Minīlik shall inform his subjects, the appointees of Shewa, that they should not forbid any Italian merchant to trade as he wishes. If these merchants are wronged the king should see to it that they receive due justice. Furthermore King Minīlik shall protect, rescue and defend these merchants from the Adal and the Somali in cooperation with the governor (*shum*) of Awsa by seeing to it that the route between Aseb and Shewa is accessible. King Minīlik shall determine the fee to be paid to the governor of Awsa by the government of Italy so that the said route remains accessible. Whenever the terms for payment expire the king shall determine the yearly payment to the governor of Awsa.

Article 11. The king of Italy shall see to it that Shewan people who come to Aseb shall receive land without the paying of money. And if they say "We shall build a house and live here", then the king shall give them control of the land which he has given them.

Article 12. The appointees of Shewa have no quarrels with the citizens of Italy. If Italians come into conflict with each other they shall be judged by an Italian consul who lives near the king, or by a person who has come by the authorization of the government. If subjects of Shewa happen to come to Aseb and quarrel with each other there they should not be judged by the government of Italy.

ክርክር የለባቸውም። የኢጣልያ ሰዎች፡ እር
ሱ፡ በርሳቸው፡ ያጠፉ እንደሆነ ወይ በኢጣ
ልያ፡ ቈንሱል ከንጉሡ በጠገብ የሚኖር፡
እለዚያ በመንግሥት ሥዞ በመጣ፡ ሰው፡ ይ
ፈረዱባቸዋል ፡ የሸዋም ዜጎች እሰብ ፍረ
ስ፡ የመጡ እንደሆነ እርሱ በርሳቸው ጥል
ቢነሳ፡ የኢጣልያ መንግሥት ሹሞች መደኛ
ት የላባቸውም ንጉሡ በሾሙት እለዚያ
ም ንጉሡ አለቃ አድርገው በላኩት ይዳኛሉ፡
በሸዋ መሬት የኢጣልያ ሰዎችና የሸዋ ሰው
የተጣሉ፡ እንደሆነ የኢጣልያው ቈንሱ
ልና፡ የአገሩ ዳኛ እንድ ዘንድ ሆነው ተቀ
ምጠው ይዳኙዋቸዋል፡ የሌላ አገር ፈረን
ጅና የኢጣሊያ ሰው የተጣሉ፡ እንደሆነ፡
ያሌላው፡ ሰው፡ ቈንስል ያለው እንደሆነ
የዚያ ቈንስልና የኢጣልያው ቈንስል ዕነቱ፡
ተቀምጠው ይዳኙዋቸዋል፡ አለዚያ የኢጣል
ያው ቈንስል ሁለቱንም ይዳኛል፡

፲፫ኛ፡ ክፍል፡

የሸዋ ንጉሥ ወደ አውሮፓ ጕዳይ እልክ
ለሁ፡ ብለው፡ ያሰቡ፡ እንደሆነ፡ የኢጣልያ ቈ
ንሰልም፡ ሆነ፡ አሰብ ላይ የሚኖረው ሹምም
በንጉሡ፡ ምኒልክ ሥልጣን ውስጥ፡ ናቸውና፡
በነዚህ፡ እጅ ወደ ፈቀደ ፡ መንግሥት፡ ል
ከው፡ ያሰቡትን፡ ጉዳይ፡ መፈፀም ይቻለዋ
ል፡ የሸዋ መንግሥት ዜጐች ፀዐ ሁሉ፡
የኢጣልያ ቈንሱል፡ ሆነ፡ በንጉሡ፡ ተልኮ
የመጣ አባሳደር፡ ካለበት ሥፍራም የተ
ገኙ፡ እንደሆነ እኒህ ሹሞች እንደ አገሩ
ቸው ልጅ፡ እንደ ኢጣልያ ሰው፡ ጥግና፡ እ
ረዳት ይሆኑዋቸዋል፡ የተበደሉም ጊዜ፡
ይረዷቸዋል

፲፬ኛ፡ ክፍል፡፡

እነዚህ ሁለቱ ወገኖች ሸዋና፡ ኢጣልያ፡ በ
ሚዋደዱ ሁለት ወገኖች እርሱ፡ በር
ሳቸው፡ የሚሰሩትን፡ የፍቅር፡ ሥራ፡ ሁለቱ
ም፡ ይሰሩታል፡፡ ይህን፡ ማለት ቸርነትና፡
ጥቅም፡ ያለው የንግድ ሥራ፡ እንደ ሕግ

They shall be judged either by someone appointed by the king or by some authority sent by the king. If Italians and Shewans quarrel the Italian consul and a judge from the country shall sit together and judge them. If another foreigner and an Italian quarrel and if the other person has a consul, that consul and the Italian consul shall sit together and judge them, otherwise the Italian consul shall judge both.

Article 13. If the king of Shewa considers sending messages to Europe, he can send what he has intended to send to whatever government it may be and thus accomplish his business through the hands of the Italian consul or the commissioner who lives in Aseb, since these people are under the authority of King Minīlik. And if citizens of the government of Shewa happen to find themselves in the same place as an Italian consul or an ambassador who has come by the accreditation of the king these Italian officials shall treat the aforementioned citizens of Shewa as if they were children of their own country and give them protection and help like Italian people, and if these people are wronged they shall help them.

Article 14. These two parties, Shewa and Italy, shall perform the deeds of love which two parties who love each other do reciprocally. And this means that the two parties will not neglect to show kindness and practise beneficial acts of trade reciprocally without the demands of the law.

Article 15. Since all people quarrel, if by chance Shewa and Italy should quarrel because of minor or major causes, the two kings shall be judged by a third king of their own choice in a spirit of friendship, and they shall accept the judgement with respect and willingness.

Il Rappresentante di S.M.
il Re d'Italia
Pietro Antonelli

Article 16. This agreement shall be translated into the languages of Shewa and Italy, adjusted, written and kept in the hands of the governments.

Article 17. Ten years after the writing down of this agreement: if one of the kings thinks of adding to or subtracting from the agreement, he can make a request to this effect one year before the end of the term of validity of the agreement. After this they should renew the agreement after having discussed the damage which each party has suffered.

Article 18. This agreement will be finished after a few days; in the city of Rome up to six months.

14th Ginbot 1875 in Ankober

Seal: Minīlik, King of Shewa. The Lion of the tribe of Judah has prevailed. The representative of His Majesty the King of Italy. Pietro Antonelli.

ASMAI 7/1–1, Amharic original and Italian translation. The Italian translation also carries Minīlik's seal. The Italian version states: "On this the 21st day of the month of May in the year 1883 (Gregorian calendar) corresponding to 14th Ginbot 1875 (Ethiopian Calendar) in the city of Ankober, the representative of His Majesty King Minīlik II and the representative of the government of His Majesty the King of Italy have hereunto affixed their respective signatures so that the treaty reaches the city of Rome as early as possible for the necessary ratification." Both Amharic and Italian drafts are found in ASMAI 36/2–13; one is also printed in *AP.DD*, XV, pp. 62–63. For context see *L'Italia in Africa*, I.1 pp. 144–146 and *Wichale*, pp. 41–43. It was the negotiation of this agreement that was the main purpose of Antonelli's mission, and it was only when he had come to an agreement with Minīlik that he placed his seal and signature on the agreement with Maḥammad Ḥanfadhē negotiated a month earlier; see doc. 118 above.

Document 123

Minīlik II to Giulio Pestalozza, 21 May 1883

Minīlik II, by the grace of God King of Shewa, of Kaffa and all the countries Galla, sends this letter to his respectable friend, Cavaliere Giulio Pestalozza, governor of the royal administration of Aseb.

How are you? I am well, by the grace of God, and my whole army is also well. I received through the hands of our friend Count Antonelli your very kind letter dated 10 January, 1883. May God repay you for all you have written to me and for the news you have given me about the services that have been rendered to my servants on the coast. May God keep you in his holy custody, since you are so well disposed to favour and protect my interests.

Our friend Count Antonelli, with all the gifts His Majesty King Umberto, and in the company of my servants, has arrived happily without losing a needle. I received with much respect and satisfaction what His Majesty, the King of Italy, sent, and above all I was delighted by the treaty of friendship and commerce that I read, accepted and returned. I was very satisfied with this treaty since I hope it will prove to be useful to the subjects of Italy and of Shewa. I hope it will be equally useful for the Bay of Aseb, as I have many hopes of progress and happiness for my kingdom from the port. For my part I will do everything possible and in my power to keep the road of Aseb open. Already today I am organizing a caravan to send it to Aseb before the rainy season, God willing

Our friend Antonelli will rest a little and after the rainy season we will have him return with one of our generals.

And now I beg you to assist me in the affair that Count Antonelli will tell you about and that make a great service to my kingdom. I also warmly beg you to protect my servants who come to Assab, as I for my part will effectively protect the Italian subjects who come to my kingdom. My hope is that the Italian merchants in my kingdom and those of Shewa in Aseb will be mutually assisted and protected and will live with full agreement among themselves with the intent to take advantage of the work begun by His Majesty King Umberto and myself.

Written in the city of Ankober on 14th May 1875 Abyssinian (calendar).

Royal Seal.

ASMAI 1/5–31. Italian translation. Printed in *l'Italia in Africa* I.3, p. 22.

Document no. 124

Minīlik II to Pasquale Stanislao Mancini, 21 May 1883

ዳግማዊ ምኒልክ በእግዚአብሔር ኃይል የሸዋና የ
ጋላም አገር ሁሉ የከፋም ንጉሥ የሆነ ይድረስ ወደ ክበሬ ወዳ ተ
ወዳጄ የባዕድ አገር ሁሉ ነገር የሚፈጽም ምኒስቴር ማንቺኒ እ
ንዴት ነህ እጅግን እኔ እግዚአብሔር ይመስገን ደኅና ነኝ ሠራዊቴ
ም ሁሉ ደኅና ነው፡ በነሐሴ ፴ ቀን ፲፰፻፸፬ የተጻፈ ደብዳቤህ እ
ጅግ ከተወዳጁ ወዳጆችን በኮንት አንቶኔሊ እጅ ከብዙ ማክበር
ና ከብዙ ደስታ ጋራ ተቀበልሁ፡ ከተጻፈው ምንም ቃል የነካስ እጅግ
ደስ አሰኘኝ፡ የኢጣልያ ኔሳችና የሸዋን ኔሳች የሚሰበስብ የፍ
ቅርና የንግድ ውል ጽፋችሁ ስለላካችሁልኝም በዚህ ደስ ስለአሰኘ
እኔም ከብዙ ደስታ ጋራ ተቀብዬ አይቼ ፈርሜ ልኬዋለሁ፡ አሁንም
የምፈልገውን ጉዳይ ከፊተኛው ይልቅ ጠንክሮ ኮንት አንቶኔሊ
ሊናገር ልኮ ከኢጣልያ አገር የተመኘሁትን ጥሎ እንዲያስመጣል
ኝ አገዛገርዋ ስለሁኔታ የተመኘሁትንም ነገር ከንጉሥ ዘንድ አስፈቅደህ
ፈቃድ እንድትሰጥልኝ ተስፋ አለኝ፡ እንሰሩም ሹም በነገሩ ሁሉ
እንድትስጠነቀቅልኝ ተስፋ አለኝ፡ ከዚህም በፊት የአሰብን ሹ
ማምት ስለኔ ጉዳይ ማስጠንቀቅህ እግዚአብሔር ያመስግንህ እኔም
ጉዳይ በመጣርህ እግዚአብሔር ያመስግንህ እኔም በተቻለኝ ነገር ሁ
ሉ የአሰብ መንገድ በጣም እንዲከፈት አደርጋለሁ፡ ከዚህም
ቀደም ኮንት አንቶኔሊ ከአሰብ ወደ ሸዋ በአውሳ መንገድ እ
ንዲመጣ የተቻለኝን ነገር ሁሉ አደረግሁ፡ ወዳጄም ኮንት አ
ንቶኔሊ ፭ መርፌ ሳፁ ጠፋበት ከኔ አሽከሮች ጋራ በደኅና
ሸዋ ደረሰ፡ በዚህም የተነሳ እግዚአብሔርን አመሰግነሁታለሁ፡ አሁን
ም ከክረምት በፊት ወደ አሰብ ሰፈር ለመሰደድ እስቤአለ

ለሁሉም ወዳጅዬን ኮንት አንቶኔሊን ጥቂት ቀን አሳርፌው መስከረ
ም ሲጠባ ከግዜር ቢወድ ከመኳንንቴ ፩ ሰው ጋራ ለ
መላክ አስቤአለሁ። ከዚህም በኋላ እኔና ንተ በኔ እኔ በናንተ
የኢጣሊያ ዜጎች በሸዋ ዜጎች የሸዋም በኢጣሊያ ደስ ብለን
ው እንዲኖሩ ተስፋ አለኝ። እነዚህም ሁሉ ዜጎች በኔና በን
ጉሥ ዑምበርቶ ለልጅ ልጅ የሚሆን ጥቅም እንዲያገኙ
ተስፋ አለኝ። እግዚአብሔር ያሰብሁትን ነገር ይፈጽምልኝ። እድሜዎን
እንዲጠብቅ እለምናለሁ። ❖ ❖ ❖

— በግንቦት ፲፬ በ፲፰፻፸፭ በአንኮበር ከተማ ተጻፈ።

The second Minīlik, who by the power of God is the King of Shewa, all of the Galla country and Kefa.

May it reach the honoured and beloved Minister Mancini. How are you, really? I am well, thanks be to God; and all my soldiers are well. I received, from the hands of our most beloved friend, Count Antonelli, your letter written on 4 Nehasē 1882 with much respect and joy. And I was very pleased with the words written [there]. I was pleased with the treaty that you wrote and sent to me and which brings together the citizens of Italy and the citizens of Shewa. And I received it with much pleasure, looked at it and sent it adding more to my earlier request to have the things I want brought from Italy by sending [a message] to you. And I hope that you will have it approved by the king and that you will give permission. And I hope that you will warn the governor (*shum*) of Aseb about all this matter. And may God thank you for being concerned about my matter. And I will do all I can to see that the route of Aseb is opened widely. Earlier I did all I could to see Count Antonelli come from Aseb to Shewa through the Awsa route. And my friend Count Antonelli safely reached Shewa with my servants without losing a single needle for this reason. I thanked God. And now I intend to send an encampment to Aseb before the rainy season. I intend, God willing, to send my friend Count Antonelli, after letting him take rest for a few days, with one man from my notables when Meskerem commences. And after this, I hope that we shall rest satisfied; you with me, I with you, the citizens of Italy with the citizens of Shewa and those of Shewa with those of Italy. I hope that all these citizens will find [our relation] an advantage until grandchildren because of me and King Umberto. I pray that God will fulfil the thing which I have planned and that he will preserve your life.

Written in the town of Ankober on 14t Ginbot 1875.

ASMAI 36/2–16, Amharic original and Italian translation. Printed in *AP.DD*, XV, pp. 135–136. When referring to Mancini's letter, to which this is a reply, Minīlik translates the month of August into Amharic Nehasē, but keeps the Gregorian year 1882.

Document no. 125

Minīlik II to Giacomo Malvano, 21 May 1883

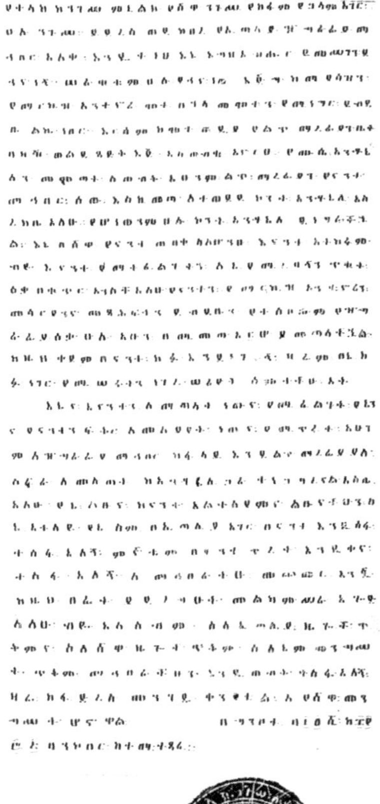

May [the letter] sent by Minīlik, King of Shewa and of Kefa and of all the countries of the Galla, reach the respected head of the Geographical Society of Italy.

How have you been? Thank God I am well and my army is well.

After the sad death of Marquis Antinori, I sent a letter that conveys news of his death. And after his death I arranged my house at Liṭ Marefīya to be guarded by *Azzazh* Welde Ṣadiq and kept waiting until the coming of M. Antonelli. And now, until a man of your Society comes, I have handed over Liṭ Marefīya to the dear Count Antonelli. And Count Antonelli will tell you all that has happened. Since I am your custodian in Shewa believing that you would not be angry, I have taken a few items reckoning that you have no use for them but they are useful to me. Your [other] articles, books, letters and collected geographical materials will reach you with a coming caravan.

Now, do not harbour ill will against me listening to those talebearers who some time ago told me bad things about you, since their desire is to make me and you quarrel and damage my and your friendship. And now I have agreed with Antonelli to give to the Geographical Society a place in Kefa similar to that of Liṭ Marefīya. I have that in mind. Since my thought is not far from you, do not distance yours from me. I hope that my name will be widely known in Italy through you. And my hope is that it [my name] will be cleared through your efforts. I am not planning to decrease all the good deeds I have done for your Society but I would rather increase [them]. I hope that your Society will be strengthened for the benefit of the Italian citizens and of the Shewan citizens and of my government. Now the route to Kefa has been opened. It [Kefa] has become one government with that of Shewa.

Written in Ginbot in 1875 in the town of Ankober.

Seal: Minīlik, King of Shewa. The Lion of the tribe of Judah has prevailed.

ASSGI, 20, 5, fol. 29, Amharic original; fols 6–7, Italian translation. The dating of the letter itself is incomplete. Space was allotted in front of "be-ginbot" but apparently left empty by oversight. The Italian agent or messenger to whom the letter was entrusted complicated the issue further. We have read his note ". . . scritta dalla città d'Ankober il 14 maggio 1875 (stile abessine)" as 14 Ginbot, thus 21 May 1883. At the end of the first paragraph the writer seems to have lost track of what he was writing and stopped in the middle of a word "*atē* . . .", most probably omitting "*qeyeben*". The addressee, Giacomo Malvano, was never President of the SGI, but director at the ministry of foreign affairs.

Document no. 126

Nigusē Tasho *et al.*, to Bengt Peter and Emelie Lundahl, 29 May 1883

May [this] message reach our master and father Lundahl and our mother Emelie.

How are you, really? Since last time we heard from you until now we are well, thank God. Amen.

By the mercy of God we have been to Jimma and returned. We travelled to Jimma with much anxiety. As we were travelling to Jimma, one day before our arrival, eight people were killed ahead of us.

We passed that place and crossed the town boundary of Jimma. Furthermore, when the people who left with us were returning, as they arrived, eighty people were killed in the wilderness of Waṣho. Those who killed are called shēh. If we had returned with them, we too would have perished. God protected us from the former and the latter [danger].

Of the cloth brought by Mihretu and Beyyene Goshu for our supplies, except one bundle (*ṭaqa*) and some gold embroidery which remain, they have been used up, namely for passage, hospitality, night lodgings and gifts to the king of Jimma.

To the king, we gave foreign-made trappings, five handkerchiefs and one mirror. He gave us a plot of land so that we could build a house. We have built a house, fenced the plot around it, and having placed a guard there, we left, saying that God knows everything. God willing, we will settle in Jimma.

Money is of no use for our daily food. Nor is it useful to facilitate our access to persons in authority. Since as gifts they like previously unseen things, send us coffee-grinders, cups of glass, mirrors, lighters (lit. lighters of light), black pepper, cloves and knives.

You can take some money from the sum set aside for our provisions, thus reducing the amount. Mekonnin has the kind of articles that we have in mind. Ask him. Send someone to him. He can make the purchase. If Beyyene Goshu happens to be there, let him assist in the purchase and bring these articles to us. If Beyyene Goshu is not around, send a strong young man to come to us with him.

Let him tell you about everything. We set out from Ballī on Tahsas the 28th and on Ṭir the 20th we arrived in Jimma. We stayed [there] three months. On the 20th day of Mīyazīya we started and on Ginbot the 12th we arrived at our home in Ballī. God reunited us with our people. May He be praised for ever. Amen.

A *ferenje* named *Ato* Moges entreated us and said: "I prefer a Protestant to an Abyssinian priest. Give me a man, someone who could teach children for me." We agreed and then we left. When we came back, we found that they had not gone. When we asked them why, they told us that he did not come at the appointed date. So we left it at that.

As to going back this year, it is too late. The rains have set in. There is a big river (lit. water). It is called Temsa. We dare not travel with women and children. You cannot cross it during the rainy season, not until Hidar. Until then send us all the things.

Convey our greetings to *Qēs* Månsson, *Imabēt* Rosa, *Qēs* Svensson, Carlsson, Mīmī, and to all the fathers whom we know and those whose names we do not know. Regarding our brothers who went to Khartoum: "Have they come back, or not?" If they have come back say on our behalf, "God be praised for delivering you from hardship and illness."

Greet those brothers of ours who are at home, the old and the young. "Our brothers! Do not forget us. We have not written to you individually, because we are exhausted from our journey."

The grace of Our Lord Jesus Christ, the love of God, the fellowship of the Holy Spirit be with us all. Amen.

Written on the 22nd of Ginbot 1883.

From Ballī to Imkullu. All the children send their greetings. Nigusē with his wife, Amanuel with his wife, Yohannis, who ever since we departed, has been sick with scabies on his hands and feet, and says, "Do not forget me", and Mihretu with his wife, we send our greetings to our beloved father and master.

EFS E I 24, Amharic text. The date in Amharic is "Ginbot the 22nd day 1883." While day and month are provided in the Julian calendar the year is almost certainly Gregorian calendar, as maintained by *Evangelical Pioneers*, p. 263. This type of inconsistency was not uncommon in correspondence at this time. Unfortunately, this volume of correspondence is so tightly bound that it has been impossible for us to photocopy it properly. For the mission station Ballī see also doc. 55.

Document no. 127

Yohannis IV to Demosthenes Mitzakis, 30 May 1883

Seal: Yohannis kings of kings of Ethiopia; Yūḥannā King of Kings of Abyssinia.

May the letter of the Elect of God Yohannis, King of Zion, King of Kings of Ethiopia, reach the Greek (Romawi) consul in Jerusalem. How are you? I, together with my army, by the grace of God and by the intercession of our Mother Zion, praised and honoured be the God of the saints, am well. I have received your dear letter with its seal. I am very happy with the words I got in the letter. Please protect the monks in Jerusalem, *Abba* Welde Sema'it and his friends so that they can build for me the church in Jerusalem without being disturbed. Take the letter, which I had written to the new king of Greece (*Rom*) George, from *Abba* Welde Sema'it and send it back quickly to me with your hands.

Written in the town of Semera on 23rd Ginbot in the year of grace 1875.

Edward Ullendorff, "Emperor Yohannes IV of Ethiopia and the Building of the Ethiopian Church of Däbrä Gännät at Jerusalem", in Alan S. Kaye (ed.), *Semitic Studies in Honour of Wolf Leslau on Occasion of his 85th Birthday 1992*, Wiesbaden, pp. 351–354, re-print of the Amharic original.

Ullendorff identifies the addressee as the Demosthenes Mitzakis who had been Greek vice-consul of Suez and who was, thanks to his good relations with Yohannis, regarded as a powerful enemy of the British. See *Yohannes IV*, pp. 137, 150–151. *Rom* (Arabic *Rūm*) was used throughout the Middle East to refer to the Byzantine empire and subsequently to Greece.

Document no. 128

Maḥammad Ḥanfadhē to Giulio Pestalozza, 2 June 1883

الحمد لله وحده والصلاة والسلام على من لا نبي بعده
الى حضرة الجناب الاجل الامجد الانجد الاكرم المكرم العزيز المحترم
الافخم المفخم اعني به جوليو بستلوسه هداه الله تعالى امين
وان سالتم عنا وعمن يلوذ بنا فاننا بخير وعافية ولا نسال صدرة الاحرف
من محروس بندر سنكوره وكل علم وخبة وصل الينا جوابكم الكريم وقرانا
مبانيه وعرفنا معانيه نحمد الله تعالى على صحتكم وعن احوالكم التي هي
غايت القصد والمراد من رب العباد نا صدرة الكتاب لاجل ارتباط المحبة
وعقد اساس المودة واعلام الحال وتعرفونا بما انتم فيه من الاحوال
وبما وصلكم منا الجواب فلا تقطعوا عنا المكاتبة عن احوالكم البارة
واخباركم السارة وذكرتم لنا عن دعوة المصريون في سكلو في ساكلوا
وانتم احسن النظر في تدبيره منا عن ذلك وانشاء الله لما يصل الجواب
اليكم من الولاية شا تعرفنا حالا بالحقائق وننتظركم واما من جناب
البسطة الذي ارسلتموها الينا مع احمد كراسو حتى نرسلها الى شوي
لكنت انتونلي وانشا الله نشيعها حال التاريخ هذا عرفناكم

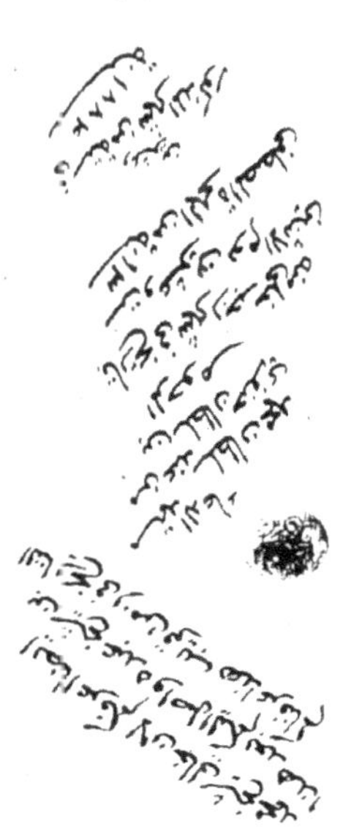

Praise be to God alone and blessings and peace be upon him after whom there is no prophet.

To His Honourable Excellency, the most illustrious, the bravest and most glorious, the most noble and most honoured, the beloved and respected, the most majestic and magnificent, by this I refer to Giulio Pestalozza. May God Almighty lead him. Amen.

If you ask about us and those who take refuge with us, we are well and healthy, and do not ask for . . .

These lines are dispatched from the capital of Sinkara, the protected; all the information we have is [good] and favourable. Your esteemed letter has reached us; we read its contents and understood its intentions. We praise God Almighty for your health and situation, which are the ultimate aim and desire of the Lord of the faithful. No letter appeared for the sake of love and the foundation of friendship and to tell us about your well-being, to inform us about your situation and to notify us that our letter reached you. Do not deprive us of your information to us about your honourable state and your pleasant news. You have mentioned to us the war cry of the Egyptians in Sagallo. Arrange this matter at your discretion. When the letter reaches you from the government, God willing, inform us immediately of the facts and we shall wait for you.

As for the mail you sent to us with Aḥmad Kirāsū in order to forward it to Count Antonelli in Shewa, if it is the will of God, we shall send it immediately. This is what we tell you

We also inform you that my uncle *Shaykh* Muḥammad bin *Shaykh* 'Abdū will reach you soon after this date. This is what we tell you.

The sender of the message is Sultan Maḥammad bin [son of] Sultan Ḥanfadhē the deceased.
Dated in the month of Rajab when 26 days had elapsed, on Monday, the year 13[00] of the *Hijra* of the chosen and the twenty-sixth of the mentioned month in the year 1883.

Seal illegible.

ASMAI 7/1–1, Arabic original. The scribe apparently forgot to complete the last sentence of the greetings.

Document no. 129

Mirça Werqē to Robert Fleming, 12 June 1883

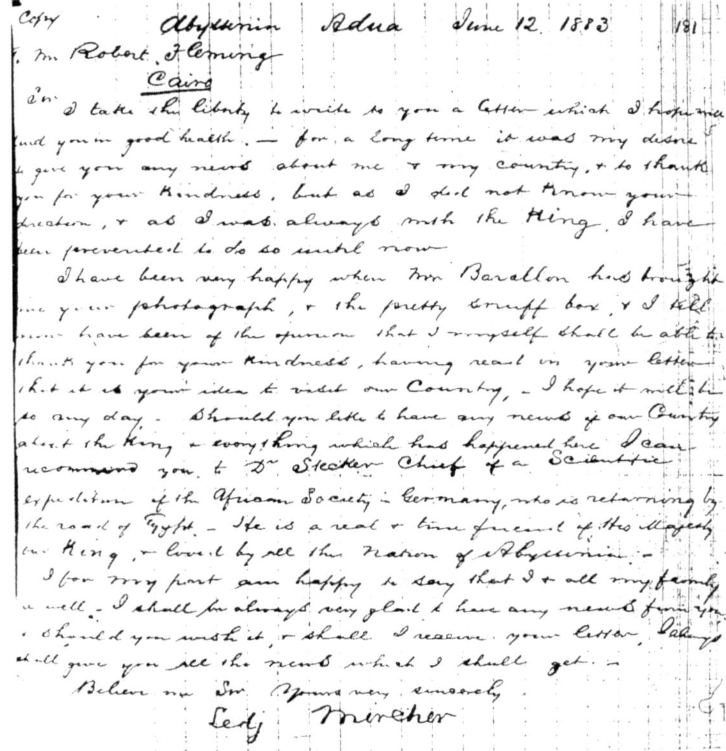

Abyssinia Adwa June 12. 1883

To Mr. Robert Fleming Cairo

Sir,

I take the liberty to write to you a letter which I hope will find you in good health. For a long time it was my desire to give you any news about me and my country, and to thank you for your kindness, but as I did not know your direction, and as I was always with the king, I have been prevented from doing so until now.

I was very happy when Mr. Baraglion brought me your photograph, and the pretty snuff box, and till now I have been of the opinion that I myself shall be able to thank you for your kindness, having read in your letter that it is your idea to visit our country. I hope it will be so any day. Should you like to have any news of our country, about the king and everything which has happened here I can recommend you to Dr. Stecker, Chief of a scientific expedition of the African Society in Germany, who is returning by the route of Egypt. He is a real and true friend of His Majesty our king, and loved by all the nation of Abyssinia.

I for my part am happy to say that I and all my family are well. I shall be always very glad to have any news from you and should you wish it, and shall I receive your letter. I shall always give you all the news which I shall get.

Believe me Sir. Yours very sincerely
Ledj Mercher (*Lij* Mirça)

FO 1/30, p. 181, English copy. The style of the letter suggests that it was almost certainly written in English, but the fact that the signature is in another hand makes it likely that it was not penned by Mirça Werqē himself, but rather dictated to a secretary. As Mirça Werqē knew English and has signed the letter, we have regarded this as a letter written by an Ethiopian and therefore reproduced the text exactly as in the preserved document, rather than editing it. For Dr. Stecker see doc. 113.

Document no. 130

Minīlik II to the Ethiopian community in Jerusalem, 25 June 1883

May [this letter] from King Minīlik reach the holy monks in Jerusalem.

My fathers, how are you, really? I am well, by the mercy of God, and your prayers. I am sending you one silver cross, one silver cup [?], one silver crown and one lectern, this I am sending. Do not forget me, my fathers.

Written in the town of Ankober on the 19th day of Senē in the year of grace 1875.

Seal: Minīlik, King of Shewa. The Lion of the tribe of Judah has prevailed.

Dayr al-Sultan, no. 32, Amharic original. The seal of the letter has not to our knowledge been used earlier by King Minīlik. It resembles the earlier European-style seal with the motto "The Lion of the tribe of Judah has prevailed", but the drawing of the lion and the crown, as well as the cross in the paw of the lion, foreshadow the later seals of Minīlik as well as of Hayle Sillasē.

Document no. 131

Minīlik II to Umberto I, 30 June 1883

ዳግማዊ፡ ምኒልክ፡ በእግዚአብሔር፡ ኃይል፡ የሸዋ፡ ንጉሥ፡ የከፋ
ም፡ የጋላም፡ አገር፡ ሁሉ፡ ንጉሥ፡ ይድረስ፡ ወዳጅ፡ ከበሩ፡ ወዳጅ፡ ተወዳጅ፡ ወንድማች
ን፡ ንጉሥ፡ ዑምበርቶ፡ መጋርመርያ፡፡ የኢጣሊያ፡ ንጉሥ፡ ሰላም፡ ለርሰዎ፡ ይሁን፡፡

ንጉሥ፡ ሆይ፡ ወዳጆችን፡ ኮንት፡ አንቶኔሊ፡ ይዞልን፡ የመጣ፡ ንጉሥ፡ የላኩ
ልን፡ በረከት፡ ከተቀበልን፡ በኋላ፡ ያማረውን፡ የተዋበውን፡ የውል፡ ደብዳቤ፡ ጨ
ርሰን፡ ከተቀበልን፡ በኋላ፡ መልእክተኛን፡ ለመስደድ፡ አሰብን፡፡ ነገር፡ ግን፡ ነገሩ፡
በመልክት፡ የማያልቅ፡ ቢሆን፡ ኮንት፡ አንቶኔሊን፡ እርሱ፡ ራሱ፡ ሂዶ፡ ነገሩን፡ እንዲ
ጨርስ፡ ወደዱን፡፡ የቀረውን፡ ያሰብነውን፡ ጉዳይ፡ ኮንት፡ አንቶኔሊ፡ ሲመለስ፡
እናደርገዋለን፡፡ እስተዚያው፡ ድረስ፡ ያሰብሁትን፡ አሰናድቼ፡ እቈያለሁ፡፡ በሐ
ዳር፡ ሰፈሩን፡ በሎሌዎቼን፡ በንጉሥ፡ ግብረ፡ ሥላሴ፡ እጅ፡ እንሰደለን፡፡ አሁን፡ ኮ
ንት፡ አንቶኔሊ፡ እንደ፡ መልእክተኛ፡ ሁኖ፡ እንዲሄድ፡ አደረግን፡፡ የሰራነውን፡ ያሰ
ብነውን፡ እርሱ፡ ይነግረዎታል፡፡ ነገሩን፡ ለማስረገጥ፡ ግን፡ የኛ፡ መልእክተኞች፡
የሄዱ፤ ዕለት፡ ያገኙታል፡፡ የየኡሮፓ፡ ነገሥታትም፡ የሁለታችንን፡ ፍቅር፡ ውነ
ታ፡ መሆኑን፡ የዚያን፡ ጊዜ፡ ያገኙታል፡፡ እኛም፡ የተመኘነውን፡ ነገር፡ በንጉሥ፡ ዘ
ንድ፡ የተወደደ፡ እንዲሆን፡ ተስፋ፡ አለኝ፡፡ ዛሬም፡ ያሰብሁትን፡ ነገር፡ እስቲደር
ስ፡ በአገሬ፡ የተገኘውን፡ የሸዋ፡ ዜጎችና፡ የኢጣሊያ፡ ዜጎች፡ የሚጠቀሙበት፡ የ
ሁሉ፡ አይነት፡ የንግድ፡ ዕቃ፡ ልኬልዎታለሁ፡፡ ይህም፡ እንደታላቅ፡ በረከት፡ አ
ርገው፡ ይቀበሉልኛል፡፡ ያሰብሁት፡ ነገር፡ ቀንቶ፡ ለልጆቻችን፡ ታላቅ፡ ጥቅም፡ እ
ንዲሆን፡ ተስፋ፡ አለኝ፡፡ ስለሕዝበዎ፡ ደስታ፡ ስለሸዋ፡ ሕዝብ፡ ጥ
ቅም፡ እግዚአብሔር፡ ዕድሜ፡ ጤና፡ እንዲያረዝም፡ እለምናለሁ፡፡ በሰ
ኔ፡ ፳፫ በእንኮበር፡ ከተማ፡ በ፲፰፻፸፭ ተጻፈ፡፡

[May this letter by] the second Minīlik, by the power of God King of Shewa, Kefa and all the Galla countries, reach our brother, the honoured and beloved King Umberto I, the Italian king. May peace be with you.

O king, we have received the present of the king, which our friend Count Antonelli had brought us, and after we have accepted completely the nice and amicable letter of the agreement, we have thought of sending a messenger. However, since the matter could not be settled through a messenger, we wanted Count Antonelli himself to finish the matter. The remaining matter which we have thought about, I will settle when Count Antonelli comes back. By then I will be ready with the matter I have in mind. In the month of Hidar, we will send [information] about our camp with our servant, Nigusē Gebre Sillasē. We have sent Count Antonelli as [our] envoy and he will tell you what we have done.

However, in order to convince you about the matter you will be assured when we send our messengers. And the European monarchs will find out the truth about our friendship. We hope that what we desire will benefit the Shewan and Italian people. Please, accept this as a big favour. I hope that what I have in mind will succeed and be of benefit to our children. I pray to God, for the happiness of your people and the benefit of the people of Shewa, to prolong your life.

Written in the town of Ankober, on 24th Senē 1875.

Seal: Minīlik, King of Shewa. The Lion of the tribe of Judah has prevailed.

ASMAI 36/2–16, Amharic original; ASMAI 36/2–12, Italian translation. This document was earlier located in 36/6–56. The messenger here called Nigusē Gebre Sillasē is most probably Gebre Sillasē Nigusē, mentioned in several documents. See *inter alia* doc. 78. Although we are not quite sure what Minīlik has in mind with the word *seferun*, the general content of the letter leads us to believe that he is referring to a boundary agreement. It seems that Minīlik does not want to mention it clearly in his letter.

Document no. 132

Tamrē *Abba* Sebsib to Umberto I, 30 June 18[83]

ይድረስ፡ ከንጉሠ፡ ኡምበርቶ፡ ፩ የኢጣሊያ፡ ንጉሠ፡ የተላከ።
ከቱርክ፡ ባሻ፡ ታምሬ፡ መድኀኔ፡ ዓለም፡ ጤና፡ ይስጥልኝ፡ ብዬ፡ እጅ፡ እነሳለሁ።
ንጉሠ፡ ሆይ።

ለሸዋ፡ ብርሃን፡ ይሁን፡ ብለው፡ ሜሳኪት፡ ኮንት፡ አንቶኔሊ፡ ወዳጅነት፡
የተነሳ፡ የንጉሠም፡ ደግነትና፡ መልካምነት፡ ከብዙ፡ ዜጎችም፡ የኢጣሊያ፡ ሰ
ዎች፡ ከሰሰማሁ፡ ከሁሉ፡ ይልቅ፡ አምነው፡ የሚስኪት፡ ኮንት፡ አንቶኔሊ፡ ንጉሠ
የሸዋን፡ ሰው፡ ብዙ፡ እንደወደዱ፡ ከሰጫ፡ ወትኛ፡ ንጉሠን፡ ቀና፡ ብዬ፡ ማየት፡
የማይገባኝ፡ እሽከርም፡ የልቤ፡ ፍቅር፡ ገፋፋ፡ ሞልቶ፡ ወደ፡ ንጉሠ፡ መላክ
አደረሰኝ። ደብዳቤ፡ ከመላክም፡ የተነሳ። ንጉሠ፡ ይህን፡ እንዩ፡ ያክቡኝ፡ ብ
ዬ፡ ለወደድ፡ ለኮንት፡ አንቶኔሊ፡ ትንሽ፡ እጅ፡ መንሻ፡ እንዲነ፡ ያሉ፡ የተሸ
ሙ፡ ቱርክ፡ ባሾች፡ በጦር፡ ጊዜ፡ የሚይዙት፡ ባንዲራችን፡ የሚገኝ፡ የጦር፡መ
ሳርያ፡ ሰድጄ፡ አለሁ። ይህንም፡ እጅ፡ መንሻዬን፡ እንዲታሳቅ፡ በረከት፡ አደ
ትው፡ ይቀበሉልኝ፡ የሰው፡ ፍቅረና፡ ሙለኝነቱ፡ ነው፡ እንጂ፡ የሚታይ፡ገን
ዘብ፡ ሳገኝ፡ እንደ፡ ሆነ፡ በንጉሠ፡ ፊት፡ ትርፍ፡ ነገር፡ ነው። እኔም፡ እሽከ
ርም፡ በሸዋ፡ ለሚሠራ፡ ጉዳይ፡ ሁሉ፡ እጠብቃለሁ። የኢጣሊያ፡ ጉ
ዳይ፡ በሸዋ፡ የሚሰራ፡ ኮንት፡ አንቶኔሊ፡ ተመልካች፡ አዉርጎ፡ ሰለ
ተወኝ፡ በተቻለኝ፡ ነገር፡ ሁሉ፡ በሸዋ፡ መሬት፡ እረዳለሁ፡ እጠብቃ
ለሁ። የኢጣሊያ፡ ዜጎችም፡ ወደ፡ ሸዋ፡ ለሚመጡት፡ እረዳለሁ።
እንደ ኮንት፡ አንቶኔሊ፡ ያሉ፡ በመልካምነታቸውና፡ በብልህነታቸው፡
የተመሰገኑ። በመልክም፡ ባህርይና፡ በሚያምር፡ ጠባይ፡ የሰውን፡ልቡ
ና፡ የሚሰብሩ፡ የኢጣሊያ፡ ሺ፡ ሰውም፡ ቢመጣ፡ አይከብደኝም፡ በሬሳ
ችንም፡ ቢሆን፡ እንሸከማለን። የንጉሠን፡ የደኅንነት፡ ወሬ፡ [illegible] ዜሁ፡ ቀደ
ም፡ የሰማሁ፡ ጊዜ፡ ብዙ፡ ውን፡ ደስ፡ እንደ፡ ለኝ። አሁንም፡ ኮንት፡ አንቶኔ
ሊ፡ በደኅና፡ ተመልሶ፡ ደኅንነትዎን፡ በደስታ፡ እንዲያሰማኝ። ዕድሜ፡ ዘመንዎ
እግዜር፡ እንዲጠብቅልኝ፡ እለምናለሁ። በሰኔ፡ በ፳፫ በአስርቱ፡ ወ
ሰመንቱ፡ ምዕት። አመት፡ ምሕረት፡ ከምልደት፡ ክርስቶስ፡ መድ
ኀኒ፡ ሰሞ፡ ሰብዓቱ። በደብረ፡ ብርሃን፡ ከተማ፡ ተጻፈ። ፈፈ።

May [this letter] sent by *Turk Basha* Tamrē reach King Umberto I, the King of Italy. Saying "May the Saviour of the World give you health for my sake", I raise my hand.

O King!

Out of the friendship [I have] with Count Antonelli whom you sent to be a light for Shewa, and since I have heard of the kindness and goodness of the king from many of your citizens, the Italian people, and moreover since Count Antonelli, whom you have sent because you have trust in him, has told me that you like the people of Shewa much, the love of my heart overflowed and caused me, your servant who is not worthy of looking at the king straight, to write a letter to the king. And dispatching the letter, I have sent, with my friend Count Antonelli, a small present a weapon of our country and which [persons] like me, appointed *turk basha*, carry in fighting, so that you may remember [me] when looking at it.

Please accept this gift of mine considering it a great present. It is the love and gratefulness of man that is desired; as for money it is of small importance before a king. And I, your servant, shall watch over any matter that is worked in Shewa.

Since Count Antonelli has left me to supervise Italian affairs undertaken in Shewa, I shall assist in everything I can in the land of Shewa. And I shall help Italian citizens who come to Shewa. Even if one thousand Italians, who are noted for their goodness and intelligence, like Count Antonelli, and who break the people's heart by their good nature and desirable conduct, come, they will not be too heavy for us; we can carry [them] even on our heads. As I was very pleased when I heard before now of the news of the well-being of the king, I pray to God that Count Antonelli may come back safely and tell me of your well-being happily and that He may give you a long life.

Written in the town of Debre Birhan, on 24th Senē in the year of grace 18[83] after the birth of our Saviour.

Seal: The seal of *Turk Basha* Tamrē.

ASMAI 36/2–16, Amharic original and Italian translation. Tamrē *Abba* Sebsib was a highly placed and influential official in the court of Minīlik. He was the commander of the regiments armed with rifles for which he was given the title. In addition, he was charged with the tasks of a *dej agafari*, which shows that his riflemen constituted the imperial guard. He carried these responsibilities all through the 1880s with the exception of 1886 when he was temporarily in disgrace and removed from his position, to be reinstated a short while later. He took part in all the important campaigns commanded by Minīlik, including the battle of Adwa. The letter shows, like many others, the friendships that developed between Pietro Antonelli and people at Minīlik's court.

Document no. 133

Alula Ingida Qubī to Augustus Blandy Wylde, [June (?) 1883]

Ras Alula, general of the regular troops, to the Agent of the Government of Massawa.

How are you? I am, thank God, all right. This son of *Ras* Ar'aya, Debbeb, if you do not catch him and send him to me, the country will be plundered by him. I shall not let the caravans come down till he is caught. If the farmer does not plough and the merchant does not buy and sell, then nothing prospers and there is no business. Debbeb killed a priest and he plundered the property of a bishop, henceforth what crime can he commit worse than that? Make him a prisoner and send him to me. You sent me word that you could not find him; he is in Arkīko or Imkullu. Works like these God does not like. Regarding the business of the son of Tesfa Haylu, the chief of the Gonder or Gojjam merchants, he is here, and has about 1,000 loads of ivory, musk and other things. He has arrived and camped here. If I send him at this moment, perhaps he will be plundered. If you want me to send them from Jenda I will protect them from that place to Sehatī, and then send up *Nā'ib* 'Abd al-Raḥīm of Imkullu, to take them down.

Written at 'Addi Teklay.

Sealed *Ras* Alula.

A. B. Wylde, *'83 to '87 in the Soudan*, vol. I, London 1888, pp. 58–59, English translation. Wylde was a British traveller and merchant who had become a friend of *Ras* Alula and a supporter of the Ethiopian cause in the negotiations of 1879–1884 to such an extent that he was reprimanded by the British authorities. See Haggai Erlich, *Ras Alula and the Scramble for Africa*, Lawrenceville 1996, pp. 31–32, 44. For Debbeb Ar'aya and the context of this and the next letter, see Erlich, *Ras Alula*, pp. 39–40.

Document no. 134

Alula Ingida Qubī to Augustus Blandy Wylde, [June (?) 1883]

From *Ras* Alula, to the Agent of the Government of Massawa.

How are you? I am, thank God, all right. The reason why I have not sent you the merchants and the caravans is that the other day I have sent to you a letter [saying] that I would send you the merchants if you catch and send me Debbeb. Now imprison him and send him to me. He is sitting with the family of the *nā'ib* of Arkīko and his children. You yourself also know it.

Written at 'Addi Teklay.

Sealed *Ras* Alula.

Wylde, *'83 to '87 in the Soudan*, vol. I, p. 59, English translation.

Document no. 135

Gobena Daçhī to Umberto I, 3 July 1883

With all respect, how is Your Majesty? I, by the grace of God, am well.

I received the gifts which Your Majesty sent me by the hands of my friend Antonelli, and I offer you my ardent thanksgiving.

Now I ask Your Majesty to accept a lion's hide, a gazelle's hide and a leopard's hide and since the departure of Count Antonelli was unexpected, I am preparing a thoroughbred so that the Italian horses together with those of Shewa would form a single race. I was glad beyond measure to be able to conclude a treaty between my king and Your Majesty and I pray to God that this friendship will be eternal.

Cimbissi, 27th Senē 1875 (Ethiopian calendar) (3 July 1883).

Seal of *Ras* Gobena.

AP.DD, XV, p. 135. Printed Italian translation, probably from a French original, as we know Gobena Daçhī was able to write in French. *Ras* Gobena was an Oromo military commander who had already supported Minīlik from the time of his escape from Tēwodros in 1868. He played a significant role in the integration of Oromo territory into the empire. See also doc. 162.

Document no. 136

Welde Ṣadiq to Umberto I, 10 July 1883

[illegible]

May [the letter] sent by *Azzazh* Welde Ṣadiq reach King Umberto, the King of Italy.

I raise my hands three times saying, "May the Saviour give [you] health on my behalf." I have received with respect and joy the gifts which you have sent me with Count Antonelli and your letter written on 29 Hamlē 1882. May God thank you on my behalf.

It does not seem to me that I did for your citizens who previously came to Shewa any good thing worth so many thanks from a king. Since they carried the little good work to the ears of the king simply because of their great kindness and gratefulness, let God thank them. In the future I shall help and assist in everything I can towards the friendship of the Italian people, the benefit of the people of Shewa and the good of the king.

And I shall work earnestly so that the route to Aseb may be cleared very well. And I hope that you the king, in your omnipotent ability, will help and straighten anything that is useful for your friend, my master. Affection overflowed and has caused me, your servant who should not look you straight in the face, to write a letter.

Now that I have dared to write a letter to a king, I have also sent ivory of an elephant that I myself killed on a hunt and a decoration, known as *addo*, which is given to hunters among the nobility in our country and which was given to me by my master for my ability as a killer. Please, accept my few presents as if they were many gifts. In the future, I shall entreat the Almighty God on my knees that He may increase my age in order that I may please the king in all my capacity, that He may increase the age of the king, and [pray] for the well-being and happiness of your people and that He may protect your government.

Although we knew that Count Antonelli came to us in the heat of the sun and [onset] of thirst, and although we were aware that the work cannot be completed without him, we decided and sent him back so that he might speed up the work which we have proposed. We hope he will come back safely. I pray to God that he may give you a long life for my sake, and a firm government for the benefit of Shewa and Italy.

Written on 4th Hamlē 1875, at Dengīya Mezgīya

Seal of *Azzazh* Welde Ṣadiq.

ASMAI 36/2–16. Italian summary printed in *AP.DD*, XV, pp. 133–134. *Azzazh* Welde Ṣadiq was an important official at Minīlik's court and governor of the district of Ankober. See *EAE* 4, 1106–1107.

Document no. 137

Maḥammad Ḥanfadhē to Pasquale Stanislao Mancini, 30 July 1883

الدعاء الوافر والثناء المتكاثر يهديان جناب عالي الجاه والجناب سلالة الاجلاء الاكابر
الاجل الافخم الاكمل الاشيم محمود السجايا والشيم الصاحب الحليم والدستور المكرم
منستر سلطان تليان حرس الباري من الاكدار ذاته وحما من الاضرار صفاته ولازال
في بارخ المجد والاجلال وشامخ العز والاقبال امين اما بعد فالباعث التحرير ذريعة
الاخلاص هو السوال عن صحة ذاتكم السنية واعتدال اوقاتكم الزكية اللتان هما
الامل من حضرة عالم الازل لازال الجناب في اكمل الخير والسرور ومحبكم العقيقي
من كرم الله تعالى في اتم الخير والسرور يسال عن حال الجناب بالغدوات والبكور
ثم لا يخفى محترم الجناب ولدكم كنت انت نلي وصل عندنا من شوي بالسلامة ومع
الكرامة وقد تسابق منا اليكم الجواب عند وصول كنت انت نلي من عصب لعله وصلكم
والان نحن والسلطان منلك قبلنا الشروط الذي وصل من طرفكم مع كنت انت نلي حتى
تكون المحبة داما واما نحن اكرمنا واويناه وارفعنا بحسله ولدكم كنت انت نلي اكراما
للسلطان تليان على حسب طاقتنا وارسلت لك هديتا منا بيد ولدكم كنت انت نلي نعامتين
تتفضل بالقبول من الخليل حتى القليل جليل ويا محب ارسل لنا من احسانك السابق ولاحق
خاخيل بلدكم مع سرجه هذا عرفناكم ختام والولد كم كنت انت نلي اعطيناله في ارضنا محل
بسكم لاجل ارتباط المحبة وعقد اساس المودة ايضا الان شيخ عبد الرحمن بن شيخ يوسف
الذي وافق بيننا وبينكم تحرسوه من كل عدوه هذا عرفناكم

مستمد الدعاء من عند سلطان محمد بن سلطان حنفري
تاريخ في شهر رمضان خمس وعشرين منه يوم الثلوث سنة ١٣٠٠ من الهجرة

Seal: Muḥammad Ḥanfadhē.

Abundant prayers and generous eulogy presented to His Honour, the high-standing and honoured, offspring of the illustrious and the majestic, the most illustrious and magnificent, the most perfect and most virtuous, the estimable and laudable of nature, the clement friend, the noble representative, the minister of the Italian sultan. May the Creator protect his person from all distress and preserve his felicity from all harm. May he live in glory and fame, and remain in might and prosperity. Amen.

And now, the reason for writing, the affirmation of our loyalty, is the inquiry about your noble health and about the harmony of your pleasant times, which are what we hope for from the Knowledgeable of eternity. May Your Honour remain in complete health and happiness. Thanks to God's kindness, your true beloved is well and pleased and prays for Your Honour's well-being morning and forenoon.

As it cannot be hidden from His Honourable Highness, your son Count Antonelli has reached us from Shewa, in safety and dignity. Before Count Antonelli returned from Aseb, we had already sent you a letter which probably reached you.

And now, we and Sultan Minīlik accepted the terms we received from you with Count Antonelli so that friendship lasts for ever. As for us, we have treated Count Antonelli hospitably, honoured him and privileged him as much as we could for the sake of the Sultan of the Italians. In addition, I have sent you two ostriches as a present with Count Antonelli. Please do accept them since even a humble [gift] from a friend is venerable. O beloved, given your former and further benevolence, send us one of your country's horses along with its saddle.

And this is what we tell you: we have given your son Count Antonelli a place in our land in your name for the sake of love and the foundation of friendship. Finally, since *Shaykh* 'Abd al-Raḥmān bin *Shaykh* Yūsif was the one who coordinated between us, guard him from all his enemies. And this is what we tell you.

The sender of the message is Sultan Maḥammad bin Sultan Ḥanfadhē.

Dated Tuesday, the 25th of Ramaḍān, the year 1300 *Hijra.*

Seal: Muḥammad Ḥanfadhē.

ASMAI 7/1–1, Arabic original, Italian translation.

Document no. 138

Maḥammad Ḥanfadhē to Pasquale Stanislao Mancini, 21 Aug. 1883

الدعا الوافر والثنا المتكاثر يهديان جناب عالي الجاه والجناب سلالة الاجلا الاكابر الاجل
الافخم المفخم الاشيم محمود السجايا والشيم المراد به الصاحب الحليم منستر حرسه الباري من الاكدار
ذاته وحما من الاضرار صفاته ولا زال في باذخ المجد والاجلال وشامخ العز والاقبال امين
اما بعد فالباعث التحرير ذريعة الاخلاص هو السوال عن صحة ذاتكم السنية واعتدال اوقاتكم الزكية اللتان
هما الامل من حضرة عالم الازل لا زال الجناب في اكمل الخير والسرور ومحبكم الحقيقي من كرم الله تعالى
في اتم الخير والسرور ويسال عن حال الجناب بالغدوات والبكور ثم لا يخفى محترم الجناب ان كتابكم
الكريم وصل وبه الانس والسرور حصل وقرانا مبانيه وعرفنا معانيه صدرة الكتاب من محروس
اوسه وكل علم خير وعافيه ولا نسال الا عنكم وان سالتم عنا عن احوال شوى من سلطان
ملك امان وضمان والحقايق تجدون بلسان كنت انتونلي وهو واصل اليكم وذكرت لنا
في كتابك فاعلم ان الطليان ليس لهم مصلحه سوى الصلح والسلم وفتح طريق المتجربين عصب
وشوي والان يا محب ولا يتحرك في قلبك شيا من الاكدار لان هذا الطريق فتحناها لكم
لاجل ارتباط المحبة وعقد اساس المودة وانا متمضن في طريقنا بان لا يقع ضرر التجار الطليان
كما تضمنتم لنا من جهة البحر لا يمسنا احد ضرر لا من جهة المصريين ولا من غيرهم
وارسلت لك هدية منا لاجل ارتباط عقد المحبة وعقد اساس المودة فهو نعامتين
بيد المحب المكرم كنت انتونلي وقد ذكرة لك مع صحبة كنت انتونلي بلسانه ان ترسل لنا خيلا
جيدا طيبا مع سرجه يكن لديك معلوم فتفضل ايضا من احسانك السابق واللاحق بنادقة
طيبات المسمى سنادر وهذا عرفناكم وان بدا لكم حاجة او خدمة فالاشارة بشارة
ايضا يا محب كذلك ارسل لنا من جنابك تابغلة بلدكم طبامع
سرجها لكن عندنا بغله وخيلا موجود الا مرادنا حق بلدكم
يكن لديكم معلوم

من محبك الداعي لكم السلطان
محمد بن السلطان حنفري
ابن السلطان ايدا احسر
تاريخ في شهر شوال يوم الثلوث
سابع عشر خلا منه
من الهجرة
سنة ١٣٠٠

Abundant prayers and generous praise presented to His Honour, the high-standing and prestigious, offspring of the illustrious and eminent, the most majestic and magnificent, the most virtuous, the estimable and laudable of nature, that is the clement friend, the Minister. May the Creator protect his person from all distress and preserve his felicity from all harm. May he live in glory and fame, and remain in might and prosperity. Amen.

And now, the reason for writing, the affirmation of our loyalty, is the inquiry about your noble health and about the harmony of your pleasant times, which are what we hope for from the Knowledgeable of eternity. May Your Honour remain in complete health and happiness. Thanks to God's kindness, your true beloved is well and pleased and prays for your well-being morning and forenoon.

As is not hidden from Your Honourable Highness, your esteemed letter reached us. It brought pleasure and delight. We read its contents and understood its intentions. The letter is dispatched from Awsa, the protected. All information is good and favourable, and we are not concerned about anything except you.

If you ask us about the situation of Shewa, Sultan Minīlik grants it safety and security. The facts you will find through Count Antonelli, who is coming back to you.

You mentioned to us in your letter that the Italians have no interest but conciliation and peace, and the opening of the commercial route between Aseb and Shewa. And now, o beloved, do not let your heart be troubled by any distress because we have opened this route for you for the sake of love and the foundation of friendship. I guarantee that no harm shall befall the Italian traders on our route, just like you guarantee us that no harm shall touch us from the sea, neither from the Egyptians nor from others.

For the sake of love and the foundation of friendship, I sent you a gift from us, which consists of two ostriches, with the honourable beloved Count Antonelli. Conversely, I have told Count Antonelli to ask you to send us a good horse along with its saddle. Let this be known to you. In addition, given your former and further benevolence, please send good rifles, a so-called snider (*sanādīr*). This is what we tell you. If you have any need or [desire] any favour, the request is good news.

And also, o beloved, send us from Your Honour, a good mule from your country with its saddle. Even though we have mules and horses here, we would like to have some from your country. Let this be known to you.

Greetings from your beloved who prays for you, Sultan Maḥammad bin Sultan Ḥanfadhē bin Sultan Īdāḥis.

Dated Tuesday, in the month of Shawwal, after 17 days have elapsed, the year 1300 *Hijra*.

Seal: illegible.

ASMAI 7/1–1, Arabic original. The letter is strangely enough missing in *L'Italia in Africa*.

Document no. 139

Yohannis IV to Umberto I, 1 Oct. 1883

In the name of Our Lord Jesus Christ. Praise be to him.

Letter from the Elect of God Yohannis, King of Zion, King of Kings of Ethiopia. May it reach the honoured and respected Umberto I, King of Italy.

How are you, really? By the mercy of God and the intercession of Our Mother Zion, I am well; may the God of the Saints be glorified and praised for his mercy lasts for ever.

It has come to my knowledge [and] I have understood that you love me and want my friendship. And now may God help us realize our friendship. As for the matter of a gate, the route through Awsa cannot be opened, for we have not yet destroyed the infidels. They have not yet been subdued. Until that [has happened], however, let the merchants, if they are united, come through Arho to my capital, to Tigrē, and trade there. Moreover, I have been surrounded on the outskirts of my kingdom on all sides by the Turks on one hand, and the infidels on the other. And now [needing] firearms with which to weaken my enemies [and] destroy all those who are in the neighbourhood, I want to buy muskets and a small cannon with my money. I would like this to be sent to me. As for the embroidered cloth, however, I am not very much in need of it so it does not matter.

Written in the town of Semera 21st Meskerem in the year of grace 1876.

Seal: King of Kings Yohannis, King of Zion in Ethiopia. The cross has defeated the tribe of Isma'ēl. Yūḥannā, King of Kings of Zion in Abyssinia. The cross has defeated the people of Ismā'īl. 1864.

ASMAI 36/2–13, Amharic original. Blue seal. Arho was a main mining place for salt in the Afar region and the beginning of the trade route to the highlands.

Document no. 140

Burhān Muḥammad to Giovanni Branchi, 9 Oct. 1883

After compliments . . .

I have received your letter through *Shaykh* 'Abd al-Raḥmān bin Yūsif and I am happy at your good intentions towards me. Regarding myself I will always make an effort to serve the royal government and be of use to it day and night, recognizing how much your government has protected me against my enemies. In writing to the government what I wrote to it relating to Markable I had in mind to let it know my position. I do not have a grudge against the government, whether the government makes a case or not of the act of which I have been a victim [and] which forced me to complain. It would never come to my mind to antagonize the government. I abstain from this claim and I expect the compensation or help which the government will accord me.

You can see how much I make an effort for the government's interests. The people of my country are Bedouins who do not know the ways of government, but I instruct them with patience and teach them to recognize the government.

For the moment I have guests from the interior who ask me for money and therefore I ask for 400 thalers. If you will help me by granting me this small sum, I do not think it will do any harm to the government, since I am confident that I will receive more important values from it. I hope that when the government recognizes my good intentions it will recompense me generously.

Seal of Burhān.

ASMAI 1/5–31 Italian translation with the title: "Translation from Arabic of a letter from Burhān, Sultan of Raḥayta to the Commander (Commissario) in Aseb, dated the 7th of Hijra the year 1300 A. H. received 10th of October 1883". The usual greetings have apparently been omitted from the translation. Printed in *L'Italia in Africa*, I.3 no. 305, allegato, p. 30.

According to Giglio, *L'Italia in Africa*, p. xliii, the original Arabic text should also be kept in ASMAI 1/5–31, R. 296, but it can no longer be found.

Document no. 141

Ḥamad La'īta to Giovanni Branchi, 27 Oct. 1883

تاريخ شهر الحجه بعد مامضى منه خمس وعشرين سنه الف وثلاث مائه

١٣

الى الاكرم المكرم المحترم المحب العزيز من حضرة حمد سلطان لعيته الى عند قنصر عسب هداه الله لعيز

اما بعد اعرفك بلغني سلامك والكلام الذي بيني وبينك ماخالفت لاكن ماامكن لي مجيئ الى

طرفكم نحن في ارض باديه وكلام البدوان ماخلا نانسير في محل بعيد والان عرفنا

اخباركم ومرادكم انكم تحبون كل الاصلاح ونحن معرفتنا قليله وكل الاخبار تحصلون

مع عبد الرحمان يوسف هو وكيل من طرفنا اعتمد وا على كلامه بمايتشاور معاكم ونحن

عرفنا انكم ماتحبون الفساد واما الطريف على مافهمنا من عبد الرحمان يوسف نفتح لكم

لا بد خل عليكم الشك من الطريق انتم احرسوا نحنا من البحر ونحن نساعدكم في برنا

الان ابطينا منكم حتى نجمع الكبار وبان حق البدوان والشرط والمكاتبه تكون بيننا

وبينكم عند السلطان منلك تحضر من طرفنا عبد الرحمان يوسف وهو وكيلنا وانتم تعرفوا

من طرفكم الى السلطان منلك والا دولتكم ان نحن ماننكر هكم هذا عرفناكم والسلام

من السلطان حمد

بن السلطان لعيته

Dated in the month of Dhū al-Ḥijja after 25 days had passed, the year 1300.

To the most noble and the most honoured, the beloved and respected, the dear, from His Excellency Ḥamad Sultan La'īta to the consul (*qunṣur*) of Aseb. May God Almighty lead him. Amen.

And now, I inform you that I received your greetings and that I have not breached our agreement. Yet, I could not come and visit you because I am in a desert. The disputes of the Bedouins do not leave us in peace and we are travelling in a distant land. And now, we were informed about your news and desire, and that you would like complete reconciliation. But we know little. You can get all news from 'Abd al-Raḥmān Yūsif, who is our representative. Rely on his words whenever he consults with you. We also heard that you do not like corruption. We understood from 'Abd al-Raḥmān Yūsif that you want us to open up our route for you. Do not have any doubt about it. You guard our coast, and we will help you in our land. And now, we are held back from you until we have gathered the chiefs of the Bedouins.

The negotiations and correspondence between us shall take place at King Minīlik's court where 'Abd al-Raḥmān Yūsif will be our representative while you assign a representative of yours there. We do not hate your government. This is what we tell you. Peace.

From Sultan Ḥamad bin Sultan La'īta.

Seal: Ḥamad La'īta.

ASMAE, AE, 2, Arabic original, ASMAI 7/1–1, Italian translation. According to the translation the letter was received in Aseb on 17 December 1882, in which case the letter must have been written in the month of al-Ḥijja 1299. Apparently either the Arabic or the Italian version has the wrong year. Unfortunately, the contents are of little help in deciding to which year the letter belongs. As the Arabic is the original, we have kept the Arabic date in spite of it being quite possible that the scribe has mistakenly written 1300 for 1299, in which case the letter should be assigned to 7 November 1882. The presence of an Italian translation, but no Arabic original, of a short and as far as content is concerned totally insignificant letter by the same Sultan Ḥamad La'īta to Antonelli, in the same file, ASMAI 7/1–1, does not help. It is also dated in the year 1300, albeit five days earlier, and has an identical note stating that it was received on 17 December 1882.

The letter is addressed to the "Consul of Aseb", which in the Italian is interpreted as being the Commissario Regio, i.e. Giovanni Branchi. For the titles of the Italian representatives in Aseb at the time, see doc. 100.

Document no. 142

Tekle Haymanot to Umberto I, 22 Nov. 1883

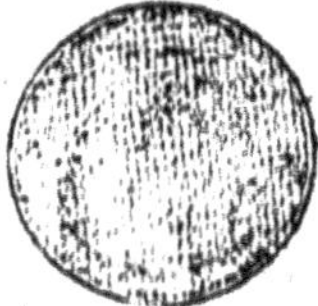

[To] King Umberto I, King of Italy. Sent from King Tekle Haymanot, the Orthodox, son of Mark, the Evangelist, the appointee of Yohannis, King of Kings of Ethiopia.

May the Saviour give you health on my behalf. How are you? I am well, thanks be to God. Your letter reached me. Your decorations and your gifts – all the gifts that you sent me – reached me through the hands of your messenger, Gustavo Bianchi, the leader of the expedition. I was very pleased with your sending of my friend Gustavo Bianchi.

And I discussed everything with him and did everything according to what you wrote to me. Earlier, as a Christian, I did what I could and had Mr. Cecchi released from where he had been imprisoned. And now, since you are a Christian like me, your friendship and love have reached me. As this friendship and love of yours are good things for me, I was very pleased. Mr. Gustavo Bianchi put on my neck a decoration of the Cross of the kingdom of Italy. I have received two guns for hunting elephants [and] your double-barrelled guns, four guns [in all] – and your diamond ring, your binoculars, your red silken umbrella, your revolver which can be fired seven times, your sheath tinged with gold and two crosses with diamonds – one for me and the other for my wife. I have received all these things that you sent to me through the hands of Gustavo Bianchi. May God reward you for all this. Four years have passed since my letter was written. It did not reach you because I did not give it to Mr. Bianchi at that time. But Mr. Bianchi performed everything that I wanted: he brought to me a mason and a stone-cutter. Also, he brought me many materials. Henceforth, we will build a bridge across the Abbay so that it may not be difficult to cross to the Galla [country]. In the Galla country ivory, gold, civet and coffee are found, and for this the bridge will be useful. Also, it will be useful for your intention for trading if Mr. Bianchi with the consent of *Aṣe* Yohannis ever opens the route through Tigrē from Tigrē to Aseb. Mr. Bianchi fulfilled whatever he had promised to me. And now, please send him to me again for my sake, for he is my close friend. Now he will go back quickly, for *Aṣe* Yohannis is waiting for him. I am not able to prepare presents for you because the time is too short for me.

My country is not like your country: nothing can be found quickly. I will have the gifts ready by the time Mr. Bianchi comes back. My gifts are trivial for you, but I am [sending them] for friendship's sake. Since Mr. Bianchi brought me the mason, the hewer and materials, I have promised to give a place near the bridge across the Abbay, a place which is better than Liṭ Marefīya in Shewa. And I have promised that this place, which I shall give to the workers, will be under the command of Mr. Bianchi because I have made him a *dejjazmach*. Also, when I have subdued the Galla, I shall add another place in the Galla country. If you will permit me, I shall call the site of the bridge [and] the bridge Umberto Adal. At the time when I discussed the matter concerning the bridge with Mr. Bianchi, my name was Adal. The land that I will give to them will be on this side, in Gojjam, and I will call it Korēntī Bir.

And I will call the place that I will give them in the Galla country Negri Agul. Mr. Bianchi will leave Mr. Salimbeni, the mason, to have the bridge across the Abbay built in his stead. About this matter I have written to your minister of foreign affairs and the president of the council for foreign countries. I have written to your chief of merchants [that] trading may be conducted from your territory Aseb up to my country. Also, I have written to the head of land revenue named Commander Malvano.

Written in the town of Debre Marqos on Thursday, 13th Hidar, in the year of Yohannis in the year of grace 1876.

Seal (twice): The seal of King Tekle Haymanot, King of Zion.

ASMAI 36/2–20, Amharic original and Italian translation. There are two versions of the Amharic text in the file, one sealed twice, the other only once. With the exception of an occasional letter missing or a misspelling, they agree perfectly. For the release of Cecchi, see docs 15–17. Gustavo Bianchi was an Italian explorer travelling in Ethiopia from 1878–1882 and again from 1883. See *EAE* 1, p. 562–563. He was killed on his way from Meqelē to Aseb in October 1884. For Salimbeni see the following note.

Document no. 143

Tekle Haymanot to Pasquale Stanislao Mancini, 22 Nov. 1883

የተ ላከ፡ከንጉሥ፡ተክለ፡ሃይማኖት፡ርቱዓ፡ሃይማኖት፡ወልዱ፡ለማርቆስ፡ወንጊላዊ
ሥዩመ፡ዮሐንስ፡ንጉሠ፡ነገሥት፡ዘኢትዮጵያ፡ይድረስ፡ለሩቅ፡ሀገር፡ጉዳይ፡ራስ፡ለ
ርእሰ፡መማክርቱ፡በእንግዳ፡ሀገር፡በይጣልያ፡መንግሥት፡እንዲት፡ነዎ፡በዜና፡
እኔ፡እግዚአብሔር፡ይመስገን፡ደኅና፡ነኝ።
የእርስዎን፡ንጉሥ፡ወረቀት፡መለሹን፡ጻፍኩ፡የንጉሥ፡ውምበርቶ፡ወረቀት፡ያመጣ
ልኝ፡አቶ፡ቢያንኬ፡ነው፡ሁሉም፡ደስ፡አለኝ፡የእርስዎ፡ንጉሥ፡ወዳጅነት፡የእርስዎ፡
ወዳጅነት፡የአቶ፡ቢያንኬ፡ወዳጅነት። እርሱ፡ያመጣልኝ፡የስራ፡በጅሮንድ፡አቶ፡ሳ
ልበኒን፡የደንጊያ፡ሰራተኛ፡አቶ፡አንድሬሆኒ፡ደግሞ፡ብዙ፡መሳሪያ፡ዓባይ፡ላይ፡፩
ድልድይ፡ለመስራት፡እኔ፡ዐ ሀገር፡አሰጣለሁ፡የስራ፡በጅሮንዱ፡የሚቀመጥበት፡ከ
ሰራተኞቹ፡ሁሉ፡ጋራ፡ዓባይ፡ከድልድዩ፡አጠገብ፡መንደር፡የምንሰራበት፡ስፍራ፡የ
ድልድዩን፡ደንጊያ፡ለመስራት። በዚያም፡ሀገር፡አቶ፡ቢያንኬ፡ነው፡የሚያዝዝበት፡
ስለ፡ምን፡ደጅ፡አዝማች፡አሰኘችዋለሁና። ያም፡ሀገር፡የሚያገለግል፡ለጅዮግራፊያ፡
ትምህርት፡ነው፡እንደ፡ሸዋ፡ልጥ፡ማረፊያ። ነገር፡ግን፡ከዚያ፡ይህ፡ይበልጣል። ደግ
ሞ፡ለአሳብ፡ንግድ፡የሚጠቅም፡ነው፡አቶ፡ቢያንኬ፡፩ጊዜ፡መንገዱን፡የጀመረ፡እንደ፡
ሆነ፡በትግሬ፡በኩል፡አሳብ፡ድረስ፡በዓፄ፡ዮሐንስ፡ፍቅር። አቶ፡ቢያንኬ፡ከዚህ፡የሚተ
ወው፡አቶ፡ሳልበኒ፡ነው፡እንደ፡ራሱ፡ዓባይ፡ድልድዩን፡የሚሰራ። በአቶ፡ሳልበኒ፡በታ
ች፡የደንጊያውን፡ሰራተኛ፡ይተዋል። እኔ፡ደግሞ፡እሰጣለሁ፡በአቶ፡ሳልበኒ፡በታች፡ከ
አቶ፡ቢያንኬ፡ጋራ፡ተማክረ፡ከለ፡ሰራ፡፩የታመነ፡መልካም፡ወታደር፡ግሪክ፡ነው፡ስ
ሙ፡ጊዮርጊስ፡ይባላል፡ዛሬ፡ግን፡ባሻ፡አምባራስ፡ጊዮርጊስ፡አሰኘሁት፡ስለ፡አገለገለ
ኝ፡እንጨቱም፡ብረቱም፡መልካም፡ይሰራል። ሁሉንም፡ሰራተኞች፡የደንጊያው
ንም፡የእንጨቱንም፡የብረቱንም፡ለአቶ፡ሳልበኒ፡እሰጣለሁ፡ለዓባይ፡ድልድይ፡ስራ፡
ለቤትም፡ለሁሉም። ደግሞ፡ለሰራተኞች፡ሁሉ፡ብዙ፡ድርጎ፡እሰጣለሁ፡ልብስም፡እሰ
ጣለሁ። ይህ፡ሁሉ፡የቀረ፡እንደ፡ሆነ፡ድልድዩም፡አይሰራ፡ይህም፡የኔ፡ቸጋር፡ነው። ዳ
ሩ፡ግን፡የሚጐድል፡ጉዳይ፡የለም። ድልድዩ፡የተሰራ፡ጊዜ፡እንደ፡ወረታው፡እሰጣ
ለሁ፡ለአቶ፡ሳልበኒ፡ለአንድሬዎኒ፡ለአቶ፡ጊዮርጊስ፡ለሁሉ። አሁንም፡አቶ፡ቢያንኬ፡
እንዳለ፡እኔ፡አዝዛለሁ። አቶ፡ሳልበኒ፡ብቻ፡ስራውን፡የሚያሳይ፡ሁሉ፡ከእርሱ፡በታች፡
ነው፡የሚሆኑ። ሀገሩን፡ለመምረጥ፡ለቤት፡መስሪት፡ለዓባይ፡ድልድይም፡ለሰራተኞች፡ለ
ባለ፡ሀገሮች፡ለእንጨት፡ለብረት፡ለደንጊያ፡ስለ፡ስራ፡ደግሞ፡ስለ፡ድርጎ፡ለዚህ፡ሁሉ፡አቶ፡
ሳልበኒ፡ለአቶ፡ጊዮርጊስ፡ይነግራል፡አቶ፡ጊዮርጊስ፡ለኔ፡የነገረኝን፡ሁሉ፡አደርጋለሁ፡ያ
አቶ፡ሳልበኒን፡ፈቃድ፡የኔን፡ትእዛዝ። አቶ፡ቢያንኬ፡በጅሮንድ፡መሳሪያ፡ዕቃ፡ቢጐድል፡እ
መጣለሁ፡አለኝ፡ለዓባይ፡ድልድይ፡መሳሪያ። እርሱም፡በፊት፡ያለኝን፡አደረሰ፡ቃሉን፡አ
ባጐደለም። እኔም፡ያልሁትን፡ሁሉ፡አላጐድልም፡አሰባለሁ። እርሱም፡አቶ፡ቢያንኬ፡ቶ
ሎ፡ይመለስ ል፡ስለምን፡ለይጣልያ፡ንጉሥ፡በረከት፡አሰናዳለሁ፡
ተጽሕፈ፡በደብረ፡ማርቆስ፡ከተማ፡በ፲ወ፰፻፸ወ፮ዓመ
ተ፡ምሕረት፡እህ፡፲ወ፫ለኅዳር፡በዕለተ፡ሐሙስ።

May [the letter] sent by King Tekle Haymanot, the Orthodox, the son of the Evangelist Mark, the appointee (*siyume*) of Yohannis, King of Kings of Ethiopia, reach the chief counsellor for foreign lands of the Italian government.

How are you [although known to me only] by hearsay? I am well, thanks be to God. I wrote a reply to the letter of your king. It was Mr. Bianchi who brought the letter of King Umberto to me. I was satisfied with everything: the friendship of your king, your friendship and the friendship of Mr. Bianchi. He brought to me Mr. Salimbeni, the engineer in charge (*yesera bejirond*), Mr. Andreoni (*Ato Indrēwonē*), the stone hewer (*yedengiya seratenya*), and also many materials [needed] for the construction of a bridge across to Abbay. I will give a place, where the mason and his workers can live, a place where we shall establish a village near the bridge, so that [they] may prepare stones for the bridge. And in that place Mr. Bianchi gives orders for I have made him a *dejjazmach*. And that country will be useful for geographical studies [just] like Liṭ Marefīya in Shewa. However, this is better than that [Liṭ Marefīya]; also it is useful for the trade to Aseb, if Mr. Bianchi with the consent of *Aṣe* Yohannis, at one time, starts [to work on] the route to Aseb through Tigrē. Mr. Bianchi will leave Mr. Salimbeni here to have the bridge across the Abbay built in his stead. He will leave the stone hewer under Mr. Salimbeni. I shall also supply [a man] for the work under Mr. Salimbeni with the consultation of Mr. Bianchi. He is a trustworthy Greek soldier, Gīyorgīs by name; now I have named him *Balambaras* Gīyorgīs because he has served me. He is good at wood and metal work. I will provide all kinds of workers – those in wood, metal and stone – to Mr. Salimbeni for the work on the Abbay bridge, for the house and for everything. Also, I will grant much allowance and clothes to all of the workers. If all these [things] are denied them, let not the bridge be built; that will be my problem. But nothing will be missing. Once the bridge has been built, I will give [rewards], according to their service, to Mr. Salimbeni, Andreoni, *Ato* Gīyorgīs, [and] all others. And now, I have given orders according to what Mr. Bianchi has told [me]. It will be Mr. Salimbeni who will direct the work; all will be under him. Concerning the choice of the place and the building of the house and also concerning all allowances, Mr. Salimbeni will tell *Ato* Gīyorgīs. I will do everything that *Ato* Gīyorgīs tells me, the wishes of Mr. Salimbeni will be my orders. Mr. Bianchi, [who is] in charge of the project (*bejirond meseriya*), told me that he would bring any missing things for the construction of the Abbay bridge. He did what he had said; he did not break his word. As for me, I will not even think of breaking my word. He, Mr. Bianchi, will come back soon, for I am preparing gifts for the king of Italy.

Written in the town of Debre Marqos on Thursday, 13th Hidar in the year of grace 1876.

Seal: The seal of King Tekle Haymanot, King of Gojjam.

ASMAI 36/2–20, Amharic original and Italian translation. There are two versions of the Amharic text, both sealed. Except for the layout they are identical and have the same seal. *Balambaras* Giyorgis (Georgios Fotis) was a Greek traveller who had married in Ethiopia and had joined *Ras* Adal's army in the 1870s. See *EAE* 2, p. 811. Count Augosto Salimbeni was an Italian explorer, engineer and later diplomat engaged in the establishment of Italian trade routes into Ethiopia. He and the Italian mason Giuseppe Andreoni came to Ethiopia in early 1883 and travelled with Bianchi to Gojjam where they were received by Tekle Haymanot on 1 November. Work on the bridge began in December 1884 and was completed on 28 March 1885.

Document no. 144

Tekle Haymanot to Pasquale Stanislao Mancini, 22 Nov. 1883

የተላከ፡ ከንጉሠ፡ተክለ፡ሃይማኖት፡ርቱዕ፡ሃይማኖ
ት፡ወልዱ፡ለማርቆስ፡ወንጌላዊ፡ሠዩመ፡ዮሐንስ፡ንጉሠ፡
ነገሥት፡ዘኢትዮጵያ፡ይድረስ፡ለሩቅ፡ሀገር፡ጉዳይ፡ለርእ
ሰ፡መማክርቱ፡በእንግዳ፡ሀገር፡በይጣልያ፡መንግሥት፡
እንዴት፡ነዎ፡በዜና፡እኔም፡እግዚአብሔር፡ይመስገን፡ደ
ኅና፡ነኝ።
አቶ፡ጉስጣቦ፡ቢያንኪ፡በይጣልያ፡ንጉሠ፡ትእዛዝ፡ወደ
ኔ፡ተልኮ፡መጣ፡ዜናዎን፡ወዳጅነትዎን፡ነገረኝ።
እኔም፡ለአቶ፡ቢያንኪ፡ለወዳጄ፡እንደኔ፡መንግሥት፡ሽለማ
ት፡የቅዱስ፡ማርቆስን፡ታላቅ፡መስቀል፡ስለ፡እርስዎ፡ሰድ
ጄለሁ፡እርሰዎም፡ተቀብለው፡በአንገትዎ፡ያድርጉልኝ፡
ለኔ፡መታሰቢያ፡ስለ፡ፍቅር። እግዚአብሔር፡ይጠብቅዎ፡
አሜን።

ተጽሕፈ፡በደብረ፡ማርቆስ፡ከተማ። በ፲፻ወ፰፻፡
፸ወ፮፡ዓመተ፡ምሕረት፡አመ፡፲ወ፫ለኅዳር፡በዕለተ፡ሐሙስ፡

May [the letter] sent by King Tekle Haymanot, the Orthodox, the son of the Evangelist Mark, the appointee (*siyume*) of Yohannis, King of Kings of Ethiopia, reach the chief counsellor for foreign affairs of the Italian government. How are you, [although known to me only] by hearsay? I am well, thank God.

Mr. Gustavo Bianchi came on a mission to me by the order of the king of Italy. He told me about your reputation and friendliness.

And I on behalf of my government, sent to you a decoration, a big cross of St. Mark, with my friend Mr. Bianchi. Please accept it and tie it around your neck for my remembrance, for the sake of friendship. May God preserve your life. Amen.

Written in the town of Debre Marqos on Thursday, 13th Hidar in the year of grace 1876.

Seal: The seal of King Tekle Haymanot, appointed by King Yohannis of Zion.

ASMAI 36/2–20, Amharic original and Italian translation.

Document no. 145

Minīlik II to Giulio Pestalozza, 3 Dec. 1883

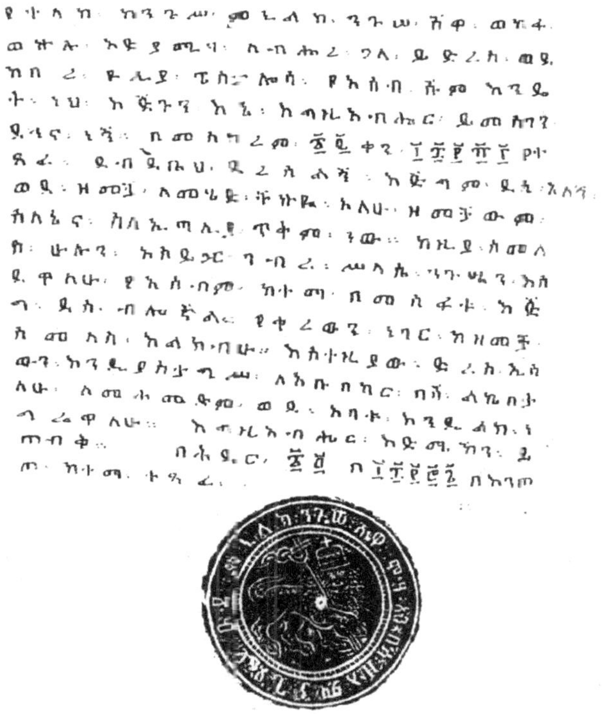

May this letter sent by King Minīlik, King of Shewa and Kefa and all the territories of the land of the Galla, reach the honoured Giulio Pestalozza, the chief of Aseb.

How are you, really? I am well, thank God. Your letter written on the 26nd day of Meskerem 1883 has reached me. I was very happy.

I am in a hurry to proceed on a campaign. The expedition is for my own benefit and for [that of] Italy. When I return, I will send *Azzazh* Gebre Sillasē Nigusē. I am very happy about the founding of the town of Aseb. I will write [about] the remaining matters when I return from the expedition.

Until then I have written to *Pasha* Abū Bakr to pacify the Īsa. I have told Muḥammad to write to his father. May God protect you (lit. your lifetime).

Written on 24th Hidar 1876 at the town of Inṭoṭṭo.

Seal: Minīlik, King of Shewa. The Lion of the tribe of Judah has prevailed.

ASMAE, AE 2, Amharic original and French translation. Muḥammad refers to the son of Abū Bakr who was active escorting European caravans between the coast and Shewa, see docs 17 and 18.

Document no. 146

Maḥammad Ḥanfadhē to Giulio Pestalozza, 16 Dec. 1883

الى حضرة الاكرم المكرم العزيز المحترم جاليوا بستلوسه هداه الله تعالى في كل وقت واوان وان سالتم
عنا وعمن يلوذ بنا فاننا بخير وعافية ولا نسال الا عنكم ونعرفكم وصل الينا الجواب من حكمدار عموم هرر وذكر لنا
في خطه ان لو دخلتم تحت حماية الحكومة المصرية وتظللتم بظلها فيكون لكم شرفا عظيم وتعيشوا مطمئنين فحين
ذلك وجب علينا التحرير الى جهتكم للتعريف وكتاب حكمدار ارسلنا اليكم مع شيخ عبد الرحمن الامام بن شيخ يوسف
ومحمد بن لعينه وتطالعوه ما فيه وتجوبوا الى حكمدار عموم هرر وعرفوه من طرفنا ومن طرفكم انك لا تتعرض
في امور الذي لا تحققت فيه الفساد الذي جرى علينا من طرف خدامهم ابو بكر محافظ زيلع ومنع الطريق وقتل
الاوادم كذلك اكتبوا له وعرفوا له ولتكم منستر الى ارض الولاية واما نحن فلا طمع لي ولا رغبة حمايتهم بل رديت
اب السكيدار عموم هرر بما لم ارغب حماية الحكومة المصرية كما ذكرت لكم في السابق لاننا في حمايتكم من جهة
بحر وحماية من جهة البر الى شوى علينا ونعرفكم من جناب الجوابات الذي وصلت مع شيخ عبد الرحمن الامام
من سابق فهمنا وعلمنا ان كلام الناس يجلب الفساد وفهمنا الامور الذي جرت كلها من عبد الرحمن الامام
نحن لا نقبل لكم بعد هذي كلام المفسدين وانتم كذلك وانما من طرفنا ما يجي احد براني وانتم لا تامنوا
اوادم البراني للحيث ما شفنا الذي يدور واصلاح بيننا وبينكم غير شيخ عبد الرحمن الامام على ما ابتدى يكون
كل الاشغال بيده اما مشايخ البلدان الا داعل عرفنا لكم حتى يساعدوني ويساعدوكم واما الواسطه الذي
بيننا وبينكم شيخ عبد الرحمن الامام المذكور لا غير نعتمد بكلامه وانتم اعتمدوا بالمذكور واما من جناب
الطريق على ما فتحنا لكم ليلا ونهارا مفتوح لكم لكن ومشيت قافلتكم كثر الفساد وصار الضرر كثير وهذي انتم
وشيخ عبد الرحمن المذكور تشاوروا في هذا الامر وبيت شيخ عبد الرحمن الامام إنه يمنع ابو بكر منكم وانتم ما
تقدروا عليه فهذي ما يلزم فيكم قوموا بهذي الدعوى عيب علينا وعيبكم لا تمسكوا كلامنا بالاصول أرضكم
أشغالكم بارضنا ونحن نشتهي لكم الاسم الطيب وهو يفتخر علينا وعلى البدوان ثم عليكم ويسمع إنه ما احد يقدر
علي اذا ما في الدوله الذي تحكم عليه وانتم ما تقدروا عليه عرفونا نحن نخاف من عيب الدوله حتى زيلع ماهي
بعيد علينا وهذا الامر لا يسهل عليكم وكل جميع الاخبار تجدون مع شيخ عبد الرحمن الامام سمعونا دعوة ابو بكر
وطفوا الفتنه الذي قامت لنا ولكم يكون لديكم معلوم ولو تعرفوا الى دولتكم وانا قبلتكم حتى توروا لنا الصدق
فتنة ابو بكر ما تخلص واذا وجدتم له حاكم الذي يرده عرفونا بالجواب حتى نقوم عليه ونرد الفتن
عرفونا سريعا سريعا

من سلطان
محمد بن سلطان
حنفذي

تاريخ في شهر ... يوم الاحد ١٣٠١

To His Excellency, the most noble and honoured, the beloved and respected Giulio Pestalozza. May God Almighty lead him at all times. If you ask about us and those who take refuge with us, we are well and healthy, and we are not concerned about anything except you.

We would like to inform you that we received a letter from the *Ḥikimdār 'Umūm* of Harer in which he wrote to us: "If you enter under the protection of the Egyptian government and remain under its auspices, you shall be given great honour and live in peace." Consequently, we had to write to you informing you of this; we have sent you the letter of the *Ḥikimdār* with *Shaykh* 'Abd al-Raḥmān al-Dhammām bin *Shaykh* Yūsif and Ḥamad bin La'īta. Read it and respond to the *Ḥikimdār 'Umūm* of Harer and inform him on both our behalf and yours, that you will not participate in the oppressive affairs which we have suffered from their servant Abū Bakr, the governor (*muḥāfiẓ*) of Zeyla. He has cut the route and killed good innocent people. Do respond to him like this. Let your government appoint a minister for the land of the province. As for us, we do not crave nor desire their protection. Rather, we reject the letter of the *Ḥikimdār 'Umūm* of Harer in that we do not desire the protection of the Egyptian government, as I told you before, because, we are under your protection from the coast while we protect the land as far as Shewa.

We inform you, in response to the letters which arrived with *Shaykh* 'Abd al-Raḥmān al-Dhammām, and given our previous understanding and knowledge, that people's gossip brings corruption. We also understood from 'Abd al-Raḥmān al-Dhammām all that happened. After this, we will not accept any corruptive talk about you, and neither should you. Do not trust any foreigner, because no foreigner will come from our side since we have not seen anyone who would work for good relations between us except *Shaykh* 'Abd al-Raḥmān al-Dhammām, who therefore holds all affairs in his hands. And now, we inform you that the *shaykhs* of the Adal countries will help him and help you. The above mentioned *Shaykh* 'Abd al-Raḥmān al-Dhammām, and no one else, is the intermediary between you and us. On his words we rely, and so shall you.

As for the route, we opened it for you day and night. But when your caravan travelled, corruption spread, and harm increased. Therefore, you need to discuss this matter with the above-mentioned *Shaykh* 'Abd al-Raḥmān.

The family of *Shaykh* 'Abd al-Raḥmān al-Dhammām prevents Abū Bakr from reaching you. You do not oppose him, which is what you need to do. In fact, you should stand up to this call; it would be a shame for both of us not to keep our promises and not to stick to our original agreement. Actually, your property and your commerce are on our land, and we wish you nothing but a good reputation. Meanwhile, he despises us, the Bedouins and you. He boasts, "No one can oppose me." If there is no one in the country who can govern him, and you do not oppose him, inform us, for we fear a failure on the part of the government. Zeyla is not far from our land. This matter is not convenient for you. You can find all the news with *Shaykh* 'Abd al-Raḥmān al-Dhammām. Let us hear a war cry against Abū Bakr. Put an end to the disturbances which have arisen for us and for you. Let this be known to you, and please do inform your government. I accepted you, thus show us loyalty. Abū Bakr's disturbances do not come to an end. If you cannot find a ruler who can oppose him, inform us by a letter so that we can confront him and put an end to his disturbances. Do inform us as soon as possible.

From Sultan Maḥammad bin Sultan Ḥanfadhē.
Seal: Sultan Muḥammad Ḥanfarī.
Dated in the blessed month of Ṣafar after 15 days had elapsed, Sunday, 1301 *Hijra*.

ASMAE, AE 2, Arabic original. The letter is, strangely enough, missing in *L'Italia in Africa.*

Document no. 147

Welde Ṣadiq to Giulio Pestalozza, 18 Dec. 1883

May this letter sent by *Azzazh* Welde Ṣadiq, reach Mr. Pestalozza, chief (*shum*) of Aseb.

How have you been, really? I am well, thank God.

The letter you sent me reached me on Meskerem 22. I have heard all the matter which is in the letter. I will not cease to correspond with Maḥammad Ḥanfadhē concerning the Awsa route. Since it is to the benefit of both countries, I would rather not be idle [in this matter]. When the king comes back from the campaign, we will send Gebre Sillasē Nigusē and others carrying the bars of salt.

We hope that you will help Count Antonelli so that he carries out all that the king has told him to do.

We will also earnestly request Maḥammad Ḥanfadhē and ʻAbd al-Raḥmān concerning the matter of Aseb. I am very happy to hear from you that ʻAbd al-Raḥmān did his best for the king. As you strive for the benefit of your country, I also strive for the benefit of my country. I will execute all that you want me to carry out; likewise, please do whatever I want you to execute for me. With this our friendship will remain strong for a long time. I beg you to hand over all the letters to Count Antonelli for us.

Written in the town of Ankober on 9th Tahsas 1876.

Seal: *Azzazh* Welde Ṣadiq.

ASMAE, AE 2, Amharic original and an Italian translation which, most unusually, bears a seal.

Document no. 148

Maḥammad Ḥanfadhē to Giulio Pestalozza, 22 Dec. [1883]

To His Honour, the most honoured and venerable, the dear and esteemed Giulio Pestalozza, may he be guided in all ages and seasons and times.

If you ask about us and those who take refuge with us, we are well and healthy, and we are not concerned about anything except you and your well-being which is the ultimate aim and desire of the Lord of the faithful. The letter is sent from Sinkara, the protected; everything is good and favourable.

Now, *Shaykh* ʻAbd al-Raḥmān al-Dhammām bin *Shaykh* Yūsif set out and left for you with the caravan on the fifteenth of Ṣafar the blessed. After this we write this letter to you while he is on the route and send our seal to him so that it catches him on the route. As for the reason why I am sending my seal to you, it is that if it is needed on our side for the issue of Abū Bakr to write on our behalf, you can stamp with our seal [which is] with *Shaykh* ʻAbd al-Raḥmān al-Dhammām, since he is instead of us. His opinion and orders are valid and effective. You should help him. Please write to the minister of your government, and to all districts, officers as well as soldiers.

We also inform Your Honour concerning the controversy of the Adal and the Ankāla. We wrote to them and we informed them that they must be reconciled and leave what was between them as it was before. Now, give the girl to the Ankāla, and the Ankāla will give a deed to the family of Sultan Burhān, and they will be reconciled and they will be to you as they were before. And you, be to them like you were before and honour them, and each tribe will help you on its land. *Shaykh* ʻAbd al-Raḥmān al-Dhammām bin *Shaykh* Yūsif will be [an intermediary] between you and them; he will see who among them is causing disturbances, and will inform us. You on the other hand, inform the above-mentioned *Shaykh* ʻAbd al-Raḥmān al-Dhammām. He holds all affairs and is informed. And this we tell you.

The sender of the message is Sultan Maḥammad bin Ḥanfadhē.

Seal: Sultan Muḥammad Hanferī.

Dated in the month of Ṣafar the blessed, the twenty-first, Saturday.

ASMAE, AE 2, Arabic original. Sultan Burhān died on 22 November 1883 as stated in a letter from the sons to Pestalozza dated 22 Muḥarram (23 November 1883) printed in *L'Italia in Africa*, II, p. 31 (writing October for November).

Document no. 149

Maḥammad Ḥanfadhē to Giovanni Branchi, 24 Dec. 1883

الى حضرة الاكرم المكرم العزيز المحترم قنصر عصب هداه الله تعالى في كل وقت واوان وحين
وان سالتم عنا وعمن يلوذ بنا فاننا بخير وعافيه ولا نسال الا عنكم وقد كنا كتبنا جميع الكتب كوكيلك بستلوسه
مع شيخ عبد الرحمن الدمام بن شيخ يوسف الان نعرف جناب حضرتك بلغنا وصولك من الحبشة الى عصب بخير
وعافية من لسان الواصلين الا وادم الذي وصلوا من طرفكم لا اتانا من جنابكم المكرم لا جواب ولا كتاب لعل
المانع عسى فيه خير والجوابات الذي ارسلنا مع شيخ عبد الرحمن الدمام بن شيخ يوسف وعرفنا مرادنا بالجوابات
للوكيل حقكم بستلوسه والان كتبنا لك انك انت تقوم في اشغالنا مع شيخ عبد الرحمن الدمام المذكور الذي في مرادنا
هو عارف حتى ختمي ارسلنا بيده لاجل الذي ربما يحتاج قولا من طرفي حتى يجوب منا هو بمساعدتكم ونحن
امنين دولتكم الطليانية بصفاء القلب الذي ما فيها خيانة ولا غش اما الفتنة والاذيه حق خدام المصريون
لاجل يخرب الطريق ما وقفوا منا عن الاذية والفتنة هذا كله من سبب ابو بكر باشه وانتم غافلين من هذا
والفرنج الذي يشتهوا الطريق ما شفنا منهم الذي يقوم بهذه الدعوى حتى بيت شيخ عبد الرحمن الدمام الذي
سعى لكم بفتح الطريق منعوا بيته من كنت انت نلي الذي سار في مركب الحرب ولم شفنا منهم اش الذي فعلوله
والان ارض سلطان رحيته الذي هو تحت حماية الطليان نزلوا فيه عساكر الترك وطرحوا فيها بنديري
وهذا من افعال ابو بكر باشه حتى يقاوي علينا البدوان ويفتن البدوان علينا ساعدوا شيخ عبد الرحمن الدمام
ونحن نساعدكم بالمحبة والصداقة وطالع كتبنا الذي كنا ارسلناه جناب بستلوسه قبلك وانت كنت غايب في الحبشة
وريحونا قلبنا من طرفكم ووقفوا منا الفاسد فعليكم بالحكمة والمساعدة للشيخ عبد الرحمن الدمام بن شيخ يوسف
فهو احد من اولادنا ومن عيالنا هو في يدنا وتحت طاعتنا وفي امرنا ورايه نافذ وحكمه نافذ جائز الحيث انه
دمام بيننا وبينكم فاعتمدوا كلامه بجميع الامور كلها واذا دعيتم فادعوه شيخ عبد الرحمن الدمام فهو
دمام بيننا وبين سلطان منلك وجميع الفرنج هذا عرفناكم لا تسمعوا كلام غيره يكن لديكم معلوم
لان شيخ عبد الرحمن الدمام بن شيخ يوسف
رجع الينا من نصف الطريق فلما
وصلنا كتبنا لك هذا الخط وعرفناك
احوالنا ولا تنقطع عنا المكاتبة
مع كل غرض بيد وجنابكم تقضا
بمحروس التحريف

تاريخ في شهر صفر
الخير ثلاث وعشرين
يوم الاثنين
سنة ١٣٠١
من الهجرة

سطره الدعاء
من تنفيذ سلطان
محمد بن سلطان
حنفذي

To His Excellency, the most noble and honourable, the beloved and respected Consul (*qunṣur*) of Aseb. May God Almighty lead him at all times.

If you ask about us and those who take refuge with us, we are well and healthy, and we are not concerned about anything except you. We previously wrote all our letters to Pestalozza as a representative and sent them with *Shaykh* ʻAbd al-Raḥmān al-Dhammām bin *Shaykh* Yūsif. And now, we inform Your Excellency that we have heard from travellers coming from your area that you have come back from Abyssinia (al-Ḥabasha) to Aseb in safety. Yet, no message or letter from Your Venerable Honour has reached us; hopefully whatever prevented it was [something] good. In the letters we sent with *Shaykh* ʻAbd al-Raḥmān al-Dhammām bin *Shaykh* Yūsif, we have clarified our demands and desires to your authorized representative, Pestalozza. Now we wrote to you that you should discuss our matters with the above-mentioned *Shaykh* ʻAbd al-Raḥmān al-Dhammām, who knows our demands and desires. We have even given him my seal in case he needs to certify a declaration on my behalf, and so that he could travel on our behalf with your help.

With a pure heart we trust your Italian government which neither betrays nor deceives, for strife and malevolence are really of the nature of the servants of the Egyptians who have ruined the route and have not stopped causing us harm and strife. This is all because of Abū Bakr *Pasha*, and you are negligent in this. We have not seen any response to this provocation from the *ferenj* who greatly want the route. Even the family of *Shaykh* ʻAbd al-Raḥmān al-Dhammām, who assisted you in opening the route, were prevented from approaching Count Antonelli, who left on the warship. And we have not seen any one of them after what they did to him.

And now they landed Turkish soldiers and raised two flags on Sultan Raḥayta's land, which is under the Italians' protection. These are the actions of Abū Bakr *Pasha* in order to incite and provoke the Bedouins against us. Help *Shaykh* ʻAbd al-Raḥmān al-Dhammām and we will help you in the name of kinship and friendship. Please read the letters that we have previously sent to his Honour Pestalozza while you were away in Abyssinia, and reassure our hearts from your side and arrest the criminal. You must honour and assist *Shaykh* ʻAbd al-Raḥmān al-Dhammām bin *Shaykh* Yūsif; he is one of our sons and a member of our family; he is at our disposal and under our authority and subject to our orders. His opinion and orders are valid and authoritative because he is the intermediary between us and you. Rely on his words in all the matters, and when you call him, address him as *Shaykh* ʻAbd al-Raḥmān al-Dhammām, for he is the intermediary between us, King Minīlik, and all the *ferenj*. This is what we tell you. Do not listen to anybody except him. Let this be known to you.

Shaykh ʻAbd al-Raḥmān al-Dhammām bin *Shaykh* Yūsif returned to us after he had travelled half way. As soon as he reached us, we wrote you this letter informing you of our situation and health. Do not deprive us of letters whenever there is an issue that Your Honour deems could be settled through written communication.

Dated Monday the 23rd of the month of Ṣafar, the blessed, the year 1301 of *Hijra*.

The sender of the message is Sultan Maḥammad bin Sultan Ḥanfadhē.

Seal: Sultan Muḥammad Ḥanfarī.

ASMAE, AE, 2. Arabic original. The letter is, like many letters, addressed to "the consul of Aseb". The title of the Italian representative was, however, *Commissario Regio*. See doc. 100 for the dates of the Italian representatives. This letter demonstrates that the term "consul" (*qunṣur*) was understood somehow differently from how Europeans defined it; a consul was not just a diplomatic representative, but acting in political issues of (land) administration and exerting his own administrative authority over political affairs or even a piece of land in the name of his government.

Document no. 150

Minīlik II to Pietro Antonelli, 24 Dec. 1883

A letter from His Majesty Minīlik II, King of Shewa, Kefa and all parts of Galla to his dear friend Count Antonelli.

How are you? I am well, by the grace of God. I am very satisfied to have received your letter dated 21 September 83 and learn that you have arrived in the colony of Aseb safe and sound and also the caravan conducted by 'Abd al-Raḥmān. I have learned from your letter that the family of Abū Bakr has tried to raise some tribes so that your caravan would be assaulted. Since I know that you never say things that are not correct, I immediately wrote to Abū Bakr to detain the 'Isa Somalis. I thought of doing this to secure the tranquillity of the route.

I am happy to know that you have succeeded in our affairs which were decided upon. I thank you for your efforts. As we have agreed I will send Gebre Sillasē Nigusē after my expedition among the Arsi Galla. If I have not sent the caravan more quickly, it is because the rainy season has been very heavy and has prevented the arrival of tributes from the Galla areas. Now, however, I act so that this delay will not repeat itself another time: I will return immediately from the expedition and send you the caravan at once. I am satisfied to hear that the colony of Aseb is definitely established to be a place for commerce between Italy and Shewa and a centre for the two countries which will never cease being friends. Gebre Sillasē will come to Aseb and when you depart to Shewa, I will write to Maḥammad Ḥanfadhē to help and escort you.

I have given orders to *Azzazh* Welde Ṣadiq to keep everything in order for the departure of the caravan as soon as I am back. Regarding Liṭ Marefīya you need not be anxious because I am the one who guards this station. I would be very content if an instructed doctor came with you to stay in Liṭ Marefīya.

Send me sounding clocks and solid chronometers as well as large quantities of medicine.

Royal Seal.
Inṭoṭṭo 24th December 1883.

ASMAI 1/5–41, Amharic original that has been lost or misplaced and could not be found. Printed Italian text in *L'Italia in Africa*, I.3 no. 312, allegato A, p. 36.

Document no. 151

Maḥammad Ḥanfadhē to Giovanni Branchi, 30 Dec. 1883

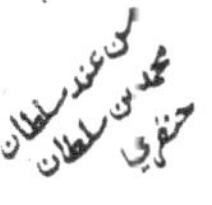

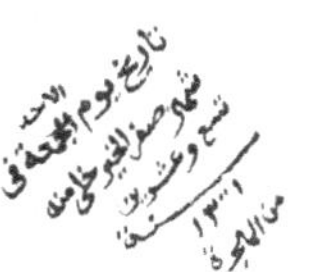

To His Excellency, the most noble and honourable, the beloved and respected Consul of Aseb. May God Almighty lead him at all times.

If you ask about us and those who take refuge with us, we are well and healthy, and we are not concerned about anything except you. These words are dispatched from Awsa, the protected; all information is good. You will find out the facts orally, sufficiently and conclusively, through the people coming from our land. I would like to inform you, o beloved, that some of the Arabs of the tribes of Modayto (Mūdīta) came to me complaining about you saying:

"The Consul of Aseb came back from Abyssinia (al-Ḥabasha) in safety and dignity, and God did not change any of his condition. However, when he came back from Kasa *Abba* Bizbiz, he started tearing down the mountains and digging for wells everywhere." And now, o beloved, you should not violate others' rights. You should remain in your land abstaining from causing any harm to the caravans of the Danākil tribes on their dominions

Now, remain in the piece of land you bought from the Ankāla tribes, and you know the boundaries of what you bought just as well as the tribes of Ankāla know what they sold you, the length and the width. You should not violate people's rights. Violating people's rights is a great offence and misdeed you have no excuse for. Beware of people's rights, o beloved. Since Sultan Minīlik did not ask anything else from me but to open the route for you, we accepted his request and agreed to open the route for him from Aseb to Shewa. The intermediary between us and all others is *Shaykh* 'Abd al-Raḥmān al-Dhammām bin *Shaykh* Yūsif. Before this, *Shaykh* 'Abd al-Raḥmān al-Dhammām bin *Shaykh* Yūsif worked with us and with Count Antonelli [for the route] to Shewa and with Sultan Minīlik for the route from Aseb to Shewa. This is what we tell you.

From Sultan Maḥammad bin Sultan Ḥanfadhē.

Dated Sunday in the month of Ṣafar the blessed after 29 days had elapsed, the year 1301 of Hijra.

ASMAE, AE, 2. Arabic original.

Document no. 152

Maḥammad Ḥanfadhē to Giovanni Branchi, 28 Jan. 1884

الى حضرة الاكرم المكرم العزيز المحترم قنصر عصب هداه الله تعالى امين

ان سالتم عنا وعمن يلوذ بنا فاننا بخير وعافيه ولا نسال الا عنكم وعن احوالكم التى هي غايت القصد
والمراد من رب العباد صدرة الاحرف من محروس سنكوه وكل علم خير وعافية فما صدرة الورقة لاجل اعلام
الحال وتعرفونا بما انتم فيه من الاحوال وبما وصلكم منا الجواب وصل الينا جوابكم الكريم وفهمنا وقرأنا مبانيه
وعرفنا معانيه فحمدت الله تعالى على صحة عافيتكم وبلغنا انك وصلت من الحبشة من عند سلطان كاسا ابا بين
سلامة والكرامة ولم غير الله عليك حال من الاحوال آنست بسلامتك من الغربة وادامك الله بالسرور
ايضا يا محب لان قبايل الدناكل الذي حواليكم يبكون عليكم فلا تبكوهم واحسنوا لهم بالاحسان منكم للحيث
انهم راع المواشي في اراضيهم فلا تتعدوا في حق الدناكل وارضكم يكفيكم وارض حقكم الذي اشتريتموه مع
معلوما طولا وعرضا من حكومة إلى بوية وان واما من جناب بيننا وبين قبايل عيسى مانرغب منكم
المعاونة منه نحن نكفيه بجيشنا وحال التاريخ جيشنا بغزوة عيسى وغزاقبل وصول خطكم الينا فالله
ينصره نصرا عزيزا وان بدالكم حاجة اوخدمة نقضا بحر التعريف
ومما اعرفك يا محب من جناب شيخ عبد الرحمن الدمام بن شيخ يوسف فهو دمام الكل فعلم بيننا وبينكم وكذلك من جناب سلطان
منلك دمام وواسط لجميعنا فلا تقبلوا كلام الخارجين من أهل عصب ومن أهل مركبلا الا كلام عبد الرحمن الدمام بن شيخ بن يوسف
وكلنا معتمدين بقول شيخ عبد الرحمن الدمام ايضا كيف سكتم عن بيت شيخ عبد الرحمن الدمام الذي في ربلع بلا اختياره
عند ابو بكر باشه عليكم باخراج بيته عن يد الظالم القاهر والسكوت فيكم من بيت عبد الرحمن الدمام عار عار ثم عار عليكم
الله الله باخراج البيت من ربلع فهو خادمكم وخادمنا والساعي من عصب الى شوى لحاجتكم فكيف يهدم بيته وانتم في الحيات
ايضا قبل ان تصل عصب من الحبشة توفا سلطان برهان في رحيته كما سمعت وخلف سلطان برهان عيال كما تعلم أنت
والوزير حمد بن محمد سلطان دبني والوزير وابن سلطان برهان ابو بكر كبيرهم وانت قم بينهم بالصلح وانا ارسلت مع شيخ عبد الرحمن
اصلحوا بينهم وحمد بن لعيته كذلك لعله واصل اليكم وانت انظرهم بعين واحد ولا تميل على احد وكذلك فى ارض سلا
لاما بين رحيته نزل فيه ابو بكر باشه عساكر الترك فى الآن عيلا وأنت عاونهم بما امكنك هذا عرفناك

To His Excellency, the most noble and most honoured, the beloved and respected Consul of Aseb. May God Almighty lead him. Amen.

If you ask about us and those who take refuge with us, we are well and healthy, and we are not concerned about anything except you and your well-being which is the ultimate aim and desire of the Lord of the faithful. These lines are dispatched from Sinkara, the protected; all the information we have is good and favourable. Not even a piece of paper appeared to tell us about your well-being, to inform us about your situation or to notify us that our letter reached you. [But now] Your esteemed letter has reached us. We read its contents and understood its intentions. So we praised the Lord for your health and well-being. We heard that you came back from Abyssinia (al-Ḥabasha) from Sultan Kasa *Abba* Bizbiz in safety and dignity, and God did not change any of your conditions. I was delighted that your journey was safe. May God perpetuate your happiness.

But in addition, o beloved, since the Danākil tribes who are your neighbours lament because of you, do not upset them. Treat them favourably since they are pasturing cattle on their own lands. So, do not invade the land of Danākil. Your land is sufficient for you. Your rightful land which you bought has well-known extension and boundaries from Kalūma to Būya. As for the [conflict between the] 'Isa tribes and ourselves, we do not need your assistance because our army is sufficient [to protect us]. Recently our army attacked the 'Isa tribes. It attacked before your letter reached us. May God favour our army with a mighty victory. Finally, if you need any favour or service, it shall be fulfilled as soon as you write to us.

And now we inform you, o beloved, that *Shaykh* 'Abd al-Raḥmān al-Dhammām bin *Shaykh* Yūsif is our representative as well as King Minīlik's representative. In fact, he is the representative and mediator of us all. Therefore, do not take into account whatever the people coming from Aseb or from Markable say. Only accept the word of *Shaykh* 'Abd al-Raḥmān al-Dhammām bin *Shaykh* Yūsif. We all stick to the statements of *Shaykh* 'Abd al-Raḥmān al-Dhammām. But why did you accept that the people of *Shaykh* 'Abd al-Raḥmān al-Dhammām were held back in Zeyla under the rule of Abū Bakr *Pasha* without his consent? You must get his people out of the hands of this unjust tyrant. Shame, shame and shame on you for your silence about the family of 'Abd al-Raḥmān al-Dhammām. In the name of God, get that family out of Zeyla. He is your and our servant. He is the bearer of your demands from Aseb to Shewa. Then how do you allow that his people suffer while you are still alive?

Furthermore, before you came back to Aseb from Abyssinia, Sultan Burhān passed away in Raḥayta as you have already heard. As you know the family of Sultan Burhān will succeed him. As for the *wazīr*, Ḥamad bin Muḥammad Sultan Dīnī, do reconcile the wazīr and the sons of Sultan Burhān, Abū Bakr being the oldest, with one another. I sent [a message] with Shaykh 'Abd al-Raḥmān: "Reconcile them as well as Ḥamad bin La'īta!". He has probably reached you. You should treat them equally without favouring any of them. Furthermore, in the land of the sultans of Raḥayta, Abū Bakr *Pasha* has landed the soldiers of the Turks in Allat 'Ayla. Help them as much as you can. This is what we tell you.

The sender of the message is Sultan Maḥammad bin Sultan Ḥanfadhē.

Dated Monday, the 29th of Rabī' al-Awwal 1301 *Hijra*.

ASMAE, AE, 2. Arabic original. Sultan Kasa *Abba* Bizbiz refers to Emperor Yohannis IV whose name before coronation was Kasa Mirçha, and who was nicknamed Bizbiz after his horse.

Document no. 153

Maḥammad Ḥanfadhē to Giovanni Branchi, 5 Feb. 1884

Abundant prayers and generous eulogy presented to His Honour, the high-standing and honoured, offspring of the illustrious and the majestic, the most illustrious, the most perfect and most virtuous, the clement friend, the consul of Aseb. May the Creator protect his person from all distress and preserve his felicity from all harm.

The reason for writing, the affirmation of our loyalty, is the inquiry about your noble health and about the harmony of your pleasant times, which are what we hope for from the Knowledgeable of eternity. May Your Honour remain in complete health and happiness. Thanks to God's kindness, your true beloved prays for Your Honour's well-being morning and forenoon. As is not hidden from Your Honourable Highness, our army has just come back from the war with the 'Isa tribes. God has favoured it with a glorious victory. It killed almost 100 men and looted and collected from the cattle, cows and camels. The looting cannot be assessed in numbers. From our army five soldiers died.

Do not deprive us of letters from Your Honour about your favourable conditions and your pleasant news, whenever there is an issue that Your Honour deems important. We also inform you, o beloved, concerning the Danākil (*Dankāra*) handed over to you by 'Abd Allāh bin Shaḥīm, he received them from Wāka bin Aḥmad. This is what we tell you.

The sender of the message is Sultan Maḥammad bin Sultan Ḥanfadhē, the deceased.

Dated in the month of Rabī' al-Thānī, Tuesday the 7th, the year 1301 *Hijra*.

ASMAE, AE, 2. Arabic original.

Document no. 154

Maḥammad Ḥanfadhē to Giovanni Branchi [March 1884]

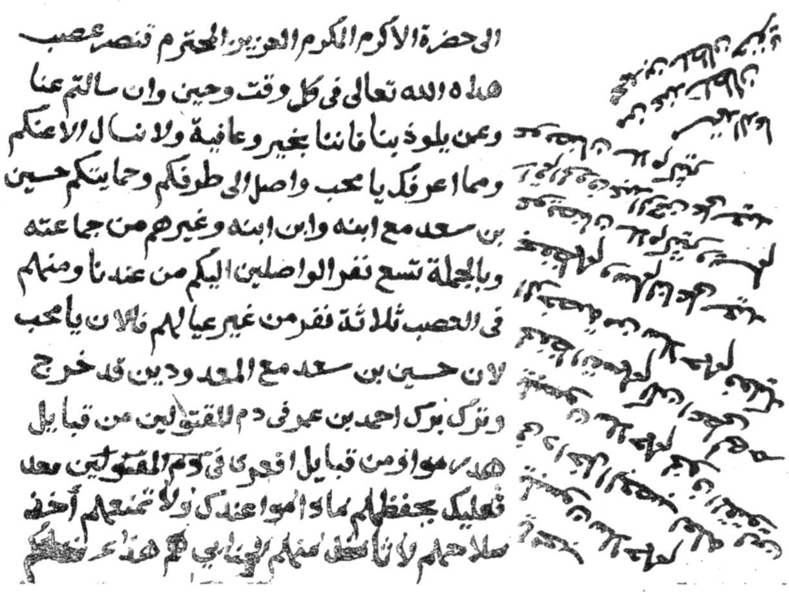

الى حضرة الاكرم المكرم العزيز المحترم قنصل عصب
هداه الله تعالى فى كل وقت وحين وان سالتم عنا
ومن يلوذ بنا فاننا بخير وعافية ولا نسال الا عنكم
ومما اعرفك يا محب واصل الى طرفكم وحمايتكم حسين
بن سعد مع ابنه وابن ابنه وغيرهم من جماعته
وبالجملة تسع نفر الواصلين اليكم من عندنا ومنهم
فى العصب ثلاثة نفر من غير عيالهم فالان يا محب
لان حسين بن سعد مع المعدودين قد خرج
وترك بورك احمد بن عمر فى دم المقتولين من قبايل
هدرموا ومن قبايل افقرى فى دم المقتولين معه
فعليك بحفظهم ما داموا عندك ولا تمنعهم اخذ
سلاحهم ولا تاخذ منهم [illegible] هذا علمكم

To His Excellency, the most noble and most honoured, the beloved and respected the Consul of Aseb. May God Almighty lead him at all times.

If you ask about us and those who take refuge with us, we are well and healthy, and we are not concerned about anything except you. And what we tell you, o beloved, [is that] Ḥusayn bin Sa'īd along with his son and his grandson will come to you and under your protection accompanied by some of his people. In total, nine of our people will reach you among whom three individuals are going to Aseb without their families. And now, o beloved, since Ḥusayn bin Sa'īd, along with the above-mentioned, has left, and left behind the corpse of Aḥmad bin 'Umar in the blood of the murdered of the tribe of Hadermū and of the tribe of Aqarā, you are to protect them as long as they stay on your land and do not forbid them to carry their weapons, and do not make them pay the blood price. This is what we tell you. O beloved, they need to keep their weapons in Aseb since they fear on account of those killed and need to protect themselves. But grant them the authorization to carry the weapons. You are to guard them. Send our regards, our best regards, to Sa'īd 'Awīḍān 'Abd al-Raḥmān, the letter's writer also sends his best regards to Sa'īd 'Awīḍān.

The sender of the message is Sultan Maḥammad bin Sultan Ḥanfadhē.

ASMAE, AE 2. Arabic original not sealed.

Document no. 155

Yohannis IV to Muḥammad Tawfīq, 14 March 1884

رسالة المويد من الله يحنا ملك صهيون ملك ملوك الحبشة

تصل الي المحب العزيز المحترم المكرم الزايد الود الثابت بالحب الصافي الضمير المجرب عند الكبير والصغير المرتفع
العز والشان بحل الممالك مع زود العز والتوقير محبنا زايد الكرم الخديوي الاجل توفيق باشا والي الديار
المصريه ادامه الله بالعز والطمانينه والرفاهيه امين
بعد السلام علي عزة مودتكم مع التوقير لاخلاص محبتكم فاذا تسالتم عنا فلله الحمد الروف متواترة علينا اولا با
وله من انعامه الغامرة فالان ايها الحبيب نعلم صدق محبتكم انه سابق تاريخه في حين الآبا الاساقفه
والمطران قد كنا ارسلنا محبين المرسلين من طرفنا مالا وجيزا لنشتري بعض الاسلحه من البنادق ولم تحضر
لنا الي الان ولما ان استخبرنا من اباتنا ارض المرسل من طرفنا سابقا فقال انه قد صار شري مطلوبكم وهو
في محروسة مصر وابونا البطريرك يعلم بذلك فالان قد حررنا جوابا لابونا البطريرك ابا كيرلس ليعلم شرفكم
بذلك ليكون تسلم الجبخانه بالارادة بارسال المطلوب والان نرجوا صدق صفو ضمير الكبير وودكم العظيم
ان يكون تسلم الجبخانه السنيه بارسال ذلك الينا ولا نريد امانتكم وفيه بعد ذلك [illegible] بديهم ما
يلزم لحب الحاصل ويتم لنا و كلم كل امل لتخطيطها م الله بغاية التساهل في ٦ [illegible] ١٨٧٦
كتب يوم الخميس [illegible]

Seal: King of Kings Yohannis of Ethiopia; Yūḥannā, King of Kings of Abyssinia.

A letter from the Elect of God, Yohannis, King of Zion, King of Kings of Abyssinia.

May it reach the dear and beloved, the respected and honoured, the excessively amicable and steadfast in pure love, the mind admired by the elderly and the youngsters, the high-ranking and influential across all kingdoms through growing might and veneration, our beloved, the overly generous, the Khedive, the most illustrious, Tawfīq *Pasha*, the ruler of the Egyptian territories. May God keep him in might, serenity and luxury. Amen.

After greetings to Your Esteemed Loving-kindness with full respect to your loyal devotion, if you inquire about us, to God a thousand ceaseless thanks for what he has bestowed upon us of his eminent favours.

And now, o beloved, we inform your honest Loving-kindness that long ago, in the time of the fathers, the bishops and the metropolitan, we sent with the envoys on our behalf a modest sum of money to buy some rifles as weapons, and they have not arrived until now. And when we inquired from *Abba* Gebre Igzī', previously sent on our behalf, he replied "The purchase of what you desired was made, and it is in Egypt, the protected, and our Father the Patriarch knows about it." And now, we wrote a letter to our Father the Patriarch *Anbā* Kīrillus to inform Your Honour to be kind and willingly send us what was requested. And now, we ask from the honesty of your pure generous mind and from your unlimited friendship to have the rigorous resolve to send us this. And we do not request anything else from Your Trustworthiness.

May God sustain the complete friendship between us. May He fulfil all your and our hopes to enjoy the grace of God [at] the highest level.

Written on Thursday 6th Baramhāt 1876.

ENA, Soudan 5/3/3b, Arabic original. The content is the same as in the letter in Amharic dated three days later (doc. 156), but the rhetoric is much more elaborate and partly almost incomprehensible. The translation of the last sentence is rather tentative. The envoy, *Abba* Gebre Igzī', is the author of letters 26 and 82.

Document no. 156

Yohannis IV to Muḥammad Tawfīq, 17 March 1884

Seal: King of Kings Yohannis of Ethiopia; Yūḥannā, King of Kings of Abyssinia.

May the letter from the Elect of God Yohannis, King of Zion, King of Kings of Ethiopia, reach the honoured and respected, intelligent and learned Khedive Tawfīq *Pasha* of the land of Egypt.

How are you since I wrote you last? By the grace of God and the intercession of our Mother Zion, praised and honoured be the Lord of the saints, I, together with my army, am well, since His forgiveness is everlasting.

When my men came to bring bishops, there was money left behind to buy firearms. They say that the rifles were bought and stored and would come to me with your permission. I have written a letter to our father, *Līqe Pappas Abba* Kīrillus stating that I now need your permission so that my property be sent to me.

The Arabic and Gi'iz words are the same.

Written in the town of Ḥashēngē, 9th Meggabīt in the year of grace 1876.

ENA, Soudan, 5/3/3a, Gi'iz/Amharic original. As indicated by the reference at the end of the letter, an Arabic version of it must have accompanied the original.

Document no. 157

Convention between Ḥamad La'īta and Italy, 17 March 1884

Convention between the government of H. M. the King of Italy and Ḥamad bin La'īta, Sultan of Gobad, of Aseb and of the land of the Adoimarà.

Article 1. The peace and friendship will be constant and perpetual between the Italian authority of Aseb and Sultan Ḥamad La'īta and between their dependents.

Article 2. Each of the two parties will nominate a representative to handle their affairs.

Article 3. Sultan Ḥamad La'īta guarantees the Italian government and H. M. Minīlik safety on the route between Aseb, Gobad and the realm of Shewa for all Italian caravans from or to the sea.

Article 4. Sultan Ḥamad La'īta in mutual agreement with the other chiefs declares all Italian caravans coming from or going to Aseb exempt from fees and taxes.

Article 5. All religions will be respected.

Article 6. The subjects of H. M. the King of Italy will travel freely all over the land subordinate to Sultan Ḥamad La'īta, and the latter's dependents will always be assisted by the Italian consular authorities.

Article 7. H. M. the King of Italy's warships will by sea watch over the security of the Danākil littoral.

Article 8. This convention will be subject to the approval of H. M. the King of Shewa and ratified in Shewa by the representative of H. M. the King of Italy's government.

Article 9. Three copies of this convention will be made, in the Italian, Arabic and Amharic languages, the respective translations being in perfect accord with one another.

Made at Aseb 17th March 1884.

Seal of Sultan Ḥamad La'īta.
Seal of the royal commissary at Aseb.
G. Branchi

ASMAI 7/1–1, Italian text with the Arabic seal of Ḥamad La'īta. Printed text *Trattati*, p. 66 and *L'Italia in Africa*, I.3 no. 317, allegato, pp. 42–43. The version printed in *Trattati*, I, 20 omits "of Aseb" in the title of Ḥamad La'īta. Although it is stated that an Arabic and even an Amharic (!) copy of the convention were to be made, no evidence has been found for any of these, and probably they were never made. A much more detailed treaty for which we have the Arabic text was concluded in November 1884. See doc. 194.

Document no. 158

Maḥammad Ḥanfadhē to Giovanni Branchi, 12 April 1884

الى حضرة الاكرم المكرم العزيز المحترم المحب صاحبنا المعروف بر صاحب
جوفي برنكي هداه الله تعالى في كل وقت وان سألتم عنا وعمن يلوذ
بنا فانا بخير وعافيه ولا نسال الا عنكم صدرت الاحرف من محروس
سنجره وكل خير وعافيه وصل الينا جوابكم الكريم وقرانا مبانيه
وعرفنا معانيه على صحة عافيتكم فحمدنا الله تعالى فيه وذكرتم لنا
بوصوله عندكم في عصب المحب المعروف صاحبنا الكونت انتونلي
من بلدكم الولاية وانكم انستم وتعظمتم بالفرح والسرور والكتا
ب الذي ارسلتم للملك منلك وصل الينا ليلة السبت مع خادمنا
في شهر جماد الاول خلا منه سبعة عشر وارسلنا كتاب منلك الى شوى حالا
يكن عندكم معلوم وخطكم الثاني وصل لنا في غرة شهر جماد الاول
فقرانا مبانيه وعرفنا معانيه وقبضنا ما ارسلت لنا
الهدية من يد خادمنا ميرم محمد نيشان وحرز فيه
فصوص سيلان فقبلنا منه يكن لديكم معلوم وذ
بان حمد بن لعيته وصل عندكم وتواجهتم فعليكم بالمشاورة
لاصلاح الارض وذكرت لنا كذلك سافر شيخ عبد الله

To His Excellency, the most noble and most honoured, the beloved and respected, the dear, our well-known friend, *Bir ṣāḥib* Giovanni Branchi. May God Almighty lead him at all times.

If you ask about us and those who take refuge with us, we are well and healthy, and we are not concerned about anything except you. The words are dispatched from Sinkara, the protected. All the information is good and favourable. Your esteemed letter has reached us; we read its contents and understood its information about your good health, and we praised God Almighty for that. You also informed us that our dear well-known friend Count Antonelli has arrived to you in Aseb coming from your sovereign state (*baladikum al-wilāya*) and that Your Highness was exalted with joy and happiness. In addition, the letter you sent to King Minīlik has reached us on Saturday evening with our servant after 17 days had elapsed of the month of Jumād al-Awwal. We sent the letter to Minīlik on to Shewa immediately. Let this be known to you. Your second letter reached us on the first day of the month of Jumād al-Awwal. We read its contents and understood its intentions. We received the gift you sent us through the hand of our servant Mīram Muḥammad, a medal and an amulet with Ceylon stones. We accepted them from him. Let this be known to you. [You also mentioned] that Ḥamad bin La'īta has reached you, and you met him in person. You have to discuss and agree in order to restore the land. You mentioned as well that Shaykh 'Abd travelled. . . .

(one line missing).

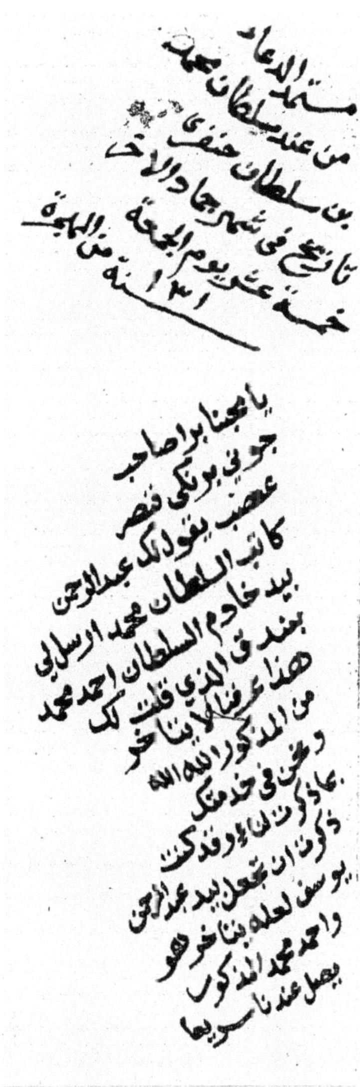

من عند سلطان محمد
بن سلطان حنفذ
تاريخ في شهر جماد الآخر
خمسة عشر يوم الجمعة من الهجرة
١٣٠١

يا محبنا بر صاحب
جوفني برنكي قنصل
عصب يقول لك عبد الرحمن
كاتب السلطان محمد ارسل لي
بيد خادم السلطان احمد محمد
بندق الذي قلت لك
هذا عرفنا لا يتأخر
من المذكور والله
ونحن في خدمتك
ما ذكرت لك وقد كنت
ذكرت ان تجعل بيد عبد الرحمن
يوسف لعله يتأخر هو
واحمد محمد المذكور
يصل عندنا سريعا

O beloved, you have to struggle with Ḥamad bin La'īta [in order to] restore the land. Likewise, the ruler of Zeyla; you have to depose him . . . the land will be ours and yours. On the other hand, we struggle . . . the 'Isa. And if it is God's will, we will know your advice through . . . when we meet him in person. This is what we tell you.

Furthermore, 'Abd al-Raḥmān bin *Shaykh* Muḥammad Turāb, Sultan Maḥammad Ḥanfadhē's secretary, asks "How are you? And how is your family and your brothers (?) from the youngest to the oldest? If it is God's will we hope you are all well and healthy (?). Our desire, given your former and further benevolence, is that you send me one rifle of 'Abū Tīz'. . . . We would have put the seal of our Sultan Maḥammad and the seal. . . ., but it is with you. God willing, we are at your service. Should you send it, please do so with *Shaykh* 'Abd al-Raḥmān al-Dhammām bin *Shaykh* Yūsif and with our beloved Count Antonelli at your discretion. This is what we tell you."

O beloved, *Bir ṣāḥib* Giovanni Branchi, Consul of Aseb, 'Abd al-Raḥmān, Sultan Maḥammad's secretary, tells you: "Send me the rifle I have told you about with Aḥmad Muḥammad, the Sultan's servant, for we were informed that this one shall not arrive later than the above mentioned. And we swear to God that we are at your service for what you have demanded. I had asked you to send it with 'Abd al-Raḥmān Yūsif, but he might be late whereas the above-mentioned Aḥmad Muḥammad will reach us soon."

The sender of the message is Sultan Maḥammad bin Sultan Ḥanfadhē.

Dated in the month of Jumād al-Ākhir, the 15th, Friday, the year 1301 *Hijra*.

ASMAE, AE 2. Arabic original. A part of the text is not clear since the edge of the paper has been cut. Thus, our translation is in some parts tentative.

Document no. 159

Minīlik II to Pietro Antonelli, 8 May 1884

352

De la part du Roi Menilek II, Roi du Choa, de Kaffa et de tous ses alentours, y compris les pays Gallas, parvienne à Monsieur le Comte Antonelli. —

Comment vous portez-vous? Moi, grâce à Dieu, je me trouve en état de bonne santé, ainsi que toute mon armée.

Après avoir reçu votre lettre, j'ai fait une expédition jusque chez les Arousies, et j'en suis revenu sain et sauf.

Il ne faut pas vous attrister en disant que je ne me suis pas pressé jusqu'ici, car il m'a été impossible. Voilà maintenant que je vous envoie Gabra-Sellassieh Negoussieh avec la caravane destinée pour vous, j'ai écrit en outre au Sultan Mohamed Hanfalieh pour qu'il fasse recevoir ladite caravane, écrivez lui vous aussi de votre côté.

Je vous écrirai, pour le reste, quand Gabra-Sellassieh viendra, faites de la sorte seulement, Monsieur le Comte, que vous puissiez venir vite. —

J'enverrai le prix entier des fusils avec la seconde caravane, je ferai de manière de pouvoir contenter et vous et le Gouvernement Italien. Ça me fait plaisir de savoir que l'affaire du traité que vous aviez emporté avec vous cette fois-ci, soit terminée, c'est pourquoi je me presse d'en connaître le mot final.

Je vais envoyer, quand Gabra-Sellassieh viendra, des cadeaux à Sa Majesté le Roi Humbert I, veuillez les faire parvenir à Sa Majesté avec tous les honneurs et tous les

From King Minīlik II, King of Shewa, Kefa, and all its dependencies, i.e. the lands of the Galla; [may it] reach Mr. Count Antonelli.

How are you? By the grace of God I find myself in a state of good health as [does] all my army.

After receiving your letter, I made an expedition as far as the Arsi, and I have returned safe and sound.

You must not be sorry saying that I have not hurried [to come] here, because it has been impossible for me. And now that I am sending you Gebre Sillasē Nigusē with the caravan destined for you, I have written also to Sultan Maḥammad Ḥanfadhē (Mohamed Hanfali) in order that he may receive the said caravan. Write to him also on your part.

Besides, I will write to you when Gebre Sillasē comes, on the only condition, Monsieur le Conte, that you can come soon.

I shall send the full price of the rifles with the second caravan; I shall do it in a manner which can satisfy both you and the Italian government. It gives me pleasure to know that the business of the treaty, which you had carried with you this time, will be completed. It is because of this that I am very anxious to know the final word.

When Gebre Sillasē comes, I will send you the gifts to His Majesty King Umberto I. Please, see to it that they reach His Majesty with all the honours and all the proper regards.

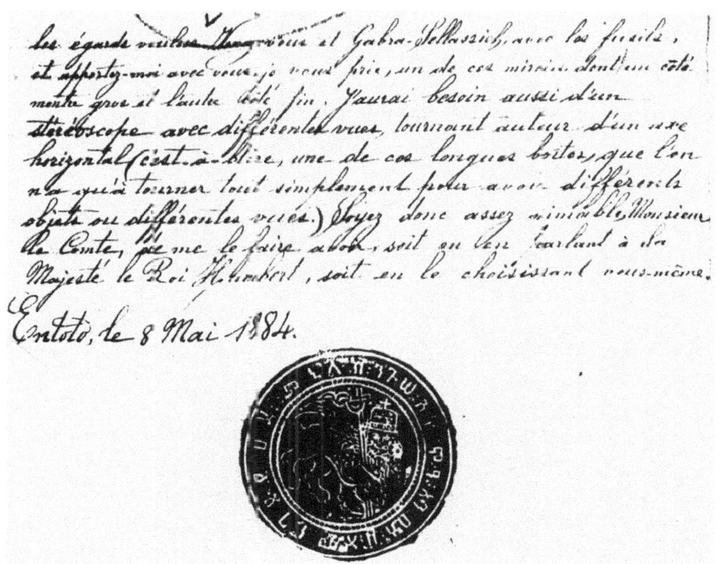

les égards [illegible] venir et Gabra-Sellassieh, avec les fusils,
et apportez-moi avec vous, je vous prie, un de ces miroirs dont un côté
monte gros et l'autre côté fin. J'aurai besoin aussi d'un
stéréoscope avec différentes vues, tournant autour d'un axe
horizontal (c'est-à-dire, une de ces longues boîtes, que l'on
n'a qu'à tourner tout simplement pour avoir différents
objets ou différentes vues.) Soyez donc assez aimable, Monsieur
le Comte, de me le faire avoir, soit en en parlant à Sa
Majesté le Roi Humbert, soit en le choisissant vous-même.

Entoto, le 8 Mai 1884.

Come, you and Gebre Sillasē, with the rifles, and bring with you to me, I beg you, one of those mirrors of which one side enlarges and the other side diminishes.

I also need a stereoscope with different views, turning around a horizontal axle (i.e. one of those long boxes which one only needs to simply turn to have different objects or different views). So please be so kind, Monsieur le Conte, to let me have it, either by talking to His Majesty King Umberto about it or by selecting it yourself.

Inṭoṭṭo, 8th May 1884.

Seal: Minīlik, King of Shewa. The Lion of the tribe of Judah has prevailed.

ASMAI 36/2–17, fol. 352, French sealed text. Italian translation printed in *AP.DD*, XV, pp. 155–156. The handwriting and the opening of the letter suggest that the letter was written by one of the Europeans at Minīlik's court.

Document no. 160

Maḥammad Ḥanfadhē to Giovanni Branchi, 8 May, 1884

To His Excellency, the most noble and most honourable, the beloved and respected, the loving and clement friend, Branchi the ruler (*ṣāḥib)* of Aseb. May God Almighty guide him.

If you ask about us and those who take refuge with us, we are well and healthy, and we are not concerned about anything except you. These lines are dispatched from Sinkara, the protected; all the information is good and favourable. The country's situation is safe and secure. You will find out orally the facts, sufficiently and conclusively, through those who come to you.

As to the news of the situation of Shewa, we have none for the time being; it has not reached us, we think it might be on its way. Your esteemed letter and eloquent correspondence has reached us; we read its contents and understood its intentions. You mentioned [to us] in your letter that Sa'īd bin 'Awīḍān has reached you. However, the reason of his visit to you is to ruin the love that binds us and the friendship that is between us. So do not listen to him and do not accept him. God knows, our friend, he did not tell us on Your Honour's behalf any good or evil and neither little nor much. Rather he came to us because of his needs and then returned to the area of Baylūl. And now, o beloved, as the above-mentioned Sa'īd has gone down to Baylūl from our part after he has come to be at our disposal and under our authority and under [our] obedience, thus he is now considered to be one of our children and among our family. We alerted the tribes about him through the crier's call. Even if he enters Aseb for his needs, do not harm him, and do not look upon him with anger. If any harm or dispute from the above-mentioned Sa'īd comes your way, do not confront him but inform us through a letter of yours about where he is so that I can catch him. If he told me anything on your behalf or mentioned words or actions, I would not hide it from you, and it cannot be hidden from you. This is what we tell you.

The sender of the message is Sultan Maḥammad bin Sultan Ḥanfadhē, the deceased.
Dated Friday, the twelfth of Rajab, the year 1301 of the *Hijra.*

ASMAE, AE 2. The same file contains a brief and rougher version of the same letter.

Document no. 161

Welde Ṣadiq to Pietro Antonelli, 22 May [1884]

How are you? I am well, by the grace of God. I have received your letter. Gebre Sillasē Nigusē should come. So far, we have not been able to send the caravan, because the king was on an expedition. Now, there is no need to be worried about this delay. When Gebre Sillasē Nigusē comes, you will find out the reason yourself. Now, until the arrival of the caravan, prepare everything carefully. As we have ordered before, the king wants a cannon to be carried on a mule and what [is used] to carry the breech. It is necessary to acquire it because the king has ordered it. We have forgotten to write this in the letter of the king, but the king has told me to write it.

Hartuma, 22nd May.

The caravan which left from Shewa has arrived at Farrē.

AP.DD, XV, p. 156, Italian translation.

Document no. 162

Gobena Daçhī to Jules Grévy [May–June 1884]

Lettre adressée à Monsieur le Président de la République française par le Ras Gobena Gouverneur de tous les Pays Gallas.

Monsieur le Président.

Comment vous portez-vous? moi par la grâce de Dieu je me porte bien ainsi que mes armées et ma famille.
Votre haute réputation m'est connue depuis longtemps et mon grand désir de voir des bonnes et amicales relations entre la France et le Choa a été comblé par la venue de l'honorable Monsieur Long-Bois que nous avons tous pris en grande estime et solide amitié.
Je lui confie pour votre auguste personne, un léger présent: le manteau Royal du + dit Kaffa, de Gimma, de Goumma etc dont ce monarque m'avait fait cadeau.

+ Souverain

Ce n'est qu'un commencement de ce que je pense faire plus tard. J'étais fort ~~embarrassé~~ embarrassé d'autant plus que j'ai déjà envoyé différents cadeaux au Gouvernement français avec lettres à l'appui et je n'en ai reçu aucune nouvelle.
Que Dieu vous ait en sa sainte garde, Monsieur le Président et veuille vous faire agréer cordialement les meilleurs sentiments de celui qui désire ardemment conserver toute l'amitié de la France puissante et glorieuse.

Letter from *Ras* Gobena, governor of all Galla lands to the president of the French Republic.

How are you, Mr. President? As for me, by the grace of God, I am well, and so are my armies and my family.

Your high reputation has been known to me since long ago, and my great desire to see good and friendly relations between France and Shewa has been satisfied by the arrival of the honourable Mr. Longbois whom we all have received in great esteem and solid friendship.

I entrust to him a small present for the august person: the royal cloak of the sovereign of Kefa, Jimma, Goma, etc., which this monarch has given to me.

This is only the beginning of what I intend to do later. I was very troubled, the more so as I have already sent various gifts to the French government with letters which support them, and have not received any news.

May God keep you in his holy care, Mr. President, and make you cordially accept the best sentiments of him who eagerly wishes to preserve all the friendship of the powerful and glorious France.

Seal: *Ras* Gobena's seal.

AED, Protocole C 41, Ethiopie, French original. The dating of this document is based on the fact that the visit of Captain Longbois referred to in the letter took place in March–May 1884 (*L'Italia in Africa*, I.1, p. 410).

Document no. 163

Minīlik II to Pietro Antonelli, 1 June 1884

Royal Seal.
Debre Birhan, 25 Ginbot [1876]

I send you the caravan with all I have put together. Altogether you will find that there is a value of around 20.000 thalers. For His Majesty the King of Italy I send gifts which I charge you to make arrive in good condition and to deliver them. I send in the same way gifts for the governor of Aseb and for the commander of the warship. I hope that all will arrive in good order. For you I send the decoration for your assiduous work and so that everyone may know that we are friends and that you work for my benefit.

Now I let you know that I expect your and Gebre Sillasē's arrival in Shewa in order to send off the other caravans. I have sent much money and many gifts to Maḥammad Ḥanfadhē so that he will be of help and work for our interests. All you need to ask him is who is in charge of providing the camels. I would myself have sent the camels, but since they die on the way I have written to Ḥanfadhē that it is more convenient to get them at the coast.

The gifts for His Majesty the King of Italy are the following: two horses with complete saddles ornamented in gold, one hide ornamented in gold, one shield and two lances ornamented in gold.

Augusto Franzoi has received my order to take the bones of Chiarini by way of Aseb, but he has not wanted to obey me. I will never abandon Aseb and I send you the declaration which I have made to signor Franzoi.

ASMAI 36/2–17, Amharic original that has been lost or misplaced and could not be found. Printed Italian text in *L'Italia in Africa*, I.3, no. 333, allegato 1, p. 57.

Document no. 164

Minīlik II to Giulio Pestalozza, 1 June 1884

Royal Seal.
Debre Birhan, 25th Ginbot 1876

How are you? I am well, by the grace of God. I have received your letter. For the moment I have succeeded in collecting some merchandise and I send it with Gebre Sillasē Nigusē.

As a token of the friendship I have towards you I send you a shield ornamented in silver, two lances and a mule with the appropriate harness.

We ask you to protect and help all Abyssinians resident close to you and those that accompany Nigusē Gebre Sillasē; he is my special agent for my merchandise and I have entrusted everything to him as a faithful servant. I recommend him to you in a special way.

ASMAI 36/2–14 R. 415, Amharic original that has been lost or misplaced and could not be found. Printed Italian text in *L'Italia in Africa*, I.3, no. 334, pp. 60–61.

Document no. 165

Minīlik II to Umberto I, 1 June 1884

ዳግማዊ፡ ምኒልክ፡ ንጉሠ፡ ሸዋ፡ ወከፋ፡ ወዥ-
ሉ፡ እንድያሜዛ፡ ለብሔረ፡ ጋላ፡ ይድረስ፡ ወደ፡ ክበረ፡ ወዲ-
ት፡ ወደደ፡ ንጉሠ፡ ዑምበርቶ፡ መጋር መርያ፡ የኢጣሊያ፡ ን
ጉሠ፡ እጅግ፡ እንዴት፡ ነዎ፡ እኔ፡ እግዚአብሔር፡ ይ
መስገን፡ ደኅና፡ ነኝ፡ ሠራዊቴም፡ ሁሉ፡ ደኅና፡ ነው።

ከኮንት፡ አንቶኔሊ፡ ጋራ፡ የላክሁት፡ ጉዳይ፡ ሁ
ሉ፡ ቀና፡ ብሎ፡ ኮንት፡ አንቶኔሊ፡ ቢልክብኝ፡ እጅግ፡
ደስ፡ ብሎኛል፡ አሁንም፡ የአሰብን፡ መንገድ፡ ስለ፡ መ
ክፈት፡ እሽክሬን፡ ገብረ፡ ሥላሴንጉሀሌን፡ ብዙ፡ ሰቈ፡
ከክዩጋር፡ ለንጉሥም፡ ጥቂት፡ የፍቅር፡ በረከት፡ ከኔ፡
ሠዐሊ፡ ጋራ፡ ከአብ፡ ድረስ፡ ከስዩጋር፡ ልኬዋለሁ።

ይህነንም፡ ጥቂቱን፡ የፍቅር፡ ምልክት፡ በረክ
ቴን፡ ከንደብዙ፡ አርገው፡ እንደቀበሉልኝ፡ እለምናለ
ሁ። ንጉሥ፡ ሆይ፡ የቱርኮች፡ ጕረቤትነት፡ ለኔ፡ መንግሥ
ት፡ አልበጀም፡ ዐሥት፡ ዐሥት፡ እጅግ፡ ከየከፉ፡ ጌዬ።፡ ከዚ
ህቀደም፡ ቱርኮች፡ ሐረርጌን፡ ቢይዙብኝ፡ ለየውሮፓ፡ ነ
ገሥታት፡ ስሞታ፡ ልኬ፡ ነበር፡ አሁን፡ ደግሞ፡ ለርስዎ፡ ለ
ወንድሜ፡ ስሞታዬን፡ ከልክ ለሁ። ሐረርጌን፡ ቢይዙ፡
እነሱቾውና፡ አልፈው፡ አገሬን፡ ወበራንና፡ ይቱን፡ ለመ
ያዝ፡ መጥተዋል። እንግዲህ፡ የተዋጋኋቸው፡ እንደሆነ፡
የየውሮፓ፡ ነገሥታት፡ በዲለኝ፡ እንዳያደርጉኝ፡ እር
ስዎ፡ ወንድሜ፡ ምስክር፡ ነዎ፡ እነሬን፡ በከንቱ፡ እም
ለቅ፡ እደደ ለሁም፡ የርስዎን፡ ምላሽ፡ በብዙ፡ መናት
ና፡ በብዙ፡ ናፍቆት፡ እየጠበቅሁ፡ ከእግዚአብሔር፡
ዘንድ፡ እድሜዎን፡ እለምናለሁ። በግንቦት፡ ፳፭ ቀን፡
በ፲፰፻፸፮ በዱብረ፡ ብርሃን፡ ከተማ፡ ተጻፈ።

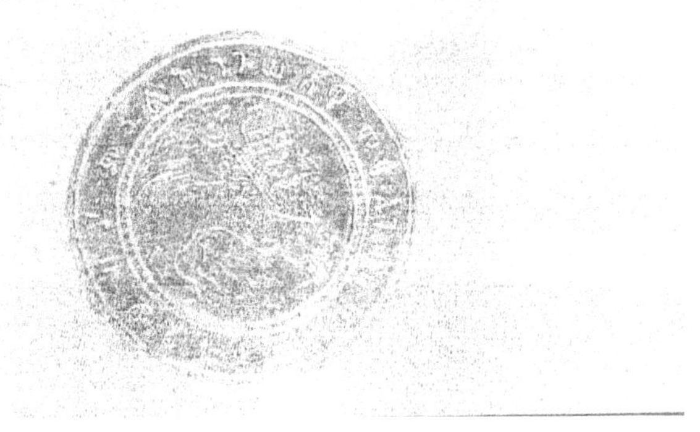

[May this letter from] the second Minīlik, King of Shewa, and of Kefa and all the districts of the Galla country, reach the honoured [and] beloved King Umberto I, King of Italy.

How are you, really? I am well, thank God, and all my soldiers are well.

I was very satisfied when Count Antonelli wrote to me that all the business which I sent with Count Antonelli had been accomplished. And now, concerning the opening of the route to Aseb, I have sent my servant Gebre Sillasē Nigusē to Aseb with much goods and some friendly gifts to the king together with my portrait. I ask that you receive these few tokens of friendship, my presents, as if they were many.

O king! the vicinity of the Turks has not been favourable to my kingdom. It is getting worse from day to day. Earlier when the Turks took Harergē from me, I sent a protest to the European sovereigns, and now I am sending my protest to you, my brother. As if their occupation of Harergē was not enough they have come to occupy my territories Webera and Yitu.

Henceforth, if I ever fight them, you, my brother, will be my witness so that the sovereigns of Europe may not take me for an offender, for I will not abandon my hold on my territory for nothing. Waiting for your reply with much desire and expectation, I pray to God [to give] you a long life.

Written in the town of Debre Birhan on the 25th day of Ginbot 1876.

Seal: Minīlik, King of Shewa. The Lion of the tribe of Judah has prevailed.

ASMAI 36/2–21 bis, Amharic original. Printed Italian translation in *L'Italia in Africa*, I.3 no. 337, allegato, p. 65.

Document no. 166

Ṭaytu to Margherita Maria Teresa Giovanna di Savoia, 1 June 1884

Letter of *Weyzero* Ṭaytu, wife of King Minīlik, King of Shewa and Kefa and all the territory of the country of Galla. May it reach the beloved, respected (lit. feared) Queen of Italy, the royal consort (*itegē*) Margherita, the honoured one. I send my greetings to the queen by asking "How is your health?"

After having seen the love between King Minīlik and King Umberto, and having heard of your kindness, I have sent a small gift, certainly not much, a token of love, consisting of a kind of mantle which empresses wear here in Ethiopia, and a decoration of gold which they hang around their necks, as well as a photo of myself, with the gifts sent to King Umberto by King Minīlik. My hope is that the love which prevails between King Minīlik and King Umberto and which has bestowed light upon the people of Italy and Shewa will create new love of a similar kind between you and me. If such be the case, what is important among kings is not a matter of visible money but rather love and treaties.

I would therefore plead with you to accept this small token of love, as if it were plentiful. And when our love grows strong, I hope that we will be able, by God's power and will and by the abundance of our love, to dispel the darkness which is among our people, and to strengthen, in our time, love between the governments of Italy and Shewa, just as the honoured monarchs in the past succeeded, through their work and their faith, in protecting their people.

As I await your beloved reply, with a fervent wish and much respect, I pray that God will protect the realm of your husband and prolong your age, for the benefit of the people of Shewa and the well-being of Italy.

Written on 25th Ginbot 1876 in the town of Debre Birhan, in the 19th year of the reign of King Minīlik.

Seal: The seal of *Weyzero* Ṭaytu.

ASMAI 36/2–21 bis, Amharic original. We have not been able to find any translation or printed version.

Document no. 167

Treaty between Ethiopia, Great Britain and Egypt, 3 June 1884

Preface

The honoured and exalted Queen Victoria, queen of the United Kingdom of Great Britain and Ireland, empress (*qisaryit*) of India, and the honoured and exalted, elect of God, Emperor Yohannis, King of Zion, King of Kings of Ethiopia and all her dependencies, and the honoured Muḥammad Tawfīq *Pasha*, khedive of Egypt, have willingly agreed to conclude a treaty in order to remove the conflict between Ethiopia and Egypt – a treaty which is to be kept by them and their heirs and successors.

Her Majesty the queen of the United Kingdom of Great Britain and Ireland, empress of India, having appointed as her representative Rear-Admiral Sir William Hewett, commander-in-chief of the warships in India, and the exalted, elect of God Emperor Yohannis, King of Zion, King of Kings of Ethiopia and all her dependencies, in his own capacity, and the honoured khedive of Egypt, having made the official who had come, i.e. Mason *Bey,* governor (*shum*) of Massawa, his representative, have agreed to confirm the following words:

[1.] Starting with the beginning of the month of Senē in the year of grace 1876 according to the Ethiopian reckoning and June 6, in the year of grace 1884 according to the English reckoning, all goods which leave and enter through the gate of Massawa shall be exempted from duties by the protection of England, even if they are the goods of merchants or weapons of war.

2. As of the beginning of Meskerem in the year of grace 1876, according to the Ethiopian reckoning, and in the year of grace 1884, according to the English reckoning, the country called Bogos shall be returned to His Majesty the King of Kings. When the soldiers of the khedive of Egypt leave Kassala, Amedib and Senḥīt, all the houses of the khedive, his goods and the munitions of war at Mogi' and all that remains at that place shall belong to His Majesty.

3. His Majesty, the King of Kings, has agreed to help and give safe conduit to the soldiers of the khedive now in Kassala, Amedib and Senḥīt when they proceed through Ethiopia on their way to Massawa.

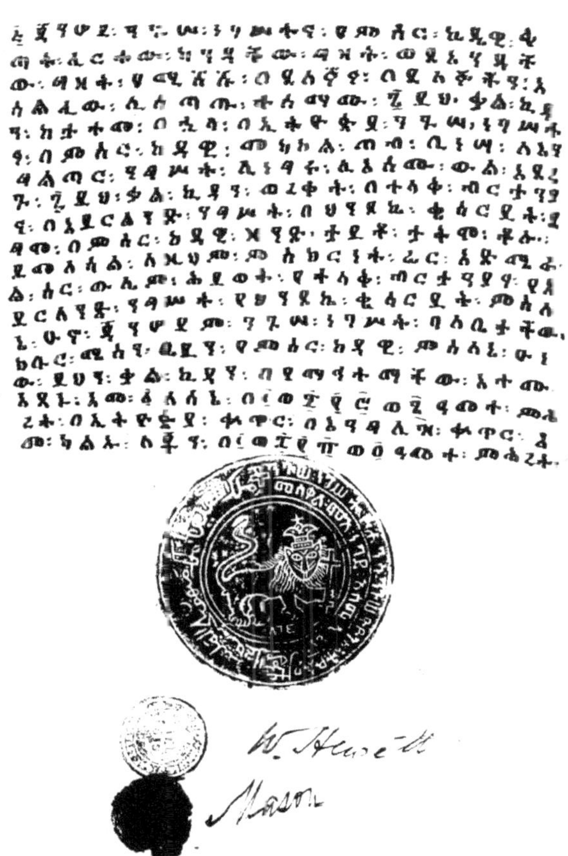

4. The khedive of Egypt will permit His Majesty the King of Kings to acquire bishops for Ethiopia.

5. His Majesty, the King of Kings, and the khedive of Egypt have agreed to extradite criminals who flee from the one realm to the other for fear of punishment.

6. If conflict arises between the King of Kings of Ethiopia and the khedive of Egypt after the signing of this treaty, they have agreed to inform and appeal to the queen of England.

7. This paper bearing the treaty shall be returned speedily after having been seen and sealed by the queen of the United Kingdom of Great Britain and Ireland, and empress of India, and by the khedive of Egypt. And as a testimony to this, Rear-Admiral Sir William Hewett as the representative of the queen of the United Kingdom of Great Britain and Ireland, empress of India, and His Majesty, the King of Kings, acting in his own capacity, and the honoured Mason *Bey* being the representative of the khedive of Egypt, have sealed and confirmed this treaty by their seals.

On the first of Senē in the year of grace 1876 according to the Ethiopian reckoning and the 2nd of June in the year of grace 1884 according to English reckoning.

Seal: King of Kings Yohannis, King of Zion in Ethiopia. The cross has defeated the tribe of Isma'ēl. Yūḥannā, King of Kings of Zion in Abyssinia. The cross has defeated the people of Ismā'īl. 1864.

Seal and signature: W. Hewett.
Seal and signature: Mason.

FO 93/2/2, Amharic original and English version. The above is a new translation of the Amharic text. The dates are confusing. The 1st Senē in the Amharic texts actually corresponds to 7 June, not to 2 June, which rather corresponds to 26 Ginbot. The English version of this treaty is dated 3 June with the correct note that this corresponds to the 27 Ginbot. Based on the English version as well as on Hewett's letter to Granville of 9 June 1884 in which he says that the treaty was sealed by Yohannis on the morning of 3 June, and on the fact that even the Amharic text reads "June" in Amharic letters, we have decided to date the treaty to 3 June. Probably the Ethiopian month Senē was equated with the European month of June, as happened in other documents and the text written one or two days before it was sealed. For Hewett see *EAE* 3, p. 26, and for an analysis of the context see *Survival*, pp. 355–362.

The designation of Victoria as *qisaryit* (feminine of Caesar) is a novelty and replaces the earlier *nigiste negestat* (Queen of Queens) in docs 113 and 119.

Document no. 168

Treaty between Ethiopia and Great Britain, 3 June 1884

Victoria, by the grace of God queen of Great Britain and Ireland and empress (*qisaryit*) of India, and the elect of God, Yohannis, King of Zion and King of Kings of Ethiopia and all its dependencies, have willingly, in love for each other, concluded a treaty between the royal house of England and the royal house of Ethiopia, that trading in slaves shall cease, that no slaves shall be sold. This shall apply eternally to all who reign as monarchs over Ethiopia and England.

The representative who has come to conclude this matter on our behalf is Rear-Admiral Sir William Hewett, the warrior (lit. annihilator) of the warship India.

The preface sent from the Queen of Great Britain and Ireland and Empress of India:

1. Your Majesty shall forbid that any slave be sold or exchanged in your realm.

2. Your Majesty, King of Kings of Ethiopia, and we have concluded a treaty, willingly, that no slaves brought in from another country or slaves from your own country and realm, shall be sold or exchanged within the country or sold to another country.

3. Your Majesty, King of Kings of Ethiopia has given permission that anyone who seizes a freed slave with the intention of re-enslaving the same, shall be punished severely.

4. The Queen of Britain has previously concluded treaties with all other monarchs against the sale of slaves. Therefore, she has ordered her appointees on the seas to keep watch. The Queen has ordered that if these appointees come upon ships transporting slaves, they should capture the ships. And if they find an Abyssinian reckoned as a slave on the ship, he should be returned to the King of Kings, to his country. Thus has the Queen ordered.

ዮሐንስ፡ ንጉሠ፡ ጽዮን፡ ንጉሠ፡ ነገሥት፡ ዘ
ኢትዮጵያ፡ ለዚህ፡ ውል፡ ሁለቱም፡ በገዛ
እጃቸው፡ ማኅተማቸውን፡ አትመዋል፡ ተ
ጽሕፈ፡ በአድዋ፡ ከተማ፡ አመ፡ ክልኤ፡ ለጁ
ን፡ በ፲ወ፰፻ወ፹ወ፬ ዓመተ፡ ምሕረት፡ በእ
ንግሊዝ፡ ቍጥር፡ በ፲ወ፰፻ወ፸ወ፮ ዓመ
ተ፡ ምሕረት፡ አመ፡ ፩ ለሰኔ፡ በኢትዮጵያ፡
ቍጥር፡

W. Hewett

5. This treaty of reconciliation shall be printed speedily and sent to Adwa. As witnesses, Rear-Admiral Sir William Hewett, the representative of the queen of Britain, empress of India and the elect of God, Yohannis, King of Zion and King of Kings of Ethiopia, have both sealed this treaty with their seals.

Written in the town of Adwa in June 1884, the year of grace, on 2 June according to the English number, and in 1876, the year of grace, on 1 Senē according to the Ethiopian number.

Seals of Yohannis and Rear-Admiral William Hewett.

Signature W. Hewett

FO 93/2/3, Amharic original and English version. The above is a new translation of the Amharic text. For dating and context, see the preceding document. The text, often referred to as the "slave treaty", is an odd combination referred to as a treaty in the prologue and the epilogue (clause 5) and a series of demands (1–4) presented as a "preface" sent by Victoria. The Amharic text is clearly a translation of an English document already prepared before the negotiations at Adwa.

Document no. 169

Maḥammad Ḥanfadhē to Giovanni Branchi, 12 June 1884

الى حضرة الاكرم المكرم العزيز المحترم برنكي حاكم عصب
هداه الله امين وان سالتم عنا وعمن يلوذ بنا فاننا بخير وعافية
ولا نسال الا عنكم وعن احوالكم التي هي غايت القصد والمراد من
رب العباد صدرة الاحرف من محروس سنكره وكل علم خير وعافية
وصل الينا جوابكم الكريم وخطابكم الجسيم فقرانا مبانيه وعرفنا معانيه
فحمدنا الله تعالى على صحة عافيتكم للحيث المكتب ار الرفن وبعده كتابكم
وصل ضحوة يوم الاثنين ستة عشر من شهر رجب وذكرتم لنا فيه
من جناب سعيد بن عويضان نعم انه وصل عندنا لكن ما ذكر منكم
لا بسوء ولا بمكروه وانما قال لنا اني خرجت من خدمة تيليان الفرنج
وشغلهم الان اني طامع وراغب حماية منك حيث ما كنت في بر عجم
وقد عرفتكم في كتابنا السابق قبل هذا الكتاب وذكرنا لكم بما قال لنا
وانتم لا تتعدوا عليه بسوء ظن فان سوء ظن اثم واما سعيد عويضان
المذكور ما دخل بيننا وبينكم بالمواصلة قبل وكيف يدخل بيننا المقاطعة
ولا هو واسط بيني وبينكم فكيف تظنون ان ارضى بكلامه الفساد
والفتنة وهذا ما هو لائق فهو رجل احد من الناس وورد عندنا كما
هو الوارد ون كثير من الخلق الينا والان انت يا حاكم عصب ارضى عنه
وسامحه ولا تمسوه ولا تنظروه بعين الغضب ولا من امواله للحيث
الله دخل في حمايتنا وتحت طاعتنا وصل عندنا هذا اعرفناكم

To His Honour, the most noble and most honoured, the beloved and respected Branch , the governor (*ḥākim*) of Aseb. May God lead him. Amen.

If you ask about us and those who take refuge with us, we are well and healthy, and we are not concerned about anything except you and your well-being which is the ultimate aim and desire of the Lord of the faithful. The words are dispatched from Sinkara, the protected, and all the information is good and favourable. We have received your esteemed letter and eloquent correspondence. We read its contents and understood its intentions. Then we praised God Almighty for your good health.

As a matter of fact, the scribe ʻAza al-Rafān arrived on Monday forenoon the 16th of the month of Rajab with the letter in his hand in which you expressed your concern about Sa'īd bin ʻAwīḍān. Yes indeed, he reached us, but he did neither insult nor defame you. Rather, he told us "I left the Italian foreigners' service and business. And now, I desire and crave your protection so that I am not on non-Arab land."

In fact, I have already informed you in a previous letter of mine what he told us. You should not mistreat him because of your misjudgement, for a misjudgement is an offence. The above-mentioned Sa'īd bin ʻAwīḍān has never before intervened in our correspondence, so how could he cause its interruption while he is not our intermediary? How could you believe that I would accept that his words lead to calamity and strife? That would not be appropriate. He is only one man among the people who came to us, just like many other people do.

And now, o governor of Aseb, pardon and forgive him, do not be angry with him, harm him, mistreat him or seize his money, for he has come to us and entered under our protection and under our authority. This is what we tell you. In fact, he presented himself to us before we wrote you a letter, which might or might not have reached you and in which we mentioned using the case of Sa'īd ʻAwīḍān. In addition, we warned all tribes that he is counted as one of our sons and one of our family. Let this be known to you.

Furthermore, our servant Muḥammad bin Aḥmad reached us on the 12th of the month of Sha'bān, Sunday evening, with your esteemed letter in his hand. We read its contents and understood its intentions. However, news not included in your letter has reached us through the travellers indicating that you have unjustly seized and squandered the money of Sa'īd ʻAwīḍān after you received our letter in which we informed you that he had come under our rule and authority. Otherwise I would not have written you a letter after you were told that he had reached me. You should not have seized and squandered the money of whoever came to me. And now, o our beloved, you have to return the money you took from Sa'īd ʻAwīḍān, for he is reckoned as one of our sons and one of our family. And we had a herald to proclaim him so warning all the tribes from Moday to Mūdīta as well as the others. Then how could you do this to him while he is under our auspices? This is a disgrace and a shame on both of us. Yet, if you have any rightful claim upon him, send us a letter and inform us.

Regarding ʻAlī Arūma from the tribe of Beylul, you mentioned to us in his case what he witnessed, and we accepted your words. May God fulfil the desire.

From our side, the Sultan*'s* secretary ʻAbd al-Rahmān bin *Shaykh* Muḥammad Turāb inquires: "How are you, and how are your servants, and soldiers? I was informed of what you have written to me in the letter you sent to our Sultan. You promised to send me the rifle I had asked for. Please send it with ʻAbd al-Raḥmān al-Dhammām bin *Shaykh* Yūsif. This is what we tell you."

The sender of the message is Sultan Maḥammad bin Sultan Ḥanfadhē.
Dated in the month of Sha'bān, on Thursday, after 17 days elapsed, the year 1301 Hijra.

The scribe ʻAza al-Rafān has been dressed in a traitor's (*ghīla)* dress. This is what we tell you.

ASMAE, AE 2. Arabic original.

Document no. 170

Yosēf Nigusē to Pietro Antonelli, 16 June 1884

Seal.
Debre Birhan, 10th Senē 1876.

After your departure my brother and I have had many troubles and we have been in the worst conditions. The persons who wanted to hurt us wanted to hurt you as well, but after having overcome many difficulties we can assure you that we are victorious. But we have been forced to spend much money and today we are poor. Above all, however, we have your safe arrival in Shewa at heart.

We are disgusted with signor Brémond because of the Aseb affairs, now I cannot tell you everything, you will know later.

Aleqa Kīdane Maryam has been chained by orders of the king. They also wanted to chain my brother and myself, but we have been liberated from this misfortune as well. The king is very worried. On our side we have worked for you and we are all tired. Brémond has tried to do me harm in my relation to the king for no other reason than knowing that I am your friend. But since it is a question of the affairs of my king, I will never get tired. I expect you impatiently and will always work for you. I recommend you not to abandon the affairs of the king, it would on the contrary be necessary to make him content by sending him a mountain cannon which is loaded from the rear. It is absolutely necessary that you get it, [since] it is something the king has long desired.

Regarding the rest, you know it from my brother Gīyorgīs Nigusē who comes to you. From a year ago to today many changes have occurred; I have worked much, God knows how much. After God, King Mīnilik and you know all my work.

There is a complete rupture with the French. All your friends in Shewa expect you impatiently. Franzoi has given us much trouble. He has refused to take the bones of Chiarini by way of Awsa. From Aseb a written explanation was sent to you by the king. All the Abyssinians in Shewa have suggested to the king the route to Aseb, but he who is an Italian does not want to and has gone with the French in Obok.

You need to make these matters known.

ASMAI 36/2–17, Amharic original that has been lost or misplaced and could not be found. Printed Italian text in *L'Italia in Africa*, I.3 no. 333, allegato 2, pp. 58–59. *Grazmach* Yosēf Nigusē was one of Minīlik's most important secretaries for his relations with the Europeans. See also doc. 180 on the author. Gīyorgīs Nigusē is commonly known as Gebre Sillasē Nigusē.

Document no. 171

Yohannis IV to Victoria, 20 June 1884

In the name of Our Lord Jesus Christ. Praise be to Him. Message from the Elect of God, Yohannis, King of Zion, King of Kings of Ethiopia and all its territories. May it reach the honoured and exalted Queen Victoria, by God's grace Queen of the United Kingdom of Britain and Ireland, sovereign over India and all its territories.

How have you been since I [last] wrote to you? I am well, by the mercy of God, and the mediatorship of our Mother Zion. The God of the saints be honoured and praised, I am well because his mercy is everlasting. Blessed was the moment when I received your honoured and glorious letter, a bestower of joy to the heart, written with your seal in 1884 in the forty-seventh year of your reign. I have also received the gift of love that you sent me: two cannons with ammunition, twelve used rifles and five new ones, one gun (*merbut*), two pistols, one colourful tent, and two carpets from the hands of the commander, the representative of India and your faithful servant, Rear-Admiral Sir William Hewett. Thank you.

Since you have opened the gate of Massawa for me to make me happy, may Christ grant you joy by opening the everlasting gate of the kingdom of heaven to you. May God grant joy in the kingdom of heaven also to the counsellors in your government for deliberating and arriving at such a counsel to make me happy. May He also enable me to agree with you in counsel and conform to your will. After all, I attained the status of emperor by God's will through the cannon, guns and ammunition that you gave me.

And now complete my joy. In the past, you have not ceased to show concern for my realm, just as a mother shows concern for her children. Though neglected for some time now, it was common knowledge with you and all the kings of Europe that the gate of Massawa belonged to our fathers, the kings of Ethiopia. Since the realm cannot succeed without a gate, I entreat you to help me secure the gate of Massawa under your mandate. Though other matters have been resolved, this one has not. Your appointed representative, Rear-Admiral Sir William Hewett, told me to keep half of the revenue of Massawa. I asked him to affix his seal to such an agreement. He has come and replied that he could not affix the seal before consulting the Queen.

Written in the town of Aksum on 14th Senē 1876.

FO 95/744, no. 174, Amharic original and English translation. The English translation, done by Mirçha Werqē, skates over the point about Massawa (see *Yohannis* IV, p. 152). The letter together with copies of the signed treaty was sent with Mirçha Werqē and Meshesha Werqē who went to England with Admiral Hewett to receive the Queen's seal on the treaty. Note that Yohannis here repeats the suggestion that the revenues from trade through Aseb should be divided and he receive half, a suggestion, originally by Mason *Bey*, that Hewett claims he had turned down in Adwa.

Document no. 172

Yohannis IV to Victoria, 25 June 1884

In the name of Our Lord Jesus Christ, praise be to him.

May [this letter] from the Elect of God Yohannis, King of Zion, King of Kings of Ethiopia, reach the honoured and exalted Queen Victoria, by the grace of God [queen of] the United Kingdom of Great Britain and Ireland, empress of India, and all their dependencies.

How have you been, really, since I wrote to you? I, together with my army, am well, by the mercy of God and the intercessions of Our Lady Zion. Honour and praise be to the Lord of the Holy. His mercy lasts forever.

I have said, "Seal the letter you have written about the reconciliation matter and return it." I have sent you my trustworthy servants *Lij* Mirçha Werqē and Meshesha.

Written at the city of Aksum on the 19th of Senē in the year of grace 1876.

Seal: King of Kings Yohannis, King of Zion in Ethiopia. The cross has defeated the tribe of Isma'ēl.
Yūḥannā, King of Kings of Zion in Abyssinia. The cross has defeated the people of Ismā'īl. 1864.

FO 95/744, no. 173, Amharic original and English translation. In this second letter sent with Mirçha and Meshesha Werqē, Yohannis points out that he expects the treaty to be signed by the Queen, as promised by Hewett, and sent back to Ethiopia. This was never done, however.

Document no. 173

Yohannis IV to Muḥammad Tawfīq, 25 June 1884

Seal: King of Kings Yohannis, King of Zion in Ethiopia. The cross has defeated the tribe of Isma'ēl. Yūḥannā, King of Kings of Zion in Abyssinia. The cross has defeated the people of Ismā'īl. 1864.

May the message from the Elect of God Yohannis, King of Zion, King of Kings of Ethiopia reach the honourable and revered, conscientious and knowledgeable Tawfīq Pasha, khedive of the land of Egypt.

How have you been since I wrote you last? By the grace of God and the intercession of our Mother Zion, praise and honour be to the Lord of saints, I, together with my army, am well, since His forgiveness is forever.

I received and accepted your esteemed letter with its seal. I have [also] received the presents which you have sent me for friendship's sake, 10 boxes of shell cases, a watch, a carpet, an umbrella, an ornamental saddle which you say you have sent (?) by the hand of your trusted servant. Thank you.

Regarding the reconciliation case – for which, by the order of the Queen Victoria, the person, the Rear-Admiral Sir William Hewett, came with your official – with the will of God it has become successful. The Lord that loves peace and who brought us to this may He be honoured and praised, and make things last forever. Since early times I did not want any quarrel with you, but only friendship.

Although this has happened and all other matters have been decided upon, however, the case of Massawa did not get any decision. It is recently that the port of Massawa has been taken away. In early days it used to belong to my fathers, the Ethiopian kings.

Written in city of Aksum, 19th Senē in the year of grace 1876.

ENA, Soudan 5/1/6, Amharic original; 5/3/4b, Arabic translation.

Document no. 174

Yohannis IV to Giovanni Branchi, 25 June 1884

Seal: King of Kings

Yohannis, King of Zion in Ethiopia. The cross has defeated the tribe of Isma'ēl. Yūḥannā, King of Kings of Zion in Abyssinia. The cross has defeated the people of Ismā'īl. 1864

May the letter from the Elect of God Yohannis, King of Zion, King of Kings of Ethiopia, and all its dependencies, reach the honourable and respected Giovanni Branchi, the consul of Italy.

How are you? I am well, thank God, and so are my soldiers. As for the matter we discussed before, although I sent Mr. Bianchi by a route where there is a river [allowing] three days of travel by boat, a route that leads to Aseb through Arho and where there is no lack of water, giving him Ṭilṭal guides to bring him along a safe route, and though the Ṭilṭal guides told him that they would accompany him, providing him with honey and butter, he went by a route where there was no water and where the sun was oppressive, saying that he had a route that he knew which left Awsa to the right. Since this route was not known to have been used by anyone, his guide left him and disappeared. And he [Bianchi] has come back to Meqelē and is residing here. It was he himself! As for me, I have not broken my word.

Written in the town of Aksum, 19th Senē in the year of grace 1876.

ASMAI 36/2–13, Amharic original with seal in blue and Italian translation. The Italian translation, strangely enough, gives the date 9 Senē. The text of this letter is printed in *Atti della Reale Accademia dei Lincei, Rendiconti,* vol. VII, Rome 1891, p. 287. For Bianchi see docs 142–143.

Document no. 175

Minīlik II to Giacomo Malvano, 9 Aug. 1884

Letter from His Majesty King Minīlik II, King of Shewa, Kefa, and all the lands of the Galla, addressed to his honourable friend Mr. Malvano, president of the Italian Geographical Society, Rome, rue du Collège Romaine no. 26.

How are you? I am very well, thank God, and so are all my armies.

I was pleased to receive your esteemed letter dated the 6th of January 1884, no. 12. I was very touched by your noble feelings of gratitude expressed in the [said] letter because these sentiments show your good and excellent heart. As for me, I have done nothing except what is appropriate to our friendship. I have likewise received your charming letter written from Rome on the 15th of August 1882, no. 633, and attached to the present letter. There I have also noticed that the attractive Italian Geographical Society has always manifested towards me the same noble sentiments of gratitude as mentioned above.

If I have made adequate arrangements for the preservation of the objects left at the station Liṭ Marefīya by the regrettably deceased Marquis Antinori, it has also been for friendship's sake.

en outre de faire transporter vos collections de Choa à Assab, c'est également par pure amitié et ce ne mérite par conséquent pas aucune récompense. c'est à moi, au contraire, de vous en connaître grès, puisque vous me procurez ainsi l'occasion de pouvoir m'associer aux louables efforts que vous faites pour le progrès du genre humain.

Mes chaleureux remerciements à la Société Géographique pour ce qu'elle a bien voulu écrire dans ses livres et ses journaux en réponse des calomnies qui ont pu être écrites par les autres à mon égard. Quant aux journaux qui ont pu parler mal de moi, je n'ai rien à leur dire, d'abord, parce que nous vivons dans une époque de liberté, et ensuite, parce que ce ne sont point leurs calomnies qui puissent tourner mes habitudes et mon caractère en mal.

La Société a très-bien agi en donnant toutes les instructions nécessaires à son digne Représentant Monsieur le Comte Antonelli, pour ce qui concerne l'établissement d'une station à Kaffa.

J'ai appris avec une extrême satisfaction, que votre société a pris la décision d'envoyer au Choa un médecin Italien savant et habile. Moi aussi je n'oublierai jamais l'amitié et la gratitude que je dois à cet effet à/.

If I also undertake to have your collections transported from Shewa to Aseb, it is also purely out of friendship and thus nothing that merits recompense. On the contrary, it is I who owe gratitude to you, since in this way you give me an opportunity to associate myself with the laudable efforts you make for the progress of mankind.

My warm gratitude to the Society for Geography for what it has been kind enough to write in its books and papers in answer to the calumnies that might have been written by others about me. As for the papers that might have spoken ill of me, I have nothing to say to them, first because we live in an era of freedom, and secondly because their calumnies are unable to change my habits and character into something bad.

It was very well done by the Society to give all the necessary instructions to its worthy representative Count Antonelli concerning the establishment of a station in Kefa.

I have learnt with extreme satisfaction that your Society has taken the decision to send a learned and skilful Italian physician to Shewa. I shall never forget the friendship and gratitude I owe to the Society for this.

à la Société, j'ai trouvé indiqué dans votre lettre tout ce dont devra s'occuper le médecin dont il s'agit, et je l'approuve. Que ledit médecin puisse venir seulement en état de bonne santé en faisant une heureuse traversée.

Quant aux liens d'amitié qui unissent déjà si étroitement l'Italie et le Choa, ils ne font, comme vous le dites vous même, que de devenir plus solides de jour en jour; c'est tout ce que nous désirons et nous désirons sans cesse.

Veuillez faire parvenir, Monsieur le Président, mes compliments de sincère amitié à Monsieur G. Dalla Vedova, Secrétaire Général ainsi qu'à tous les autres Membres de votre Société.

Que le Tout-Puissant daigne vous accorder une longue et heureuse vie et bénisse tous les louables efforts de la Société!

Boru Méda, le 9 Août 1884.

I have found indicated in your letter everything that the physician in question shall busy himself with, and I approve of it. May this physician only come here in good health and have a fortunate passage.

As for the bonds of friendship that already unite Italy and Shewa so closely, they only become, as you say yourself, more and more solid every day. This is all that we wish, and we wish it constantly.

Please, Mr. President, send my compliments of sincere friendship to Mr. G. Dalla Vedova, Secretary-General, as well as to all the other members of your Society.

May the Almighty deign to grant you a long and happy life and to bless all the laudable efforts of the Society.

Boru Mēda, 9th August 1884.

Seal: Minīlik, King of Shewa. The Lion of the tribe of Judah has prevailed.

ASSGI, 20, 5, fols 20–21, French original in the handwriting of Gebri'ēl Welde Gobena (see his own letter, doc. 177).

Document no. 176

Minīlik II to Giovanni Branchi, 9 Aug. 1884

625-

Lettre de Sa Majesté le Roi Ménilek II
Roi du Choa, de Kaffa et de tous les pays
Gallas, adressée à son honorable ami Monsieur
G. Bianchi, Commissaire Royal, Consul de
Sa Majesté le Roi d'Italie dans la mer
Rouge, à Assab.—
Comment vous portez-vous? Moi,
grâce à Dieu, je me porte bien, et
toutes mes armées aussi.
Le courrier de Monsieur le Comte
Antonelli m'a remis votre aimable lettre
datée du 29 juin 1884. J'ai été très-content
en lisant toutes les charmantes paroles que
vous m'avez écrites, pour me souhaiter bonne
et heureuse année à l'occasion du prochain
changement de celle qui court. Que le Seigneur
daigne accorder à vous aussi une longue
et heureuse vie, et vous fasse voir, en bonne
et parfaite santé, plusieurs années abondantes.
Tout ce que Monsieur le Comte
Antonelli vous a fait savoir, relativement
à la caravane et aux cadeaux, est vrai.
Cette caravane n'aurait pas tardé jusqu'à
ce jour, si, au moment où la nouvelle
de l'arrivée à Assab de Monsieur le Comte
Antonelli et des marchandises fut parvenue
au Choa, je n'aurais pas été en expédition.
Je suis en train de faire préparer
actuellement la seconde caravane, pour
vous faire plaisir comme vous autres
me...

Letter from His Majesty King Minīlik II, King of Shewa, of Kefa, and all the lands of the Galla, addressed to his honoured friend Monsieur G. Bianchi (*sic*), royal commissioner, consul of His Majesty the King of Italy at Aseb in the Red Sea.

How are you? As for me, thank God, I am well, and so is all my army. The messenger of Monsieur Count Antonelli has transmitted your friendly letter dated the 29th of June 1884. I am very satisfied reading all the delightful words which you have written to me to wish me a nice and happy year on the occasion of the near turn of that which ends. May the Lord deign to grant you a long and happy life and make you experience many plentiful years in good and perfect health.

Everything which M. Count Antonelli has informed you of with regard to the caravan and the gifts is true. This caravan would not have been delayed until now if I had not been on an expedition, at the moment when the news of the arrival of M. Count Antonelli and the goods at Massawa reached Shewa.

me l'avez faites. — J'ai été très-content aussi en apprenant qu'un de vos grands navires de guerre a été jusqu'à Zeyla, et a termin[é] l'affaire d'intérêt que mon ami Abdarrahman Youssef avait avec Abou-Baker-Pacha. Je Vous prie, Monsieur le Commissaire Royal, de vouloir bien faire parvenir à cet effet mes sincères remerciements, tant au Gouvernement Italien, qu'à l'honorable Commandant du-dit navires; car ils ont agi en ami, en terminant l'affaire de mon serviteur Abdarrahman. J'ai trouvé très-intéressant aussi, ce que Vous m'avez écrit pour m'informer qu'Abou Baker-Pacha a promis solennellement de ne plus attaquer ou déranger la route entre Assab et le Choa.

Que Dieu Vous conserve, mon honorable ami, et Vous préserve de tout mal.

Borou-Mieda, le 9 Août 1884.

I am now about to prepare the second caravan to give you the same pleasure that you have granted me. I am also very satisfied by learning that one of your large warships has remained until now at Zeyla and has completed the business of interest which my friend ‘Abd al-Raḥmān Yūsif had with Abū Bakr Pasha. I beg you, Monsieur Royal Commissioner, to be so kind as to convey to this effect my sincere gratitude both to the Italian government and to the honoured commander of the said ships, because they have acted as friends in terminating the business of my servant ‘Abd al-Raḥmān. I have also found very interesting what you have written in order to inform me that Abū Bakr Pasha has solemnly promised not to attack or disturb the route between Aseb and Shewa.

May God keep you, my honoured friend, and preserve you from all evil.

Boru Mēda, 9th August 1884.

Seal: Minīlik, King of Shewa. The Lion of the tribe of Judah has prevailed.

ASMAE, AE, French original in the handwriting of Gebri’ēl Welde Gobena (see his own letter, doc. 177). Printed Italian text in *L'Italia in Africa*, I.3 no. 335, allegato 1, pp. 61–62. Although the text has G. Bianchi, the letter is clearly written to the civil administrator of Aseb, Giovanni Branchi, as also observed by Giglio, *L'Italia in Africa*.

Document no. 177

Gebri'ēl Welde Gobena to Giacomo Malvano, 9 Aug. 1884

Boru Mēda (Galla village), the 9th of August 1884.

Mr. President,

Although I have not yet had the honour of making your desirable acquaintance, the utility of the humanitarian and essentially civilizing work that your honourable Society pursues with such success, the inclination I have for that branch of science that is your principal concern and of which even the sovereigns of the world are honoured to become members, and in one word, the love that I myself have for the progress of all countries in general and my own in particular, all these reasons, I say, encourage me to respectfully address these few lines to you.

A native of the Galla country, chance, or rather the impenetrable will of Divine Providence, made me at an early age leave my native country and I was able to attain a certain degree of education. I write six languages and speak seven fluently, having studied in Cairo (Egypt) and in Jerusalem. I have served the Egyptian government for about four years, attached as under-secretary at the Ministry of Justice under the paternal direction of the commander Mr. J. Haimann, who was head of the department there. The honourable Mr. Haimann, the commander Mr. Ara, the likeable consul Count Gloria, as well as all the other Italians who knew me in Egypt, will be able to tell you more about me.

Lastly, having received news from His Majesty King Minīlik II, who is more of a European sovereign than an African monarch, I resigned from the ministry and broke voluntarily my future . . . and returned to my native country in order to find, if God wishes, my ignorant parents (who will have deplored the loss of me since about twenty-two years) and to be of use more closely to my compatriots, for my own future is none other than the progress and welfare of my country, and I had the incomparable luck of finding myself since almost two years together with a sovereign who is able to understand me, being animated himself by the same feelings, a sovereign who is more than exceptional for Ethiopia and who, I am sure, will with God's help lead his country on the road of civilization that is appropriate for the nineteenth century and allows Abyssinia to occupy the rank that befits its past and its intelligence

If I have permitted myself to write all this to you at length, it is not, Mr. President, to boast about myself, far from it, it is simply to tell you that a young man who finds himself in such circumstances, who has experienced so many adventures, could be useful to you within the limits of the possible for the laudable efforts you make with such energy for universal progress.

If I am pained by anything here, it is by not having any papers or journals to read in order to instruct myself further and know what is happening in Europe and in other parts of the world. I therefore permit myself to ask you (for you are the only person who can exactly understand the sentiments that guide me) to be so kind as to make a subscription in my name for a serious journal and to extend your kindness to sending me some issues with the courier that will be possible for you, if you wish to honour my humble letter with an answer.

n'y a que Vous qui puissiez comprendre exactement
le sentiment qui me guide, de vouloir bien prendre,
en mon nom, un abonnement à un journal sérieux,
et d'avoir l'extrême bonté de m'en envoyer quelques numéros avec le courrier qu'il Vous sera
possible, dans le cas que Vous voudriez honorer
d'une réponse mon humble lettre. Le journal
peut être en Italien ou en français. Je Vous ferai
parvenir le prix d'abonnement d'une année à l'a-
vance, par l'intermédiaire de la personne que
Vous aurez la bonté de m'indiquer. J'aurais
préféré, si c'est possible, un journal hebdomadaire
grand format qui puisse contenir quelques
gravures intéressantes.

Votre Société pourra disposer de moi,
pour tout ce qui peut être dans l'intérêt
de la noble Italie, de ma chère patrie et
du progrès en général.

Veuillez agréer, Monsieur le Président,
avec mes remerciements anticipés, l'expression
de mon profond respect et de mon sincère
dévouement.

Votre humble serviteur,
Gabriel W. Gobana
Secrétaire-Interprète
de S.M. le Roi
Minilek II

The journal may be in Italian or in French. I will send you the subscription fee for a year in advance through the intermediary of the person that you will have the goodness to indicate. I would prefer, if this is possible, a large-sized weekly journal that might contain some interesting engravings.

Your Society will be able to have me at its disposal for anything that might be in the interest of noble Italy, of my beloved country and of progress in general. Please accept, Mr. President, together with my thanks in advance, the expression of my profound respect and sincere devotion.

Your humble servant
Gebri'ēl W. Gobena, secretary-interpreter to His Majesty King Minīlik II

ASSGI, 20, 5, fols 23–24, French text. Gebri'ēl Welde Gobena had, according to his own testimony, left Ethiopia ca. 1862, studied in Cairo and Jerusalem, learned to write six languages and speak seven, and worked as an undersecretary for the ministry of justice in Cairo before returning to his own country in 1882. He then became one of Minīlik's secretaries. The two previous letters of the same date are both in his handwriting.

Document no. 178

Minīlik II to Pietro Antonelli, 9 Aug. 1884

How are you? I, thank God, am well and so is all my army.

It is with great pleasure that I have received your letter dated in Aseb 29 June 1884. I am very happy to hear that you have brought everything I wanted from Italy to Aseb. When you come to Shewa with Gebre Sillasē Nigusē and ʻAbd al-Raḥmān Yūsif bringing me all the merchandise, I will tell orally all the gratitude which I feel in my heart for you and for the Italian government.

I shall do what is due because of your friendship and what can make you content, because my word is one only. The caravan would not have been delayed from its descent to Aseb until now, if I had not been on an expedition when the news of your return arrived from Aseb. As for the caravan, which I have just sent with Gebre Sillasē, I have taken all the actions necessary in order that no interference stops it on the way, and in order that it will not take some other direction; so be patient. As you have said yourself, as soon as Gebre Sillasē arrives, come quickly with the merchandise, so that we may speak together about all our affairs. You have done well in not entrusting [to somebody else] the letter and the gifts which are addressed to me; it is better that you bring them with you.

Oh my friend, while I wait for your arrival, I will prepare a second caravan which will compensate you for what you have expended to satisfy me; only come quickly with all the merchandise.

In case it might be possible for you to return here at the time of the feast of the Cross, or even before the end of the month of Meskerem, which coincides with the beginning of the month of October, bring the merchandise to Boru Mēda by the route of Gerfa. But send me, in advance, a fast messenger so that I know about your arrival in order to send a person to meet you. Otherwise, if you cannot arrive [here] at the time indicated, follow the route to Shewa and come straight to Ankober, since I expect to leave Boru Mēda at the end of the month of Meskerem.

As for the camel issue, or the fact that every time I send camels from here a number of them die, I have written to ʻAbd al-Raḥmān and to Sultan Maḥammad Ḥanfadhē asking them to find there as many as will be needed, and promising to reimburse them for their expenses for renting the camels as soon as the camels arrive here with the merchandise. I shall forget neither Sultan Maḥammad Ḥanfadhē nor ʻAbd al-Raḥmān; if the merchandise arrives soon and in good condition, I shall do everything to satisfy them. It was right of you also to write to the Sultan about the caravan. As for the station of Liṭ Marefīya, do not worry, because I am always there to protect it. My sincere thanks to the Italian government, to you and to the Italian Society of Geography for the decision taken by this Society to send a learned and skilful Italian physician to Shewa.

ASMAI 36/2–14, Amharic original that has been lost or misplaced and could not be found. Printed Italian text in *L'Italia in Africa*, I.3 no. 335, allegato 2, pp. 62–63. As is often the case in *L'Italia in Africa*, the opening phrases have been omitted.

Document no. 179

Treaty between Ḥamad La'īta and France, 9 Aug. 1884

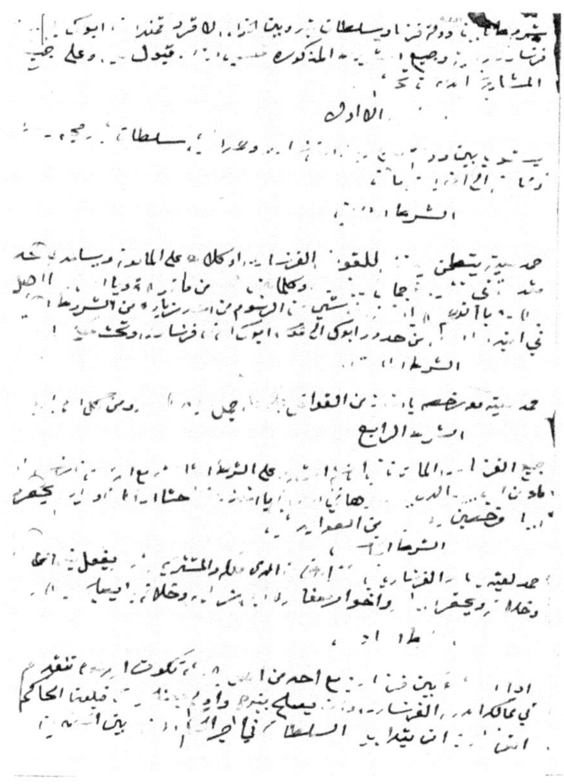

Between Mr. Lagarde, Commander of Obok, acting in the name of the French government, and Ḥamad La'īta, acting in his own name and in the name of the officials under his orders, has been concluded the following treaty:

Article 1: There shall be between the government of the French Republic and Ḥamad La'īta, Sultan of Gobad, constant peace and eternal friendship.

Article 2: Ḥamad La'īta undertakes to protect the French and the caravans of the French and their merchants, and to open the most convenient route and to offer them, by the means in his power, the best opportunities for the purchase of camels, mules and provisions of all sorts, and to prohibit their becoming subject to any fee other than that set by article 3, from the borders of the colony of Obok until those of Awsa itself, as the colony of Obok is a French territory directly subject to French laws.

Article 3: Ḥamad La'īta has the right to collect a caravan fee of one thaler per camel and per European individual.

Article 4: In return for the fee provided by Article 3, the French caravans and travellers have the right to get fresh supplies of water from all wells they will come across or from wells they deem right to dig for that purpose and shall be exempt from all additional fees.

Article 5: Ḥamad La'īta undertakes to grant the French all rights to acquire property with full ownership on his territory, to build constructions of all sorts, to dig wells and canals, and undertake other works that will be considered beneficial to aid the transportation of respective possessions of the contracting parties and promote common prosperity.

Article 6: In case of a dispute between a French person and a subject of the Sultan, it shall be brought before the chief of the French colony who will strive to reach an amicable settlement. Should this not happen, the chief of the French colony will agree with the Sultan to jointly examine the matter and rule on the basis of equity.

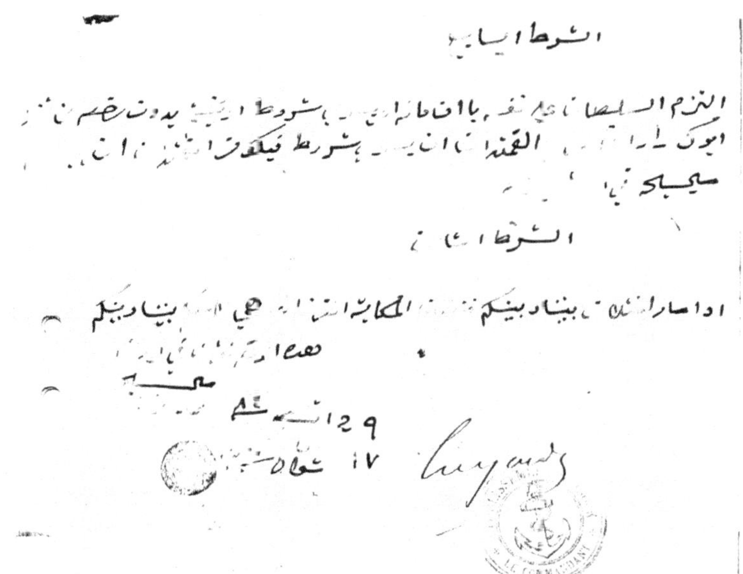

Article 7: The Sultan promises not to conclude any agreement nor to sign any treaty without the agreement of the chief of Obok, who should countersign every act of such a nature.

Article 8: In case of disagreement, the French text will prevail.

Written in Obok on 9th August 1884.

Seal of Ḥamad La'īta
LAGARDE
Seal of Lagarde
(Etablissement d'Obok * Le commandant *)

ANOM.OI, Arabic and French originals. French text printed in *Trattati*, pp. 67–68. Although we present the Arabic text, the translation has been made from the French since this is stated to be the only valid text and since the Arabic copy is unfortunately barely legible. The French and Arabic have identical seals and signatures and are both dated 9 August 1884 as well as 17 Shawwal 1301. The reference to 9 April in the heading in *Trattati* and in Hertslet, no. 70, is evidently a mistake.

Document no. 180

Gīyorgīs Gebre Sillasē Nigusē to Pietro Antonelli, 11 Aug. 1884

Awsa, 6 Nehasē 1876
Greetings.

We are well and have happily arrived in Awsa. I have with me the caravan destined for Aseb and the one destined for Obok. When I was in Shewa, as soon as I received your first letter I asked His Majesty to send me at once to Aseb, but I was detained till today. I will begin by bringing you the camels, and if their number is not sufficient, I will try to find other ones. With these few, however, I have arrived in Awsa, and here I have not found any camels, because water is lacking along the route.

I had to leave the hides and the coffee in Awsa, but Maḥammad Ḥanfadhē has undertaken to send everything himself to Aseb. The ivory, the musk and so on I have brought with me. I have some gifts for His Majesty the King of Italy, for the Royal Commissioner of Aseb and for the commander stationed here, which I shall deliver to you from my king.

It is only that my king has ordered me to go first to Obok and then to come to Aseb. I cannot do otherwise, because this is the order I received from the king. Do not think I am a friend of Brémond's; indeed we have completely broken with each other.

I send Goshu to you, so that you will get to know that the caravan is near. I wish you all the best.

ASMAI 36/2–17, Amharic original that has been lost or misplaced and could not be found. Printed Italian text in *L'Italia in Africa*, I.3 no. 333, allegato 3, p. 58. For the author, often simply referred to as Gebre Sillasē Nigusē or Gīyorgīs Nigusē, see doc. 78.

Document no. 181

Yosēf Nigusē to Pietro Antonelli [Aug. 1884]

Seal.

Greetings!
After I had received your three envoys, I immediately went to the king four times to remind him of the affairs of Aseb. The king always answered me: "I will send the caravan to Aseb at once, yes, yes." But afterwards he received the Europeans and they always succeeded in changing his mind. Signor Brémond has more than others intrigued with the king, giving much money to the interpreters whose name I do not say, so that the caravan destined for Aseb should not depart before him and before the caravan to Obok. Signor Brémond is in agreement with signor Ilg and signor Franzoi who always says he is an Italian author. For my part I find that this man is nothing but a slanderer of people. All three of them are against me because of the question of the bones of the deceased engineer Chiarini.

The king had decided that the remains of Chiarini should remain in his house in order to be sent to Italy later together with those of Marquis Antinori, but one day Brémond, Ilg and Franzoi went to the king and insisted that His Majesty should send the remains of Chiarini by way of Obok and not by way of Aseb. The king made Franzoi aware that having a treaty with His Majesty the King of Italy, it would be appropriate for all Italian subjects to use the route to Aseb. Franzoi replied to him that he was not a slave to anybody and that he was free to choose the route which pleased him most. Then the king finished, saying to him: "Then go wherever you like with the body of Chiarini, but first write a declaration through which it is clear that you yourself have refused the route of Aseb." The king then gave Franzoi 50 thaler and three camels for his journey to the coast.

The cause of all this is signor Brémond, who by having credit in Italy is in fact said to be planning to start a commercial company with Franzoi. Doctor Alfieri has received some gifts from Brémond and is reconciled with Franzoi, having given him a certificate on the authenticity of the skeleton of poor Chiarini. I have always said that it was not the intention of the Geographical Society to let the remains of the deceased leave, at least for the moment, and that we should wait for an order from the coast. I think I know that signor Franzoi will slander you in the journals and write against the Geographical Society and against me.

The king has reunited Gīyorgīs Gebre Sillasē with Brémond. Gīyorgīs will go with the caravan first to Obok and then to Aseb. This is what the French have tried to obtain.

An envoy of the French government stays here in Shewa. He does not do anything but speaks ill of Italy and says that the Italians want to take Shewa from the king.

ASMAI 36/2–17, Amharic original that has been lost or misplaced and could not be found. Printed Italian text in *L'Italia in Africa*, I.3 no. 333, allegato 4, pp. 58–59. The printed Italian text introduces the author as "L'interprete di Let-Marefia". *Grazmach* Yosēf Nigusē had studied at the French school in Massawa and thus knew French. As the heading of this letter shows, he was well known as the interpreter of the Italian explorers at Liṭ Marefīya. Gīyorgīs Gebre Sillasē was his brother and is in most letters known as Gebre Sillasē Nigusē.

Document no. 182

Yohannis IV to Gebre Igzī', 10 Sept. 1884

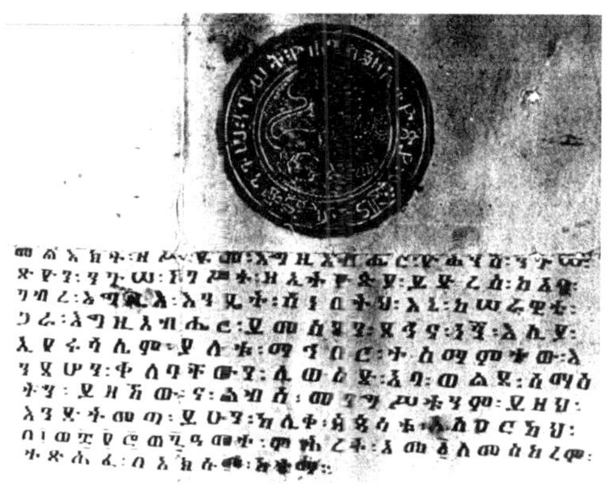

Seal: King of Kings Yohannis of Ethiopia; Yūḥannā, King of Kings of Abyssinia.

May this message from the Elect of God Yohannis, King of Zion, King of Kings of Ethiopia, reach *Abba* Gebre Igzī'.

I am well together with my army, thank God. If the community in Jerusalem have agreed, bring with you *Abba* Welde Sema'it in order that he may take their provisions. Bring also the royal dress after having it blessed by the patriarch.

Written in the year of grace 1877 on 1st Meskerem at the town of Aksum.

Dayr al-Sultan, no 10, Gi'iz/Amharic original. Printed with English translation in *Chronicle*, no. 22, pp. 184–187.

Document no. 183

Maḥammad Ḥanfadhē to Giulio Pestalozza, 16 Sept. 1884

بندر سنجوال بندر عصب في تاريخ ١٨٨٤ سنة الموافق ٢٠ شهر ذي القعدة ١٣٠١ سنة من الهجرة

الى حضرة الجناب الاكرم المكرم العزيز المحترم الامجد الانجد المحب المحبوب غايت كل طالب ومطلوب جوليو بستالوسه هداه الله
بعد السوال عن صحتكم انشاء الله ان تكونوت في خير وعافيه وان سالتم عنا فنحن بخير مع تمام وسرور وبلغنا كتابكم الكريم
مع ولدنا سعيد وقرانا مبانيه وعرفنا معانيه وقبضنا ما ارسل لنا دولة ايتليا بغلة والخيل تاخر في اثناء الطريق
ولعله نظن انه مات وكذلك قبضنا من يد الولد سعيد كوسيه واثنين وثلثين بندق حسب مرغوبنا فجزاكم
الله وكذلك ليس لاجلنا فجزاكم الله وذكرت لنا من جناب محبنا كنت انت نلي متوجه الى طرفكم مع صحبت شيخ عبد الرحمن الامام
بدري ما اخرهم لعله النافع عسى فيه خير ومن جنابه خصوص سعيد عويضات ذكرتم لنا في خطكم ما صدرنا عليه
فنشوف عاقبة الحكم منكم ومن جناب الخيل الذي ارسل لي دولة ايتليا مات كما بلغكم خبره لكن يلزمكم ان
تعرفوه لدولة ايتليا بما مات في اثناء الطريق والان نرغب من الدولة المذكوره فرسا خيلا جيدا والخيل
موجود لا معدوم وانما مرادنا بالخيل واصل من بعيد لا لغرض آخر وانت عرف الدولة ايتليا نيابة عنا وبلغنا
ان الخيل الذي مات كان مقطوع الذنب وان ارسل لي لا مقطوع ذنب سالما في كل عضوه هذا عرفناك

مستمد الدعاء
من عند سلطان
كاتب محمد بن سلطان حنفري
ويقول الفقير سلطان محمد بن سلطان حنفري
يسئل عن حال المحب الفقير عبد الرحمن بن شيخ محمد نواب
نرغب منكم المحبة والمعرفة هذا عرفناكم
يسئل عن حال المحب المكرم الاكرم جوليو بستالوسه
ويسئل عن حال العسكر سعيد مع احد افكم

From Sinkara, the capital, to the port of Aseb in the year 1884 which falls on the 25th of the month of Dhū al-Qa'da in the year 1301 of *Hijra*.

To His Honour, the most noble and honourable, the beloved and respected, the bravest and most glorious, the loving and dear, the aim of every aspirant and aspiration, Giulio Pestalozza. May God lead him.

After inquiring about Your Loving-kindness, God willing you are well and healthy. If you inquire about us, we are perfectly well and happy. Your esteemed letter has reached us with our son Sa'īd, we read its contents and understood its intentions. We also received the female mule the Italian government sent us. However, the horse was delayed on the way, and we think it probably died. In addition, we received from our son Sa'īd a small drum (?) (*kūsiyya*) and 32 rifles, just as we had requested – may God reward you – and also clothes for ourselves. May God reward you.

Furthermore, you mentioned to us that our beloved Count Antonelli accompanied by *Shaykh* 'Abd al-Raḥmān al-Dhammām is heading towards you; we do not know what kept them late, but perhaps whatever prevented them was [something] good. As for Sa'īd 'Awīḍān, we have not issued . . . [a verdict?] on him. We will see the consequence of your verdict.

And the horse that the Italian government sent, it died as you were informed. It is necessary that you inform the Italian government that it died on its way here. We would like from the mentioned government a horse, a very good mare. Not that we do not have any horses, but we would like to have a horse coming from such a distant country and not for any other reason. Do inform the Italian government on our behalf that the horse that died had its tail cut, and if they desire to send me a horse, please tell them not to cut its tail, but to send one with all of its body parts. This is what we tell you.

The sender of the message is Sultan Maḥammad bin Sultan Ḥanfadhē.

Maḥammad bin Sultan Ḥanfadhē's secretary, poor 'Abd al-Raḥmān bin *Shaykh* Muḥammad Turāb, prays for the well-being of the honourable and most noble Giulio Pestalozza saying: "We desire friendship and news from you. This is what we tell you." He prays for your well-being, the happiness of [your] soldiers and your servants.

ASMAE, AE (650), Arabic original. Pestalozza actually left his post in August 1884.

Document no. 184

Treaty between Ḥamad Muḥammad and Léonce Lagarde, 21 Sept. 1884

Entre Mr Lagarde ([illegible]) Commandant à Obock agissant au nom du Gouvernement français et Hamed ben Mohamed sultan sultan de Tadjourah qui commande de Ras Ali à Goubbet Kharab et dans l'intérieur jusqu'à Assal a été conclu le traité suivant.

Article 1er

Il y aura désormais entre la France et le sultan Hamed une amitié éternelle

Article 2

Le sultan Hamed donne son pays à la France pour qu'elle le protège contre tout étranger.

Article 3

Le Gouvernement français ne changera rien aux lois établies dans le pays du sultan Mohamed

Article 4

Le sultan Hamed en son nom et au nom de ses successeurs s'engage à aider les Français dans la construction de maisons et achats de terrains

Article 5

Le sultan Hamed s'engage à ne signer de traité avec aucun autre pays sans l'assentiment du Commandant d'Obock

Article 6

Le Gouvernement français s'engage à servir mensuellement une pension de 100 (cent) thalers au sultan Hamed et 80 (quatre-vingts) [illegible]

Article 7

En cas de contestation le texte français seul fera foi.

Fait à Obock le 21 septembre 1884

[illegible]

ابرهيم وزير ابو حمد

أول شرط

[illegible]

شرط تني

[illegible]

شرط ثلاث

[illegible]

شرط ربع

[illegible]

شرط خميس

[illegible]

شرط سبع

[illegible]

Between Mr. Lagarde Commandant of Obok, in the name of the French government, and Sultan Ḥamad bin Muḥammad, Sultan of Tajura, who governs from Rayshālī (Raysālī) to Qubbat al-Kharāb, and in the interior until 'Assal, and Ibrāhīm bin Ḥamad, the Sultan, the *wazīr* of Sultan Ḥamad, the articles included here, have been agreed upon.

First article
There will be eternal friendship and kinship between Sultan Ḥamad and his successors and the French government.

Second article
Sultan Ḥamad gives his country to the French to protect so that no one may enter it.

Third article
The French government will not change anything in the laws which are established in the lands of Sultan Ḥamad.

Fourth article
Sultan Ḥamad in his name, and in the name of his successors, promises to aid the French in the construction of houses and buying land.

Fifth article
Sultan Ḥamad promises not to sign a treaty with any other country without the agreement of the Commander of Obok.

Sixth article
The French government promises a monthly payment of 100 Riyāl to Sultan Ḥamad and 80 Riyāl to *Wazīr* Ibrāhīm.

Seventh article
In case of disagreement, only the French text is the ultimate witness.

Written at Obok 21st September 1884.

Seal illegible
Signatures:
Ibrāhīm *Wazīr* Ḥamad (two words illegible)
Lagarde

ANOM.OI; Arabic and French originals. French text printed in *Trattati*, p. 77. The Arabic seems to be a rather poor translation of the French, which is stated to be the only valid version in the last article. The Arabic is even dated with the European month and year: 21 September (*ṣibat mibir*) 1884. The inclusion of Ibrāhīm, the *wazīr* in the prologue, is, however, missing in the French, and in article 3 the French erroneously and in contrast to the Arabic writes Muḥammad for Ḥamad. Owing to the nature of the Arabic text and the stipulation that the French version is the only valid one, the translation above is based on the French text, taking the Arabic version into consideration. An English summarizing translation is printed in Hertslet, no. 71, with a map and a comparison with the treaty between Great Britain and the Sultan of Tajura on 18 August 1840. The treaty, which makes the sultanate of Tajura into a French protectorate, was followed by a so-called donation some weeks later; see doc. 190.

Document no. 185

Maḥammad Ḥanfadhē to Pasquale Stanislao Mancini, 5 Oct. 1884

To His Excellency, the most noble and most honourable, the beloved and respected, the venerable official, the Minister of Foreign Affairs of His Excellency the exalted Sultan, the first emperor, the King of Italy, the Commander, Minister Mancini. May God Almighty bless him and bless all his treasures. If you ask about us and those who take refuge with us, we are well and healthy, and we are not concerned about anything except you. The [reason for] sending this letter is news about the situation and to inform us about your well-being and to know if our letter reached you. So, how are you, how is your situation and your soldiers? God willing you are well and healthy. Your esteemed letter has reached us. We read its contents and understood its intentions. In addition, your envoy Count Antonelli, with a physician, Ragazzi, and *Shaykh* ʻAbd al-Raḥmān al-Dhammām bin *Shaykh* Yūsif, have reached us in safety and dignity. God did not change any of their conditions. For the binding of love and foundation of friendship we welcomed them, honoured them, and settled them as much as we could. You will find out the facts in their letter.

We received from them the female mule and the horse that were sent from Your Eminence. However, the horse died on the way before reaching us. We liked the female mule that we have received since we do not have one of such a race in our area. We were exceedingly happy with it.

And the arrangements you made with *Shaykh* ʻAbd al-Raḥmān al-Dhammām bin *Shaykh* Yūsif suit us perfectly. We heard about the assistance you gave him and the ship you equipped, which is called Castalfidardo. Furthermore, we were informed in your letter about the arrangements of Markable. What you have done for us delighted our minds and made our hearts rejoice. We shall not reward you but with good deeds, honesty, friendship, love and friendliness. May God Almighty make your government superior to all its rivals. Your benevolence reached its peak when you assisted the people of the Danākil. In return, we shall protect and guard the travellers on our land as far as Shewa and make sure they have all they need as long as we live; you are neither to worry nor grieve. We also offer assistance to the people of Aseb who are collaborating with the Danākil people since they have no discord with the Danākil people. You informed us through Count Antonelli, who reached us, and from whom we happily accepted it with honour and pride, that the medallion you sent to me is for honour and tribute for opening the route. It reached us and we saw that you engraved my name on it for glory. O God, may your desire, aim and intent be fulfilled.

As for the route, we have opened it for you, so it is open for you, with honesty and truthfulness. Whoever comes from the side of the sea or from Shewa shall not be bothered or disturbed.

As for *Shaykh* ʻAbd al-Raḥmān al-Dhammām bin *Shaykh* Yūsif, whom we sent on our behalf, we have heard that you received him in honour and dignity, and that you have fulfilled all his needs and have protected his tribe and family, all this because you love us and want to help us. We ask God for assistance and love for ever and ever. In addition, we heard the word you gave Abū Bakr *Pasha* and rejoiced greatly. Also, we ask one thing from you, which will not be convenient for us and will not be convenient for you either. What this thing is we will tell you and we have told Count Antonelli and he will let you know in his own handwriting and in his letter. What harms us and harms your people on the route is what Abū Bakr *Pasha* wrote to me in a letter, and that was not to open the route for Aseb. This is a vicious matter. Furthermore, the letter he sent did not have his seal, but the person who wrote for him is known and cannot deny the accusation. You judge this matter at your discretion. On the other hand, Abū Bakr Pasha and his sons will not cease their mischief among us as long as he is in this life. And you should not ignore him. So do not take this matter for granted. This is what we tell you.

From Sultan Maḥammad bin Sultan Ḥanfadhē.

Dated in the month of Dhū al-Ḥijja on Saturday after 14 days had elapsed, the year 1301 of Hijra.

Seal: Muḥammad Ḥanfadhē.

ASMAI 7/1–1. Arabic original and Italian translation. Ragazzi was a medical officer who had arrived with Antonelli in February 1884. He later replaced Antonelli as director of the station at Liṭ Marefīya.

Document no. 186

Maḥammad Ḥanfadhē to Pasquale Stanislao Mancini, 5 Oct. 1884

من سلطان محمد
بن سلطان حنفري

تاريخ في شهر الحجة يوم السبت
خلي منه اربعة عشر سنة ١٣٠١
من الهجرة

الى حضرة الاكرم المكرم العزيز المحترم المحب المحبوب غايت كل طالب ومطلوب وزير امور
الخارجيه للحضرة سلطان المعظم امبرطو الاول مالك ايطاليا الكمندار تور منسنر مانجيني
وفقه البارئ تعالى بكامل خيراته وان سالتم عنا وعن يلوذ بنا فاننا بخير وعافيه ولا نسال الا
عنكم ومما اعرفكم نخبركم في ما حصل لنا في المدة الاولى سنة اثنين وتسعين بعد الف ومائتين
من الهجرة لان دولة مصريون غزوا علينا بجيشهم وتقاتلنا بالاشر قتلت من الطرفين ونحن
كنا غافلين عن غزوتهم ونصرنا الله عليهم نصرا عزيزا ثم رجعوا الي تجرة واقاموا في بلدة
تجرة هي بطرف البحر ملكوا مننا قهرا وغصبا وجلسوا فيها وانا منعت نفسي من الحرب وكا
تبت اليهم مرارا الان هذا الامر ما يليق في اصول الدول ولم حصل لنا رد الجواب منهم
الان نسمع اخبار من الجانب يقولون الانكليز ناوي يدخل بلدة تجرة للملك وهو من طرف
المصريون اخذ قالوا الان نعلمكم انا مالك ارض الدناكل ما احد غيري الذي ساكنين
بطرف البحر انا سلطان تجرة من لهم واحد كجسد واحد وعيال اعمام وانا لم اتعرض في ملك
غيري وانتم يا اصحابي انظروا لي في حقوقي وبلدة حقنا تجرة حقنا اعرضوا لنا ههنا
الجواب عند الدول وثانيا نسمع اوادم من طرف دولة فرنساويون اشتروا امينة البحر من
الدناكل وانا لم علمت وبعد ما علمنا ما كرهنا بجاورت الاربا ويون قبلنا وصونهم
ومجاورتهم الان نسمع منهم طالبين ارض كبير الذي ما احد باع عليهم نطلب منهم
شهادة الذي اشتروا فيه والا يستنعوا من مطالبة زياده عن حقوقنا ابا
انا ودولة ايطاليا الان لي وداد انتم ما ترضوا تضيع حقوقنا ونحن ما رضينا بطرفنا
بتضيع حقوقكم هذا عرفناكم خير ختام

To His Excellency, the most noble and most honourable, the beloved and respected, the loving and dear, the aim of every aspirant and aspiration, the Minister of Foreign Affairs of His Excellency the exalted Sultan Umberto I, the King of Italy, the Commander Minister Mancini. May God Almighty bless him and bless all his treasures.

If you ask about us and those who take refuge with us, we are well and healthy, and we are not concerned about anything except you. What I would like to tell you is: we tell you what befell us in the first period of the year ninety-two after one thousand and two hundred of the Hijra when the Egyptian government invaded us with their army, and we fought the fiercest battles on both sides. We had no knowledge of their attacks, but Allah vindicated us with a mighty victory. Then, they retreated to Tajura and settled in the town of Tajura, which is by the coast. They took it from us by force and by extortion and settled in it. I restrained myself from [going to] war, and I wrote to them many times because this [thing] does not befit the principles of governments, but we did not receive a response from them.

And now, we hear news from abroad saying that the English plan to invade the city of Tajura to appropriate it, and it is said that they took the side of the Egyptians.

And now, we inform you that I am the possessor of the land of Danākil, and not any other person among those who live by the coast. The Sultan of Tajura and I are from the same blood and flesh and are cousins. I did not violate any possession of others. And you, my friends, behold my rights; and the town of Tajura is our right. Present these words to the governments.

Then, we heard [the words of] people from [the side of] the French government that they bought a port from the Danākil, but I was not informed about this. After we were informed, we did not despise the neighbourliness of the Europeans (*irabbāwīyūn*); we accepted their arrival and neighbourliness.

Now, we hear from them that they are claiming a vast land that no one sold them. We request the certificate that they bought the land, otherwise they are to cease claiming more of our rights. The government of Italy and I are hence [the same] flesh and blood: you do not accept that our rights be lost, and we, on our part, do not accept that your rights be lost. This is what we tell you. Concluding greetings.

From Sultan Maḥammad bin Sultan Ḥanfadhē.
Seal.

Dated in the month of Ḥijja, Saturday after fourteen days have elapsed in the year 1301 of Hijra.

ASMAI 7/1–1, Arabic original and Italian translation.

Document no. 187

‘Abd al-Raḥmān Yūsif to Pasquale Stanislao Mancini, 5 Oct. 1884

الي حضرة سعادة الامجد الانجد وزير ملك طليا مستر منسني طيبه رعاه المولي
من كل سوء وآفات فان سالتم عنا فنحن علي جناح السلامه ولا نسال الا عن صحتكم ان
شا الله ان تكونوا بعافيه نحن خرجنا من بندر عصب مع الكنت انتونلي ودكتر
ركاسي وصلنا عند سعادة السلطان محمد حنفري بالسلامه واكرم نحنا ورحبهم
وعزاهم معزا كبيرة وكان الوادي هواش مليان من المويه وخرجنا الي الحبشه
من طريق كرفه وهذي لاجل اكرامكم وانا اخبرته له جميع ما فعلتوا معيا و
مع الله تاكل والنيه الصالحه الذي انتم عندكم لا الله تاكل انكم انتم قايمين و
مجتهدين بمحبتكم مع الله تاكل بكل همه وفرحناه من طرفكم غاية الفرح
وتجدون كل اخبار في جواب لننا انتونلي ودكتر ركاسي اما انا ما ننسا فضل
دولتكم ديما ما نقدر نجاريكم الا نخدم دولة طليا بالصداقه ديما وان شا
الله تشوفوا منا ديما كل طيب والسلام وسلم لنا علي عيالك الله يسلم

من شيخ عبد الرحمن الله
ابن امام شيخ يوسف

تاريخ شهر ذ
الحجة يوم
١٤

سنة ١٣٠١

To His Excellency, the bravest and most glorious, the Minister of the King of Italy, Minister Mancini. May God Almighty protect him from all harm and illnesses.

If you inquire about us, we are well. We are not concerned about anything except your well-being. God willing, may you be healthy.

We left the port of Aseb with Count Antonelli and Dr. Ragazzi; we safely reached His Excellency Sultan Maḥammad Ḥanfadhē, who treated us hospitably, welcomed them and honoured them greatly, and the [river in the] Awash valley was full flowing. We left for Abyssinia (al-Ḥabasha) taking the Gerfa route. This was in your honour. I told him all that you have done for me and for the Danākil and of the good intention you have, but not the Danākil, and that you are settled and working hard under his protection with the Danākil in full ardour. We made him rejoice greatly on your behalf. You will find all the news in the letter of Count Antonelli and Dr. Ragazzi. On the other hand, I shall never forget the favour of your government. We cannot reward it, except by serving the government of Italy with friendship forever. God willing, you will always witness our good deeds. Greetings. Send our greetings a thousandfold to the members of your family.

Shaykh ʻAbd al-Raḥmān al-Dhammām bin *Shaykh* Yūsif

Seal.

Dated in the month of Ḥijja the day 14, the year 1301.

ASMAI 7/1–1, Arabic original and Italian translation.

Document no. 188

Ḥamad La'īta and 'Abd al-Qādir Ibrāhīm to Giulio Pestalozza, 11 Oct. 1884

الحمد لله وحده والصلاة والسلام
على من لا نبي بعده الى حضرة الجناب الاكرم المكرم العزيز اعني به قنصل طليان
الذي [illegible] في عصب هداه الله تعالى امين فاذا سالت عنا وعن بلادنا بالجميع [illegible]
وعافيه ونعمه [illegible] جعلكم الله [illegible] بل احسن من ذلك [illegible] امين
وبعد الذي نعرفكم من جنابكم الجمال الذي طلبتم منا ما حصلناها بالسهل
وشفنا فيه تعب كبير والمشقة لانه والجمال [illegible] علينا غالي بسبب قلة
الامطار والحشيش ولكن خرجنا الجمال بعد التعب الكبير وان شاء الله تعالى بعد
اخر الجمعة نوصل الى طرفكم مع الجمال [illegible] تحقيق [illegible] وبعثنا من جناب
البلد بيره علام الذي ارسلتوا انتم وعبد الرحمن وصلني وقريت الكلام
واعرفنا من جنابكم الجمال في عصب البدوان فانا بي مده ما يرضونا وان كان
مرادكم بالمحل الطيب من ارضنا الذي فيه مصلحة السفر وقريب الى
عسل [illegible] الملح قريب ساكنوه والمحل فيه ماء طيب حالي اسم المحل
دابكل اصلح منه في هذه الاطرف ما فيش وان كان انتم مرادكم في شغل
السنوق بنادق [illegible] فلس [illegible] اقرب من هذا المحل واسهل من هذا المحل ما فيش
في برناهن وانتم [illegible] وصلوا في البابور الى طرفنا لما ان يوصلكم عبد القادر
ابن ابرهيم مع الجمال طلعوهم في الوابور وهو يجيبكم وان صبر لكم في [illegible]
وانتم لما ان يوصل عبد القادر [illegible] فلم تنساو وكلكم حتى الى [illegible]
به الطلبات هذا اصلح لكم واما الغرنج فرنساوي مرادهم باخذ [illegible] ولكن
نحنا ما نشتي نعطيهم وان كان امكن لكم انتم [illegible] وان كان ما تبغون انتم
نحنا بعرفي رضنا والسلام

Praise be to God alone and blessings and peace be upon him after whom there is no prophet.

To His Excellency, the venerable and most noble, the most honourable and beloved, with this I refer to the Consul of the Italians, who resides in Aseb. May God Almighty lead him. Amen.

If you ask about us and those who take refuge with us, everyone is well and healthy, and [enjoying] constant blessings. May God keep you likewise and even better by God's and Muḥammad's Glory. Amen.

As for the trouble with the camels you requested, we inform you that it was not easy for us since we faced a lot of hardship and toil to obtain them. In addition, the camels cost us a lot due to the scarcity of rain and grass.

However, after great effort, we were able to obtain the camels. If it is the will of God the Almighty, we will reach you after the end of al-Ḥijja with the camels. This would be an achievement on my part. And as for the pennon you and 'Abd al-Raḥmān sent as a sign, I received it and accepted the sign.

Furthermore, we inform you concerning the trouble with the camels in Aseb, the Bedouins Qānīr Murra do not accept it. If you desire a good location on our land, where there are good opportunities for travel and which is close to 'Assal, the salt place, and close to Saklawa as well, a place where there is good water in the area, that would be Dābbukan. There is no better place in this area. Furthermore, if you desire dealing in rifles in Shewa for King (*nikus*) Minīlik, there is on our land neither a closer nor an easier place than this. And you (O) God (O) God (O) God, come to us on a steamship (*bābūr*). And when 'Abd al-Qādir bin Ibrāhīm reaches you with the camels, board him on your steamship. He will bring you while I wait for you in Tajura. When 'Abd al-Qādir reaches you, all of you are to discuss my rights in relation to the Italian government. This would be the best for you. As for the French foreigners, they are taking what they desire, but we do not wish to give them what they want. If it is possible for you, you are more suitable. However, if you do not wish so, we are more insightful as to our land.

Greetings.

The sender of the message is Ḥamad La'īta and 'Abd al-Qādir Ibrāhīm.

May God Almighty protect them. Amen
Dated in the month of al-Ḥijja 20, 13[01]

ASMAE, AE 2. Arabic original. Italian translation printed in *L'Italia in Africa*, I.3 no. 342, allegato 1, p. 68. The year is not fully written, but an Italian marginal note says 1301.

Document no. 189

Maḥammad Ḥanfadhē to Giulio Pestalozza, 17 Oct. 1884

اهدى السؤال لا يقاس والاحوال والكمال بعدد الانفاس تهدى
وتحل وتتشرف الى جناب العاقل الكامل الفاضل الاجل الاعز الامجد
الاكرم المكرم المحب المحب غايت كل طالب ومطلوب العزيز المحترم
جوليو بستالوسا هداه الله تعالى في كل وقت واوان وحماه ومن
المكاره ووقاه وحرسه من كل مكروه وبلغه غايت مناه على الدوام
مد الايام الى يوم المرجع ومن هذه الاطراف لم تجدد اخبار يجب
رفعها اليكم بل هي تجدون على لسان القادمين لطرفكم كفاية ونهاية
وحيث وجدنا القاصدين اليكم وجب علينا تحرير هذه الاحرف
لابلاغكم واوفر الجواب المستطابه وان الامل منكم ان لا
تقطعون عنا المكاتبة عن احوالكم البارة واخباركم السارة مع كل
غرض يبدو لجنابكم تقضا بمحو التعريف وصل الينا مكتب حامل
البسطة فهو كذلك ابن كامل قرانا مبانيه وعرفنا معانيه فحمدنا
الله على صحة عافيتكم ومن جناب ما ذكرت لنا من طبع العبيد الذي
كانوا عندكم مقيمين مدة قليل للتعليم ضرب البندق نعم الامر كما
ذكرت قلة أدبهم ولكن مع قلة أدبهم علمتهم وأفطنتهم بضرب
البندقية تجزاكم الله خيرا والان يا محب لان شيخ عبد الرحمن الزو
وكنت انت تلي قد غنياهم ووصلنا خطا منهم وهم في اثناء الطريق
طالعين الى كفرا ذكر والثاني خطهم قالوا سمعنا ان اوادم الفرنجي
نازلين من طرف بوريه كاسا بو تقتلوا هم تحت الحبشة مسيرة يوم منه

The most proper innumerable inquiries and boundless power and perfection are offered with honour and veneration to His Honour, the wise and perfect, the virtuous and most illustrious, the bravest and most glorious, the most noble and most honourable, the dear, the aim of every aspirant and aspiration, the beloved and respected Giulio Pestalozza. May God lead him at all times. May He protect him from all calamities. May He preserve him and guard him from all evil. May he attain all his goals for ever and ever till the Judgement Day. There is no recent news to advance to you, but you will find out the facts orally, sufficiently and conclusively through the people who come to you. And since we met the people who are heading towards you, we had to write these lines to inform you, for the best letter is the pleasant one. Our hope is that you do not deprive us of your letters informing us about your honourable state and your pleasant news, and whenever there is an issue that Your Honour deems could be settled through written communication.

Your scribe Kuddalī bin Kāmil, the carrier of the mail, has reached us. We read its contents and understood its intentions. We praised God for your good health. As for what you mentioned to us about the character of the slaves who stayed at your place for a short period of time to learn how to use a rifle, yes you are right; they have bad manners. However, despite their ill-behaviour, you trained and educated them on how to use a rifle: may God reward you with good things.

And now, o beloved, we have bidden *Shaykh* 'Abd al-Raḥmān al-Dhammām and Count Antonelli farewell. And while they were still on their way out of Gerfa (Kafrā), their letter reached us and they mentioned to us that they heard that the *ferenj* people from Kasa Bizbiz were killed beneath Abyssinia (al-Ḥabasha) at a distance of one day's journey. When the news reached us, we informed you. As is not hidden from you, not all of the land is under our authority. The people who live beneath Abyssinia are neither reliable nor trustworthy since they have no business and no transactions on our land.

We also sent you nine of our slaves that are to join our army with Dummū 'Alī and the scribe [Kuddalī] bin 'Ablā Kāmil. We would like you to train them on how to use a rifle, just like you have done with our slaves before. As a matter of fact, our dear Count Antonelli . . . (two words missing) that the slaves have arrived to Aseb. You are to guard them and . . . (one word missing) as long as they are with you. As for their expenses and their provisions, . . . (two words missing) Count Antonelli, and they lacked nothing, so you . . . (two words missing) to satisfy their needs.

In addition, do discipline them, . . . (one word missing) and warn them, and confine them in accordance with your training, for . . . (words missing) the one who is present is better-sighted than the one absent. Furthermore, I sent seven men to Obok to be trained on how to use a rifle. However . . . (words missing), news has reached me that Ḥamad bin La'īta had to send the above-mentioned . . . to Aseb. Maybe there was no . . . (one word missing) for them. So if he sent them, and they reached you, you have to accept them . . . (two lines missing) . . . our desire to use a rifle. Also discipline and confine them in accordance with your training. In addition, o beloved, if they learn and grasp how to use a rifle, you are to send them back, and you have to give each one of them a rifle with its provisions. And be kind, for kindness among great men is a synonym of elegance and sublimity.

And also, o beloved, Mehammad Ḥanfadhē's secretary, 'Abd al-Raḥmān bin *Shaykh* Muḥammad Turāb, prays for your Honour's well-being and that of your soldiers morning and forenoon. As is not hidden from your respectable Honour, I desire that you send us a good rifle, Abū Tīz with its provisions in accordance with your former and further benevolence. May God reward you with the best things for ever and ever. We shall always be at your service. We read your letters to the most illustrious Sultan Mehammad word by word. Previously we sent a letter and asked the ruler of Aseb, Branchi, to send us a rifle, and he replied in his letter that he accepted sending the rifle with its provisions. He mentioned [this] in three letters and he promised us to send [it], yet he did not send it to us. Then he left without sending any letter. I wanted to write a separate letter, another than this one, but I obtained the permission from Sultan Maḥammad [to include my words]. So please do not deprive me of my wish, and my wish is an Abū Tīz rifle with its provisions and good clothes, a loincloth, and a prayer carpet for correct prayer. Send them to us through the hand of *Shaykh* 'Abd al-Raḥmān al-Dhammām Yūsif or else through the hand of your scribe Kuddalī bin Kāmil, for he is a member of our tribes and our cousin, so be kind to him for he is at your service and has never let you down, by God, by God, by God. This is what we tell you.

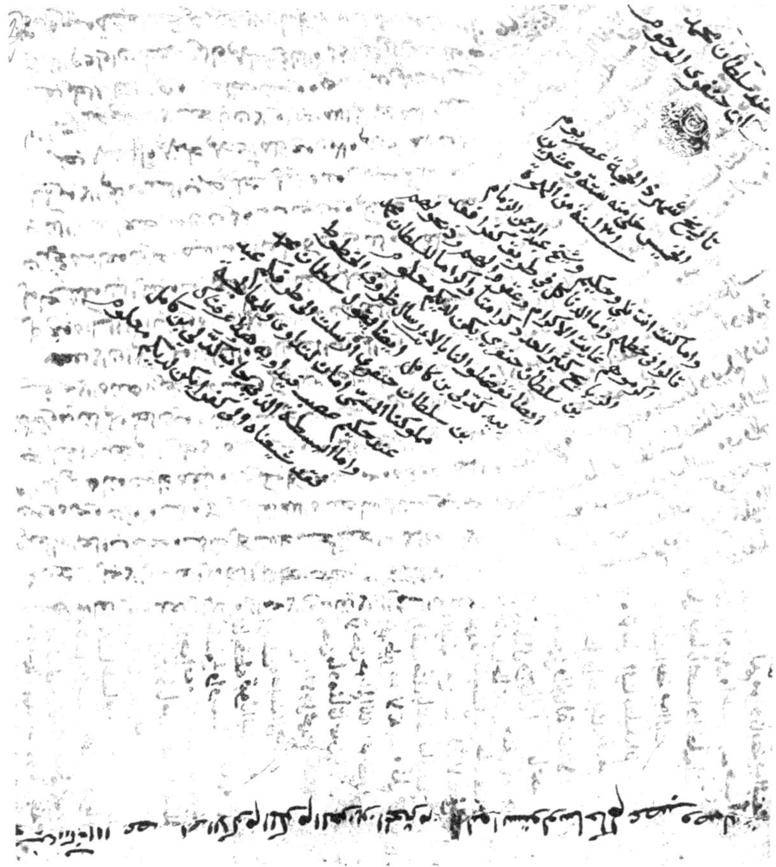

Count Antonelli, the physician and *Shaykh* ‘Abd-al-Raḥmān al-Dhammām wrote in their letter that the Danākil on the Kafrā route honoured them greatly and protected them and butchered many animals in honour of Sultan Maḥammad bin Sultan Ḥanfadhē. Let this be known to you. Also, please send us the letter envelopes through the hands of Kuddalī bin Kāmel. Furthermore, Sultan Moḥammad bin Sultan Ḥanfadhē says: “I sent to you our own slave named Amān to be treated and cured by the physician of Aseb. Let him cure him”. This is what we tell you. As for the mail that Kuddalī bin Kāmel brought, we sent it to Kafrā. Let this be known to you.

From Sultan Maḥammad bin [son of] Sultan Ḥanfadhē the deceased.

Seal: illegible.

Dated in the month of Dhū al-Ḥijjā, Thursday afternoon, after 26 days have elapsed, the year 13[0]1 of Hijrā.

ASMAE, AE 2. Arabic original. The Arabic text is unfortunately partly destroyed and thus the translation at times somewhat tentative. Note the reference to Emperor Yohannis as Kasa Bizbiz.

Document no. 190

Donation by Ḥamad Muḥammad et al. of territory to France, 18 Oct. 1884

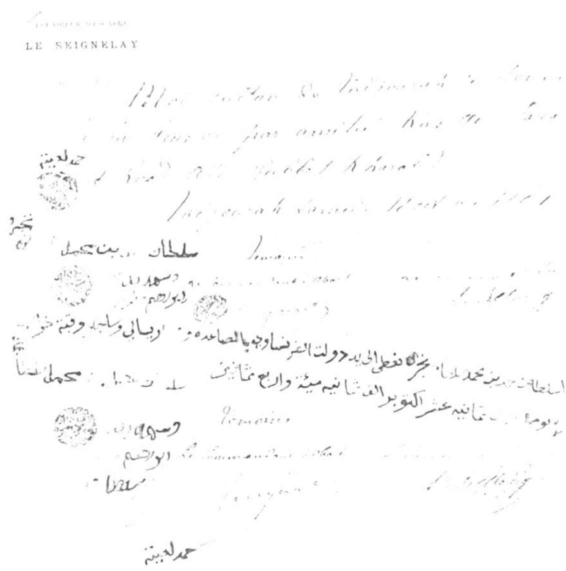
LE SEIGNELAY

Sultan Ḥamad bin Muhammad. Sultan of Tajura, present to the French government for friendship's sake Rayshālī (Raysālī), Sagallo and Qubbat al-Kharāb.

Tajura, Saturday 18th October 1884.

Sultan Ḥamad bin Muḥammad, Sultan of Tajura.

Ḥamad La'īta; Seal: Hamad La'īta.

Sultan Ḥamad bin Muḥammad, Sultan of Tajura; Seal: Sultan Ḥamad bin Muḥammad.

Certified by Ibrāhīm, *wazīr*; Seal: Ibrāhīm, sultan.

Sultan Ḥamad bin Muḥammad, Sultan of Tajura; Seal: Sultan Ḥamad bin Muḥammad.

Certified by Ibrāhīm, *wazīr* of Ḥamad, the sultan; Seal: Ibrāhīm, sultan.

Ḥamad La'īta; Seal: Ḥamad La'īta.

Witnesses:
The commander of Obok, Lagarde; Seal: Établissement d'Obock. Le Commendant.

The commander of the "Seignelay", A. Bellanger; Seal: illegible.

ANOM.OI, French/Arabic original. French text printed in *Trattati*, p. 78. The printed French text erroneously identifies Qubbat al-Kharāb as Rood Ali. The Arabic text seems to be written across an already finished French document written on the paper of the French vessel "Le Seignelay". Even in the Arabic text the date is given as 18 October (Aktūbir). The "donation" was preceded by a treaty only a few weeks earlier; see doc. 184.

Document no. 191

Minīlik II to Giulio Pestalozza, 4 Nov. 1884

Seal.
Boru Mēda, 26th Ṭiqimt 1877

Letter from His Majesty Minīlik II, King of Shewa, Kefa and all the lands of the Galla, to the honourable Cavaliere Giulio Pestalozza, head of the civil administration of His Majesty the King of Italy in Aseb.

How are you? We are well, by the grace of God, and so are our armies. It is with great pleasure that we have received your letter dated 23rd August 1884 which Count Pietro Antonelli has delivered to us. He has arrived to us safe and sound, as has his travel companion Doctor Ragazzi. We have received them with much joy and honour. We have talked with the count about all our affairs, which we have concluded. Regarding the day of departure of our envoys, we will decide and let you know as soon as the affairs related to this are finished.

We will also send a letter to Sultan Maḥammad Ḥanfadhē together with thirty (30) elephant tusks so that he supervises the safety of the route and provides the necessary camels. We will also send 'Abd al-Raḥmān to the coast again.

We hope, royal governor, that you will take care of Gebre Sillasē Nigusē and all those accompanying him and support them with what they might need.

May the Almighty be with you, Royal Governor, and preserve you from all evil.

ASMAI 36/2–17, Amharic or probably French original that has been lost or misplaced and could not be found. Printed French text in *L'Italia in Africa*, I.3 no. 372, allegato 2, p. 92.

Document no. 192

Yohannis IV to Welde Sema'it Welde Yohannis, 5 Nov. 1884

Seal: King of Kings Yohannis of Ethiopia; Yūḥannā, King of Kings of Abyssinia.

May the message from the Elect of God Yohannis, King of Zion, King of Kings of Ethiopia, reach our father Welde Sema'it, teacher of the Ethiopians who are in Jerusalem at Dayr al-Sultan.

How are you? I am well together with my army, praise be to God. The king of Greece (*Rom*) always sends people with presents. So far I have not sent people. Today, however, I have sent him five ramrod rifles (*neft qwad*) as a souvenir and a women's gear for his wife. Let it be that you deliver these things and take counsel on all issues on my behalf and return after discussing and listening to everything.

As to what I had informed you, that you should come here, do not come.

Written on the 27th day of Ṭeqemt, 1877 of the year of mercy, in the camp of Shīma Nigus.

Dayr al-Sultan, no 14, Gi'iz/Amharic original. Printed with English translation in *Chronicle*, no. 24, pp. 186–187 with notes on the *neft qwad* and the identification of the place called Shīma Nigus. The "king of Rom" refers to the king of Greece; see doc. 127.

Document no. 193

Maḥammad Ḥanfadhē to Giulio Pestalozza, 11 Nov. 1884

الى حضرة الاكرم المكرم العزيز المحترم الحاكم المعتبر المحب
الاكبر صاحبنا ومحبنا جوليو بستلولسه حاكم عصب
هداه الله تعالى امين وان سالتم عنا وعمن يلوذ بنا فاننا
بخير وعافية ولا نسال الا عنكم وصل الينا جوابكم الكريم
وقرانا مبانيه وعرفنا معانيه نحمد الله تعالى على صحة عافيتكم
صدرة الحروف من محروس سنكره وكل علم خير وسرور
وانتم كذلك على كمال العافية انشاء الله وذكرتم لنا من جناب
الفرنج المقتولين تحت الحبشة قد عرفناكم كما بلغنا خبرهم
فى خط الشيخ عبد الرحمن الزمام بن شيخ يوسف والمحب كنت انا
مع صحبة المكتب كذلك بن كامل والحقايق تجدون فى بسطة
عبد الرحمن الزمام وصاحبنا كنت انت تلى والبسطة واصل اليكم
مع خطنا هذا بيد مكتبكم فهو محمد كما بلغكم فى السابق والمحل الذى
قتلوهم ما هي بحكمنا ليس لهم الا ستعمال في اراضينا ومن جناب
ما ذكرتم لنا من عبيدنا العساكر بوصولهم عندكم ومرغوبنا تعليم
ضرب البندق كما عرفناكم حيث ما داموا عندكم ربوهم وعرفوهم وعلموا
وفي ظننا لم تقصروا بالتعليم فلا تقطعوا عنا المكاتبة عن احوالكم
واخباركم مع كل غرض بيد والجابكم تقضا بحر التعريف

To His Excellency, the most noble and most honourable, the beloved and respected, the esteemed ruler (*ḥākim*), the dearest, our friend and our dear Giulio Pestalozza, the ruler (*ḥākim*) of Aseb. May God Almighty lead him. Amen.

If you ask about us and those who take refuge with us, we are well and healthy, and we are not concerned about anything except you. Your esteemed letter has reached us; we read its contents and understood its intentions. So we praised the Lord for your good health. These lines are dispatched from Sinkara the protected; all information is good and favourable. May you be likewise in complete health if it is God's will.

You mentioned to us the case of the foreigners killed beneath Abyssinia. We informed you about them as soon as the news reached us in the letter of *Shaykh* 'Abd al-Raḥmān al-Dhammām and the beloved Count Antonelli accompanied by the scribe Kuddalī bin Kāmil. The facts are to be found in the mail of 'Abd al-Raḥmān al-Dhammām and our friend Count Antonelli. The mail will reach you along with this letter of ours through the hand of your scribe, who is Muḥammad. As you were previously informed, the place where they were killed is not under our authority and they had no business on our land. As for what you mentioned about our slave soldiers when they reached you, our desire is that you train them on how to use the rifle as we informed you. As long as they are staying at your place, discipline them and train them, for we believe that you have never failed in training. Do not deprive us of your letters whenever there is an issue that your honour deems could be settled through written communication.

The sender of the message is Sultan Mehammad bin Sultan Ḥanfadhē.

Dated on Tuesday in the month of Muḥarram after 22 days had elapsed, the year 1302 of Hijra.

Also Sultan Maḥammad bin Sultan Ḥanfadhē asks you to send him bullets for the Filī rifles, a sample of which was sent through the hands of your scribe Muḥammad; collect it from him and send [them] fast.

Sultan Maḥammad bin Sultan Ḥanfadhē's secretary, Muḥammad Turāb, inquires about your well-being and tells you "We were informed of what you wrote to us in the letter. May God reward you with good things. And you informed us of what you have written for our sake. This is the right affection. May you live long in peace."

ASMAE, AE 2. Arabic original. No seal. The foreigners referred to as killed beneath Ethiopia were Gustavo Bianchi and his associates. In spite of being warned and asked to take another route, he went from Meqelē to Aseb and was killed in the Danākil in October 1884. See further doc. 174.

Document no. 194

Treaty between Ḥamad La'īta and Italy, Nov. 1884

Praise be to God

List of clauses of the treaty of peace and protection between Sultan Ḥamad bin Sultan La'īta, the deceased, and the illustrious Italian government represented by its Consul in Aseb:

Article 1
There will be constant friendship and peace between Sultan Ḥamad La'īta and his dependents and the Italian governments and all its dependents. In order to affirm that, Sultan Ḥamad La'īta demands that the Italian government protects him, his dependents and all the lands under his reign.

Article 2
The Italian government, at the request of Sultan Ḥamad La'īta and the desire of the Danākil, has accepted and placed under their protection Sultan Ḥamad La'īta, his dependents and all the lands under his reign. The borders are from the eastern cape of the gulf of Qubbat al-Khārāb until the lake of 'Assal or the Salt lake, and all the gulf of Qubbat al-Kharāb and its shore from all sides, and also, outside the gulf of Qubbat, the coast of Baḥr al-Ladhaq (?) until the lands of the Danākil on the side of the 'Isa; and from the lake of 'Assal the lands of the sultan stretches to the lands of Arar (?). All of the above lands will be under the protection of the Italian government.

Article 3
Sultan Ḥamad La'īta keeps his exclusive rule and his sovereign rights over the Danākil in all the lands enlisted.

Article 4
Sultan Ḥamad La'īta grants the government of Italy Dabbakan, situated on the beach of Qubbat al-Kharāb, and another place outside the gulf mentioned, so that the government can according to its wish in these places build two towns or stations for its caravans and raise its flag and exercise its jurisdiction.

Article 5
Sultan Ḥamad bin La'īta undertakes neither to sell, nor to break up, any of his possessions or his lands without the approval of the Italian government, especially the 'Assal lake; furthermore, the salt extracted from it will exclusively be for Ḥamad bin La'īta and his people, and for Sultan Maḥammad

Ḥanfadhē, and for Sultan Minīlik, the King of Shewa, and it will be forbidden to export this salt by sea in the interest of foreign nations.

Article 6

Sultan Ḥamad bin La'īta commits himself to granting all dependents of the king of Italy the total freedom to reside and travel in all places of his sultanate whether it be for commercial or other purposes without having to pay any taxes for travel or residence

Article 7

Sultan Ḥamad bin La'īta commits himself to defending the rights of Italy and protects its stations on all parts of the land, whether they are Danākil or others, from the 'Isa tribes; all caravans heading from or to the Italian stations will be under his protection and the protection of his dependents. The sultan has to determine what is best for the nation of Italy and its merchants. His efforts and assistance shall in particular be for the increase of business and for the merchants of all the Italian stations and the kingdom of the dear and respected King Minīlik and all the lands of Abyssinia.

Article 8

In exchange for this the Italian government will protect Sultan Ḥamad bin La'īta and all his land from the coast by a proper perpetual protection while his dependents in foreign lands are protected by the consuls of the Italian government.

Article 9

Furthermore, the Italian government will assign in writing a permanent monthly payment for Sultan Ḥamad bin La'īta to be paid in Aseb or in Dabbakan (*Dabbākan*) when the government settles there.

Article 10

The previous articles that have been agreed upon between Sultan Ḥamad bin La'īta and the Italian government representatives in Aseb and dated on the 19th of Jumād al-Awwal 1301, corresponding to 17 March 1884, remain in their essence accepted and compelling for both parties.

This treaty is to be presented to the illustrious Italian government to ratify it, and its articles will be communicated to His Majesty King Minīlik, King of Shewa, and to His High Honour, Sultan Maḥammad bin Sultan Ḥanfadhē. This treaty has two copies: one is given to the Italian government, and the second is given to Sultan Ḥamad bin La'īta.

Dated in November 1884, which corresponds to the month of Ṣafar in the year 1302.

Verified like this.

Seals: Ḥamad La'īta
R. Commissario Civile in Aseb.

Signed: Pestalozza

ASMAE, AE 2, Arabic original. Printed Italian text in *Trattati*, pp. 79–81 where it refers back to the convention of 17 March 1884 and a note states that it was ratified by the Italian government in November 1884.

Document no. 195

Yohannis IV to Welde Sema'it Welde Yohannis, 22 Nov. 1884

Seal: King of Kings Yohannis of Ethiopia; Yūḥannā, King of Kings of Abyssinia.

Message from the Elect of God Yohannis, King of Zion, King of Kings of Ethiopia, to our father *memhir* Welde Sema'it, teacher of the Ethiopians who are in Jerusalem at *Dayr al-Sultan*.

How are you since I wrote to you? I am well with my army, praise be to God. I had given an order that 500 thalers should be allotted to you from the money that was sent for the purchase of the royal dress, assuming that the dress had not been bought yet. But now, it has been found that [the sum] has been used for the purchase. And now, borrow 500 thalers for your provisions and go. I shall repay the money. I sent you not because I lack people, but rather because you know the language and the secrets.

Written on the 14th of Hidar in the year of grace 1877 in the camp of Gura.

Dayr al-Sultan, no 13, Gi'iz/Amharic original. Printed with English translation in *Chronicle*, no. 23, pp. 186–187.

Document no. 196

Minīlik II to Umberto I, 1 Dec. 1884

ዳግማዊ፡ ምኒልክ፡ በጸጋ፡ እግዚአብሔር፡

ንጉሠ፡ ሸዋ፡ ወከፋ፡ ወኵሉ፡ አድባራቲሃ፡ ለብሔረ፡ ጋላ፡

ይድረስ፡ ወደ፡ ተወደዱ፡ ወደ፡ ክቡሩ፡ ወዳጃችን፡ ወንድ

ማችንም፡ ንጉሥ፡ ኡምበርቶ፡ በስም፡ መጀመሪያ፡ የኢጣ

ሊያ፡ ንጉሥ፡፡ እጅግ፡ እንደቆዩ፡ ነው፡ እኔ፡ እግዚአብሔር፡

ይመስገን፡ ደኅና፡ ነኝ፡ ሠራዊቴም፡ ሁሉ፡ ደኅና፡ ነው፡

ከርስዎ፡ ዘንድ፡ ተልኮ፡ የመጣው፡ ኮንት፡ አንቶኔሊ፡

ከኔ፡ ዘንድ፡ በደኅና፡ ደረሰ፡፡ ከንጉሥ፡ ዘንድ፡ የመጣው

ን፡ በረከትና፡ ደብዳቤዎም፡ በታላቅ፡ ደስታ፡ ተቀበል

ሁ፡ በጥር፡ ፫ ቀን፡ በ፲፰፻፹፬ የተጻፈ፡ እግዚአብሔር፡

ይስጥልኝ፡፡

ኮንት፡ አንቶኔሊ፡ የመጣ፡ ጊዜ፡ ወደ፡ ወሎ፡ ዘምቼ፡ ሳለሁ፡

በገርፋ፡ በኩል፡ መጣ፡ እኔም፡ ገርፋ፡ ድረስ፡ ጦር፡ ሰድጄ፡ ተ

ቀበልሁት፡፡ ይህም፡ ገርፋ፡ የወሎ፡ መሬት፡ ነው፡፡ እኔም፡ በ

ዚያን፡ ጊዜ፡ በጦርነት፡ ነበርሁ፡፡ ንጉሥ፡ በደብዳቤዎ፡ የነ

ገሩኝ፡ ነገር፡ እኔም፡ ከዚህ፡ ቀድሞ፡ የነገ፡ ታላላቅ፡ መልእ

ተኞቼ፡ ውሉን፡ ለመፈጸም፡ እልካለሁ፡ ያልሁትም፡ ከኮ

ንት፡ አንቶኔሊ፡ ጋራ፡ ተነጋግረን፡ ጨርሰናል፡፡ አሁን፡ ኮን

ት፡ አንቶኔሊን፡ ሸዋ፡ እስክገባ፡ ድረስ፡ ስለኔ፡ ብለህ፡ ቆይ፡ ብዬ፡

ለምኜአለሁና፡ ለምን፡ ዘገየ፡ ብለው፡ እንዳያዝኑብኝ፡ ተ

ስፋ፡ አለኝ፡፡ ተጻፈ፡ [illegible]

[May this letter from] the second Minīlik, by the grace of God King of Shewa and Kefa and all the districts of the Galla country, reach the beloved [and] honoured, our friend and brother King Umberto I, the King of Italy.

How are you, really? I am well, thank God, and all my soldiers are well. Count Antonelli who was sent by you has arrived to me safely. I have received the gifts which came from the king and your letter written on 3 Ṭirr 1884 with great joy; may God reward you on my behalf. When Count Antonelli came when I had gone on an expedition to Wello, he came through Gerfa and I received him by sending soldiers as far as Gerfa. This Gerfa is a territory of Wello.

At that time I was at war. I and Count Antonelli have discussed and have come to a conclusion in the matter that you, the king, told me about in your letter and about which I had said to you earlier that I would send my great messengers to conclude the treaty.

Now, I have asked Count Antonelli to stay [with me] for my sake until I enter Shewa, and I hope that you will not be sad because he has tarried.

About the remaining things: On my part I have done everything you, the king, said. The only thing that remains for me is to send the messengers, even this matter has been completed.

But I am sorry for its delay because the time was not convenient to me; if it were as my wish, I would have liked to send [them] immediately. And now, I will send [them] when I enter Shewa, and I shall inform the consul of Aseb of the day of their departure. Do not suspect that they have delayed because something bad has happened. I pray God that He may protect your kingdom and that He may prolong your life for what you have done for the tranquillity and peace of the people of Italy, for all the kindness you have shown to me and for all the good deeds that you are going to do in the future for the benefit of the people of Shewa.

Written at Boru Mēda on the 23th day of Hidar in the year of grace 1877, the Evangelist Matthew.

Seal: Minīlik, King of Shewa. The Lion of the tribe of Judah has prevailed.

ASMAI 36/2–21bis, Amharic original. Italian translation printed in *L'Italia in Africa*, I.3 no. 36[illegible], allegato, p. 86.

Document no. 197

Minīlik II to Pasquale Stanislao Mancini, 2 Dec. 1884

[May the letter from] the second Minīlik, King of Shewa and Kefa and all the districts of the Galla country, reach the honoured foreign minister of Italy.

How are you, really? I am well, thank God, and my soldiers are well. Your letter, written on the 3rd of Ṭirr 1884, has reached me with great honour through the hand of Count Antonelli. Count Antonelli came through Gerfa while I was on an expedition in Wello. I had him brought from Gerfa to Boru Mēda by sending an army.

[I] and Count Antonelli have discussed and have come to a final conclusion on what you and King Umberto said and about which I had earlier said that I would send important people as ambassadors to conclude the treaty. We are very pleased with all the good things that Count Antonelli has done for us, by his work and his conduct. Now that I am on an expedition, I have asked Count Antonelli saying "Stay with me until I enter Shewa", and have kept him. For this reason, I hope that you will not suspect that Count Antonelli has tarried because something bad has happened. We have completed the matter. And having determined the day on which the ambassador will leave, I shall inform the consul at Aseb.

As for the salt, I sent [some] earlier with Gebre Sillasē Nigusē, and now I have prepared some [more] to be sent. Also, I will send some after the messengers, when the caravan comes from the sea. For this reason do not have any doubt about my part; I shall make everything straight in due time. And now let me ask you for one thing. I hope that you will write to me immediately whenever a new governmental affair about Abyssinia comes up, even if the decisions remain as taken. I ask God that he may prolong your life so that we may fulfil our friendship.

Written at Boru Mēda on 24 Hidar 1877; by the [calendar] of the *ferenj* on 1 Tahsas 1884 in the year of grace.

Seal: Minīlik, King of Shewa. The Lion of the tribe of Judah has prevailed.

ASMAI 36/2–21bis, Amharic original. 24 Hidar 1877 was 2 December 1884, not the 1st, as in the Amharic text.

Document no. 198

Donation by Ḥamad of Tajura and Ḥamad La'īta, 14 Dec. 1884

Ḥamad, Sultan of Tajura, has donated his lands to the French government as far as Adaéli, and I, Ḥamad La'īta do the same and give to the said government from Adéli to Ambado.

Obok, the 14 December 1884.

Signatures and seals of Ḥamad, Sultan of Tajura and Ibrāhīm, *wazīr* of the same which testify to the authenticity of the declaration.

Signatures and seal of Ḥamad La'īta who verifies the authenticity of this statement.

Ogschlager, military interpreter.

Lagarde
Commandant of Obok.

Trattati, p. 84. French text. Unfortunately, we have not been able to locate any original of this document. It can be doubted that there ever was an Arabic original. Since we have not been able to identify with certainty the places named as Adaéli and Ambado, we have preserved the spelling of the French printed version of these.

This document is published by Hertslet no. 186, as follows: "Hamed, Sultan of Tajurah, having given to the French government his territory as far as the place called Adaeli. I, Hamed-Laita, do the same thing, and I give to the said government from Adaeli to Ambado. Obok, 14th December, 1884 (Signature and Seal of Hamed, Sultan of Tajurah and of Brahim, Vizir of the same place, who bear witness to the authenticity of the said declaration.) (Signature and Seal of Hamed-Laita, who certifies to the authenticity of what he has said.)"

INDEXES

Numerals refer to documents, not pages.

Authors of letters, parties to treaties and conventions

Persons mentioned in texts and footnotes

Scholars, editors and publishers referred to in the notes are not included.

Countries, districts, places and peoples

Ingram Content Group UK Ltd.
Milton Keynes UK
UKHW051325250423
420753UK00014B/168